AN ENSIGN IN THE PENINSULAR WAR

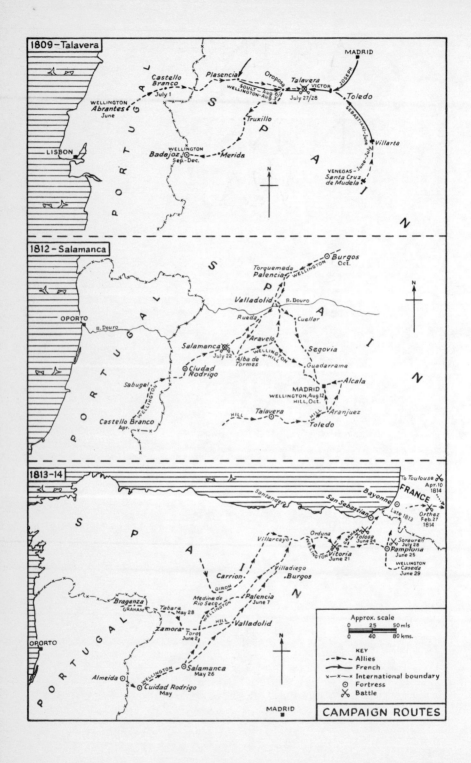

1809 – Talavera

MADRID
JOSEPH
PORTUGAL
Castello Branco
July 1
Plasencia
Oropesa
Talavera
VICTOR
July 27/28
SOUL – Aug 6/7
WELLINGTON – Aug 3/4
Toledo
WELLINGTON
Abrantes
June
SEBASTIANI – June
SPAIN
Truxillo
Villarta
LISBON
WELLINGTON
Badajoz
Sep.-Dec.
Merida
VENEGAS –
Santa Cruz
de Mudela
N

1812 – Salamanca

SPAIN
Burgos
Oct.
Torquemada
Palencia
WELLINGTON
Valladolid
R. Douro
OPORTO
R. Douro
Rueda
Cuellar
Aravelo
Segovia
Salamanca
July 22
WELLINGTON
HILL
Alba de Tormes
Guadarrama
Ciudad Rodrigo
Alcala
Sabugal
WELLINGTON
MADRID
Aug. 12
HILL, Oct.
Aranjuez
PORTUGAL
Castello Branco
Apr.
HILL
Talavera
HILL
Toledo
N

1813-14

To Toulouse
Apr. 10
1814
FRANCE
Santander
San Sebastian
Bayonne
Late 1813
Orthez
Feb. 27
1814
SPAIN
Villarcayo
Orduna
URDAZ?
Tolosa
June 24
Sorauren
July 28
PORTUGAL
WELLINGTON
Vitoria
June 21
Pamplona
June 25
WELLINGTON
Caseda
June 29
Carrion
GIRON
Villadiego
Burgos
Medina de
Rio Seco
Palencia
June 7
Braganza
GRAHAM
Tabara
May 28
WELLINGTON
HILL
Valladolid
Zamora
Toro
June 2
OPORTO
Almeida
WELLINGTON
Salamanca
May 26
Ciudad Rodrigo
May
N
MADRID

Approx. scale
0   25   50 mls
0   40   80 kms.

KEY
- - - - ▶ Allies
————▶ French
×—×—× International boundary
⊙ Fortress
✕ Battle

CAMPAIGN ROUTES

AN ENSIGN
IN THE
PENINSULAR
WAR

THE LETTERS OF JOHN AITCHISON

Edited by W.F.K. Thompson

MICHAEL JOSEPH
LONDON

To Rosemary

MICHAEL JOSEPH LTD

Published by the Penguin Group
27 Wrights Lane, London W8 5TZ
Viking Penguin Inc., 375 Hudson Street, New York, New York 10014, USA
Penguin Books Australia Ltd, Ringwood, Victoria, Australia
Penguin Books Canada Ltd, 10 Alcorn Avenue, Toronto, Ontario, Canada M4V 3B2
Penguin Books (NZ) Ltd, 182–190 Wairau Road, Auckland 10, New Zealand

Penguin Books Ltd, Registered Offices: Harmondsworth, Middlesex, England

First published in Great Britain 1981
First published in this paperback edition 1994

Printed in Great Britain by Clays Ltd, St Ives plc

ISBN 0 7181 3840 6

Contents

List of Maps

Introduction

THIS account of Wellington's campaigns in Spain and Portugal from 1809 to 1814 has at its core the letters and diaries of General Sir John Aitchison G.C.B., written by him while serving in the Peninsula as a junior officer in the 3rd Regiment of Guards, now the Scots Guards.

So far as operations would allow, John Aitchison wrote a weekly letter to his father, William Aitchison of Drummore, Musselburgh, East Lothian, and on occasions to his four brothers and his sister, Helen. I have excised most of the family gossip from the letters, but they show the Aitchisons to have been a close-knit family much concerned with each other's welfare. William, the eldest son, helped his father manage the estate to which he succeeded; James had business interests in the East Indies; John came next, and then George, who in many ways seems to have been closest to him. George hankered after a career in the regular Army, but John did much to dissuade him, and George eventually made do with a commission in the East Lothian Militia and set up a business in Leith to take advantage of the reopening of the Baltic to British trade. Robert, the youngest, entered the Royal Navy. He was a midshipman in the *Impétueux* (74 guns) at Lisbon when John returned to Portugal in 1812, and subsequently sailed for the East Coast of America where he played a very active part in small boat operations during the War of 1812. He was promoted post captain in 1827.

The letters and diaries add fresh nuance to well-known characters and events as seen through the eyes of a junior subaltern. Aitchison does not hesitate to criticize Wellington and other senior commanders, notably Sir Thomas Graham, later Lord Lyndoch, but where this criticism is adverse it is made without malice. John Aitchison was a countryman at heart and not least in interest are his descriptions of the people and agriculture in the countryside which he passed.

For so junior an officer he exhibits a remarkably wide grasp of affairs in the Peninsula and throughout the whole theatre of war. It could be argued that the Guards were exceptionally well placed for receiving news, being often stationed close to Wellington's headquarters, but the Duke was notorious for holding his cards close to his chest and Aitchison's letters show how often in deluding the enemy the Duke also led his own officers into misconception of his intentions.

There was no censorship of the mail, and much criticism and many details of matters of operational importance found their way into the press, to the delight of the enemy and the indignation of the Duke. Public opinion at home often reflected the views of officers in Wellington's army, who were not necessarily well informed or qualified to pass judgment on events.

John Aitchison's appraisal of the contribution made by the Spanish, and more particularly the Portuguese forces, is fair and of special interest. The regular forces of both these nations demonstrated the truth of the old adage that 'there are no bad soldiers, only bad officers'. The improvement made in the Portuguese forces by Marshal Beresford and the British officers seconded for service with them was remarkable, and it was a pity that Spanish pride prevented similar steps being taken with their own regular forces. The part played by the Portuguese in Wellington's army seldom receives the recognition it deserves. Nevertheless, in a letter to Lord Liverpool on 25 July 1813, Wellington was to say, 'The Portuguese are now the fighting cocks of the army. . . . I believe we owe their merits more to the care we have taken of their pockets and their bellies than to the instruction we have given them'. Apart from the Portuguese Division and a number of independent Portuguese brigades of cavalry and infantry, each of the apparently British divisions was in fact an Allied division. In the course of 1810 all but the 1st Division came to include a Portuguese brigade which, with four to five battalions, was much stronger than the normal British infantry brigade, and the 1st division had a brigade of the King's German Legion. The famous Light Division was formed by Craufurd's Light Brigade being split to form two brigades each including Portuguese Caçadores, or light infantry battalions.

The action of the Spanish guerrillas under such leaders as Martin Diaz ('El Empecinado'), Mina, Longa and a score of others in keeping the French forces dispersed throughout the Peninsula was essential to the success of Wellington's strategy. The Spanish provincial armies also played a part, for although they were beaten in open battle time after time they were never wholly destroyed. Spanish soldiers, too, made an important but seldom noticed contribution to Wellington's army; Harry Smith in his memoirs relates that 'We had also ten men a company in our British Regiments, Spaniards, many of them the most daring of sharpshooters in our corps, who nobly regained the distinction attached to the Spanish infantry of Charles v.'[1]

From his letters the young Aitchison emerges as an intelligent man with a strong sense of duty and a determination to do well in all circumstances. He was evidently also a rather private man. That he was courageous and efficient is certified by being given the honour of carrying the King's Colour of his battalion at the battle of Talavera, in which he was wounded, and by being selected for command of the Light Company of that battalion. What is surprising in one who was to reach the highest rank in the Army was that John Aitchison was a reluctant, though a perceptive, soldier, only entering the army to please his father. Having done so, he would have preferred a commission in the Royal Artillery; however, his father thought otherwise and in 1805 bought him an ensign's commission in the 3rd Regiment of Guards, with whose 2nd Battalion John, after serving at the siege of Copenhagen in 1807, went to Portugal in 1809.

The most revealing analysis of himself and his attitude to the army is contained in a diary entry of March 1811, when he was home from Portugal and serving in London. He takes a particularly gloomy view of his own prospects, partly, no doubt, because he was suffering from a bout of malaria.

Diary
Tuesday 26th March 1811

Wrote a very long letter to my Brother George at Palermo in obedience to my father's direction, to give him my opinion – 'that if he is still inclined to enter the army my Father *would allow him*, but if not a keen soldier never to think of it'. I gave my opinion against his entering the army, because it does not seem to me so likely to promote what I suppose every man has in his view, viz *his advancement in the world*. I stated what occurred to me for and against the army, and I revealed to him, with injunctions not to disclose it, that I really regretted having entered the army myself and I desired him to keep it from my Father because I am firmly persuaded that he would be *truly* uncomfortable in the idea that I was so. But, I stated, it would become *me* to persevere in and endeavour to overcome all difficulties, to promotion, for I am quite unacquainted with business, and now weaned from the necessary habits. To one so sensible as yourself, my Dear George, it would be absurd to hold out as the life of a soldier what he leads at home, and there is too great a contrast between his life on service for me to describe adequately, but there is something in the life of a subaltern on service so nearly approaching slavery as generally disgusts – I was completely so, but my comfort was greatly increased by the liberal allowance of my father which enabled me to live better than a Captain on the Line.

Were any misfortune to deprive my worthy parent of the means of supporting me . . . how could I live? Not by my pay for that is barely sufficient for my cloths! . . . Do not imagine from this that I absolutely hate my profession – by no means – the profession of arms always has been and ever will be respectable – I rejoice in contributing in any way my assistance to add to the renown of my country, and I glory in having acted in deeds which have immortalised my regiment and have enhanced the character of the army – but how dearly purchased! – at two and twenty I find myself unequal to extraordinary exertion, and I am compelled to live as *cautiously* abstemious as a ruined *debauchee* and what is worse, I am left in doubt whether I shall ever be restored to my former health, but I am galled most at *the want of independence* which I can never gain.[2]

My aristocratic principles forbid me to hold out wealth as the basis of happiness . . . but there is, in this demi-democratic country, a necessity for a considerable income to keep up the appearance of rank and independence, and then in the army, my total lack of interest[3] added to my unconquerable superciliously reserved disposition debar me the hope of ever attaining. These unhappy reflections never occurred to me but lately, but now in many sleepless nights, I have too much time to indulge in melancholy.

In short, you will perceive, but should your inclination still be *strong* for it, far be it from me to oppose it, for I am convinced that when inclination runs strong for any pursuit, it *will go* to it some time or other, but with my father I agree that an experiment in the army for one year or two would only be so much time lost.

On 15 May 1875 this obituary notice appeared in *The Times*.

We have to announce the death of General Sir John Aitchison G.C.B., Colonel of the Royal Scots Fusilier Guards, on Thursday night, at his residence in Devonshire Place, at the advanced age of 87 years.[4]

He entered the Army just 70 years since – namely, in October 1805. He served in 1807 at the siege and capture of Copenhagen, and the following year embarked for the Peninsula. In 1809 he was present at the passage of the Douro, capture of Oporto and subsequent pursuit of Soult's Army to Salamanca. At the battle of Talavera he was wounded in the arm while carrying the King's Colour, which was also shot through. Sir John also served in the campaigns of 1810, 1812, 1813 and 1814, and was present at the battle of Busaco and the retreat to the lines of Torres Vedras; the battle of Salamanca, the capture of Madrid, the siege of Burgos and the retreat from thence into Portugal; the affair of Osma, the battle of Vittoria, affair at Tolosa, the siege of San Sebastian, the battles of the Nivelle and Nive, passage of the Ardour, investment of Bayonne, siege of the citadel, and repulse of the sortie. The veteran General had received the war medal with six clasps.

He commanded the Scots Fusilier Guards for upwards of four years till promoted to Major General. Sir John served in India from June 1845 to November 1851, as Major General on the staff of the Madras Presidency, in command of the Mysore Division (including Coorg) and of the Province of Malabar and Canara. In 1851 he was appointed Colonel of the 72nd Highlanders, and was transferred as Colonel to the Scots Fusilier Guards in 1870. In 1859 he had been made a Knight Commander of the Bath and promoted to General in the following year. In 1867 he received the Grand Cross of the Order of the Bath.

At the end of the Napoleonic Wars the Navy and Army were greatly reduced, but Aitchison stayed on to achieve high rank in command and on the staff. Taking his soldiering seriously, he decided that he would not marry until he ceased to be actively employed. Accordingly at the age of sixty-eight he married Ellen Mayhew, by whom he had a son and two daughters. The girls were tragically drowned when young, and it is through his son that the letters and diaries of his youth have been preserved.

In editing the letters the reading and spelling of place names created a particular difficulty. I have adopted the current British spelling of such well-known names as the River Tagus and Corunna; for simplicity I have used 'Douro' for the river throughout, rather than changing to 'Duero' when the narrative moves to Spain. In general, I have followed modern spelling of

Portuguese, Spanish and French place names. I have tended to retain Aitchison's own somewhat idiosyncratic punctuation, only amending this where I thought it necessary for the reader's comprehension. Letters have only been cut where the subject matter has been of purely family interest, or where it has been duplicated by extracts from Aitchison's diaries.

W.F.K. Thompson

Prologue

THE significance of the events described in John Aitchison's letters can only be judged within the context of the world-wide struggle for power between Britain and France covered by the Revolutionary and Napoleonic Wars. When the first of these letters was written, in October 1808, Britain and France had been continuously at war since February 1793, except for a fourteen-month interlude during the uneasy Peace of Amiens (1802–3).

It was a struggle between the world's greatest naval and commercial power, and a far more populous country borne up by revolutionary fervour and a longing for 'la Gloire', and latterly directed by the restless ambition and military genius of Napoleon. It was prolonged by the inability of either side to destroy the other's power base, for Napoleon's victorious armies could not destroy the Royal Navy or sweep British commerce from the seas, neither could Britain's maritime power crush the armies of France.

In accordance with tradition, Britain began the war with an army which in size, organization and equipment was wholly inadequate. The total force available at home for overseas service fell short of 20,000, from which some of the best infantry had to be embarked with the Fleet to act as marines.

Throughout the war Britain's army had been frittered away on numerous, and too often disastrous, diversions, while the penchant of politicians, under the influence of the City of London, for 'picking up sugar islands' in the Caribbean led to the death or crippling for life of some 100,000 soldiers. A costly strategy, that did nothing to undermine the power of France. Coupled with ill-conceived recruiting methods, these policies ensured that the British Army never acquired a strategic reserve – despite the Duke of York's extensive administrative reforms – of a size and quality to exploit adequately the strategic opportunities which sea-power provided for bringing succour to her allies.

The main tasks of the Royal Navy had been to blockade the enemy's ports and coastline, strangling their trade and confining the hostile navies to their bases, while protecting British commerce and keeping open the markets of Europe, the Levant and North Africa and North America to British trade. As Napoleon's grip on Europe increased, Britain looked for new markets in South America, an economic version of Canning's post-war policy of calling in the New World to redress the balance of the Old.

Britain used her wealth to hire mercenaries and subsidize Continental allies to do battle for her against the armies of revolutionary France and later of Napoleon. While Britain could not bring France to her knees by blockade, Europe as a whole being self-sufficient, Napoleon sought to isolate Britain and bring her to terms by commercial strangulation and the threat or fact of invasion.

Plans for the invasion of England, directly across the Channel and via Ireland – which was in an actual or incipient state of rebellion – were being prepared from 1794 onwards and on occasion were attempted, though on a small and ineffectual scale. Periodically, formidable land forces were assembled for invasion together with large flotillas of special craft to carry them across the Channel for three days. It was the task of the French and their allied navies to establish this control.

As a prelude to the Peninsular War a summary of events from 1804, the year in which Napoleon crowned himself Emperor and Pitt returned to power, will be helpful. Pitt set about creating a Third Coalition with Austria and Sweden as founder members, shortly to be joined by Russia. Napoleon had again turned his attention to the invasion of England. His 'Army of England', comprising more than 150,000 men, was encamped along the Channel coast, centred on Boulogne, ready to embark in 2,000 invasion craft. Spain had re-entered the war against Britain in 1804, and it was planned that the combined French and Spanish fleets from Toulon and Cadiz should lure the Mediterranean Fleet, under Nelson, across the Atlantic, then double back and, with the squadrons from the Atlantic ports, proceed to wrest control of the Channel.

These manoeuvres ended in Nelson's great victory off Cape Trafalgar on 21 October 1805. In retrospect, Trafalgar set the seal on British maritime supremacy for more than a century. At the time it greatly raised morale at home and British prestige abroad, though it had little direct effect on the war. How far Napoleon believed in the feasibility of his invasion plans is not known, but well before Trafalgar, at the end of August, he decided that the necessary conditions could not be established while he remained menaced by Russia and Austria in the east. He therefore broke up his camps on the Channel coast and marched swiftly to the Danube.

Four days before the battle of Trafalgar an Austrian army was defeated at Ulm and 23,000 men surrendered. Napoleon then occupied Vienna, and at Austerlitz on 2 December he decisively defeated the Russian and Austrian armies. Tsar Alexander I and the Russians retreated to the north-east to carry on the war, but the Emperor Francis II sued for peace. By the Treaty of Pressburg, Austria lost her remaining possessions in Italy and on the Adriatic, and the Emperor his souzerainty over the south German states. From these, Napoleon created a subservient Federation of the Rhine. In effect, Austerlitz put an end to the Holy Roman Empire.

On 23 January 1806, Pitt died. He was succeeded by a Whig administration under Grenville, with Charles James Fox as Foreign Secretary. As Leader of the Opposition in the House of Commons, Fox had strongly opposed the war. In power he found that even he could not stomach the only terms on which Napoleon was prepared to make peace, so the war went on. Fox died in September but the Whigs carried on – little suited for pursuing the war with vigour, despite having a great admiral, Lord St Vincent, at the Admiralty.

In the same month Frederick William King of Prussia, who had followed a pusillanimous and equivocal policy, declared war on France. On 14 October, at the battles of Jena and Auerstadt, the army created by the genius of Frederick the Great was heavily defeated. Napoleon pursued the Prussians with extraordinary energy, covering 170 miles in eight days, and at Prenslau accepted the surrender of 120,000 men under Prince Hohenlohe. Continuing his eastern march, Napoleon covered 375 miles in twenty-three days, occupying all Prussia west of the Vistula except Silesia.

Napoleon wintered in Warsaw. Danzig fell in May, and on 14 June 1807 the Russians were decisively beaten at Friedland. By the nineteenth, Napoleon had reached the River Niemen at Tilist. Here, in a pavilion erected on a raft, the Emperor of the French and the Tsar of All the Russians embraced in mid-stream, and after 'exchanging Ribbons and Gew-Gaws' sat down together in surroundings of considerable splendour 'to drink coffee' and divide Europe between them.[1]

The young Tsar Alexander I, who had set out to liberate Europe from Napoleon, now recognized all the latter's satellite republics, and is said to have greeted Napoleon with the words, 'I hate the English as much as you do' – to which Napoleon allegedly replied: 'Then peace is made'.[2] The Tsar's disillusionment with Britain stemmed from her failure to bring him any substantial aid or divert Napoleon's forces by opening up a second front in northern Europe or the Mediterranean. The view was growing on the Continent that Britain was always prepared to fight to the last Austrian or the last Russian.

The Treaty of Tilsit, signed on 9 July, established Napoleon at the height of his power. The Third Coalition had collapsed and Britain was virtually isolated. Only Sweden, under a mad king; Portugal, with an imbecile queen and a weak regent; and Sicily, with a feeble king and an unpredictable queen, and with some 10,000 British troops for its defence, continued to support her. All Europe other than these minor territories and those of the Ottoman Empire was ruled by Napoleon or members of his family, by subservient republics created by him, or by regimes in alliance or treaty relationship with him.

Under the treaty the Tsar received Swedish Finland, some of Prussian Poland, and the promise of Napoleon's support againt Turkey. Previously, Napoleon had supported Turkey against Russia and Britain had mounted expeditions against the Dardanelles and staged a landing at Alexandria, all unsuccessful, to persuade the Turks to sever their French connection. In return the Tsar gave up some strategic positions in the Adriatic to France. The remainder of Prussia's Polish territories were taken from her to form the Grand Duchy of Warsaw, while Danzig became a free city, and some of Prussia's western provinces were formed into the Kingdom of Westphalia under Napoleon's brother Jerome.

The secret clauses of the treaty were more menacing for Britain. The Tsar agreed to close his ports to British commerce and to declare war on Britain should she not have accepted him by November as the arbiter of peace between Britain and France. Sweden, Denmark and Portugal were to be coerced into an alliance against her.

Should Britain refuse peace on his terms, Napoleon was determined to step up the trade war, and, despite Trafalgar, to outbuild the Royal Navy. After Jena Napoleon entered Berlin, where on 21 November he gave a fresh, and internationally illegal, turn of the screw in his war on British commerce, from which came Britain's ability to subsidize allies against him. From Berlin he decreed 'the British Isles to be in a state of blockade'; all commerce and communication with her was to be prohibited and all goods belonging to or coming from Britain and her colonies were to be seized. It was a measure by which Napoleon, in his own words, hoped 'to strike England to the heart'. He also planned to isolate Britain from her markets. France would occupy Constantinople, the Ottoman Empire would be partitioned with Austria and Russia, and the road to India opened. Brother Joseph would occupy Sicily, and French armies would garrison Gibraltar and Cadiz and cross into Africa.

On 24 March 1807, the Grenville administration resigned over the question of Catholic emancipation, and a Tory government came to power under the elderly Duke of Portland. It contained two men of character and energy who unfortunately detested each other – Canning, the Foreign Secretary, and Castlereagh, the Secretary for War. The Secretary to the Viceroy of Ireland was another man of character, Major-General Sir Arthur Wellesley.

The new government inherited failures in the Dardanelles, in Egypt and at Buenos Aires, but proceeded to act with resolution. In reply to the Berlin Decrees they sought to bring all neutral shipping under control. By Orders in Council all vessels going to or from neutral ports were to travel via Britain, where they would be subjected to customs charges and would have to buy licences to proceed. Napoleon replied by new decrees from Milan, on 23 November 1807, by which all ships touching at English ports were to be confiscated. Many commodities would be deemed to be English, and therefore subject to confiscation, unless it could be proved otherwise. This trade war brought the major contestants into conflict with the neutrals, but fortunately the most important of these, the United States, did not declare war on Britain until 1812 when it was already too late to turn the tide of victory.

The secret clauses in the Treaty of Tilsit quickly became known to Canning, and the government determined to prevent the Danish and Portuguese Fleets from falling into French hands. After Trafalgar, France still had thirty-two battleships afloat and a further twenty-one under construction. When the Treaty of Tilsit was signed it is estimated that the combined French and Dutch Fleets had seventy-five battleships, to which Napoleon's allies, Spain and Russia, could add thirty and twenty-four respectively. If to these could be added seventeen from Denmark and ten from Portugal this would be a good start towards Napoleon's goal of outnumbering the Royal Navy by three to two, say 150 to 100 ships of the line.

Control of the Baltic by the enemy denied Britain her main source of supply for naval stores – spars and timber for shipbuilding, rope and Stockholm tar.

Britain had difficulty in finding the men to maintain more than one hundred battleships in commission and these had to be spread from the Atlantic to the Indian Ocean. For France Europe's mercantile marine, confined to port by the Royal Navy, provided an ample supply of trained seamen. While his warships lay in port under blockade, Napoleon would wage a guerrilla war at sea against British commerce by means of privateers.

Castlereagh quickly overhauled the army and set about creating a well-equipped and well-trained reserve of 30,000 men. Canning also acted with vigour, though he inherited that flaw of English politicians of wanting to employ the army on numerous petty diversions. He demanded that the Danes surrender their Fleet into British hands for safe keeping until the end of the hostilities. When this was refused, an amphibious expedition of twenty-five battleships, forty frigates and smaller warships, accompanied by 27,000 troops, was sent to Denmark. They started to land on 15 August and, after the bombardment of Copenhagen, the Danes surrendered on 7 September. Fifteen Danish battleships laden with valuable stores from the dockyard were escorted to England, though only one 80-gun and three 74-gun ships were considered worth incorporating into the Royal Navy. On Britain's withdrawal, the forces with which Napoleon had intended to forestall Britain occupied Denmark. With the British forces was Ensign John Aitchison of the 3rd Regiment of Guards. For the start of this story, attention must now be focused on the Iberian Peninsula.

Spain, under the feeble rule of Charles IV, had re-entered the war against Britain in 1804. In fact, the real ruler of Spain was the king's first minister – and the queen's lover – Godoy, whose main opponent was the Crown Prince, Ferdinand. Portugal, 'England's oldest ally', was ruled by the irresolute Regent, John, Prince of Brazil, since Queen Maria was mentally deranged. Portugal was virtually an economic colony of Britain, and would starve if the sea communications to her overseas Empire were cut.

The success or failure of Napoleon's trade war depended on establishing control over the ports and coasts of the Peninsula. He also wanted to topple the Bourbons in Spain, to secure his own dynasty. Having failed to secure the Danish Fleet, it was even more important to gain control of that of Portugal. On 19 July 1807, only ten days after signing the Treaty of Tilsit, Napoleon demanded that Portugal should close her ports to British ships and confiscate British property. Three weeks later he demanded that Portugal should declare war on Britain. Caught between the French and the British, the Regent prevaricated.

Castlereagh ordered 8,000 men under Sir John Moore to be relieved in Sicily by troops evacuated from Alexandria, and to be embarked for Gibraltar to await instructions. On 27 August, Lieutenant-General Lord Cathcart was ordered to release 10,000 of his troops, now returned from Denmark. These included Major-General Sir Arthur Wellesley, who had commanded a brigade while he was still Irish Secretary.

On 19 October, Junot crossed into Spain at the head of 28,000 men, with orders to be in Lisbon by 1 December and gain control of the Portuguese Fleet. A week later the secret Treaty of Fontainebleau established a joint

Spanish–French interest in the occupation and partition of Portugal. Napoleon, fearing another Copenhagen, pressed Junot to make all possible speed and not to delay for want of supplies; '20,000 men can live anywhere, even in a desert',[3] he was told.

At the beginning of November, to appease Napoleon, the Regent showed hostility to Britain, but was secretely preparing to sail to Brazil if the French invaded Portugal. On the sixteenth a squadron of six battleships under Rear-Admiral Sir Sydney Smith arrived in the Tagus, where they found a Russian squadron *en route* from the Mediterranean to the Baltic. Smith arrived with dispatches for the British Ambassador who was instructed that if the removal of the Royal Family and Portuguese Fleet to Brazil was not agreed upon, Portuguese shipping in the Tagus would be taken by force.

Junot marching over inhospitable country in appalling weather, entered Lisbon on 30 November, with some 1,500 exhausted and near-starving infantry, all he had left from the 28,000 with which he had set out. For the moment his army had ceased to exist, though many of his men were to come in over the next three weeks. He was just in time to see the white sails of the Portuguese Fleet flying the Royal Standard as they cleared the Tagus with the Royal Family on board. Portugal occupied by French and Spanish troops, fell into a mood of sullen discontent which from time to time broke out in rioting.

The Treaty of Fontainebleau had allowed Napoleon to march up to 40,000 men through Spain to reinforce Junot. At the beginning of 1808, without consulting the Spanish authorities, he sent 75,000 men under Murat into Spain. By a series of tricks the frontier fortresses and the citadel of Barcelona (hardly *en route* for Portugal!) were seized. Murat was ordered to occupy Madrid under cover of marching against Gibraltar. He was a tough fighting soldier without a shred of political acumen, and when Napoleon sent him into Spain he took the first step in creating the 'Spanish ulcer' that contributed so greatly to his own downfall.

Riots followed, calling for the blood of Godoy, and King Charles abdicated in favour of Crown Prince Ferdinand. Ferdinand was not a strong man, and little better than his father, but he was young and bitterly anti-French, and the Spanish people – proud, xenophobic, and deeply attached to the Church of Rome – rallied to him. Napoleon offered to mediate between Charles IV, who regretted his abdication, and Ferdinand while planning to have one of his own brothers offered the crown of Spain with some semblance of constitutional legality.

Ferdinand was tricked into visiting his parents in Bayonne, where great pressure to abdicate was brought on him by Napoleon. Rumours of this reached Madrid, which Murat had entered as a conqueror, and on 2 May the mob rose and killed every Frenchman on the streets. Murat took drastic reprisals, Charles and Ferdinand were made to abdicate, and a subservient Council of Regency was prevailed upon to offer the crown to Joseph Bonaparte, King of Naples. Madrid once more rose against the French. Rebellion quickly spread to all the provinces, each of which set up its own junta to conduct the resistance and raise forces. Spanish forces withdrew from Portugal, which in turn declared its independence.

The Spanish regular Army was in poor shape. Fifteen thousand of its best troops were serving in north Germany under the Marquis de la Romana, and from these some 9,000 were to be extracted by a clandestine operation under Rear-Admiral Keats. Most of the Spanish officers were ignorant, inexperienced and too proud to learn. The rank and file, however, were peasants — brave, hardy and frugal; potentially they were excellent fighting material. The main bodies of the Spanish Army were in Galicia, from where they could threaten the French lines of communication and expect outside help through the northern ports, and in Andalusia in the south.

To crush the insurrection, the French had some 91,000 troops in Spain. However they were mainly inexperienced recruits and soon they were in trouble everywhere. Individuals and small parties were ambushed and killed, often with great brutality. Nowhere were their lines of communication secure — the French controlled only the ground that lay within range of the cannon. The guerrilla war which was to provide the framework within which Wellington's regulars were to triumph had started.

Two events that took place in Spain prior to British intervention deserve special notice. General Dupont, commanding one of the French armies, was sent to crush resistance in the south, with orders to occupy Seville and Cadiz. *En route* he sacked Cordova, and then, finding himself isolated and his communications cut, and in the presence of vastly superior forces, capitulated on 23 July at Bailen, where 18,000 of his men laid down their arms to General Castaños. The other event was the heroic defence of the strategically important city of Zaragoza at the main crossing of the Ebro. Here a largely volunteer force of Spaniards, manning improvised defences, repelled three attempts by 17,000 French troops to take the place by storm. Such heroism in defence of fortified places was to be repeated throughout the war.

The defeat of the French Army at Bailen had a great psychological effect on both sides. However, whereas the defeat of the French by the British at Maida in Calabria in July 1806 demonstrated that defence by well-disciplined troops in line, two-deep, could defeat this *élan* of the French attacking in column, a lesson taken to heart by Sir Arthur Wellesley, misled the British into overestimating the capabilities of the Spanish, which led to some costly mistakes and missed opportunities.

On 8 June, while Dupont's troops were sacking Cordova, the first delegates arrived in London from the Spanish provinces and from Portugal, seeking arms and money. The British government expressed its determination to help, and on 4 July Spain was formally declared an ally. Joseph Bonaparte crossed into Spain on the ninth to ascend his throne. He could not enter Madrid until the fifteenth, when he found a dead city without a single Spaniard on the streets. Napoleon had believed that there would be little difficulty in putting down the insurrection, but French arms had failed everywhere except in Léon, where the Spanish General Cuesta blundered. By the end of August, Joseph had to evacuate Madrid. Zaragoza had been relieved and French power had virtually been confined to north of the Ebro. The French now had some 60,000 men in north-east Spain, having lost 40,000 in action.

The French had been humiliated without any outside intervention on the side of Spain. This gave the Spaniards unjustified confidence in their own prowess, and similarly deceived the British government. Before tracing the early course of British intervention in the Peninsula it is worth considering two errors of judgment by Napoleon which were to persist throughout the war and carried the seeds of disaster. Firstly, he under-rated his enemy, despising them and entirely failing to understand their patriotism and their loathing for their French 'liberators'. Secondly, and more surprisingly, he ignored the effects of terrain on operations in Spain and Portugal.

Communications play some part in all military campaigns. In the Peninsula they were vital. Throughout, Napoleon seems to have seen the Peninsula in terms of his first brilliantly successful campaign in Italy, where he was welcomed as a liberator and could live off the land. This enabled him to move with remarkable speed and out-manoeuvre the Austrians, who were tied to depots and fixed lines of communication. That Napoleon should have believed that the same system would work in the Peninsula is the more surprising after his experience of campaigning under desert conditions in the Middle East. Wellington, on the other hand, from his experiences in India as a 'Sepoy General', understood very well the problems of supply where food is scarce, population scanty and roads few and bad. Moreover, Wellington understood from the beginning the importance of not despoiling the inhabitants, for he relied upon their supporting the guerrilla forces to tie down and disrupt the lines of communication of his numerically superior enemy. It has been well said that 'in Spain large armies starve and small armies are beaten'.[4]

Operating against the British in Portugal, the French had long land-lines of communication which were exposed everywhere to guerrilla attack. The British, however, had their lines of communication with their main base secured by the Royal Navy's command of the sea. Sea-power also enabled them to change their own lines of communication according to the position of the army and to threaten the French communications with landings in the rear. Because they lacked a proper system of supply the French armies were only able to remain concentrated for a few days, after which they had to scatter to areas where food could be obtained, or starve. Part of Wellington's genius lay in his ability to build up a supply system which ensured that administration served, but did not control, the movement of his army. John Aitchison, with a farming background and lively interest in what went on around him, pays considerable attention to this aspect of the war in his letters home.

We must now look at those events which led Britain into choosing the Iberian Peninsula as the theatre in which sea-power, combined with a comparatively small but well-trained and well-led army, would enable a successful war of attrition to be waged against Napoleon's might and unlimited manpower. Sir John Moore, with 7,258 men, left Sicily on 30 October 1807 for Gibraltar to await orders. The intention was to use these troops to help the Portuguese resist the French, but when they arrived Portugal was already occupied, so Moore was ordered to leave two battalions there and bring home the rest. Major-General Brent Spencer, with 5,000 men evacuated from Buenos Aires, had also been sent to the Tagus but was subsequently ordered to maintain his force in floating reserve at Gibraltar.

While this was going on, Major-General William Carr-Beresford was sent with an occupation force to Madeira, and an expeditionary force of 8,000 was assembled at Cork under Sir Arthur Wellesley, aged thirty-nine and recently promoted lieutenant-general. Sir Arthur's force was ordered in June 1808 to the Iberian Peninsula, the British government having heard that the insurrection in Spain had caused Junot to abandon north and south Portugal and concentrate his forces around Lisbon. On arrival, Sir Arthur was to add Spencer's force to his command.

Wellesley first made contact with the Galician junta at Corunna, where he found enthusiasm and a desire for arms and money but none for British soldiers. He sailed on to consult Admiral Sir Charles Cotton on landing his force at Figueira, the port of Coimbra in Portugal. Wellesley then received dispatches informing him of the government's intention to send out a further 16,000 troops with Sir Harry Burrard and Sir John Moore. Burrard would be second-in-command to Sir Hew Dalrymple when Dalrymple arrived from Gibraltar, where he was governor.

Dalrymple and Burrard were both senior to Moore, who in turn was senior to Wellesley. Dalrymple, who had seen no active service since the Flanders campaign of 1793–4, was reluctant to leave Gibraltar, while Burrard made no pretence of being a great soldier. Wellesley, who would have been most happy to have served under Moore, was affronted by these purely political appointments, arising from Canning's determination to keep Moore out of the principal command. Wellesley was therefore determined to defeat Junot before being superseded.

At Vimeiro he achieved his first major victory in the Peninsula, but the fruits of victory were denied him, for Burrard arrived to take command in the middle of the action and failed to exploit Wellesley's success. This inaction was confirmed by Dalrymple when he arrived the next day. The defeated French were now cut off from their communications and Junot asked to open negotiations, which ended on 31 August in the Convention of Cintra. Though he had had no hand in the negotiations, Wellesley added his signature to those of Dalrymple and Burrard. Under the Convention, Junot's force was to be shipped back to France with their arms and loot. Admiral Cotton insisted, fortunately, that the Russian ships trapped in the Tagus should be handed into custody for safe keeping until the end of hostilities. This squadron had taken refuge in Lisbon from a storm on 10 November 1807 (not knowing that the Tsar had declared war on England on the second), and had been blockaded by the Royal Navy ever since.

Burrard's reinforcements were now landed and Lisbon occupied. Dalrymple was kept busy setting up a Council of Regency, while the affairs of the army fell into disarray. On the nineteenth Sir Arthur met Moore for the first time, and promised to use his influence at home to get Moore the chief command. Next day Wellesley left for England on leave.

When the conditions of the Convention of Cintra became known in England they created uproar. An enquiry was demanded and Dalrymple went home to face the music. John Aitchison's letter from Chatham, dated 5 October, typifies this reaction:

Chatham
To my dear Father,   *5th October 1808*

There are several queries to which you desire answers, I think best to notice according to their order in your letter (of the 27th).

You express a hope that Hew Dalrymple has by this time shot himself. I must confess I have no such desire, nay, I should feel disappointed did it take place, but, as far as I can judge of his conduct, I see no reason to entertain the hope that he will have so much resolution, for I cannot conceive that any man who could act so basely irresolute as Sir Hew appears to have acted throughout could meet death with such coolness. I hope he is destined to receive the punishment he appears to deserve, that will serve to warn those officers who may be appointed to high commands. We have acted with too much lenity to all the officers commanding expeditions that have failed, and the evil has now risen to such a height as to require a dreadful example on some.

The French papers say immense armies are on the march to Spain, and Bonaparte himself says he will immediately send 200,000 men there.

I, however, do not believe it. I am of opinion there will be no active operations there *for six months at least,* as I cannot believe that Bonaparte, who has hitherto acted with such judgement in the direction of his military operations, will now commit himself by sending an army into Spain at this season of the year to act offensively. There are only five passes across the Pyrenees, three of which are impassable from November to May, but the two principal ones are always passable. They lie at each extremity; one leads from Bayonne to Vitoria, the other leads into Catalonia through Gerona to Barcelona; this latter is guarded by the Spaniards and Gerona is in their possession.

I am aware that the plea of the season may appear frivolous when we recollect Bonaparte's winter campaign in Poland, but let it be considered he had then to fight against governments supported by mercenary armies, in a country the inhabitants of which were not unfavourable to his cause, but that he has now to fight in a country against *its whole population.* Let it also be considered that he will have to draw his whole supplies from that country – mountainous, thinly populated and in consequence badly culti- vated – and although every pass in the Pyrenees were practicable at all seasons, the difficulty of transporting supplies for a beleaguered army on muleback would almost amount to an impossibility.

The French army in Spain by the greatest [*sic*] accounts does not exceed 75,000 men including the different garrisons, yet it has taken up a *defen- sive* position with the River Ebro in its front, and extending through Vitoria to the sea, thus occupying a distance of about 150 miles covering the western passes of the Pyrenees.

I certainly believe that Bonaparte will send more troops into Spain, but I think it will be with a view to endeavour to maintain the present position, for should Barcelona hold out it will enable him to attack Zaragoza with great advantage at the opening of the campaign, and this town is of the utmost importance to him to possess.

But on the other hand, while the French remain behind Ebro *inactive*, the Patriotic army will every day increase and improve, as it now possesses the uncommon advantage of having to attend to only one point. Their force will soon amount to a number sufficient to resist any attack or that will enable them to act on the offensive should they judge it most advantageous. This certainly is a strong reason why the French should act offensively – but it does not appear that any reinforcements have actually entered Spain, and yet we are told of the immense number of troops marching through every part of France and from Italy *all* towards the Pyrenees. Perhaps they are collecting to enter in one body with the hope of wearing down all opposition. This has been the practice of Bonaparte in all the campaigns in which he succeeded, but let it be remembered the French themselves, at the commencement of the revolution in driving back the *Austrians and Prussians united*, gave a strong proof that *no regular army could possess a country defended by inhabitants, although unorganized, if determined to be free.* I therefore entertain the most sanguine hope that however great be the force sent against Spain it will not be subdued.

In speculating on the efforts of the Spaniards I have not calculated on the probable assistance of Austria, I mean in the event of her going to war with France. Should this take place, and it now seems beyond doubt, France will be unable to prosecute the war in Spain with vigour, and Italy already drained of troops will be exposed to attack on the side of Sicily.

There is no doubt the British army in Spain would render considerable assistance, but it seems to be the general opinion that it might be employed in another quarter to better account, for situated advantageously as is Spain in having to fear attack from only one point, and being so much intersected by ranges of mountains, *if her inhabitants remain unanimous and firm* they must eventually succeed. Yet if the French can bring a considerable army into the field, in the first encounters, it will be successful, but it is not to be supposed successes are to be gained without some loss on their side. The Spaniards, however, will always be able to replace theirs, however great, and by infinity of numbers they must at least accomplish the overthrow of the French, without the co-operation of any foreign army.

Of our brigade going on service, opinions are different. Those in the regiment generally seem to think we shall go, but after the very shameful behaviour of the Commander-in-Chief[5] nothing induces me to think we shall go abroad but the injustice of keeping us at home.

> Remember me to all the Family
> I remain my dear Father
> your most affectionate son.

Inspired by the victory at Bailen and by reports of other Spanish successes, mostly fictitious, the government reversed their views and ordered Sir Harry Burrard to retain 10,000 men for the defence of Portugal and dispatched Sir

John Moore with the remaining 22,000 to co-operate with the Spanish armies in northern Spain. Fresh reinforcements under Lieutenant-General Sir David Baird would be sent to Moore to bring his force up to 35,000 men, 'the finest command held by a British officer since Marlborough'.[6]

Moore decided to enter Spain overland. Speed was essential, as the high mountains along the frontier had to be crossed before the rainy season. The bad roads caused him to march by several routes and to send his reserve artillery by a separate, circuitous route escorted by two infantry brigades and most of the cavalry. The administrative difficulties were immense. He had virtually no military transport and no money to hire transport, buy provisions or pay the troops.

Baird arrived at Corunna with 12,000 reinforcements on 13 October, but was prevented by the Galician junta from disembarking until 4 November. At the end of that month Moore set out for Burgos to take his place in the line of Spanish armies facing the Ebro. He intended first, however, to concentrate his force at Salamanca. He relied on improvised transport and on the Spaniards to provide food and forage.

The central junta in Madrid could not agree on the appointment of a commander-in-chief. Their collective strategic concepts were ill-defined, the intelligence they passed to Moore was usually faulty and often grossly misleading, and the commanders of the provincial armies were very much a law unto themselves. Proper co-ordination of plans with the Spanish was therefore impossible.

Napoleon had already announced his intention of leading an army in person to the conquest of Spain and Portugal. He had assembled a striking force of 152,000 behind the Ebro, organized into six corps including many veterans from his triumphs in central Europe. Before long the French were to have some 250,000 men in the Peninsula. The day Baird arrived at Corunna, Napoleon arrived at Joseph's headquarters at Vitoria. By the time Moore reached Salamanca with two-thirds of his force, Baird was still 120 miles to the west, and the situation had completely changed. Burgos had fallen and the two Spanish armies which were to have covered Moore's flanks had been beaten and dispersed.

Moore was in a dilemma. The Spanish armies, to which his expeditionary force was to be auxiliary, had collapsed before the French – and he now heard of the defeat of Castaños at Tudela. He was left facing overwhelming odds, in command of Britain's only substantial and irreplaceable army, whose loss would radically change the course of the war. Militarily this was the time to retire, and he ordered Baird to do so while making preparations for his own force to follow. On the other hand, calls for aid came to him from every side, not least from Madrid which a staff officer, Colonel Thomas Graham (the future General Lord Lyndock), had recently reported that the Spaniards were preparing for defence.

A change of leadership in the central junta nursed the hope that the flame of resistance would be rekindled. Napoleon was concentrating on the capture of Madrid, and Moore, at last reunited with his artillery, decided to make a thrust towards Valladolid, threatening the French lines of communication, with the intention of drawing off the French forces and so giving the Spanish armies a breathing space. Baird's orders were countermanded. Instead, he was to advance to Astorga, but remain prepared for a rapid retreat. Moore now heard from Castlereagh that Sir John Cradock was to relieve Burrard as Commander-in-Chief in Portugal, and that fresh reinforcements were to be sent out to him. Among them, would be John Aitchison, with the 1st Battalion, 3rd Regiment of Guards.

The central junta had left Madrid for Badajoz in November, and when Moore set out towards Valladolid the French had already reoccupied the capital. The Spanish garrison had surrendered without firing a shot and had not thought fit to inform Moore.

On 13 December a French staff officer, killed by guerrillas, was found to be carrying dispatches from Napoleon to Soult. Sold to an officer on Moore's staff for twenty dollars, they gave the disposition and order of battle of Napoleon's forces in Spain and, *inter alia*, disclosed that Soult, with 20,000 men, was isolated north of Valladolid, the nearest French forces being around Madrid. They also disclosed that Napoleon believed Moore to be retreating on Lisbon, where the Emperor intended to follow and destroy the British army.

Moore turned north to move against Soult, but on 23 December, when the opposing forces were very close, news arrived that Ney had left Madrid three days before to cut Moore's line of retreat. Napoleon, though still not clear as to the exact location of the British, had realized that Moore had shifted his lines of communication to Corunna, and, appreciating the importance of destroying the British army, was exerting every effort to cut him off.

Moore had no choice but to make a rapid retreat. Baird's column had joined him on the twenty-second, the day after a smart cavalry action by the 15th Hussars, under Lord Paget, earned them the battle honour 'Sahagun'. Moore's force was on the river Cea, his left column at Sahagun and his right at Benavente. The great retreat started in bitter weather on Christmas Eve. On 26 December, Ney, commanding the French advance guard, reached Mayorga, on the Cea, between Moore's two columns, and was joined two days later by Napoleon.

The British rearguards retired on the twenty-ninth, covered by the cavalry; the 10th Hussars fought a notable action at Benavente on the thirty-first. The retreat was not to end until the army reached Corunna on 11 January, having lost a fifth of its strength. The suffering was appalling, and morale – which had been high – and discipline broke down in all but the best corps. Fortunately the discipline of the rearguard division, including the 52nd Light Infantry and the 95th Rifles, never wavered. In terrible weather, and constantly without food, many perished from cold and fatigue. Many women and children also died, and men deserted in search of food, drink and plunder.

When Moore entered Corunna on 11 January his army, strung out over many miles, was, with the exception of some élite corps, a rabble – starved, emaciated, filthy and many without boots. However, he had gained the necessary time to prepare defences to check Soult and so make embarkation possible. After the British had passed through Astorga, Napoleon realized that Moore had escaped his trap, and on 4 January, leaving the pursuit to Soult and Ney, he turned back, for he had received disturbing reports of the rearming of Austria.

Unfavourable winds kept the transport out of Corunna until 15 January, so that Moore had to take up positions capable of being held for several days with the number of men available. The days after the transports got in, Soult made his main attack. Able at last to grapple with the enemy, the effect on British morale was miraculous. Moore rode the battlefield, encouraging his men wherever the fire was hottest. French attempts to carry the position were thrown back with heavy casualties. British losses were not light – the most grievous being that of Moore himself. He fell in the thick of the fighting at the moment of victory, his shoulder carried away by a cannonball. Next morning he was buried on the ramparts of Corunna. By then Soult had been fought to a standstill and, helped by local Spanish men, women and children manning the ramparts, the expeditionary force embarked without molestation.

It took a long time for the British people to appreciate and understand Moore's achievement in drawing away Napoleon's forces from the south of Spain and the conquest of Lisbon. In later years Wellington, who inherited the situation, looked back on his own triumphs and paid Moore this compliment, 'You know, we'd not, I think, have won without him'.

Napoleon left Spain with the Imperial Guard. He left behind 191,000 men organized in six corps and a reserve, each under a marshal, five of whom were dukes, each jealous of one another and contemptuous of King Joseph and his Chief of Staff, Marshal Jourdan, whose orders they ignored. Napoleon wrote to his brother Jerome, King of Westphalia, 'The Spanish business is finished. . . . If the Emperor of Austria makes the slightest hostile movement, he will soon cease to reign. That is very clear. As for the Russians, we have never been on better terms with them.'[7]

In Britain the uproar over the evacuation of the British forces after the loss of 6,000 men was predictable. Indignation over the Convention of Cintra had hardly died down. The reactions of an intelligent and keen young officer of the Scots Guards to these events will be seen in Chapter 1.

This Prologue will, it is hoped, have illustrated those features which were to influence the course of the war in the Peninsula over the next four years: the difficulties of the terrain, lack of transport, scarcity of provisions, prevalence of disease, harshness of climate and, in the case of the British, the chronic lack of an adequate military chest. As for the Spanish ally, co-operation was to prove most difficult. Their armies, though unable to withstand the French in the field, proved to be remarkably resilient after defeat, and their citizens frequently exhibited extraordinary valour and determination in defence of fortified places (the outstanding example being the two-month defence of Zaragoza). But most significant was the burgeoning of the guerrilla war which was to deny the French control of Spanish territory beyond the range of their guns and, by tying down their forces and cutting their communications, enabled Wellington, with far fewer troops, to triumph in the field. Lastly, the campaign illustrated the close inter-relationship between the war in the Peninsula and that in central Europe.

CHAPTER ONE

1809
The Year of Talavera

T the beginning of December 1808, General Sir John Moore received news that further reinforcements were to be sent to him, under the command of Major-General John Sherbrooke, of which the 2nd Guards Brigade, commanded by Brigadier-General Henry Campbell and comprising the 1st Battalion Coldstream Guards, and 1st Battalion, 3rd Regiment of Guards, would form a part.

The brigade was stationed at Chatham from where John Aitchison wrote early in December to his father:

Chatham
6th December 1808

My dear Father,

I have at length the pleasure to inform you that we are to be sent to Spain immediately – the order for our embarkation arrived this morning. The transports sailed from Portsmouth last Saturday and we are to embark as soon as they arrive at Sheerness – this will be in two or three days at furthest.

Ministers are now acting as they ought – and sending the whole of our disposable force – the present embarkation will amount to 12,000 men but they will sail by brigades as soon as they have embarked. The cavalry are embarking at Cork, Falmouth and Portsmouth and the infantry at Sheerness, Ramsgate and Harwich.

The north-east winds which usually prevail at this season are the fairest for us and we shall have arrived at Corunna in three or four days' sail.

The whole of my field equipment has been packed since the first order – I am now packing up my heavy baggage.

I shall write to you again in the day we embark and before we sail.

Love to all the family

John Aitchison's cavalier attitude towards Portugal in his next letter reflects public opinion at the time. It did not, however, reflect naval opinion, which regarded the use of Lisbon as of great importance. Then came news of the Spanish defeats and the possibility that the British expeditionary force might have to be evacuated.

Chatham

My dear Father,   *11th December 1808*

It was but the other day I had the great satisfaction to acquaint you with the determination of Ministers to send immediately reinforcements to our army in Spain, but I have now the mortification to state that the disastrous turn of the cause of the patriots has completely changed that laudable resolution, and no more troops are for the present to be embarked; on the contrary, the few that were ready to sail have been relanded and the whole of the transports in England, and every ship of war in the Southern ports, has been ordered to proceed to Corunna and go forthwith.

The accounts from Spain were indeed melancholy, and they produced a gloom which operated on the extreme ardour of our expectation, but it did not damp our enthusiasm in the cause – we did expect that the resolutions of our Government were founded on a basis not to be shaken by misfortune, and that *that*, instead of intimidating or inducing them to relax, would stimulate exertion correspondent to the exigency; in fine, that regiment after regiment will be sent to assist the Spaniards while there was the most distant prospect of an effectual resistance – but these expectations were transient – and to say the least the honour of our country has been most shamefully sacrificed, for what can be thought of a people who by pompous assurances of powerful assistance encouraged a nation to resist the oppression of a foreign yoke – and when the moment of danger arrived withdrew without an effort? – that people must I think be cursed – but enough – the heart sickens at the thought.

To look to what is yet possible to be done – the Spaniards have dispersed but they are not subdued. I by no means despair of the final success if they be but firm. Let Portugal, if it is necessary, be abandoned to its fate and the whole of our forces be sent into Andalusia; it was here the first blow was struck against the French and the country is naturally strong – besides if at last it should be found necessary to desist – our retreat will be so secure to Cadiz and Gibraltar and once there no enemy can affect us.

I shall not yet despair of seeing service – for I hope ministers will be compelled to continue the army in Spain – should any reinforcement be sent this is the first brigade to go.

The government began to see the south of Spain as the most suitable area for British intervention. Moore had always held this view. To be effective, however, it would be necessary to have Cadiz as a secure base and although there was evidence that the inhabitants would not have resisted British troops, governing circles opposed the suggestion, fearing to create a second Gibraltar.

Cradock was ordered to leave the general defence of Portugal to the Portuguese and to concentrate his troops for the defence of Lisbon, releasing as many as possible for Cadiz. British troops were ordered not to land at Cadiz except with Spanish permission. Major-Gen. Alexander Mackenzie and four infantry battalions were embarked for Cadiz and the 40th Foot was sent overland via Seville. Sherbrooke's force, originally intended for Corunna, was now ordered to the Tagus to await orders, and then on 16 January received secret orders to go straight to Cadiz.

The embarkation strength of the 1st Battalion 3rd Guards was 1,375.[1]

Between December 1808 and February 1809, Aitchison's letters contain details of regimental preparations for the coming campaign and his reactions to them:

> The whole of the servants of this battalion are to join the ranks on service; in consequence the officers have provided themselves with knap-sacks to carry their necessaries themselves. This is a most commendable regulation of Sir John Moore which besides lessening the baggage of the British army, that has been so enormous hitherto,[2] will add forty effective men to each battalion, and increase the army by one-thirtieth. It will no doubt render the situation of officers not quite so comfortable, but they possess the same feelings as the rest of the nation in the cause of the Spaniards, and whatever is conducive to the general good, it requires but example and a little persuasion to make them adapt. I have weighed what I have to carry and find it amounts to 27 pounds.

On Christmas Day the Guards received orders to prepare to embark at Ramsgate. Aitchison arrived at Portsmouth on 2 January in the *Queen* transport where they waited for a convoy before going to Falmouth. The ships of the Russian squadron which had been interned at Lisbon were lying off Mother-bank, manned by their officers and crews but with all their sails and ammunition put ashore. Aitchison remarks that some of the ships were thought uncommonly fine. There followed a period of frustration because of contrary winds and uncertainty from news filtering home from Spain.

They were still at Portsmouth on 11 January, and sailing was postponed at the news of Moore's retreat. There were rumours of some other destination than Corunna. John Aitchison wrote:

> Lord Castlereagh, I have heard, is not for assisting the Spaniards with men and it has been asserted by those likely to know . . . that no one question relative to sending troops to Spain has been carried without a *division* (of the cabinet). . . . My Lord C. has, I think, in most instances shown himself eminently *un*qualified for the office he holds (Secretary for War) and I sincerely trust if it does appear he opposed supporting a cause which the people called their own and for which his Majesty pledged himself to assist in carrying into immediate execution . . . he will suffer such a punishment as will secure all others from undertaking the duties of an office they are not qualified to discharge.

This is unfair to Castlereagh, for it was Canning who was opposed to sending British forces into Spain.

Three days out from Portsmouth they ran into a severe storm which scattered the convoy, and the *Queen* lost her main yard. They got into the Cove of Cork on 3 February. It was 13 February before all the convoy were accounted for, when Aitchison wrote:

The greatest exertions are still made to revictual the fleet and it is still given out that we are to sail as soon as the wind is fair without instructions from England – from several circumstances, however, that have transpired I am myself induced to believe we shall not sail until orders are received from Ministers.

Colonel Duff, who commands the 88th Regiment, has been permitted to go to London on private business, and General Sherbrooke has sent dispatches by him. Provisions at this place, although exorbitant for Ireland, are very cheap compared to England. Potatoes sell 25 lbs for 2½ pence. Beef and mutton 4½ pence a pound, eggs 10 pence a dozen – butter 18 pence, but this since the fleet arrived has risen to 2/- and eggs 13 pence – the other articles are considerably advanced – the prices I have mentioned are what the natives pay generally, we are obliged to give more. . . .

Having embarked a further 5,200 men and 400 horses, and taken on board six months' supply of water, they set sail on 23 February 1809 under the overall command of General Beresford, for a rendezvous off Cadiz which they expected to reach in eight days.

> *Queen Transport 415 Lisbon*
> *11th March 1809*

Who could have thought that the high-minded, generous, patriotic Spaniards, our allies, the Spaniards who scorn to receive as a gift the money sent from Britain at the commencement of their revolution, who pledged themselves to repay or remunerate us as soon as circumstances would permit, who could believe the same Spaniards now their cause begins to appear hopeless would refuse admittance to our army into Cadiz? Such however has been their return for our generous conduct and it was fallen to our lot to suffer the mortification of the refusal.

By a succession of moderate weather and by an almost uninterrupted continuance of northerly winds we had the good fortune to reach our intended destination early on Wednesday, 8th. The whole fleet was within sight of Cadiz and some of the transports had actually entered the roads, when the signal was hoisted to rendezvous in the Tagus. Accordingly we immediately put about when, most fortunately, the wind changed from the north-east to the south and we arrived here at 12 this day.

As the ship I am in did not enter the roads I had not an opportunity to learn the cause of this most extraordinary behaviour on the part of the Spaniards – but we hailed one of the transports that had been at the mouth of the harbour and the Master of it told us he had heard from the British Admiral's boat that the French had gained a battle and taken a large town and arrived in force in the neighbourhood which occasioned our non-admittance – and that 3,000 British troops had returned to Lisbon from the same reason three days before.[3]

This is the whole of the information we could collect and I cannot, you will perceive, vouch for its correctness nor am I inclined to place much reliance on it. But there seems very little doubt that the Spaniards, whatever should happen, will not deliver up their fleet nor will they permit us to carry off the French ships in their ports – we went near enough to see the French fleet in the harbour – they appeared dismantled and there were no preparations making to equip them.

Lord Collingwood[4] and Admiral Purvis were in Cadiz with about 5 sail of the line. The Brest fleet you will have heard put to sea yesterday week – it passed Cadiz at 15 leagues distance on the 7th. *Sunday 12th* I had written thus far before we came to anchor. We are to land tomorrow morning at 9 and we are for the present to be in barracks at Belem, which is about 5 miles from Lisbon. I have been on shore for about an hour and I find the belief that the Spaniards will not permit us to carry off their fleet confirmed. The reports at Lisbon are as you may suppose very numerous and uncommonly favourable. The French it appears have evacuated Corunna and Vigo and are withdrawing from the whole of the North of Spain and retreating upon Madrid with a view, it is said, of evacuating the Peninsula. This last, people will believe as they think proper, but it has been published in the *Lisbon Gazette* that the French had retreated as far as Toledo, which place was also evacuated, and that Sir Robert Wilson[5] had advanced to Salamanca with the Portuguese legion without meeting any French troops. Several vessels are now in this port which left Vigo at a week, since at that time there were no French there. The Portuguese, it is said, are arming in great numbers and there is already a respectable army well clothed and accoutred – General Beresford[6] is at Lisbon and has been gazetted Commander-in-Chief and he has brought with him a number of British officers to organize the Portuguese.

I have written this in a hurry to take advantage of a frigate which sails for England tomorrow but I shall write again by the packet on Tuesday.

I remain etc.

Belem Lisbon
Tuesday 14th March 1809

We landed yesterday morning – The men are in barracks and the officers are billeted, but in such houses as the lowest servant in England would object to. . . . I walked the whole of yesterday without being able to find a lodging – although accompanied by an officer of police – I am going again to the Intendant to renew my search. I trust therefore you will excuse my giving any news as the packet sails at 3 o'clock.

We have not met with the kind reception we expected but it would not be fair to judge a whole nation by the behaviour of a few tiresome individuals in the suburbs of Lisbon, which is I believe the most inhospitable part of Portugal. I shall write again to you or William as soon as I am settled.

On failing to obtain Spanish permission to use Cadiz as a base, the government ordered the recall of Mackenzie and Sherbrooke to Lisbon. 'Without a fortress to fall back upon we will not commit our troops in the heart of Spain, nor will we fritter our forces away among the Spanish armies. If the Spanish do not desire our assitance we have no desire to press it on them,' wrote Canning.

Sir Arthur Wellesley was also making his influence felt. Moore, who only had a very brief experience of Portugal and believed the Portuguese Army to be useless, considered that with Spain in the hands of the French, Portugal could not be held. Wellesley expressed a more positive view. The natural defences of Portugal are weak, since her frontiers are pierced by rivers flowing east to west, but he believed that, provided the Spanish continued their insurgency, Portugal could be held by 30,000 British troops while the Portuguese forces were retrained and brought up to a strength of 30,000 regulars and 40,000 militia; the British troops could then be reduced to 20,000.

Wellesley was now appointed marshal-general of all the troops in Portugal, with the task of defending it, but was not to enter Spain without the British government's permission. Aitchison's letter below reflects the false optimism which had been generated by erroneous reports from Spain about a French withdrawal. In fact Napoleon had left orders for the subjugation of Spain and the conquest of Portugal. Soult was ordered to march south, occupying first Oporto and then Lisbon. Victor was to march on Badajoz down the Guadiana valley, and between them Lapisse was to advance from Salamanca. In Galicia, Ney was immobilized by a small Spanish force under Romana and harassed by guerrillas. The revolt in Catalonia had, for the time being, been quelled – in February, 16,000 of the heroic defenders of Zaragoza had marched out, leaving 40,000 dead from war and disease amidst its ruins. Zaragoza's citizens under General José Palafox (afterwards Duke of Zaragoza) heroically withstood siege by immensely superior forces, from 15 June to 14 August 1808, and from 20 December 1808 to 20 February 1809.

Soult marched on 30 January but his advance was slowed by bad roads, and the action of a few Portuguese regulars and guerrillas. Oporto fell by assault on 29 March and for twenty-four hours was given over to rape, destruction and pillage. Some 8,000 Portuguese were killed or drowned in the Douro.

Lapisse was held in check by Sir Robert Wilson's Loyal Lusitanian Legion, and Victor, after defeating a Spanish army under Cuesta at Medellin on 27 March, remained at Merida awaiting reinforcements. Wilson meanwhile had seized the Pass of Baños, cutting communication between Victor and Lapisse.

With the arrival of Sherbrooke, Sir John Cradock had some 16,000 men. On 4 April, Major-General Rowland Hill arrived with a further 4,000 and Cradock, urged by Beresford, decided to advance. Wellesley is usually credited with the plan to hold Victor and Lapisse in check while concentrating against Soult. John Aitchison makes it clear that Cradock, whose difficulties have been overlooked by some historians, and who is commonly accused of over-caution, was the author of this plan which Sir Arthur approved and executed.

Carregado
12th April 1809

The letter which I wrote to you from Sacavem on the 3rd inst would inform you it had been determined not to quit Portugal but in the last extremity, and with that view to advance to a position at greater distance from Lisbon.

The army having been considerably increased by the arrival of the forces from Cork under Major-General Hill commenced its march in three columns early on Sunday. The right column, composed of one Brigade of Light Artillery,[7] two squadrons of Cavalry, the Brigade of Guards, with the 7th and 53rd Regiments of Foot, moved along the left bank of the Tagus from Sacavem by Pavoa and Alverca to Alhandra, and the next day by Villafranca and Castanheira to Carregado and Villa Nova, where it halted to admit the centre and left columns (whose march was considerably longer) to come up.

The arrangements for our further advance will be completed by Friday, and we are to march early on that day. The position originally intended to be occupied was to extend from Santarem to Obidos. This was thought the best for defending Lisbon, as the supplies could be easily transported from thence by water and in the event of suffering such reverses as to make it most expedient to retreat, there would remain the possibility of re-embarking the army at Peniche. But it is *now* understood the advance of Marshal Victor with 30,000 men, who was believed to have reached Badajoz, is not so rapid as was reported, and *in consequence* we are to take the route to Oporto with a view to attacking Marshal Soult. His corps amounts to 25,000 men of whom a great proportion are cavalry and his advance division has already reached Coimbra, but from the garrison it is supposed he will find necessary to leave in Oporto and the detachments to occupy the different posts on his advance, our army is expected nearly to equal his in the field – it amounts to 20,000 on paper.

Upon a reference to the map you will perceive it is a very bold measure our marching against Soult, and that *its* success will in a great degree depend on the rapidity of our movement – not that I have the least doubt of victory if he accepts battle, but, as it is evidently his interest, I suspect he will retire on our approach, in order to draw us to such a distance from Lisbon before he fights as to make it impossible for us, even if we be successful, to arrest the progress of Sabastiani and Victor, who are to advance along the banks of the Tagus.

While we remain in a position with our right supported by the Tagus and our left by the sea, Lisbon will be perfectly secure, but by quitting it we expose our right flank and we open Lisbon to attack on its least assailable point. The approaches are naturally difficult and would be impracticable if defended by *Saragopean hearts*,[8] but such a defence is not to be looked for by any town in Portugal, and least of all by the Capital. I shall give credit to a few of its inhabitants for hatred of the French, but there is too great a want of energy to make it have effect. From the little opportunity I have yet had to judge of the disposition of the peasantry I believe it decidely hostile to the French, but even amongst them there is too great a want of proper leaders to make my hopes very sanguine of their exertions.

All accounts agree that it was want of proper example that caused the fall of Oporto, and there is very little doubt that had 1,000 British soldiers been in that town it would *yet* have been possessed by the Portuguese. Upon the whole therefore (notwithstanding Lisbon is almost to a certainty lost by our advance) our marching against Soult must be approved, for it will imprint the natives of the provinces, if they are to be inspired, with confidence, as we have no doubt of the issue if we can but bring him into battle.

Marshal Beresford has 45,000 Portuguese under him – his headquarters at present are at Thomar.

The country we have passed through is in a respectable state of cultivation but manure does not appear to be in general use. Beans are already large in the pod, rye is in ear and the other grains common in England are advanced in proportion. We are about 36 miles from Lisbon; all the way there was a great want of population although on the best post road in the kingdom.

Leiria
Monday evening 24th April 1809

The column marched on 14th to Alcoentre and the next day to Rio Mayor, where we halted till the 21st. We then marched to Albrahao and afterwards to this town, where it is supposed we shall remain some days.

It will appear extraordinary in a friendly country there should be a want of information for the movements of the enemy but this seems to prevail to great degree in Portugal, at least it is to this that we ascribe the indecision of our Commander-in-Chief. We marched to Rio Mayor with a view to proceeding to attack Soult, but we were halted six days at that town and during that time it was determined we should not advance further, nay, it was actually given in orders that the right column should proceed to Santarem and the left and centre of the army be thrown forward to maintain a defensive position. But the night before we were to march an express arrived changing our route to Batalha, as it was subsequently resolved we should act offensively – it is in this manner things are managed and it can proceed from nothing but the want of correct information.

The accounts of the French are more favourable than before. An Aide-de-Camp of General Cotton has arrived from Cuesta's army. It has taken up a position in the mountains and Victor is kept in check by it – it amounts to 14,000 regulars. These are new raised soldiers in a good state of discipline and well appointed. General Lapisse (not Sabastiani) with 8,000 men after having summonsed Ciudad Rodrigo marched away and is now at Alcantara. Sir Robert Wilson watches his motions – he has under him 1,500 Portuguese infantry and 200 cavalry. He has been successful in cutting off some convoys of provisions and stragglers.

Soult it appears is now only at Vouga and Aveiro [on the river Vouga] with 18,700 men . . . he has divided his force into three columns and has made a demonstration of attacking us, and we as certainly are determined to attack him. Magazines are forming in this town of salt provisions and indeed of every sort of supply. The whole army with the exception of the infantry of the German Legion are in the neighbourhood – and the 14th and 20th Dragoons with the light troops are about three leagues on the road to Coimbra in advance. Sir Arthur Wellesley has arrived and is expected here tomorrow to assume the Command-in-Chief. We shall advance as soon as the magazines are completed and from every appearance at present the determination of the contending commanders in less than a fortnight will be brought to issue. Soult has already been opposed to the British and we confidently hope that our first encounter will again prove that the British soldiers, like British sailors, are superior to the French. Adieu! I shall always have a letter to dispatch.

The next three letters give a very good account of the taking of Oporto, the operations leading up to it and the subsequent pursuit. Before leaving Coimbra Sir Arthur formed his brigades into a cavalry and four infantry divisions. The Guards Brigade (Brigadier-General Henry Campbell), 2nd Brigade (Brigadier-General Alan Campbell, and the 3rd Brigade (Brigadier-General Sontag) comprised the 1st Division under Major-General Sherbrooke who also became Wellesley's second-in-command with local rank of lieutenant-general. Sontag's brigade included two battalions formed from detached men from various regiments of the German Legion left behind when Corunna was evacuated.

Wellesley planned to turn Soult's left and cut his communications. Beresford was sent wide to the east to join the Portuguese force under Silveira at Lamego on the Douro, fifty miles from Oporto. Sir Arthur advanced directly on Oporto and attempted to cut off Soult's rearguard by an amphibious landing in its rear, at Ovar. Tactically this failed but it confirmed Soult in the opinion that Wellesley would attempt to land from the sea behind the Douro; Soult therefore stationed the bulk of his force to guard the mouth of the river, and neglected the river above the city except for ordering all boats to be brought over to the north side, and the bridge at Oporto to be destroyed.

Sir Arthur decided to cross the river, which at Oporto was as wide as the Thames at Westminster, above the city. A skiff hidden on the south bank was disclosed by a Portuguese barber to Colonel John Waters, an adventurous volunteer on Wellesley's staff who had been brought up in Oporto. This enabled four wine barges to be brought across. The Buffs, under Major-General Paget, commanding the 2nd Division, were ordered to cross, thirty men to a barge, and seize a seminary just above the city. At the same time Major-General John Murray with the King's German Legion, equivalent to a division in strength, would cross the river by the Avintes ferry five miles above the city.

On 12 May, with the high tide slowing the current, the first of the Buffs crossed the river and established themselves firmly in the seminary before they were discovered. After his first attempt to dislodge them had failed, Soult was compelled to move his troops guarding the mouth of the river in a further attempt. This enabled the fishermen to bring across their boats to Villa Nova, the suburb at the southern end of the Oporto bridge, and to ferry the Guards into the heart of the city.

Major-General John Murray, who had obtained his rank through political patronage, crossed at Avinches in time to see the demoralized French crossing his front pursued by the Guards, but remained inactive. However, the 14th Light Dragoons, who were with him greatly distinguished themselves. Wellesley, like other commanders-in-chief, naval and military, suffered throughout the war from inefficient senior officers with political influence.

Coimbra
5th May 1809

Sir Arthur Wellesley, having assumed the command on the 27th, made his debut by ordering the army to advance. The express did not arrive at Leiria till 10 o'clock on Saturday morning, but before 12 the Brigade of Guards, one brigade of artillery, one squadron of Cavalry and Brigadier-General R. Stewart's brigade of the line were on the march and they reached Pombal, a distance of eighteen miles, by half-past six the same evening although the roads in many places were very heavy from the great quantities of rain that had fallen on the day and the two days preceding.

We continued the next day and we entered Coimbra at 11 o'clock on Monday amidst the joyful exclamations of an immense concourse of people collected to welcome our arrival.

Sir Arthur arrived the day after and he was received as at Lisbon with the most marked demonstrations of applause; indeed, so much does he appear to possess the confidence of the people that it was with difficulty that he could pass through the streets, and flowers were strewn before him even from the prison. There was a general illumination the evening we arrived and it has been continued ever since.

The arrival this day of the 16th Dragoons has completed the army destined to attack Soult. It amounts to about 18,000 men exclusive of five regiments of Portuguese infantry that arrived last evening – they have been attached to different brigades, one regiment to each – none have been attached to the Brigade of Guards but it has been increased by a company of riflemen[9] and one has likewise been added to each of the other brigades composing the army going against Soult. Of the 18,000 British there are almost 1,400 cavalry. There are also artillerymen for twenty-four guns – these guns are all light except the six heavy six-pounders – the shot principally to be used is shrapnel.[10] Major-General Mackenzie was detached from Leiria on 29th with three regiments of foot to Abrantes, and the 3rd and 4th Dragoons and the 24th Regiment which have since arrived at Lisbon have likewise been ordered thence. They are to form a corps of observation and are to dispute the passage of the Tagus should Victor have the temerity to approach. Several gunboats carrying heavy metal and manned by seamen, volunteers from the transports, are moored at Astigo, at which place the Tagus is sometimes fordable.

We are now 140 miles from Lisbon, 80 from Oporto and about 30 from the French, a small corps being on the northside of the Vouga. The main body have withdrawn to the other side of the Douro and it is expected they will there await our attack. Douro is a very steep, scarped river – and is passable for an army only at Oporto and Lamego, which is about fifty miles higher up. The Portuguese general Silveira had taken up a position at Amarante with a view to securing the passage at Lamego, but he has been attacked by a detachment of French and beaten with considerable loss. In consequence, Major-General Tilson with his brigade was sent in advance this morning under the orders of Marshal Beresford – it consists of two battalions of the line, one battalion of Portuguese Grenadiers and five companies of riflemen. A squadron of the 14th Dragoons and the Hussars of the German Legion were likewise sent with the Marshal.

These troops are to march by Vizeu to Lamego to endeavour to secure the passage of the army. Should they not arrive in time to secure the bridge the operations against Soult will be very much protracted, and their final success becomes very precarious. I am not inclined to despond, for with the whole of the army in Portugal I feel more confidence in the Commander-in-Chief than I should under any other officer in the service, but I do not wish to give a more flattering description of the state of affairs than circumstances will warrant. Reverses must be expected and are likely to happen and if severe losses before taking a place can be called so, we are likely to suffer them soon. Oporto defended by the French will not surrender so soon as when defended by the Portuguese – nay, Soult will make a desperate resistance, there is every reason to believe, and if we have not been fortunate enough to secure the passage of the Douro at Lamego we shall make but little impression for some time. It is said to be possible to bombard it from this side, but it remains to be proved whether we shall not, in this instance, from a foolish delicacy for our allies, lay aside the only means in our power to accelerate its fall.

I trust Sir Arthur's experience of the last campaign in Portugal will have shown him the necessity of using every extremity in annoying the French, although in some instances it may affect the Portuguese.

The plan at present arranged is – the greater part of the army cross the Douro at Lamego while the remainder prevents the French from advancing from Oporto.

The 14th Dragoons marched out of Coimbra this morning to occupy the village in front and the army will be put in motion tomorrow or the day after. It will not perhaps be quite fair to judge the merits of the Portuguese troops by their appearance, but compared with the men of our army the contrast is certainly very striking. There are a great proportion of boys amongst them and they are all I believe newly raised. On this account the propriety of incorporating them with our troops appears to be questionable, for but a few young soldiers of any nation will stand fire well and if they are at once thrown into confusion and retire this confusion will soon spread amongst the veterans, and the bad effects are incalculable. Marshal Beresford is confident they will fight well and so says every British officer in their service – I sincerely trust they will, but if bodily strength adds much to the effects of an army armed with muskets I fear the Portuguese troops will make little impression on the French. I am the more surprised their army should be composed of boys and weak men because the peasantry in the country we have marched through are as fine a race as are to be seen, and they all appear to have the utmost detestation of the French. This can arrive only from want of example in the nobility – there certainly is great want of exertion in the higher orders.

This induces some to believe that unless the Austrian war[11] has the effect of diminishing the French force in the Peninsula it will be finally under the domination of France. In England you hear everybody is in arms here. That is literally true, for there was a picquet of pike men in the smallest village we passed through – but what can be expected from men without leaders, a body of twenty or thirty who, if collected together, would be without provisions and all sorts of supplies twenty miles from the spot of rendezvous – opposed to a regular army? – it may be said that the army's supplies would be intercepted – the warfare thus carried on may be protracted but it can never be successful, it will oblige the enemy to keep on being a large force – but that will be all.[12]

The town of Coimbra has certainly done its duty in defending the kingdom – it is the seat of the University and all the students have been formed into corps of infantry and artillery.

Oporto
13th May 1809

The Almighty God has blessed the indefatigable exertions of Sir Arthur Wellesley with a great victory over the French yesterday morning. I have not time to relate particulars – but the passage of the Douro has immortalized the troops engaged – it will be the admiration of the present generation and is of such a nature as posterity will not credit.

The Guards had no share in the action. I shall write again at the first opportunity.

Oporto
25th May 1809

The very short notice I had that letters would be forwarded after the battle of Oporto prevented me doing more than simply announcing a victory but the early termination of the campaign – the most brilliant that has for a long time honoured the British arms, will now permit me to relate the few particulars that have fallen within my own observation.

The moment Sir Arthur Wellesley assumed the command he ordered the army to advance and assemble at Coimbra. This was completed on the 5th inst. by the arrival of the 16th Dragoons. On that morning, Major-General

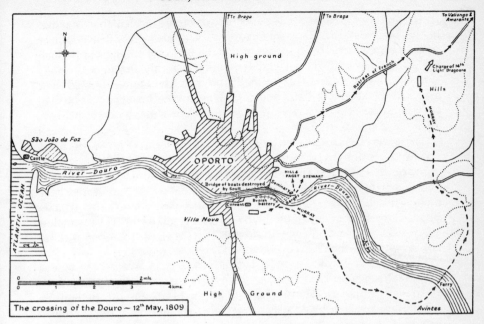

The crossing of the Douro – 12ᵗʰ May, 1809

Tilson, with his brigade and the Portuguese regiment attached, were sent under Marshal Beresford with two squadrons of Dragoons to Lamego to secure the passage of the Douro at that place. Sir Arthur proceeded with the main body by the coast and at daybreak on the 10th, the second day after leaving Coimbra, he came up with a corps of the enemy on the north side of the Vouga and put it to flight with the cavalry, only assisted by a small number of armed peasants. This corps was pursued immediately and it was brought to action the next day by our infantry at about three leagues from Oporto and again obliged to retreat with losses of 150 prisoners and several pieces of artillery. It afterwards showed a disposition to resist and took up a most advantageous position on a hill, but it withdrew under cover of the night.

They were followed at daybreak by the cavalry and the brigades under Generals Hill, Paget and Cameron; these were quickly succeeded by the Germans under Major-General Murray, and the Guards with the artillery, and afterwards by the brigades of General Alexander Campbell and Stuart. Upon reaching the Douro it was found that the bridge had been blown up and the means of crossing in boats prevented by their being moored on the opposite side. These difficulties, however, did not for a moment daunt the enterprising mind of the Commander-in-Chief – he resolved to force the passage at all hazards and the success which has attended this bold measure fully justifies the resolution.

A battery of twelve light pieces was immediately formed on a rising ground to cover the troops, and the other dispositions being completed the French began to retire, *panic struck*, upon which the Buffs under General Paget sprang into a few boats which had now been collected and crossed under a heavy fire in face of the enemy's strongest post. Three companies of this regiment formed as well as the circumstances would permit and attacked and carried this strong point at the point of the bayonet, in opposition to the efforts of a whole column which defended it. At the same time, the Germans and General Hill's brigade having crossed higher up attacked the enemy in flank and rear. The natives, being encouraged by these successes, cut the boats adrift and conveyed across a squadron of the 14th Dragoons.

These were the troops which bore the brunt of the action and they were several times obliged by the superiority of the enemy to fall back, but the appearance of Lieutenant-General Sherbrooke with the Guards on the enemy's right flank and the charge of the 14th Dragoons at the same instant decided victory. The enemy retreated from every point and was pursued for four miles by the Light troops – he afterwards took up the position in view on a hill but withdrew during the night and was pursued in the morning by the Germans and the Cavalry.

He (the enemy) at first commenced his retreat upon Amarante intending to join Loison, who had taken a strong position at that place after 17 days' resistance by Silveira, but on reaching Penafiel he found Loison himself, having been beaten by Marshal Beresford, was on the retreat. Finding himself thus situated he resolved to endeavour to save his army by flight and he immediately blew up all his ammunition and spiked all his artillery and began to retreat by crossroads upon Tuy, but on getting to Guimaraes he heard a strong division of our army was at Braga. This obliged him to change his route and he now directed his retreat on Chaves, but finding Marshal Beresford, who had marched that way, on his front he again altered his route – fled across the mountains . . . and thus escaped into Galicia with a few thousand men, dispirited and disarmed, without ammunition, artillery and indeed every sort of store.

This occupied the army from the 13th in the morning till the evening of the 18th. During the whole of that time it rained without an hour's intermission and was excessively cold. The Guards marched on the 19th on the road to Braga and, after two marches of 24 miles, on the 16th they came up with the rearguard of the enemy at a small village at Salamonde. Our eight companies in front immediately attacked and drove them from the village, but the road unfortunately being on the side of a mountain and extremely narrow did not admit the brigade to come up before the enemy had formed – as soon, however, as the dispositions could be made, which was not until late in the afternoon from the irregularity of the ground, he was attacked by the Light Companies supported by the brigade and two light field pieces and driven from his position. He was pursued for three miles but we were then obliged to halt from night coming on. Had we had but one hour's more light we should have taken the whole of the rear-guard, which amounted to 2,000 infantry and 500 cavalry – as it was, several hundred prisoners and two squadrons of Dragoons lost their horses – a great quantity of plunder was likewise taken – several of our soldiers took to the value of £100. There was no possibility of finding covering that night and we slept on the field of battle – it rained the whole time. From the 16th a great number of stragglers were made prisoner, several were found on the roads dying of hunger and fatigue and many were dead who had been shot by the peasantry – so closely had we followed them that they had not time to dress the animals they had killed, and on the 18th in the morning they shot a great number of horses and hamstrung all their mules to prevent their accelerating our march. They burnt the villages as they proceeded.

The army turned left in front and we as the rearguard arrived yesterday. It has already set out for the South, after one day's halt at Oporto, supposed in consequence of Victor's showing a disposition to advance – his advanced corps was said to have reached Castello Branco from Alcantara. We are to follow immediately and are to be hutted for the present around about Agueda on the coast – it is 50 miles from Oporto. The more you consider this campaign the more you will admire the genius who could plan it and the manner in which it has been executed. In the short space of ten days one of the greatest generals in Europe has been driven from a post he occupied six weeks, naturally strong, and pursued for 200 miles through a country hitherto supposed impassable for an army and which might have everywhere been defended by a handful of men. It has immortalized the hero of Vimiero and it has proved that even in rapidity of movement no soldiers can equal the British.

We are very much in want of shoes, and when you know that for six days not one man or officer in the army had on dry clothes you will believe the number of sick very great – I hear nearly 2,000 will be left in this town.

Punhete near Abrantes
[To his brother, William]   *Tuesday 13th June 1809*

In the short space of thirteen days (inclusive of a halt for two) we traversed upwards of 240 miles of a country extremely unfavourable to the operation of an army, of which 130 were in pursuit of a vanquished enemy, and during the greater part of this time we were exposed to weather the most severe that has ever been remembered at this season – suffering all the privations instant to war in a mountainous country – occasionally passing the night without shelter in the open air, in incessant rain sometimes accompanied by hail. Such indeed was the difference that the thermometer, which in Oporto stood at 65 in the shade, during over eight days' continuance in the mountains varied between 46 and 54.

The campaign has been highly creditable so far as regards the conduct of the troops, and all circumstances considered it has been brilliant, but it perhaps never before fell to the lot of any general to witness the result of so admirably a laid plan being so unequal to the expectations at first entertained. No circumstance can palliate Soult's error in suffering us to force the passage of the Douro in the manner we accomplished it. An isolated situation might have paralysed his efforts in offensive operations but this could not have affected him on the defensive – yet it must be allowed the manner in which he conducted his retreat after he had lost his position and finally effected his escape will add to the high character as a general he already bears.

Our gaining possession of Oporto was a scene the most animating and impressive I shall most probably ever witness. Where we crossed the river a large white flag with a black cross was hoisted, fragments of the bridge, and those burning, were floating on the water, reports of cannon and musketry were heard in every direction, and the waving of handkerchiefs by the nuns through the grating of their convent accompanied by loud acclamations of 'Deliverers' from every window increased the natural eagerness of our soldiers to meet the French – they passed the river with astonishing rapidity and ran up the steep streets totally forgetting the fatigue of a twenty-mile march under a scorching sun – over the dead bodies of men and horses, some yet wallowing in their blood in the agonies of death.

The inhabitants of Oporto were most severely punished for their insubordination and want of animosity, but they provoked the cruelties that were practised by the French. They cut to pieces one officer and injured another who were sent on the first arrival of the French to offer terms of surrender, but on the appearance of the main body they changed their tune and to excuse their cowardice they began to accuse every man of influence of treachery, and had the French not entered at the time they did but few respectable individuals would have escaped murder.

It was given up to plunder for 24 hours but the licentiousness of the soldiery was not to be stopped and it continued for three days – many persons were most wantonly murdered and neither age nor sex was respected; indeed, the older women suffered the most even after, and during their continuing in the town it was common for both officers and soldiers after dinner *aller a la chasse des filles* and this in the streets. While they triumphed thus over the wretched inhabitants, a great conspiracy exists in their army. Finding that they could nowhere move in small bodies without some being murdered, and seeing little hope of enjoying their wealth at home, both officers and men became disgusted and one general of division, nine colonels and a considerable number of inferior officers conspired to desert to us, but they were betrayed by a young officer of cavalry and the officer who was negotiating with our Quartermaster-General on terms of desertion was tried and sentenced to be shot – he was to have been executed on the 13th but in the confusion on the 12th at our entering Oporto he had the good fortune to escape and he is now in quarters.

I have myself spoken to several prisoners and they say their army in general was disgusted with the war and, had it not been the dread of being murdered by the peasants who give no quarter, many would have come over to us. Portugal is the best suited to defence by peasants possible to conceive. Indeed, Alemtego is the only province where the regular soldier would have advantage. The Portuguese troops have behaved well in every action and have done wonders – left to themselves they will do little, but with British officers they will do very well.

Rapidity is the order of the day – the plan of a new campaign is already decided on and we are to march into Spain as soon as the arrangements are completed. Major-General Mackenzie with his corps has advanced to Castello Branco, and Sabastiani (who succeeded Victor in the command of the French at Alcantara) has retired. Major-General Tilson's brigade is with the Portuguese army at Guarda. The Light Cavalry have been ordered to march from Oporto to Vigo to proceed across the country to join and support our left flank near Castello Branco, and the rest of the army is concentrated in the villages and in huts around about Abrantes where headquarters are at present. I have not yet received the box with books and newspapers you mentioned having been sent from London. I have now newspapers to the 22nd ult and I have been much astonished at their ignorance of the real state of affairs in this country.

The weather begins to be very hot – at this moment the thermometer in the shade stands at 77 and has been so for several days – our march into Spain will be severe. The reflection from the sand is inconceivably great and it will sometimes continue for 100 miles on a stretch. Bill-books have been issued in the proportion of one to every ten men as we shall often be lodged in huts – our heavy baggage has been landed and there is every possibility of our remaining out of England for a long time – I wish you were at this moment within call – I have a thousand things to tell you that cannot be communicated in a letter.

Adieu.

TALAVERA

Soult had been expelled from northern Portugal with the loss of 4,500 men, and all his artillery, baggage and military chest, and for some time could be no threat. Sir Arthur, therefore, turned his army about and marched to Abrantes to make joint plans with the senior Spanish commander on the central front, Cuesta. After its defeat at the battle of Medellin, Cuesta's Army of Estremadura had been reconstituted and now numbered 35,000. Subordinate to him was Venegas's 22,000-strong Army of La Mancha, south of Ciudad Real, due south of Madrid.

At the start of the Talavera campaign, Soult and Ney were engaged in pacifying Galicia, and the former in re-equipping. Mortier was on the Ebro, and Sabastiani with 15,000 men faced Venegas about Villarta, on the upper Guadiana, south of Madrid. Victor was at Merida on the Guadiana near the Portuguese frontier, with 22,000 men, and King Joseph with a reserve of 8,000 was at Toledo.

Allied strategy was for the combined forces of Cuesta and Wellesley to overcome Victor, thus opening the road to Madrid, while Venegas held Sabastiani in check by an advance to the Tagus from the south. In this he failed and before the battle of Talavera Sabastiani's force was concentrated with that of Victor under Joseph. Venegas, however, did at last make his weight felt and on 28 July at the end of the battle, Joseph, ignoring Victor's plea for one more attempt to dislodge the British, dispatched Sabastiani to deal with the developing threat to Madrid from Venegas.

About this time Wellesley received reports of a French army approaching Plasencia from the north, on his line of communication with Portugal. Believing this to be Mortier with 15,000 men, he left his wounded with Cuesta at Talavera and marched to intercept him, but on learning that it was Soult with 30,000 (in fact he had nearer 50,000) Wellesley was forced to cross the Tagus and establish a new line of communication through Badajoz on the Guadiana.

French losses in the battle of Talavera were 7,268 men and seventeen guns. The British, who bore the brunt of the French attacks, had 5,263 casualties, of whom some 800 were dead. Wellesley, who as a reward for the victory was created Viscount Wellington of Talavera and Baron Douro, had discovered the futility of concerting plans with the Spanish commanders, for whom, in Wellington's words, 'nothing will answer excepting to fight great battles in plains, in which their defeat is as certain as the commencement of battle'.[13] In future the British Army would no longer act as auxiliary to Spanish forces, though the determination shown by the Spanish people in waging guerrilla war and in defence of fortified places was an essential contribution to the eventual success of British arms.

Among the senior officers, Mackenzie and Langwerth were killed on the British side, and Lapisse on the French. In Wellington's opinion 'the battle of Talavera was the hardest fought in modern times. The fire at Assaye was heavier while it lasted; but the battle of Talavera lasted for two days and a night'.[14] Victor might have won a great victory had he planned to put everything into a concerted effort to turn Wellington's left which had been left dangerously weak, while holding the allies elsewhere. As it was he dispersed his effort in isolated and ill-planned attacks.

The Light Brigade under 'Black Bob' Robert Craufurd arrived on the field of battle the following morning with bugles playing 'merrily'. Though they had marched forty-two miles in twenty-six hours, they immediately relieved their exhausted comrades on outpost duty, and in collecting the mass of dead bodies, already putrefying in the heat, into large heaps for cremation. John Aitchison gives some graphic descriptions of the campaign and subsequent battle:

Punhete near Abrantes
Thursday 23rd June 1809

I wrote to you on the 26th ult from Oporto – it would inform you of our returning to the south of Portugal. We have remained so short a time in any place and I have had so little intercourse with the inhabitants that it has been impossible to write to you of their manners and customs. All I can say is that from what I have seen the impression has not been favourable. In regard to their behaviour to me I have almost everywhere met with the greatest civility and I shall always be ready to acknowledge it.

The country north of Coimbra is infinitely better cultivated than to the south; indeed, the people seem a superior race and under any other government it would flourish. At present it is at least a century behind Britain in (I may say) civilisation and there seems little prospect of its making progress under its present rulers. On this account it admits a doubt whether the expectation of the French was an object [to be] desired – I myself should conceive not, for they appear to be the only people incapable of regenerating the Portuguese. Insolence is inherent and to such a degree as to stagger credulity and, with it, filth and its accompanying miseries. The land is uncommonly fertile and without manure it produces crops that in England would be called good. There is but a very small proportion under the plough but it is certainly made the most of. The rain which we felt so severely has been the most fortunate occurrence that could have happened to Portugal. The French had cut nearly all the corn green for forage for their horses, but there has been planted on the lands which nurtured it an uncommonly great quantity of Indian corn and it requires much rain to make it spring. This will secure the natives against a scarcity; indeed, at this moment there is a prospect of Portugal being better supplied than is general from its own production. The provinces north of the Douro produce the most corn and it has been these suffered the most from the war – Alemtejo is the only province in Portugal for grazing and the bullocks reared are larger and finer than are generally to be seen in England – these now, however, begin to be scarce and we are already *feeding* on salt provisions and this we fear will be our principal food during our continuance in Portugal.

In a letter to William on the 13th I mentioned it was believed we were to march to Spain – the arrangements for our advance have since been completed and the army will be put in action on Saturday. On that day we are to march but to what place we do not yet know – everybody says to Spain.[15]

In regard to the situation of that country, people seem to say it is favourable and circumstances certainly agree in warranting the belief that the assistance of a British force might be attended with benefit to the Spaniards.

After the battle of Medellin, when Cuesta's force was dispersed, Victor it was expected would take the opportunity of our moving against Soult to advance with a view to capturing Lisbon, and it is evident from Sir Arthur Wellesley's anxiety to return to the banks of the Tagus that he entertained that apprehension – this apprehension however is now completely removed and it says much for the cause of the Patriots that Victor, although reinforced by the column under Lapisse from Alcantara, has not only not been able to advance but he has been obliged to withdraw from dispositions between the rivers Tagus and Guadiana.[16] He at first retired to *Truxillo* but he has since crossed the Tagus at *Almaraz,* which lies on the great road to Madrid and about 100 miles from it, and he had manifested such eagerness to cross it that when the movement came off he had passed three divisions of his army in a *single* boat which held only 80 men although the bridge, which had been destroyed, was but of two arches.

His proceedings previous to this sudden retreat excited a suspicion that it would soon take place, for after he had concentrated his force near to the Guadiana he sent a detachment of a few thousand men to show themselves opposite to Alcantara. These alarmed the Portuguese so much as to make them blow up the bridge, which the French no sooner observed than they withdrew – its destruction has been supposed their object, as it was the finest stone bridge over the Tagus, and it would impede our advance had we been disposed to annoy their retreat.

Cuesta's force is now greater than it was before and the officer who brought this report says it was daily increasing; he adds it is not so forward in discipline as might have been expected nor was much pain taken to instruct the levies and that Cuesta himself is of known probity and bravery but that he never was a general. . . .[17]

While things appear then so favourable in the South of the Peninsula it is said *Soult,* who had effected a junction with Ney in Galicia, has been reinforced by a division under Mortier and half of this army has penetrated the North of Portugal and reoccupied Chaves – I know not on what authority this report rests but I do not myself conceive it improbable.[18] It was at Orense he formed his magazines when he first entered Portugal and this town is only nine leagues from Chaves. He effected his retreat upon Orense and a scarcity of supplies may have induced him to detach a force to Chaves with a view to collect provisions.

It is a post of no consequence because it is not tenable. It cannot therefore be of importance to an army not in possession of the North of Portugal, and if I were to judge from the specimen of roads we saw when in pursuit of the French I should pronounce it impracticable for the enemy again to advance although thus reinforced, but through the most criminal neglect on the part of the present Governors of Portugal. Precautions certainly appear to be taking [sic] as the Portuguese army are assembling about Lamego, and Marshal Beresford (who with our ambassador and the admiral had a consultation for a few days with Sir A.W. at Abrantes)set out some days since to Lisbon previous to rejoining the army.[19]

A levy of 50,000 men which has been sometime ordered is now completing with expedition, but I regret the government·have thought it necessary to use compulsory means – and instead of every man coming forward with an offer of voluntary service one sees them marched under an escort of regulars chained to one another like French conscripts.

Today, Sir A.W. is said to have received official communciation of victory by the Archduke Charles over the French.[20] I shall rejoice that it is true – if the Austrians will but fight – all is not over and much will be done. We have been so often deceived by reports that we are now cautious of giving credit.

The despatch of Sir A.W. on our crossing the Douro has much disappointed the whole army – some part of it is almost unintelligible to us who saw all the movements he describes. The people in England make very light of our success – the army think otherwise.

23rd June

The campaign has increased the high character which all who knew this brigade of Guards had given it – the line even look up with admiration, and so much has its conduct meant for the approbation of the Commander-in-Chief that he has written a private letter to the King in the strongest terms of recommendation. This is some consolation but Englishmen are never contented. We have great difficulty in getting money – but very little is with the army and little in consequence is to be had from the Paymaster, and a bill on England is not to be negotiated but at Lisbon.[21] I should wish therefore, if you think proper, that I had letters of credit on Lisbon, Madrid and Oporto. By lodging so much in the hands of a banker (Coutts for instance) a letter of credit will be given their correspondent at these places. This I believe necessitates they should have my signature.

All letters to me must be sent by the post – inland postage being paid they will be forwarded. I have received the box of books with a letter from you – I am disappointed so few Collets [?] were sent – here they are really a great treat. I have written to Mr Thomson about letters of credit and I have requested him to enquire about how it is to be done – before you receive this therefore he will most likely be master of the subject. I have not yet had occasion for much more money than that I brought with me besides my allowances and pay, but as there is a possibility of remaining long in this quarter I have proposed paying into Coutts about 300£.

I have received your letter of the 2nd inst from London – William wrote to me Robert was going on board the *Dryad* – but I suppose it has now been changed although he is yet young. Nothing will give me greater pleasure than meeting him, but I doubt I shall have an opportunity unless a retreat up Corunna again takes place, which I assure you we are at this moment far from expecting.

> *Punhete near Abrantes*
> *26th June 1809*

The order for our advance has at length arrived and we are to march tomorrow to Abrantes, from whence we are to proceed to Spain direct.

The route we shall take and the place we are going is not yet known but it is generally believed we shall keep this side of the Tagus and the army will be assembled about Plasencia. Victor is reputed to be in that neighbourhood, having, it is said, halted after crossing the Tagus at Almaraz. I fear however we shall have a longer march before we overtake him. Several regiments are due from England but none have yet arrived.

It is prodigiously hot – the march will be severe – the thermometer at present stands at 78 in the shade. . . .

> *Continued at Abrantes – 27th*

Sir Arthur Wellesley has received dispatches this morning from Spain – Victor is retreating and the whole of our army is in motion and will assemble at Zarza la Mayor – on the frontiers of Estremadura by the 5th July – I have just seen the route. Headquarters in advance this afternoon – the King's messenger accompanies so orders may be expected in a day or two.

Spanish Estremadura, Galisteo near Plasencia
10th July 1809

I wrote to you from Abrantes on 27th inst that the army had been put in motion and would be assembled at Zarza la Mayor on the 5th instant. Accordingly, about half-past eight in the morning of that day we forded the river Tagus and entered Spain and soon afterwards camped about four miles to the east of Zarza. The several divisions of the army which had preceded ours marched again the next day and we followed the day after. We arrived at this place yesterday, where we are to remain encamped until further orders. Headquarters is at Plasencia, where our two divisions of the army and Major-General Mackenzie with his division is a little in advance. A brigade of Light Troops under General Craufurd which have arrived from England are on the march to join us.[22]

These and the Light Dragoons are the only part of the army not yet come up and as soon as they shall have arrived the whole will march forward to attack Victor in co-operation with the Spanish force under Cuesta. He has been reinforced by 6,000 infantry from the garrison of Madrid and his army is now said to amount to 48,000 men, of which 12,000 are cavalry. Cuesta, it is calculated, will bring into the field about 30,000 men of which 10,000 are mounted and Sir Arthur expects to have about the same number, including 4,000 cavalry. The united force will thus exceed that of the enemy and we anticipate a successful result of the battle about to take place.

A courier arrived from England two days ago and Sir Arthur has immediately set off to a conference with General Cuesta – he is expected to return today.

Victor has taken up a formidable position in the neighbourhood of Talavera on the Tagus with a view to await our attack. Cuesta is on the south side and occupies a position around the bridge of Almaraz. He will cross the river on our approach.

These are, I believe, the positions of the two armies, though it is reported differently and some even say the French are only ten leagues off – but a few days will decide beyond the possibility of doubt. The 21st is said to be fixed on for the joint attack on the enemy and that day we look to as likely to prove as glorious to the British army as any yet reported. The enemy, if he fights at all, has every inducement to resist with desperation, but Spanish patriotism supported by British courage will overcome every obstacle.

In the English papers which have arrived to the 16th ult, they talk of our final success as a matter of course and they even chalk out a plan for us to act upon after the expulsion of the French from the Peninsula. We are not, however, in this quarter yet so sanguine – the French have got a force of 120,000 men – these are at present scattered but they will nevertheless require a proportionate force and great perseverance to expel them – and the Spaniards, besides the army of Cuesta, have no force of any consequence and it added to the British is far inferior to the numbers of the enemy.

Much in my opinion depends upon the resistance of Austria – for when the French find themselves worsted they will retire behind the Ebro, and with the chain of fortresses which they possess from Pamplona to Monzon they will be enabled to make such a protracted resistance that, if Austria is in the meantime disposed of the reinforcements which will be sent, will again force us to retire. This certainly is what at this time we do not expect; on the contrary I trust I shall have only to recruit a succession of victories until we reach the passes of the Pyrenees.

I hear today couriers are constantly arriving from Marshal Beresford – he is apprehensive of an attack from Ney and Soult.

The weather is dry but uncommonly hot. In the whole of our march we have encamped every night – the men make huts and the few officers who have tents make use of them – we march every morning at half-past two. Our division amounts to about 7,000. On the march we have had to pass many rivers, some of which were of a considerable depth but we forded them all. The country in Portugal was very wild and mountainous and the few inhabitants had abandoned their houses on the approach of the French and retired to the mountains. On crossing the Tagus we came at once into a different country well cultivated and flat – the appearance of the people and the houses much changed for the better. The whole country to this place has been in general plane, well-cultivated and well-wooded and watered. From our present situation, however, we can see mountains with their tops covered in snow, they are distant about seven leagues.

Pray write often – Adieu.

Talavera de la Reyna
25th July 1809

I did entertain a hope that in the first letter under this date I should have to announce a most complete victory over the French, and perhaps the annihilation of Marshal Victor's army, but I have been disappointed, and the circumstances which have led to it, when they come to be known at home, will, I am persuaded, excite feelings of a stronger nature throughout the whole kingdom.

The British army was put in motion from Plasencia on 17th inst and by *forced* marches reached Oropesa on 20th, where it halted in order to allow the Spanish army to advance as they *claimed* the honour of leading. Accordingly, on the 21st the army of Cuesta passed through our camp and on the same evening we were inspected by him, after which the whole of the Cavalry and the advanced guard of the army and the Lusitanian Legion proceeded two leagues on the road to Talavera.

The next morning the whole were in motion by daybreak – the picquets of Spanish cavalry were attacked by the French early in the day and driven in, but these being soon supported by the British Dragoons the enemy in turn was forced to fall back and he was finally obliged to retire. About 10 of the main body of the combined cavalry came up with the outposts of the enemy about two miles from Talavera, which were immediately attacked and forced, and after skirmishing for a short time the enemy withdrew from Talavera to behind the Alberche and as usual in his retreat signalled

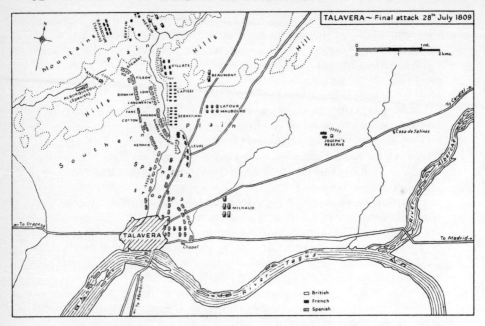

himself by the most wanton acts of cruelty. All the detached houses and
convents were burnt and whole fields of standing corn were set fire to by his
order, which in this country, being without enclosures, extended many miles.

Having thus succeeded in gaining possession of Talavera, Sir Arthur
wished to follow up and attempt his main body, which was drawn up on a
very formidable position about five miles beyond Talavera. This position
was across a neck of land formed by the conflux of the rivers, Alberche and
Tagus. He had thus both flanks supported and he was protected in his
front by the former river, the banks, except at the regular fords, being in
general too steep to approach beyond the river, and from the water's edge
the ground rose in gradual ascent for three miles to the village of Monte de
Salinas, where he had his headquarters and where there is a plane well
suited to his numerous cavalry. Availing himself of this advantageous
position Marshal Victor appeared determined to await our attack.

On Sunday 23rd the combined army was under arms before daybreak
and by 12 the several columns of British had nearly reached their points of
attack when they were ordered to halt and afterwards return to their camp.
In the operations of a combined attacking army a retrograde movement, as
it manifests want of confidence or unanimity of the chiefs so it tends
strongly to damp the ardour, diminish the hope and excite the apprehension of the troops – this order to retire therefore produced in all a sensation
– possible to conceive but which I cannot describe. However, we were
again under arms by half-past four in the morning of the 24th. Several
columns both Spanish and British again arrived at their attack stations, but
no enemy was now to be seen, the vedettes having withdrawn on the
approach of our advance division – the Spanish army crossed the Alberche

in pursuit, as did likewise the British dragoons and a division of infantry, but the whole of the British have been ordered to halt – the advance occupies what was the headquarters of the French and the main body are encamped within a mile of Talavera.

I have not been able to ascertain positively what caused the enemy to retire or what led to this incomprehensible conduct of the allies, but it is generally said Victor acted in consequence of hearing that the French from Toledo were advancing to join him, and Cuesta having declared himself unprepared on Sunday,[23] the attack was not made on that day. We are all so virulent against the Spaniards that I shall leave them to your own reflections, observing that Sir Arthur acted under the orders of Cuesta but he was always prepared.

Our prospect is now unhappy in that the enemy will either come upon us with superiority of force or, if it suits him better, he will retire (avoiding a general action) behind the Ebro – how we are to follow him, God knows, we are destitute of means of transport and already short of bread.[24] Reports say the French are retreating on Avila towards Madrid. King Joseph commands. The Spaniards have about 9,000 cavalry and 30,000 infantry under Cuesta and Alburquerque, cavalry are well mounted and the men, both cavalry and infantry, in appearance good.

John Aitchison evidently went through his letters during his period of home service in the middle of the Peninsular War and on 26 January 1812 he added the following note:

The above letter was written during a moment of disappointment at Talavera, but could not be forwarded being too late for the post – I was at the time very unwell and in consequence weak – the exertion to write was very great – life was indifferent and never did I expect to see home again – but I am in health and I thank God for his mercy.

My dear Father,

Talavera de la Reyna
29th July 1809

The most severe and obstinately contested battle was fought yesterday in front of this town. The French were 45,000 strong and commanded by Marshal Victor – the combined army were 57,000 of which about 17,500 were British and the French were the attackers and they were repulsed three different times, the first of which was in the night between 27th and 28th but although they maintained their own position they did not gain an inch of ground in any point and they suffered so much that they finally withdrew between the night of 28th and 29th, leaving behind nineteen pieces of ordnance.

The British army has suffered seriously. The loss is calculated at about 5,000. We have lost eleven officers – I received, while carrying the colours, a contusion in the right shoulder-blade from a musket ball – but my wound is slight. It is stiff at present but I shall write in a day or two more fully.

Adieu.

To follow John Aitchison's descriptions of the battle of Talavera an understanding of the dispositions of the Allied Army and the overall course of events is necessary.

While Cuesta was following up Victor, against Wellington's advice, Wellington selected a defensive position on the west bank of the Portina stream, which rose in the nearby Sierra de Segurilla and ran due south through the town of Talavera into the Tagus. The key to this position was a steep and prominent feature which marked the left flank, the Cerro de Medellin. Here Wellington deployed Hill's 2nd Division. Opposite it, across the Portina, a similar feature, the Cerro de Cascajal, was used by Victor for the mass deployment of thirty guns.

Wellington persuaded Cuesta, who was the overall Allied commander, to deploy his Spaniards on the right flank around Talavera, where walled enclosures favoured defence and where the inexperienced and ill-disciplined part of his force would come to least harm. On the low ground between the Cerro de Medellin and the Spanish left, Wellington positioned Sherbrooke's 1st Division, which included the Guards and King's German Legion, with, on their right, Campbell's 4th Division, with Mackenzie's 3rd Division, in rear, after having covered Cuesta's withdrawal. The Light Cavalry was stationed to watch the chief weakness of this position, the gap between the Medellin and the Sierra. The whole front extended over some three miles.

Victor surprised and drove in the covering force under Mackenzie on the afternoon of 27 July. Thus encouraged, he decided to attempt to take the Cerro de Medellin that night by a silent *coup-de-main*. Owing to some confusion of orders, he nearly succeeded, but Hill managed to retrieve the situation. In the early hours of the twenty-eighth some nervous firing in the Spanish lines soon spread to the whole Spanish corps. Although no move had been made by the enemy, four battalions of inexperienced Spanish troops panicked and fled. At 5 a.m. Victor made a second attempt to carry the Cerro de Medellin with Ruffin's division supported by very heavy fire from the guns on the Cerro de Cascajal. The British skirmishing line retired on to the main line beyond the crest, where Wellington stood close to the colours of the 29th. As the French reached the crest they were met by a devastating volley. Wellington ordered a charge and with a tremendous shout the 29th and 48th hurled themselves on the enemy, bayoneting and tumbling them back beyond the stream.

After this second repulse there was a pause while Joseph took counsel of his generals. Both sides collected their wounded, and since the day was extremely hot mingled while drinking from the Portina. It was an interesting strategic situation. Venegas, advancing on Madrid from the south, would soon threaten the French lines of communication, while Soult, with Mortier and Ney, was advancing on Plasencia from the north and would soon menace those of the British. Victor proposed that Sabastiani's corp should attack the British centre and right while he made a third attempt to carry the Medellin, and the cavalry demonstrated against the Spaniards on the right. Jourdan, the chief of staff, and Sabastiani favoured delay but when it was learnt that Soult's advance was behind time, and the choice lay between an immediate attack or withdrawal to cover Madrid, Joseph gave way to Victor's forceful arguments.

This third attack took place about mid-day. Joseph launched some 30,000 infantry against Wellington's 17,000, while his cavalry contained 30,000 Spaniards. Sabastiani's left column was directed against the 4th Division and was repulsed at close quarters by withering fire from the 7th and 53rd Foot. His right column came nearer success when they attacked the most exposed part of the Allied position held by the 1st Division, but this is part of the battle best left for Aitchison to describe.

Victor's third attack on the Medellin with Ruffin's by now exhausted troops never looked like achieving success. Previous attacks against his left had impressed upon Wellington its exposed situation. Cuesta, when asked for troops to reinforce this flank sent him a Spanish division and some cavalry to cover the gap between the Medellin and the Sierra. Into this gap Victor now directed a division. Picking a moment when the enemy appeared to falter, Wellington ordered Anson's cavalry to charge. The ground was unreconnoitered and the result disastrous, for the long grass hid a steep ravine in the path of the galloping horses. A few managed to pull up, some jibbed, some cleared the obstacle, but many fell in. The result was chaos. Major Ponsonby of the 23rd wrote: 'We had a pleasing amusement of charging five solid squares [the French infantry had formed 'square'] with a ditch in their front. After losing 180 men and 222 horses, we found it not so agreeable and that Frenchmen will not always run away when they see British cavalry. . . .'[25] Victor wanted to make a third attempt on the Medellin but was over-ruled. The fighting now petered out. It had been a most bloody battle. The grass on the battlefield caught fire roasting the dead bodies of men and horses and scorching the wounded. 'I never saw a field of battle which struck me with such horror as Talavera', wrote George Napier.[26]

Talavera de la Reyna
31st July 1809

I wrote after the great battle of 28th, but as it has not been sent off and as I have some chance of getting this forwarded sooner I think it proper to write to you again. My wound has been very slight and the stiffness has left my arm and now only on the part struck by the ball. I expect in a day or two to join the regiment.

The French retired about a league and a half to a strong position on the other side of the river Alberche, which runs into the Tagus, the morning after the battle. They have since withdrawn from there except the rear guard, which is very strong. They, it is supposed, will also retire as soon as their wounded are at a considerable distance.

It appears that after the French had retired from their original position on the 24th Sir Arthur Wellesley was of opinion no part of the combined army should advance beyond this position, but Cuesta, from a foolish vanity of wishing to enter Madrid first, resolved and did follow them with the whole of the Spanish Army. The consequence was the enemy the moment he received his reinforcements, which increased his army from 25 to 42,000 men, now turned about and compelled the advance guard of the Spaniards to fall back, and it was then Cuesta[27] saw the propriety of Sir Arthur's advice and ordered his army to retreat. Accordingly, the Spaniards arrived here early on the morning of the 27th covered by the advance division of British, who were the whole of the day engaged with the French, and Major-General Mackenzie, who commanded, found it necessary to fall back on our main body late in the afternoon. The whole of the French afterwards crossed the River Alberche and were drawn out in front of our position. On the left our position was strong being supported by a range of hills of gradual ascent. This was occupied by one division of the army – from thence to the right is a plain covered with vines and olives and other trees. Here to the right there was a small rising ground on which we had erected a small battery. Behind this and to its right were the whole of the Spanish army in three lines, each line three deep. In this position the French attacked us about 9 in the evening with their usual impetuosity on both flanks but they were successfully repelled.[28]

They renewed the attack at daybreak and were again beaten back. Their attention was finally directed to our left and they made prodigious efforts to turn it, but British hearts overcame every one and they were obliged to fall back with great loss. Having been foiled in every attempt to force our flanks they resolved on attempting our centre, and it was here their grand push was made. Accordingly, having refreshed, about 1 o'clock they advanced with great numbers both of infantry and artillery and they had strong divisions of cavalry in the wood immediately in their rear.[29]

On their approaching within 200 yards we were ordered to advance without firing a shot and afterwards to charge this *we* did as became British officers. The enemy did not wait for us, we carried everything before us, but unfortunately the infantry of the German Legion, which formed the left of our division, gave way and this made it necessary for our brigade to retire. When we faced about, the enemy that were flying rallied and opened a heavy fire and we were taken in our left flank by that part of the enemy which ought to have been driven back by the Germans.

It was in this retrograde movement that I was wounded and I was shortly after obliged to quit the field. It was not, however, until our men had formed round their colours in a drill[30] and had opened a most destructive fire on the enemy who, not withstanding our misfortune, was not able to gain one inch of ground even by redoubling efforts with fresh troops, and at the close of the action we occupied a more advanced line than at its commencement. But we suffered severely, having lost in killed and wounded 23 officers and upwards of 500 men, of whom there were of the 3rd Regiment five officers killed, six wounded and 290 men killed and wounded.

The loss of the enemy exceeds 8,000, ours is about 5,000, but this is small when it is considered it was a contest of 18,000 against 42,000, for the Spaniards had very little to do. We have since been reinforced by one light brigade amounting to 3,000 men and we expect a troop of horse artillery today.[31] Six regiments are on the march who will arrive in less than a fortnight.

The 28th July has indeed been a glorious day for the British Army but it has been a lamentable one also. Venegas is at Toledo with 22,000 Spaniards.

My love to all at home.

Belem
14th September 1809

I shall not accuse you of negligence – I am persuaded it would be unjust, but must express my sincere regret at receiving so very few letters from home. You have experienced disappointment at not receiving a letter from me – *judge my feelings by your own.*

I am to remain here till my shoulder is quite well and perhaps afterwards in charge of sick. The Lisbon mail is made up in London every Wednesday evening and it sails from Falmouth on Saturday, so write your letters so as to arrive in *London* on each *Wednesday* and thus no time will be lost.

I have seen Sir Arthur's account of the battle of Talavera.[32] It is not very minute but it is clear – it will not perhaps appear so to one not having seen the ground, but such was its nature that I should conceive it very difficult to convey a clear idea of the whole affair in writing; at least, its description would be too long for dispatch.

From the numerous instances recorded, even in my own time, of the intrepidity of the British troops, I have formed an idea of the coolness with which they would oppose the impetuosity of a French attack and their bravery in advancing to the charge, but in the battle of Talavera I witnessed courage beyond what I could have conceived even of them, and which I am persuaded but few persons who have not seen it, will credit. Till about two o'clock on the 28th our men from daybreak were for the greater part exposed to a tremendous cannonade – shots and shells were falling in every direction – but none of the enemy were to be seen – the men were all the while lying in the ranks, and except at the very spot where a shot or shell fell, there was not the least motion – I have seen men killed in the ranks by cannon shots – those immediately round the spot would remove the mutilated corpse to the rear, they would then lie down as if nothing had occurred and remain in the ranks, steady as before. That common men could be brought to face the greatest danger, there is a spirit within which tells me it is possible, but I could not believe they could be brought to remain without emotion, when attacked, not knowing from whence. Such, however, was the conduct of our men (I speak particularly of the Brigade) on 28 July, and from this steadiness so few suffered as by remaining quiet the shots bounded over their heads.

On the left and the right of our positions, where the attacks were most frequent, the men ordered to remain on the ground till the French came within 40 yards. They then rose, gave the enemy a volley, and repulsed them with the bayonet. This coolness on our part staggered the resolution of the enemy, and instead of being the assailants they *by it* became the assailed, and the confidence this gave to our men of their superiority over the enemy had the same effect as addition to their numbers; in short, the enemy in every attack was repulsed with prodigious slaughter.

In the centre where at last the enemy made his grand push,[33] we charged when he was within 100 yards, and our fire was reserved until they were flying. The eagerness of *our* men in advancing without support, beyond the distance intended, had nearly proved fatal, for we had no sooner passed the ravine in our front than the enemy perceived the troops on our left halted,[34] took us in our left flank by his retiring columns and the columns which we posted in our front in a wood behind the bank of a vineyard. Thus gaining confidence, nearly turned our right, they stood till the grenadiers were actually within double musket length, but they then retired in great confusion. At this point of the action our numbers were diminishing very fast, and it being impossible to maintain this advance position we were ordered to be withdrawn. Accordingly we faced about, retired to the ravine, slower and in better order than we advanced.[35] Here we made a stand and did considerable execution, but the enemy having come on with all those troops that had been flying, supported by strong columns which concealed in the wood, it was deemed necessary to order another retirement, and we once again faced about – the enemy by this time having advanced within a few yards, the havoc was great, and we were thrown into momentary confusion – but the same ardent spirit which had urged our men to advance beyond the point originally intended still operated – they rallied with astonishing rapidity and their exertions keeping pace with the exigencies, success crowned their efforts in the complete rout of the enemy.

The length of the action makes the victory the more brilliant, but it is not gained without great loss. We lost a third of our men present and the regiments which supported us about the same proportions. These were the 24th, 61st, 83rd, 48th Foot and the Germans, who were on our left.[36]

Thanks from His Majesty conveyed in a letter through My Lord Castlereagh are as great as can be expressed but having been most pointedly expressed to the non-commissioned officers and men it is much regretted the medals struck on the occasion will only be given to the commanders of the corps.[37]

My letter of the 21st ult you will have by this time received. I spoke of George's desire to enter the army feelingly – I was at that time completely exhausted and in low spirits; perhaps like a person with the jaundice sees everything yellow, I may have seen everything in its worst light. I do not recollect exactly what I said, but I think I may have been stronger in my opinion against the army than I would have expressed at any other time. I am now quite well as to spirits, and I am still of opinion (nor shall I, I think, ever alter it) it is the worst profession that any young man can follow. As I have been in now four years it becomes me to persevere and I think it improper being indetermined.

In giving my opinion of the regiment George should go into in the event of his persisting, I said a regiment of the Line in preference to the Guards because in the Line the promotion is so much the quicker. He is already three years older than I was when I entered and were he to come into the Guards now he would be the 32nd, instead of the 21st ensign which I was, and as to his promotion and a Lieutenancy (*calculating that promotion will be as quick as it has been and he so fortunate as I am*) he will be two years *longer* in getting it than I was.

The Ensign just promoted has been one and a half years longer in than me, and there seems every chance of me getting a Lieutenancy in a few months, at all events in one year's less time than they have been.

The regulation says he must be three years subaltern before he can get a company; now even if he were to serve these three years as Ensign in the Guards[38] I should object to it, because it is now next to an impossibility, without great interest, to purchase a company in the Line from an Ensignery in the Guards. But if he were at first to enter a regiment of the Line there is a chance of his being able to purchase a company as soon as he is eligible, but I do not conceive there is the least chance of his having to serve 6 years in the line before he can get a company and this I have shown he would most probably have to serve before he could obtain the same rank by service in the Guards – the promotion is 2 to 1 in favour of the line in the lower ranks. I have shown it to be so to the rank of Captain and I am persuaded it is much more – this much for the army.

Sir Arthur (as he still so calls himself) is at Badajoz – it is the frontier town of Spain but the army extends from Talavera de la Reyna in Spain to Camp Mayor in Portugal – they are still in huts and yet very sickly; all the wounded and some of the sick are at Elvas – but 1,500 of them are to be sent here. The mortality in the Guards has been very great: thirteen died two weeks running and many die every week; indeed, the brigade is completely cut up.[39] 8th inst there were only 10 doing duty. We are very much at a loss to conceive what is to be done – the drafts which had actually left London en route were to join us, have been countermanded and many empty transports have within these few days arrived in the Tagus, while on the other hand a regiment of cavalry and detachments for different regiments have likewise arrived and it is reported part of the expedition from Antwerp are to reinforce us.[40]

It is reported here that the army is to march to Cadiz and be embarked in the Spanish fleet – and the sick and wounded are to be embarked here. Some transports are to sail immediately to England for ordnance stores.

In the midst of all this uncertainty the Portuguese are busily raising a levy of 50,000 men[41] – they are pressed like seamen in England, and bound together they are conveyed immediately under escort to the army – and there they desert as fast as possible. In the streets of Lisbon, horse and foot soldiers are parading with arms in every quarter to keep the people in awe while this is going on – so much for patriotic enthusiasm. But after all, the Portuguese have more to boast of than the Spaniards. The Portuguese armed peasantry always accompanied us and did wonders, but in Spain I never saw one armed peasant and indeed not one person seemed to have the least interest in the cause we came to support. We are good mercenaries but we are not strong enough, nor is it to be expected we can transform the war – the Spaniards have shown *they will not fight* – and without their assistance we can do no good. I wrote to William on the 8th – this I sent to England by our quartermaster who is home for the benefit of his health. Remember me to all friends. My shoulder is healing fast.

Following the battle of Talavera, Joseph retired to cover Madrid, while Victor's corps were left on the direct road to the capital. Sabastiani had already been sent off to intercept Venegas who on 11 August was brought to battle and defeated at Almonacid, south east of Toledo, the French suffering 2,000 casualties.

On 29 July, Wellington was still contemplating an advance on Madrid, after his men had rested, with Cuesta, whose corps had hardly been engaged, but on condition that he was fully provided with supplies and transport. On the thirty-first Wellington heard that Soult's men had entered Plasencia on his line of communication. Before thrusting into Spain, Wellington agreed that Cuesta would provide forces to hold the passes of Perales and Baños, which gave access to his left flank, and for further insurance ordered Robert Wilson with the Loyal Lusitanian Legion to raid into Spain towards Madrid.

On 20 June, Soult had received a letter from Napoleon saying that 'Wellesley will most likely advance by the Tagus on Madrid; in that case pass the mountains, fall on his flank and rear and crush him'.[42] Soult now concentrated his own corps with those of Ney and Mortier, and on 30 July his advanced troops, who had had no difficulty in brushing aside the Spanish force occupying the highly defensible Pass of Banos, were marching on Plasencia. This created a crisis for Wellington; if the French could seize the bridge at Almaraz and pass a considerable force south of the Tagus, the alternative British line of communication to Portugal would be cut and it would be necessary to open up communications to Cadiz, leaving Portugal open to invasion.

As yet Wellington believed that the French at Plasencia comprised not more than 15,000 men of Mortier's corps. Those he could deal with, and it was decided that Cuesta should remain with his army and the British wounded at Talavera while the British marched against Mortier. Wellesley left Talavera on 4 August and the next day learnt that at least 30,000 French were already in Navalmoral, blocking the road to Almaraz. The British turned south through Oropesa, crossed the Tagus at Arzobispo and made their way by side roads to rejoin the main road to Badajoz at Jaracego. The Light Brigade raced across country through the mountains in extreme heat and forestalled the French at the bridge and ford of Almaraz after a fifteen-hour march. The army reached Jaracego on 10 August, on which day John Aitchison left for Belem to look after the sick and wounded of his regiment. On arrival he wrote to his father:

Belem
26th September 1809

I do not recollect whether what I mentioned in respect of the state of the army was sufficiently explicit to remedy the great uneasiness which the contradictory accounts in the newspapers appear to have caused you. But I shall now state as far as came under my knowledge the situation of the army at that time. All sorts of supplies were extremely scarce and in general very bad. The troops sometimes wanted bread for several days together. On the 27th in the morning we have served out about ¾lb of bread and a pound of meat to each man and on the 28th, late in the evening, the same quantity of meat but without bread was all they received. This meat was old goats – lean and very tough. During the halt after the battle of Talavera supplies were equally scanty and from the 2nd, the day before the army began to retire, until the 10th, the day on which I left, the troops used to receive about 2 ozs of bread divided amongst eight with more than a pound of meat to each person and they once received a pound of flour in addition.

But the meat was killed in a high state of fever from being drove, it was cooked before it was cold and eaten without salt and the consequence, as was to be expected in a hot climate, was fatal. Many men were sent to the hospitals and the whole army was reduced to a miserable condition. The army, however, is now well supplied with both bread and meat but the number of sick does not yet diminish. Indeed, with all the reinforcements we are not so strong as when we marched to Oporto.

Of the Spanish army that was with us I have already told you they are dismayed and dispersed, and Romana has I since understand been at our headquarters in Badajoz, (and it is repeated and believed at the army) stating that his army had almost all deserted. In short, from every account, nothing more is to be expected from the Spaniards – they will not make the sacrifices and exertions which are absolutely necessary to oppose the invading army.

I ascribe it all to the nobility – they really are a despicable set. The men composing the Spanish army are remarkably fine and I am yet persuaded that if they were well officered they would fight. But they have no example shown them – their officers are miserable beyond conception and they were always the first to desert. Soult is at Plasencia awaiting reinforcement to penetrate Portugal. Victor is at Talavera and occupies Arzobispo with his advance guard. When we marched against the French the combined army was not numerically stronger than the enemy – it is now much weaker.

Sir Arthur is very ill with ague and it is reported that he is coming here. General Beresford has cantoned his army and he is now in Lisbon. What is to be done everybody is at a loss to conceive – transports are sent off every week to England for stores but the cavalry which lately arrived are ordered to remain at Belem till further orders and they do not expect to join the army. Brigadier General Campbell, who was wounded in the thigh, has sailed to England after being quite recovered – he was much in the confidence of Sir Arthur and it is believed by many that he has been sent home confidentially for the purpose of representing to Ministers the state of affairs, the same as General Stewart was sent from Sir John Moore. . . .

The mail closes at 11 o'clock and it is now past ten so I must stop.

Remember me to all friends. My shoulder is almost quite healed – I shall be ready to join the army in a fortnight!

Belem
1st October 1809

The truth must at last appear. I expected it would and I was prepared for all the clamour at present at home. How I pity fallen greatness – for rapidity of movement and able dispositions in a battle my Lord Wellington certainly merits much applause, but the late campaign in Spain has diminished in a considerable degree the credit for Generalship which he acquired by the brilliant success that attended his former operations.

There is now but one opinion of the late campaign – the army in the Peninsula are unanimous and the nation appears to be of their opinion. In arranging and directing his operations with the Spaniards my Lord Wellington appears entirely to have forgot the indolent habit and inactive disposition of the people with whom he had to co-operate, nor does he appear to have bestowed much consideration on the nature of the country through which he had to march, and the small supply, nay, *extreme deficiency* of medical stores showed he entertained no apprehension of a reverse – in short, ere he had quitted Albrantes with his army, he had already in imagination triumphed in Madrid.

This hazardous boldness and apparent confidence of the chief had the effect to produce a corresponding feeling in the troops, yet flushed with recollection of their former success – attack and victory became synonymous in idea, and although the letters of Sir John Moore proclaimed the reception we were likely to experience from the Spaniards, and the reports – strengthened as we proceeded – acquainted us with the vast superiority of the French (inspired as we almost had been by the conduct of our commander), we nevertheless proceeded with cheerfulness, impatient only for the day we should measure our strength with that of the enemy.

Thus much, perhaps, the conduct of Lord Wellington may be applauded. It is right to keep up the spirits of the soldiers by prospects of success, but unfortunately when these visionary hopes are carried beyond probability, reverses when they do come are the more severely felt.

The grand error of our Commander-in-Chief seems to me to have been too much reliance on the professions of ability and execution in Spain and the Spaniards – from this has resulted the discomfiture of the combined army. But I am also of an opinion the great miseries which our troops have suffered are in no small degree to be attributed to a presumption of infallibility, which Lord Wellington appears to have entertained for his own plans. . . . I think every man ought to have confidence in his own abilities and as every, the most and boldest, plan there is always a chance of success when the stake is great I have no objection to risk it; *but* ere the safety of an army be committed, the commander-in-chief ought first to weigh well all circumstances. That in the present instance it has been neglected is what I complain.

While I say this much against Lord Wellington I am far from thinking with many (what the French wish to inculcate) that eventual success was ever beyond the power of possibility – on the contrary I am firmly persuaded had the attack on Talavera on 22 August been followed up on that day or the following by an attack on the French position on the left of the Alberche, success would have been consequent.

Victor beaten must have retreated and the effect of a defeated army falling back on its reinforcements, if it had not been sufficient to induce the whole French force to retire, and perhaps for the moment to withdraw from Madrid, yet it would have enabled the combined army to gain sufficient in advance to form a junction with Venegas and Toledo. Had this happily been the case, Soult, with his whole army at the distance of twelve days' march from us, *must of necessity* have changed his route to endeavour to unite with the other corps, and Madrid would in the meantime have fallen.

Such would have been the brilliant consequence of an attack on the 23rd and to the delay must be ascribed all the humiliations the armies have been compelled to endure. We (I mean the British) expected to attack – we were prepared for it and in spirits. After remaining under arms six hours we were ordered to march and we (the right column) arrived within a mile of our point of attack by 12 – here we were ordered to halt and afterwards to return to our original position. . . . A retrograde movement, as it manifests a want of confidence or uncertainty in the chief, so it tends thoroughly to damp the ardour, diminish the hope and excite the apprehension of the troops. The order therefore to retire produced in all a sensation which it may be possible to conceive but not to describe.

Reports, as is usual on such occasions, were numerous and various – by some it was said that the Spaniards would not attack – but the position was so formidable we could not, with chance of success – in short, such was the effect produced that when we were ordered to re-advance by moonlight at midnight the spirits were depressed and every man believed himself marching to his grave. This, however, did not last long, and by 4 of the morning the state of things was known – day by day the incapacity and indifference of the Spanish generals became more apparent – we determined to do our best notwithstanding – firing at a distance soon told us our time was approaching – we regained our spirits and ere the French returned on the 27th we were fully prepared to sacrifice our all. We did what we could and our efforts were rewarded with victory on the 28th. Victory achieved by the sacrifice of a quarter of our army – a sacrifice trifling were it in assistance to a people hearty in so good a cause – but this experience denies – more than regret follows those who have fallen and whether a title to one's general will be sufficient to appease the manes of the departed, heaven only can reveal. The course of the battle belongs to the Spanish, the honour and the dreadful consequences to the *British* – the retreat while it lasted was indeed melancholy – conceive the feeling of a soldier forced to shoot his horse, the sharer of his toils, worn out by want of food; conceive the feeling of a soldier in seeing his comrade drooping exhausted by extreme fatigue and bad food – conceive the feeling of a soldier, perhaps his brother, under excruciating agonies of a wound dying for want of dressing. These and more than these were the melancholy scenes on the retreat in one part, while in another the emaciated soldier yoked to the guns, and with the noble spirit of a man striving against nature, in the cause of honour performing prodigies of strength. The mind by sweet success is warmed and exalted. I shall never forget the impression it made. The consequence of a severe campaign is felt when the body becomes inactive. I am happy to say I am now quite recovered from the weakness I felt in my legs and my shoulder wound is healed – there is yet a very small piece of proud flesh to burn but I have no pain. I begin to pick up flesh – the army, however, I am sorry to say – if we judge by our brigade – is very sickly and rather increasing: we have upwards of 800, besides those who have died or were killed.

Belem
7th October

There has been no packet arrived since that on 30th ult. The next is looked for with great anxiety by every person here, as by it we expect to learn what is to be the fate of the army in the Peninsula. We have heard of the quarrel amongst Ministers, and as Mr Canning was the chief advocate for the Spaniards, the recall of his army is anticipated in consequence of his resignation.[43]

I am not yet however myself over-sanguine that this will take place, for notwithstanding our ineffectual sacrifices in assistance to the Spaniards had sufficiently demonstrated their incapacity to resist the French, yet the Ministers, in opposition to the opinion of everyone acquainted with the true state of affairs, persisted a second time in hazarding the existence of our army in co-operation. Although the result was a dreadful corroboration of former experiment, they *still* persevered in a determination to sacrifice men to their inconsiderate contract; while therefore there remains in power one man who lent his support to such measures, I am debarred the hope that a measure so reasonable as the recall of the army will be resorted to, especially at a time when a rupture between Russia and France is so confidently talked of, and while Austria maintains negative hostility.

If Austria continues the war with the French, those troops in Spain must of necessity be withdrawn, and if peace is concluded, all Spain organized as is her armies at present, *even* with the co-operation of a powerful British force, will be insufficient to withstand the host of enemies that will be brought against her. The opportunity for freeing Spain has I fear already passed, and if she, with augmented resources after a fourteen months' experience in war, be not able to bring into the field a force *numerically equal* to a reduced and enfeebled French army, I confess I cannot see what circumstances will enable her to overcome the tyrants of oppression.

Such was the situation of Spain previous to the battle of Talavera when, *with* her forces *united* to an army of 19,000 British, they did not exceed in number *those* armies of the French which immediately opposed them. This I believe is a circumstance not generally known in Britain, at least not generally credited. From the moment I had an opportunity to witness myself the state of affairs of this country I had but little hope of success – the more I have seen the less has been my hope and I have been much surprised that in England people should remain so ignorant of the true state of things in the Peninsula – their eyes now begin to open and I fear only in time to be dazzled.

The Brigade of Guards has added much in this campaign to the high character which it always bore. It is a real pride to belong to a corps so highly thought of by all ranks in the army – many compliments are paid in general orders – the other day alluding to inaccuracies in returns – 'it is but justice to both battalions of Guards to state their returns have always been accurate in every particular, as the *conduct* of these excellent corps in the field has been regular and examplary throughout.'

The invalided sick are all to embark tomorrow for England – the two battalions of detachments have arrived from the army and they are to be sent home.

The 1st Dragoons which arrived here some weeks ago have received their route and they are to join the army tomorrow. All the English generals in the Portuguese service set off in a hurry several days ago to their commands in the country. Both Soult and Victor are said to be in motion and advancing. Most of the rich merchants have packed up ready to be off to England and the Brazils. We are all very anxious to know what is going on in England – write me your opinion. My remembrances to all my friends. Adieu.

I am here now in charge of the sick of our brigade – how long I shall remain is uncertain.

Belem
9th October 1809

My late letters will show you so completely what is my opinion of the Spaniards that I shall not now say anything of them – Sir Arthur says he did not *urge* them to make any movement on the enemy's flank but it is not to be inferred he did not wish it. They were drawn up in three lines and they all remained as unconcerned spectators in their positions, which in front was of difficult access but not strong.

The officer you observed who was appointed as adjutant was junior to me and by that appointment I lose a step. He is not approved of in this battalion and the officer commanding it wrote to recommend an officer of service now in the 2nd Battalion senior to me, but the Ensign having been promised it at headquarters he was appointed and I did not apply for it as I knew the state of things. I am now 3rd Ensign but the senior expects his Lieutenancy every day (if he has not already got it) and should the battalion be ordered home I shall get mine in a few weeks. Without great reinforcements we can do no good here – wherever the French are sufficiently strong to advance we must retire – on 24th of last month the sick amounted to 10,300 and they rather increased. The average deaths at Elvas were 80 a week, here they are 7 per day. The rainy season has begun and the men are still in camp.

Give my love to all

Belem
11th October 1809

Dispatches received for Lord Wellington are supposed to relate to the withdrawing of the Army from *Spain*; indeed, I learnt yesterday, from Authority which I have generally found correct, that the army was to retire immediately to Abrantes, with a view to its embarkation at Peniche, should it be found expedient. I am however at a loss to reconcile this with the late proceedings here, and if this measure has been resolved upon it must have been decided lately – for although the whole of the non-effectives of the army amount to little short of 15,000 men, no measures have yet been adopted for moving the hospitals to Lisbon, and in a few days it will be impracticable. The rainy season will begin about the middle of this month and during its continuance it is impossible for an army to move, much less for a hospital.

We have it reported Lord Wellington was appointed War Secretary. I have not seen any late newspaper – I wish I had one sent me occasionally. Your last letters have not been numbered – it would be convenient to me did you continue to number them.

Of the Spanish armies we have not lately heard anything and their operations begin to lose all interest. The French are said to be in force on the north side of the Tagus and a corps has already crossed the bridge at Arzobispo.

The packet sails tomorrow – another I believe will sail next Sunday – by it I shall write to William and it will I think be my last letter from Lisbon. Adieu.

Belem
21st October 1809

In consequence of the non-arrival of another packet, the one which was to have sailed on Thursday morning has been detained and it will not sail until tomorrow.

The drafts for our brigade have at length arrived but they only amount to 200 men in all; there are 11 officers for our regiment and eight for the Coldsteam. Draft for several other regiments have likewise arrived by the same convoy, but in the whole there are not 1,200 men – a great number of empty transports came in the same fleet – they have each provisions for three months for the number of men they can hold. These few men will have no effect on the army as a reinforcement but no more troops are to be sent here – the armies, both British and French, remain where they have been since the retreat and they wait the issue of the negotiations with Austria.

The Royal Dragoons, which had received orders to join the army, has been countermanded and Lord Wellington has received orders not to risk a general action but to withdraw for embarkation should the French advance in force. We have it from the French army that peace was signed on 1 October – they say Bonaparte himself is to come into Spain with re-inforcements and after they have conquered all Spain (which they talk of as the work of a day) the 15,000 men are to be stationed in each province. . . .

I believe I shall set off to join the regiment again very soon – Colonel Stopford has sent to request I would enter the Light company and I think it right to comply – I shall get a jacket made up in Lisbon and when equipped I shall set off. The Light[44] company has been unfortunate in its officers in not one out of six now doing duty – two were wounded and taken prisoner, one is knocked up and not likely again to join while here – one was put on the staff and two went home on promotion.

Belem
23rd October 1809

Lord Wellington having again detained the packet to carry dispatches, I embrace the opportunity the delay affords me to send the news.

Within these few days Lord Wellington has employed himself in[45] reconnoitring the country round about Lisbon on the north side of the Tagus and yesterday he was to Cascaes Bay and examined it most minutely – the dispatches which the packet is to carry home are supposed to be his opinion of the practicability of embarking troops pressed by an enemy on this side of the Tagus and on the defence Lisbon is capable of making.

It has been in report here and believed that the army was to retreat from the frontier to take up the defensive position in front of Lisbon on the north, and I have a letter from the army today which says the sick from the General Hospital at Elvas are to be sent to Lisbon immediately as fast as they can be moved.

It is said Bonaparte himself is now on his way to Madrid and the French army is already in motion. Peace with Austria was signed on 1 October.[46]

If all this be correct (and it comes from the French army, whose information here has lately been found so) I should suppose our stay in this country will be very short. The French will not advance upon us till they have such a force as to set resistance at defiance. In my last, of 21, I told you I was posted to our Light Company – if we retreat our situation will be an arduous one – the Brigade of Guards will cover the retreat and embarkation of the army and its Light companies will cover it.

The regiments of Portuguese Militia and Volunteers which were raised for the defence of Lisbon have been ordered by Lord Wellington to practise walking two days every week – they began yesterday˙and all was in a bustle.

Adieu.

The British Army remained in the Jaracejo–Truxillo area until 20 August. Cuesta had left a covering force at Talavera and, without informing Wellington, marched and joined him, in opposing Soult, on 4 August. He left some 1,500 wounded British to the French, from whom, however, they received excellent treatment. Cuesta was then holding Oropesa and Arzobispo. On 6 August the main body of Cuesta's army moved south of the Tagus. Two days later their rearguard was attacked and put to flight. Soult's army, by this time suffering for want of supplies, did not exploit this success. Joseph now ordered the army to be broken up, Ney turning north to deal with partisan troubles in Léon stirred up by Romana.

By this time Wellington's half-starved army was low in morale and discipline – 'With the army which a fortnight ago beat double their numbers, I should now hesitate to meet a French corps of half their strength,' he wrote.[47] British troops seized Spanish army rations, Spanish troops attacked British foraging parties and threatened to sack any village providing their allies with bread. The troops plundered under the eyes of their officers. Soldiers' wives offered themselves for a loaf of bread and those caught plundering, at which they were at least as ardent as the men, were given 'six and thirty lashes a piece on the bare doup',[48] an action for which Wellington was later to be taken to task.

On 10 August, Cuesta, having suffered a stroke, resigned. The next day Wellington informed his deputy that either the army must receive proper rations or he would withdraw to Portugal. The central junta continued to draw up impractical military plans. Wellington's threat they considered desertion and they still hoped to get him involved, but he would have none of it. The French already had 200,000 troops in Spain, and with peace declared between France and Austria there was no limit, other than logistics, to the numbers Napoleon could deploy there. The Spanish field armies numbered 80,000, not all of whom were armed, and the 25,000 British could not tip the balance.

In Wellington's view the correct strategy for Britain was to ensure the security of Lisbon and the mouth of the Tagus while Spain concentrated on the defence of Andalusia, and both built up their military strength. The British position in Portugal would assist in the defence of Andalusia by posing a threat to the French lines of communication, in the event of an advance against Seville. Though the central junta had made him Marshal General of Spain after Talavera, Wellington was determined never again to act as auxiliary to Spanish forces. By 3 September he had withdrawn his headquarters to Badajoz.

On 10 September, Wellington was in Lisbon for three weeks' reconnaissance of the Lisbon peninsula, accompanied by his chief engineer, Lt-Col

Richard Fletcher R.E. This resulted in a memorandum on the construction of the now famous Lines of Torres Vedras. It would be a year before the lines would be occupied by an Anglo-Portuguese army, a year in which 10,000 Portuguese labourers were continuously at work strengthening a naturally strong position by every known artifice. Unknown to the French, the Lisbon peninsula was turned into an almost impregnable redoubt from which, as a last resort, the army could be evacuated by sea.

Wellington had by now evolved a very clear strategy from which he was prepared to resign rather than deviate. No unnecessary risks would be taken with Britain's only effective army and he would, therefore, confine himself to the defence of Portugal and the Lisbon base until such time as he had trained and organized an Anglo–Portuguese army capable of a sustained offensive, and the time was right for it. In the meantime he would wear down the French by offering them defensive battles whenever a favourable opportunity occurred and by encouraging partisan forces to operate against the enemy's long lines of communication and to deny them local sources of supply.

It was a strategy that in the coming years was to put a great strain on the morale of his forces, on that of the Portuguese people and their leaders, and on the British people. The latter were by now thoroughly tired of the war in general and the expense of war in the Peninsula in particular; the political opposition made full use of the distorted reports which the French government released to their press; the Portuguese always suspected that any retreat by the British was but a preliminary to their re-embarkation, leaving them to the mercy of the French. Wellington's 'scorched earth' policy did not arouse enthusiasm for the war in the hearts of the Portuguese peasantry, though experience had taught them that French occupation was worse, nor did the British troops find it easy to understand why every triumph over the 'Frogs' was rewarded by an arduous retreat through inhospitable country.

His officers praised him in victory and censured him for lack of judgment when things appeared to go wrong for reasons they often did not understand. John Aitchison's letters are typical of many. Wellington often complained of 'croakers', as did Montgomery of 'bellyachers', and of matters appearing in the press, clearly inspired by letters home, that were likely to bring comfort to the enemy. There was no censorship of mail and it is striking how closely the tenor of discontent at home reflected that felt by many in the field. Unlike Montgomery, Wellington did not believe in explanation, much less in apology, and it is a measure of his remarkable powers of leadership that the army came to trust his judgment in all things, even when they did not understand it.

Belem
4th November 1809

Invention is on the rack. We have reports every day so contradictory that it is impossible to learn anything in respect to the situation of Austria and France. Peace or war between[49] these powers is to us now immediately of consequence, for on the decision must wholly depend the future proceedings of this army – the absence of certain information, the reports from Spain are, I'm sorry to say, on the whole unfavourable. It certainly appears the French were foiled in their attempt on the Duc del Parque's army in position, and this by numbers but little superior, but the division of the main army under Venegas, after having made a forward movement in the direction of Toledo, have retired precipitately, without even encountering the advance posts of the enemy. From Seville we hear Lord Wellesley was hooted by the populace before his departure – this from a belief that the British Army was about to be withdrawn from Spain.

Since I wrote to you on the 23rd, Lord Wellington has been at Bucellas reconnoitring – he went from this on 27th and he has since left the army for Seville. The army remains in cantonments and it is expected it will be gradually withdrawn from Spain and retire upon this part of Portugal. There are several circumstances that encourage this belief – the artillery stores at Lisbon (under the denomination *Spare*) have in part been embarked already, and a battery is now being erected on a hill which commands Fort St Julien on the land side, to secure the road to Cascaes. These I consider more as precautions against extremities than indications of immediate retreat. They are, however, decisive in as much as they show there is no idea of the army acting offensively.

Sickness is not decreasing but I am happy to say deaths had not lately been so frequent. We have had a good deal of rain here and on Monday there was a shock of an earthquake. It was not, however, severe and no damage has been done – I am not yet completely equipped for the Light Company; the moment I am I shall leave Lisbon for Badajoz, where the brigade is at present cantoned – the officer commanding will be here tomorrow on sick leave. Mr Villiers sails tomorrow on the *Norge* (74)[50] and by her this letter goes. I have none from home of later date than 16 September.

Adieu.

Badajoz
30th November 1809

The defeat of the Spaniards on 19th has been the most complete they have yet suffered and by them the least expected. The general who commanded has been sent to retrieve the character of the main army, but unfortunately for him the soldiers had been so completely cowed by seven defeats that on the first approach of the enemy the cavalry gave way to and overthrew the columns of their own infantry which were immediately in rear.

The French were 20,000 strong, the Spaniards 50,000 and they lost in killed 5,000 and prisoners 15,000 and about 55 out of 70 pieces of artillery. The remains of this army are now in the Sierra Morena, eighty miles from the scene of action. Between us and the French there is now no force but a small corps of Spaniards under the Duc de Alburquerque which was at Talavera de la Reyna before 19th, but it will now be obliged to fall back in consequence of the defeat of the main army. All our prisoners have been moved to Madrid, whence they are to be sent to France as fast as they can be moved. They have been remarkably well treated.

The sickness in our army has decreased but in a very small degree, but deaths are as frequent as ever and for the last month I hear they exceed 1,000. Hospitals are now established in the rear on the road to Lisbon and they are removing the sick as fast as possible.

You are mistaken in your idea about Belem. There is only a fort which commands the river but it is not formidable on the land side; indeed, there is no place near Lisbon which could resist a well-provided army one week, not excepting Fort Julien. All the forts in the Tagus are built for its defence and against ships only, but they are formidable. The weather has been dry and fine for the last fortnight but generally cold and frosty, and if it continues the hospitals will diminish very fast.

There is no talk of the French advancing yet. There is no chance whatever of my eating a Christmas dinner at home; you must suppose me there as I am sure my thoughts will be.

Badajoz
6th December 1809

There is such an inconceivable difference between the state of cultivation in the Peninsula and Great Britain that in calculating on the operations of an *auxiliary* army in Spain you must divest yourself on every recollection of the *improved condition* of Scotland and particularly of the highly cultivated part which you are the most accustomed to see. So much indeed is Spain behind the improvement that I have doubts whether the strongest language I could make use of in a letter would be sufficient to convey to you an idea of the extreme barbarity of the inhabitants and the consequent impoverished state of the soil.

It is certainly natural enough, with plenty before you at home and a knowledge of the conditions of our countrymen, that you should be surprised at the deficiencies of supplies of our small army in Spain but this arises from the supposition that the Spaniards in their husbandry are now what we were formerly; there is not however any analogy. In the whole extent of country we passed over there was not one farmhouse – the Spaniards live in towns and except immediately around them there is nothing in the appearance of the land that would lead you to suppose that the country is populated. Everything is left to nature, and from July to January the grass in the plains (which by much exceeds in excellence that in the mountains) is completely burnt up. The supply of animal food is consequently small, and as the inhabitants are obliged by their religion to eat but little, no pains are taken to rear horned cattle, there is no commerce and therefore no encouragement to the farmer to grow grain above home consumption; this too is the cause of want of carriages.

In summer the Spaniards live on watermelons, which grow with little trouble in the sand, and on grapes; and in winter on eggs, onions, garlic with bread and, occasionally, salt fish and meat.

Their middlemen make them extremely tenacious of their property and although they are avaricious beyond conception, yet the trouble in getting paid for what they sell us, the exertions necessary to bring their things to market and their jealousy of us will always prevent our being easily supplied even in a plentiful part of Spain. While in an unproductive part of Spain we shall always starve – because means of carrying provisions are not to be procured and *force* only will make the Spaniards assist us.

The French say to be treated like men by the Spaniards you must treat them as brutes – this we have invariably found the case. I am persuaded it always will be so and hence the French army will be pretty well supplied and fit for service while ours is *starving and sickly*. I have often thought the great sickness in our army must in some degree be owing to bad quarters and I am more convinced of it as the sick of a regiment of the line which has *beds* for all the men bears no proportion to the other regiments which are all without beds or straw and who have only one blanket between two men.

I shall be better able to explain to you in conversation the cultivation of Spain. What I have said will perhaps be sufficient to convince you the fault of our deficiencies was not Lord Wellington's.

As you observe in your last letter it certainly is a paradox, in condemning the exertions of the Spaniards while the French make but little progress against them. To me, however, it is not so. When you come to have a more intimate knowledge of their character you will yourself be persuaded the French *will be* masters of Spain. I have always given (and I do yet give) the Spaniards credit for a hatred of the French – but it is hatred only – they want determination and whenever the French have a force sufficient to garrison every town the Spaniards will not long delay accord. At present the French force is [indecipherable], and from the little the Spaniards have done against it, it is evident they will do nothing more. There must be revolution in everything in Spain – government and religion – before she can resist France.

I regret to see you accuse me with having *permitted* a junior officer to have been put over me – rest assured no person is more zealous for my interest than myself – I shall say no more till I see you, I shall then explain all to your satisfaction and I must now beg of you to spare my feelings and never again allude to what you have already said – you have fallen into a misconception and do not argue as from a fact.

Since I wrote to you on the 30th the French are reported to have advanced from Talavera and Oropesa in the direction of Truxillo. The Duc de Alburquerque has his headquarters there and the French have certainly showed themselves around Almaraz but it is not ascertained in what degree – the officers of our staff corps were sent to reconnoitre – we are moving our sick to the rear and the Purveyor of the hospital at Elvas had been ordered to have everything packed up and ready to move off at a moment's notice. Nothing can equal the incivility of the inhabitants here – I should almost rejoice to see the French amongst them tomorrow – there have been several little quarrels with our men and I should not be surprised that it becomes serious before we leave this.

The weather has continued very fine and for some days warmer, today it is a keen frost and very cold but fine.

Badajoz
7th December 1809

Since I did myself the pleasure to write to you yesterday, appearances have so much changed as to induce me to trouble you with another letter. I acquainted you last week with the complete defeat and dispersion of the main Spanish army at Ocaña on the 19th. I have now to mention my official dispatch was this day received by Lord Wellington announcing the overthrow of the army under the Duc del Parque on 29th ult at the town of Alba de Tormes, about three leagues south-east of Salamanca. It appears that Mortier retured from Salamanca after the check he had received from the Spaniards and the Duc del Parque was induced to follow him from the good behaviour of his troops but the French attacked him on the 29th and took all his artillery, which consisted of 30 pieces. Their loss of men has been very great, I have heard upwards of half the army – the remainder are now on the retreat of Ciudad Rodrigo.

Several of our regiments of infantry have already moved about four leagues to the rear of the frontiers of Portugal and there is now every reason to suppose the whole army will quit Spain immediately. The sick from the outposts have been sent to Elvas and the *whole* of the sick in this town were sent off early this morning in consequence of an order issued late yesterday. The hospitals in the rear of Elvas have been ordered to be ready to move at any moment's notice, and I have just seen a field officer of the artillery and he tells me they received orders this morning to hold themselves prepared to march.

We have not yet been warned but we do not expect to remain here a week longer. The Spaniards are likely to be punished very soon for their inhospitable behaviour to us – Marshall Oudinot[51] has already passed the Pyrenees with 20,000 men. Those at Talavera de la Reyna are expected to advance immediately – they have passed the Tagus in small ferries at Almaraz.

Everything is extremely dear here and all have been doubled in price since our entering this town – wine costs 4/6d and 7/6d a litre, butter 3/- a pound, barley for horses 4½d a pound, this paper 2½d a sheet, quarto 2/- a hundred and everything else in proportion.

I have just received your last letter and notice your remark on the advance of the Guards in the battle of Talavera – the *Gazette* certainly leaves the impression that they committed an error; it is, however, now thought a most fortunate thing they went beyond the point intended, as the French were so much intimidated that they did not bring into action their reserve columns of infantry and cavalry which were in their rear[52] – should we be pressed by the enemy on a retreat you will find the Guards will again distinguish themselves and their services be as beneficial to the army.

It is supposed we shall only for the present retire to Abrantes, where if assited by the Portuguese we shall be able to make some stand. I am in very good health and strength and all our men who are not in the hospitals look remarkably well.

I shall write you again the first opportunity when I expect to be able to tell you some thing has been decided on. The weather has the appearance of continuing fine. The French advanced posts are yet upwards of 100 miles from this town.

Abrantes
17th December 1809

The next day after I wrote to you last from Badajoz we received our route to proceed to Vizeu with one brigade of artillery. The army is withdrawing in Spain; the last division was to leave Badajoz on the 15th and the whole is on the march for the province of Beira, where it is to take up a position of two lines for the protection of Portugal. This measure *is said* to be rendered necessary by the movements of the French army under Mortier, who, since his success against the Duc del Parque, has threatened to pass the frontier. There are, however, several circumstances which incline me to believe the course assigned is merely to blind the Spaniards, and the operations of the army (if it is thought advisable to attempt a retention of Portugal) will be confined to a defence at Lisbon and the country between the rivers Tagus and Mondego.

This is in the first instance we have had of any brigade being at once made acquainted with the ultimate point of its destination – a division of the army under General Hill which was to have passed the Tagus at Villa Velha to form the right of the first line has been ordered to march by Abrantes, and we are now to halt at *Coimbra* till the rear comes up, although in the original order we were to have remained there only one day.

We march tomorrow to Punhete whence we proceed by Thomar to Leyria, where we are to halt one day, and afterwards by Pombal we go to Coimbra. All the sick have not yet been removed from Elvas, indeed Lord Wellington is thought to have received orders to withdraw forthwith from Spain by dispatches which came by the *Juno* to Lisbon only four days before our march.

I have already hazarded so often my opinion on the state of Portugal that I shall not now risk another speculation, but I think it must be evident to everyone, even those not possessing a local knowledge, that with a luke-warm assistance which only we shall receive from the natives of Portugal, an attempt at defence with an army so reduced and enfeebled as ours will have annihilation for its result.

I do not myself despond, I know the bottom of the British soldiers; all that can be done will be affected by them – but I state things as they appear and when we know the worst we are forewarned.

We have yet been fortunate in the weather. It has sometimes been dry and frosty and the worst day has been like a good November one at home.

Coimbra
26th December 1809

Since I wrote to you from Abrantes the whole of the disposition of the army has been changed and an express from Lord Wellington overtook us at Pombal with orders for our brigade to proceed to Vizeu. Sir John Sherbrooke[53] had intended to halt us for ten days at Coimbra to allow the division to close, but in consequence of the Commander-in-Chief's order we march again tomorrow. Lord Wellington had not left Badajoz on the 18th and the cavalry had not then received the order to quit Spain. The whole of the infantry, however, have entered Portugal and are now on the march by different routes to take up the position on the frontier in the province of Beira.

The civility we have received in Portugal has formed a contrast to the brutal coldness of the Spaniards towards us. We are everywhere met with open arms and the Portuguese, sensible of their own weakness, are emulous of the appearance and conduct of our men – they in most regiments really seem desirous to learn and they have already approached a degree of perfection under the tuition of British officers which astonishes themselves and commands our respect. It is, however, to be feared that the same servility of disposition which makes them learn, sooner than the British soldier, will act on their spirit of resistance in defence and that they will sooner abandon their posts.

I had at one time hoped to have spent Christmas at home with my friends but it has been deemed I should spend it at Coimbra. Two other officers who mess with me had a very happy dinner after our march and each drank to his family and a happy meeting.

It seems determined we shall defend Portugal to extremity. The country north of the Tagus is capable of much resistance and the French know it. They will therefore perhaps not molest us for some time, but when Spain has surrendered they will bring against us a force sufficient for Portugal and we will then retire. It is reported here 12,000 men are ordered from England to reinforce. We stand much in need of it as I believe our present force fit for duty does not amount to 18,000 men, notwithstanding that they say it is 22,000. The men have been very healthy since they began the march – we have been very lucky in the weather, there has been little rain and not very cold – it is now frosty and fine.

Remember me to all the family.

PS I shall write from Vizeu

CHAPTER TWO

1810
The Year of Busaco

AT peace once more with the rest of Europe, following his victory at
Wagram, Napoleon was free to concentrate on the subjugation of
Spain and the invasion of Portugal. His plans remained faulty for he
continued to misjudge the temper of the Spanish people, to overestimate
the resources of the Peninsula, and to underestimate the effect of its terrain.
First priority was to be the elimination of the British: 'The English are
the only danger in Spain. The rest can never keep up a campaign.'[1] On
4 December he declared: 'When I shall show myself beyond the Pyrenees the
frightened leopard [Britain] will fly to the ocean, to avoid shame, defeat or
death.'[2]

The leopard, in the form of Wellington, was far from frightened and
convinced Percival, the Prime Minister, and Liverpool, the War Secretary,
that with 30,000 British troops and a like number of Portuguese supported by
militia and partisans, and by fixed defences across the Lisbon peninsula (the
lines of Torres Vedras), he could hold Lisbon and the Tagus estuary against
any force the French could maintain against him, and that, if wrong, he could
still extricate the British.

Nor were the 'partisans' to be lightly dismissed. Xenophobia was a Spanish
characteristic but it was fierce provincial loyalties that, while making an
overall strategy difficult, fuelled the flame of resistance. The year 1809 had
been a disastrous one for Spain's immature regular armies whenever they
sought to challenge the French in the plains. While Napoleon continued to
ignore the effect on operations of the mountains and the barrenness of much
of the land, the Spanish equally failed to exploit these peculiar features for
defence purposes. Nevertheless, in the face of frequent defeat the Spanish
provincial armies had shown themselves remarkably resilient. Lessons were
being learnt and inefficient generals eliminated. However, the most significant event of 1809 was the rise of the guerrilla movement. Bands under local
leaders, drawn from all walks of life, established bases in mountain strong-
holds from where they could harass the French lines of communication.
Their activities ranged from knifing senior officials to ambushing an isolated
battalion. They intercepted French official mail providing Wellington with
much valuable information.

From October onwards thousands of Portuguese peasants were employed
constructing the lines of Torres Vedras and other defensive works in Por-

tugal. The whole country was surveyed and mapped for the first time. Some roads were improved to make defence more flexible, others were destroyed to make attack more difficult. A naval signal system was established from Lisbon to centres at the front, and depots and garrisons were stocked and provisioned.

Wellington expected to be attacked from the direction of Salamanca, via Ciudad Rodrigo and Almeida, which indeed was Napoleon's plan. He therefore established his headquarters at Celorico and the bulk of the British army in the Mondego valley with Craufurd's Light Division thrown forward across the Coa on outpost duty. The 1st Division, now commanded by Stapleton Cotton, afterwards Lord Combermere, Sherbrooke having been invalided with Stopford commanding the Guards Brigade, was in reserve with the 3rd Regiment of Guards of Vizeu. To watch the approaches to Badajoz, Wellington stationed Hill's 2nd Division with an equal number of Portuguese troops south of the Tagus. The Portuguese army garrisoned a number of strong points and fortresses and the bulk of their mobile reserve was around Thomar.

In preparation for a fresh campaign in the Peninsula, Napoleon had assembled, in the autumn 1809, 100,000 men between Orleans and Bayonne. French military strength in the Peninsula was to rise to 336,000 during 1810, very large numbers being required to protect their lines of communication. In January, King Joseph, without Napoleon's specific permission, had assembled an army of 60,000 men under Soult along the Sierra Morena with the intention of adding rich and populous Andalusia to his kingdom. To oppose him the Spaniards had an army of 25,000 stretched out over a 160-mile front under Areizaga. Cordova was occupied on the twenty-fourth and on the twenty-ninth Joseph had the choice of occupying Seville or pressing on to Cadiz, where members of the central junta had fled. On Soult's advice he chose the former and this enabled the Duque de Alburquerque, who had been commanding an army near Merida on the Guadiana, to use his initiative and throw an army of 10,000 men into Cadiz.

Cadiz became the seat of the Regency under a triumvirate headed by General Castaños. An important, highly defensible naval base, it had hitherto been practically undefended. This time British help was sought and Wellington sent reinforcements under Major-General the Hon. William Stewart, which, with a further 3,000 Spanish reinforcements, brought the garrison to 17,000. On 26th March further British and Portuguese forces under Lieutenant-General Thomas Graham brought the British contingent up to 8,000 men.

When Alburquerque moved to Cadiz, the Marquis Romana, another Spanish general with whom Wellington found he could work, took over command from the Duque del Parque around Ciudad Rodrigo. Reorganizing his 20,000 men into formations of 3,000, he deployed them to cover the Portuguese frontier from the pass of Perales to Zafra. Without naval support, Cadiz could not be taken and Victor, whose corps were operating against it, was forced to withdraw. Given a free hand, Joseph might have had some success in pacifying Andalusia, but Napoleon was intent on extracting as much money from Spain as possible to pay for his armies and in February divided Spain into four areas of military government – Catalonia, Aragon, Navarre, and Biscay – which virtually deprived Joseph of all power.

Napoleon had intended to lead the 'Army of Portugal', which was being assembled around Salamanca, in person but he soon lost interest and handed over the 70,000 troops to Massena's command, which was independent of Joseph, and had corps under Ney, Junot and Reynier, Napoleon tried to conduct the war from Paris while engrossing himself in dynastic affairs, for Josephine had failed to produce an heir and he had had their marriage declared void in December 1809. The Tsar had declined Napoleon as a possible brother-in-law but not so the Emperor Francis II, and in February he was officially engaged to marry the Emperor's daughter, the Archduchess Marie-Louise.

Massena was told by Napoleon that his invasion of Portugal should not be precipitate. When the British had been expelled they would continue to blockade Lisbon and he did not want responsibility for feeding that city until after the harvest. Wellington would also do nothing to precipitate the conflict, nor would he allow himself to become involved in support of Spanish forces – time, he believed, was on his side. Massena opened the campaign in early June by sending Ney to invest Ciudad Rodrigo.

By this time the British troops had been hutted and well fed throughout the winter; they were in good health but they were living in wine country and their behaviour in their cups worried Wellington. 'We are an excellent army on parade,' he wrote, 'an excellent one to fight; but we are worse than an enemy in a country; and take my word for it, either defeat or success would dissolve us.'[3] Raising and training the Portuguese Army had progressed well under Beresford. All they now required was the confidence which only success in battle can bring. The tranquillity of the first six months of 1810 enabled John Aitchison to send a weekly letter home. It no doubt also allowed more time for gossip and the spread of rumour, and for him to dwell upon the complications and prospects of promotion.

Vizeu
13th January 1810

I must beg of you not to execute the determination you had formed at not writing to me from a belief of the army's return to England.[4] Do not pay attention to any reports about us, there will be many and contradictory. When anything relative *to our recall is certainly decided on* I shall take an early opportunity to inform you, but, until I do this, I expect you will continue to favour me with your communications as frequently as you have done. News from home is the most interesting to be received from any quarter – indeed, were it not from what we learn from England one would be perfectly ignorant of what is going on in the rest of the world. This, I am persuaded, will be to you a sufficient reason for continuing to write to me, although many of your letters were to miscarry – I should not have thought it necessary even to urge this in support of my request had it not appeared to me from 1 December, being the date of your last letter, that you were inclined to suppose your letters to me less valuable than I feel them.

Mr Thomson at last has had the goodness to send me newspapers by post, and I have received a weekly one from 17 December, but as the expense is so much beyond what I had conceived I have thought it proper to beg him not to send any more by *that conveyance* for the present; yet, having found out that newsmen are in the position of getting papers sent abroad through the under-clerks at the Foreign Office (by paying five guineas a year in addition) I have requested him to endeavour to get me a daily paper forwarded in that manner, and should he succeed two other officers of the regiment will go shares.

There seems at present no chance of our being recalled. Nay, it evidently is resolved we shall attempt a defence of Portugal to extremity. That we shall succeed, no one who knows the country and the people entertains a hope; *but there certainly is no immediate cause why the army should be withdrawn.*

We are now too well acquainted with the nature of the Spanish force to suppose that as an army they can withstand the efforts of the French. In fact, intersected by rivers and mountains they may yet offer great resistance if well disposed – the movement of the British from Estremadura to the north of Portugal has had the effect to prevent the remnants of Areizaga's army being molested. And *while we remain north of the Mondego and on the frontiers,* the French will not dare to attempt the passes of the Sierra Morena;[5] at least, till they have such a force besides sufficient to prevent our acting offensively in their rear, and this they cannot well have sooner than three months.

After the defeat and dispersion therefore of the principal Spanish army and the reverse immediately after sustained by the Duc del Parque, it became indispensably necessary to make a movement with the British army and Lord Wellington has made a judicious one. In the positions now occupied, we may make a great resistance to a much superior force, and, if from one point we are obliged to retire, we can with safety to another at a short distance and stronger; while an attacking army if he suffers reverse in attempting positions so difficult of approach will be exposed to destruction.

While we continued in the extensive plains of Spanish Estremadura, had we suffered reverse in defending a position we must have retreated, and retreat in an open country before an enemy so numerous as the French would be destruction. In the mountainous tracts of Beira, however, small as is the British force it will nevertheless be formidable, and if well seconded by natives as irregulars it may yet avert the fate of the Peninsula, as at least it may protract the war in Spain to an incalculable period. If forced to withdraw into Portuguese Estremadura we shall lose all our cannon, but at Abrantes we shall find a good position and if from thence we are further obliged to retire we shall move to Santarem, a point formidable by nature and improved by art, from whence to at last we can retire with the Tagus on our flank to Villa Franca. . . .

It is to this we all expect it will at last come, but the termination thus will leave to posterity a noble example of the disinterested exertions of a brave people in endeavours to give to others that freedom which they themselves gained and preserved by the greatest sacrifices.

We hear for certain that about 4,000 men are immediately to come out to reinforce us. Our present effective strength is *given out* here at 25,000 – I do not myself believe it near that, for notwithstanding the guards brigade has received 200 men from London, our Regiment has, only on paper, effective 1,140 rank and file and we have lost by battle and sickness 583 and have now in hospital 736; and we have generally been more healthy than the rest of the army.

We have had a few days wet, but it is now clearing up again. The winter has been remarkably fine – we are in grand spirits and health and well quartered. My love to all at home and may you enjoy the New Year and have many returns is my morning and evening prayer.

Vizeu
17th January 1810

The French are reported to have crossed the Tagus at Arzobispo and advanced a little. It is even said they have appeared on the frontier at Salvatierra but that they could not advance for want of supplies. I do not, however, believe these reports are correct. We do not expect they will molest us before the beginning of May.

Lord Wellington went off the day before yesterday to inspect the outposts and the positions now occupied – he is not to return for eight days, when he will soon remove his quarters to Lisbon to make arrangements. Marshal Beresford has gone on a tour to the Minho to inspect the frontiers. The Portuguese troops in several parts have been moved from their cantonments in the interior to the frontiers.

The weather continues wet and it has been and still is very cold – the hills around about are covered with snow and the thermometer here stands between 45 and 46.

I have just been told by Colonel Stopford that he now considers me Senior Ensign and I am in hopes that I shall be Lieutenant in a few months.

I am not myself very sanguine, though I certainly think there is a chance of my coming home on promotion before the regiment, whose stay in this country it is supposed will be protracted until July.

I have some thought just now of applying for leave to make a small tour of Lamego and Amarante to Oporto to see the different positions defended by the Portuguese and the French. When at Oporto, if I can get any very good wine and have an opportunity of freighting it for Leith, I may probably send some home a pipe of red port. This year's vintage has been very indifferent and the quantity not half the usual. I understand, including the duty in England, the cost little exceeds £70 per pipe.

Vizeu
24th January 1810

Since my last Lord Wellington has been inspecting the outposts. A strong patrol of French cavalry made its appearance in the neighbourhood of Pinhel and ordered 30,000 rations, but they ran off precipitately and have not since been seen. One company of our infantry has been advanced two leagues. It is reported the French which were in Salamanca have moved south towards Puerto de Baños and left only a small corps of observation. This movement is said to have been made in consequence of the army from Madrid having advanced with an intention of proceeding to Seville, where it is supposed they wish to arrive before the meeting of the Cortes which will assemble their next month. The Spanish officers here do not seem to think much resistance will be made just now if the French try to advance. We know they are assembling a large army at Merida and the neighbourhood but the object is not yet ascertained.

From the Spanish papers we learn that Bonaparte has divorced the Empress to marry a princess of Baden – that Joseph is to be made King of Italy and that Bonaparte himself is to be King of Spain.[6] The Duc del Parque is to move with his army by Almeida into Galicia – they are very much in want of provisions and so are the French in the Fortress on this front. We are very well off – the country is naturally rocky but the inhabitants are industrious and every *inch* that can be is cultivated – the bullocks are very fine and fat. There has been a fall of snow and the ground has been covered an inch deep for five days and the frost is very hard and likely to continue.

From the number of steps that were talked of after the battle of Talavera I have reason to expect my Lieutenancy in a month or two – I was however disappointed but I am now happy to say I consider myself certain of getting it in May at latest by purchase. In that case I shall get leave to go to the second battalion as soon as an officer arrives from London to relieve me. I have not yet made up my mind about what I shall do in the event of my promotion being before the regiment is ordered home. . . .

Vizeu
31st January 1810

The affairs of Spain have assumed an appearance rather more unfavourable than when I last wrote to you. The enemy have an army of 80,000 men advanced from Madrid to the Sierra Morena – they are in full possession of a pass and there are no Spanish troops to prevent their march to Seville – the Junta have removed to Cadiz. At Valladolid the French are in great force and it is said they are even advanced and increasing at Zamora. Be this as it may, the Duc del Parque who was to have moved with his army into Galicia[7] is now on the march to cross the Tagus at Villa Velha to endeavour to unite with the Duc de Alburquerque. For ourselves we remain as we were – well supplied with provisions, in good spirits and very healthy. The small reinforcements have arrived at Lisbon.[8]

Marshal Beresford was here the other day on his return to Lisbon from his tour of the northern frontiers. Lord Wellington moves his headquarters tomorrow to Torres Vedras to inspect the works throwing up there and at Peniche etc. You will before this have heard of Massena with his army having declared themselves enemies of Bonaparte. We have it from authority better than such reports generally rest on but are nevertheless giving it no credit.

Love to all the family. Adieu.

Vizeu
8th February 1810

I have not yet seen the news brought by the last packet but I understand London papers are of 24 January.

The success of the Spaniards in obliging the advance guard of the French to retire which was pushed forward from Cordova appears to have been occasioned more by the weakness of the enemy than the strength and enterprise of the Spanish force. Indeed, from the accounts which we have received here there is no reason to suppose the enemy will experience much resistance to their approach to Seville.

The Junta, it seems, have retired to Cadiz to avoid being deposed by the people, who on the advance of the enemy rose and put the Marquis of Romana at their head and since declared him the Spanish governor. This is a measure which has long been wished for by most Spaniards – it is believed to have come too late. But it will nevertheless give satisfaction. I am myself very happy at it. It may not perhaps be of much service but it shows a good disposition and if at the assembly of the Cortes next month the other provinces appear so well disposed a great deal may be done. The resources of the country directed by an energetic governor are yet sufficient to maintain an army more numerous than those French who have crossed the Sierra Morena.

I do not expect much will now be done in Spain, although I believe much might be done – the French, however, appear to dread the assembling of the Cortes. To prevent this is believed the reason for the rapid advance in the north of Spain, as . . . troops which they had about Salamanca have even been withdrawn towards Madrid, and after Spain, Portugal they look on as certain even when defended by British troops. This, every officer in Portugal likewise considers certain. But it appears we are to attempt its retention, at least of Lisbon. Works have been thrown up at Torres Vedras and provisions have been sent there from Lisbon.

Lord Wellington has gone to inspect them. Precautions are taken against any rapid movement of the French into Portugal, all our heavy baggage has been embarked and I understand the reserve stores at Lisbon are embarking.

There appears something mysterious going on in France. We have heard from various quarters of insurrections in the southern provinces. Massena with his army is said to have declared themselves displeased with Bonaparte[9] and we had it the other day that the French general who was at Salamanca received confirmation of it and that several regiments which had come into Navarre had been ordered to recross the Pyrenees. Reports of this kind have been so very frequent that not much credit was attached to the present one, but it is strange if true – it has come from different quarters but the different accounts agree in particulars. The belief of our being about to retire to the defensive position in front of Lisbon is very general – a fortnight will perhaps be our utmost stay in this town.

I am glad to hear that the disturbances in India are at an end.[10] You heard me express my opinion of Merchants – (I do not mean individually) and the army of Merchants I have always looked on as despicable. The officers were wrong in supporting their claims by threats but the company were more so in reducing it to this alternative. They must have been well aware of the object of every individual on entering their service. When hope of gain is the only stimulus to exertion, the zeal for the service becomes negative, the noble qualities of the soldier are forgot and the character is degraded.

Vizeu
14th February 1810

You will by this time have heard of the French having appeared before Cadiz and that 2,000 British troops have been sent from the Tagus to assist the garrison[11] – they were to have sailed on the 7th but I believe it is by no means certain they will be admitted into Cadiz.

So much folly or treachery has not yet been shown in Spain as the management of the troops south of the Sierra Morena. At the passes by which the French crossed, there was stationed a Spanish corps, but it appears that either from ignorance, treachery or stupidity on the part of the officer commanding or, perhaps a combination of all, *the roads only were occupied and not the positions;* this was immediately observed and taken advantage of by the enemy,[12] and, while a small party engaged the attention of the Spaniards by a false attack in the front, a strong corps moved on their flank, turned and occupied the position successively, and thus obliged the Spaniards to retire and crossed themselves without loss. But the French, notwithstanding, were under the necessary of leaving behind them most of their heavy ordnance from the badness of the roads.

They however proceeded with such rapidity that the Spanish army in the rear were surprised and so unprepared that no obstacle was thrown in their way until, on the approach in the first instance of the advanced guard from Cordova towards Seville, they fell in with and were obliged to fall back by the Duc de Alburquerque, who had just arrived with 25,000 men[13] between that town and Carmona.

This unfortunately was an obstacle as easily overcome as all the others and it did not for a moment retard the progress of the enemy, for the

French generals, knowing the composition of the Spanish force and the ability of its commander, sent but a corps of 5,000 men against the Duc de Alburquerque with a view only to mask his intentions, and he proceeded himself with his main body by a road to the *South*. The Spanish position was thus turned – the Spaniards forced to retire, Seville was left open and the enemy proceeded without further molestation and arrived before Cadiz.

On reviewing the circumstances of the enemy's movement, and the motives which could have induced the French Commander to move with such rapidity though in an enemy's country, so adverse to the operations of an army, and at the season most unfavourable, I confess my jealous apprehension began to be excited for the good dispositions of the inhabitants of Cadiz and I fear the more one considers, the more likely will my jealousy appear to be well founded. For I conceive it will hardly admit of doubt that a general so experienced as Marshal Victor must be [aware] of the universal hostility of Spain, would proceed upwards of 300 miles in it, *against any town*, with his rear exposed to the attack of 25,000 *organized* troops and his supplies and communications liable to be cut off by peasants in arms unless he had some strong reason to hope that town would easily fall. Much less can it be imagined that he would do this against a town *rendered almost impregnable*, and, though a part of Spain is in manner severed from the rest by the formidable Sierra Morena, over a tract of country too where a recollection of brilliant success, *under every disadvantage* against the *same experienced enemy*, would raise almost to inspiration the desire of the peasants to emulate their former exertions in avenging the invasion of their country unless, you knew almost to a certainty, *that town* would be given up.

In short, I am rather at a loss what to decide, but a reliance on *the ability and precaution of a French general*, and a *knowledge* of the cowardly behaviour of the Spaniards, appear to me on the one side, while a hope that the Spaniards will improve, and a recollection of their gallant conduct in defence of walled towns are the other – the weight I confess I feel much inclined to give the former, and to conclude, if Cadiz is not already in possession of the French it will soon be surrendered to them through fear.

I understand the Duc de Alburquerque retired to Ayamonte and embarked part of his army for Cadiz – the remains of Areizaga's force is likewise said to have embarked at Algeciras for the same place but I fear both will be too late. The French took possession of Seville without resistance and they found plenty of battering cannon.

Vizeu
21st February 1810

From every account which we have received during the week from Spain, it appears the enemy are gathering round us on all the frontiers, but we have not heard that they are in great numbers. On the 12th, the day on which they made the false attack on Ciudad Rodrigo, they pushed forward a small corps from Talavera de la Reyna and summoned Badajoz to surrender, but the Spaniards sent back the messenger to tell the French general that no more flags of truce would be received, and they would answer all from the walls.

Badajoz is not a town of such strength; the walls are in good repair but they are commanded on three sides, and the place might easily be taken in a week by a well-supplied army. From its situation, however, it will be of great importance to the French, because they can there form the magazines necessary to enable them to penetrate Alemtejo [province], and there is an arsenal in it well-supplied with battering ordnance. The guns on the works, too, are very good and there is every requisite in the town to mount them for the field.

Olivenza, another frontier town, has already been taken possession of by the enemy and they get well supplied from it for 9,000 men, *although three months since there was the greatest difficulty in supplying a small British brigade in it*. When Badajoz therefore is taken the French will be well prepared to besiege Elvas should they judge it expedient. Elvas is a place of great strength, it is on the top of the hill and the works are modern and in excellent order – the town is chiefly supplied with water conveyed in an aqueduct from a distance, which may easily be cut off: it is therefore to be doubted whether it will offer great resistance garrisoned by the Portuguese. Elvas itself, however, is commanded by Leite, *a fort supposed impregnable* situated on top of a still higher hill – and whoever has this fort will possess the town.

The garrison of Badajoz is not strong but the Marquis of Romana who is there has gone out several times and skirmished with the enemy in the pine woods between Badajoz and Talavera, and many have been lost on both sides. He wrote here on the 15th, after a severe skirmish, that the Spaniards have behaved remarkably well in every affair, and *as the enemy are not strong* he has urged Lord Wellington to order the troops from Abrantes under General Hill to advance and co-operate in destroying them.

It is not supposed Lord Wellington will agree to the Marquis' request, but General Hill has advanced to Portalegre and it is said the Royal Dragoons from Lisbon are ordered to join him. This movement we imagined to have been made with a view to cover the retreat of the sick from Elvas. Our hospital in Alemtejo were all removed into that place, and the sick there are yet said to amount to 3,000. About 1,000 convalescents arrived here a few days since and have gone to their regiments. We have had no certain account from Cadiz since I last wrote you, but reports say the French have left it for the present and entered Algarve [province] by Ayamonte. . . . Algarve has not yet had to supply any troops and it is very productive.

It did not at first seem to me that the French were likely to enter Portugal by Algarve, but as Portugal without us would offer little resistance, I think it probable the French will attack the British army in every point they possibly can, and as Lisbon can be bombarded from the opposite side of the Tagus at Almada, it seems most likely the French will send a force into Estremadura both by the Algarve and Alemtejo.

Junot has arrived at Benavente, and it is even said that he is advancing with 15,000 men into Galicia, to be ready to penetrate Portugal by Chaves. Marchand, who was at Ciudad Rodrigo on the 12th with 11,000 men, has returned to San Felices which he has destroyed. There is a road from that town along the Douro to Lamego.

Soult is at Plasencia. Junot entered Portugal in 1807 from thence by Castello Branco. Mortier commands the French who have attacked Badajoz, and Victor those who are said to have entered Algarve.

From each of these five different points where the French are assembling there is a road directed to Portugal, and from the stations of their generals it would appear they are determined to attack the British army.

It is the interest of the enemy to advance as soon as possible and we shall find they will, as soon as their corps are strong, without the fear of being starved, but the sooner they do advance, the more likely are they to be well provisioned.

On a reference to the map you will perceive that in advancing from the different points I have stated, the enemy will have an army on *each* of our flanks, and three corps in our front. The corps in our front and on our left flank will be sufficient to force us to retire from our present position towards Lisbon. It is Lisbon we are principally to attempt to retain, but Lisbon can be bombarded from Almada and as I have no doubt the patriotism of her inhabitants will be too weak to resist yielding to the enemy when their houses shall be in flames and *we* obliged to retire to the position in its immediate front, I think our best effort will be ineffectual and I should not be surprised that those arms which we have sent to the natives to assist us were turned into weapons of offence against us – *nay, I expect it*. Lord Wellington returned here on Saturday – Mr Stuart, the new Minister at Lisbon[14] was with him several days after he landed. Nothing has yet transpired relative to our movements.

The weather has become very warm here and we have had no rain for several days. We are in good spirits and extremely healthy. Whatever be our situation the British army will behave well and the French will again learn the superiority of their enemy.

Vizeu
7th March 1810

Since Sunday morning it has rained in torrents without an hour's intermission – it still continues and the natives say it will probably do so for ten days more. Such generally is Portugal at this time that rivulets which two months hence are nearly dry are now so deep as to be impassable.

I am happy to say all our sick from Elvas have left that place and either joined the army or gone to Lisbon. Since we left Badajoz we have been uncommonly healthy – with the regiment there are not twenty men in hospital and no bad cases – indeed of 300 which we had sick in Spain, we have now no more than 60. The rest of the army I believe are nearly as healthy as the Guards.

From what I have been told by the commanding officer, and the communications I had myself, I expected to have been Lieutenant long before this – many steps were talked of and four seemed likely to take place, but I now fear none of them will take place soon, they are all certain in time, and two others are still talked of as settled, but I have been so much disappointed I shall not rely on any till they are gazetted.

I confess I think I have served long enough in the subordinate situation of Ensign and I long to be promoted – that promotion will come some time – there is a great deal in chance – and were we to go home tomorrow I should be Lieutenant myself and have several under me in less than a month – so at least say those likely to know. If the money is lodged in Coutts & Co. I have[15] only to regret it should be there so long without being turned to account, I am anxious as little should be lost as anyone can be; at the same time I must say steps in the army, and particularly in the Guards, often come so sudden that I should hardly think it prudent to take the money from the bankers and employ it. Perhaps in stock, it might be turned into money again in one or two days? This you of course know and if it could – I see no reason why it should not be employed in that way – but you are the best judge and you will of course do as you think most convenient.

No talk of moving yet – while the effects of the rain continue the French cannot advance, therefore there is no reason why we should retire.

Remember me to all the family.

Vizeu
16th March 1810

It does not appear that the enemy are increasing on the frontiers in our front; Marchand is with most of his corps at Salamanca and only 3,000 men are now at San Felices, but hardly a day has passed lately without an affair of picquets. The enemy in cavalry are much more numerous than we are; they have already gained so much the superiority that the German Hussars (which are the only dragoons we have in advance) generally retire on their approach. Indeed, the enemy have become so confident that they have several times sent to say that they were coming in force; the Germans on this have withdrawn.

In consequence, a company of the 95th (riflemen) were the other day posted in a deserted village, and when the French came on they were so well received with a fire from every house that they were obliged to retreat in confusion, with the loss of eight men.

It is much to be regretted that the French should be permitted to acquire any superiority over our cavalry – hussars are the best description of force for the duties of an outpost, and the Germans understand it well, but when once they are accustomed to retire before the enemy there is no getting them to make a stand, and the consequence of their being cowed so early in the campaign may hereafter be most seriously felt. Their colonel was here yesterday urging Lord Wellington either to diminish the extent of our outposts, or to send the 16th Dragoons to the front and drive back the French advanced posts[16]. . . . There is not one good cavalry officer in command in Portugal and it will not be said of General Payne what Sir John Moore said of Lieutenant Paget that 'by his example he had infused the proper spirit into his men'.

There have been several fine days since I wrote to you, but the day before yesterday and today have been uncommonly wet. The rains have brought on the corn wonderfully and rye is already in most places full in the ear and barley will be very soon. I am very well. We have only nine men in the regiment in hospital so healthy are we.

Vizeu
28th March 1810

In my last letter I mentioned that there had been frequent little affairs at the outposts between our hussars and the French Cavalry – there has since been a considerable affair at a bridge on the Agueda near to San Felices. It appears in consequence of the very great desertion of the *foreign regiments* (which had in a smaller degree begun even amongst the French); the enemy removed every one of them to the rear and sent fresh regiments (chiefly composed of *French* conscripts) to take the duty of the outposts. The Agueda, from the immense quantities of rain which have lately fallen, has been for some time so high as to render the ford by which the French used to cross quite impassable, and they were therefore under the necessity of attempting the bridge near to San Felices.[17] On this bridge there was stationed a picquet of 95th (riflemen) supported immediately in the rear by four companies of the same regiment.

On the 19th, at midnight, the enemy approached the opposite bank of the Agueda with four battalions (in all 1,900 men) and they immediately pushed across the bridge 400 men, which drove in our picquet on the bridge and came upon the four companies at the same time. These luckily were prepared – they fired a volley and afterwards charged the enemy with the bayonet down the bank, and forced them to recross the bridge. But we have lost one officer and five men killed and seven wounded from the fire of the 1,500 French from the opposite bank of the river; the loss of the enemy has not been considerable: only five men and three officers were left dead.

It is supposed the enemy came on in hopes of surprising our men and making prisoners to gain intelligence. We have had only two instances of desertion: these were two hussars of the German Legion. Deserters from the enemy arrive here about three times a week and they have almost all been taken into our service – the Germans with the German Legion; the Freemen[18] into the 5th battalion of the 60 Regiment (riflemen), and the Italians etc are sent to England for the York Rangers in the West Indies. Three deserters were brought here this morning.

From Spain you will have heard the Marquis Romana has divided his army into small corps and given command of each to enterprising young men. As yet this mode has turned out well. At Zafra they attacked the enemy and obliged them to retire to Monesterio, which is the first town on the Bodon – the French who were in Merida have withdrawn, it is supposed with a view to reinforce those in the south of Spain. It is reported King Joseph is shut up in Malaga by the Spaniards – this I have no doubt, like most reports from Spain, is without foundation.

On the arrival of a packet Lord Wellington intends to remove his headquarters to Cea. But it is not yet decided whether he will remain there. Cea is a few leagues to the south of Mondego upon a road which has been made to communicate freely with the frontier from Coimbra. The Brigade of Guards will move to St Romoa and Martinhel should headquarters be established at Cea. This movement will make it evident that our defence will be confined to the country between the Tagus and Mondego. Our first stand (with the army) is to be at the Ponte de Murcella[19] across the river Alva. It here joins the Mondego and the high roads from Thomar and Coimbra join close to it. Since I last wrote to you it has rained very heavy without 12 hours' intermission. Today however is fine and warm and as the moon has entered her last quarter it is hoped we shall have fair weather. We are very healthy.[20] At Lisbon the people will not produce their dollars and we are in consequence in want of money.

Vizeu
29th March 1810

I had written this much, when another mail arrived and brought me a letter from George of 2nd inst announcing that it was finally fixed he should set off for Lisbon immediately. For the first time in my life a letter from a brother has been unwelcome; and I now feel so much perplexed at the idea of seeing George immediately in this country that I shall hardly be able to communicate to you what I wish. I feel so much more annoyed at George's coming at this time, because I fear that what I mentioned about an intended tour has been the sole cause of exciting his desire, and I have been much too inexplicit to make him in the most distant degree aware of the preparations absolutely necessary for him to make before he leaves England.

But as I have thus committed myself I must now state everything to you *without the least reserve*. When I stated my intention of visiting the south of Spain it was provisionally that I was promoted and had permission to leave this battalion.[21] I should have gone from Lisbon by sea to Cadiz, thence by land to Gibraltar etc. George might have accompanied me and there would have not been the least difficulty, for in these large towns accommodation is to be had for payment as at home, but this is by no means the case off the highroads in other parts of the Peninsula, and from what I have seen, I do not hesitate to say *it is quite impossible for a person not in the army* to travel here at any time and more particularly at present. In Portugal, except in the large towns, there is not an inn which affords accommodation the 1/20th part so good as any gin shop in England – how then is George to travel while we remain here ... and *he* as well as ourselves and animals receive rations of food from the Quartermaster, *without which we could not exist*? As, in most places, it is not to be bought – being universally embargoed for the troops. But these would not be allowed to a person not an officer and not in the army, and without it, it is impracticable to travel. There are *no carriages of any description* in this country, for travellers and the stores and baggage even of the army are carried on mules and small carts drawn by two oxen. To describe (so as to give an idea of) the impracticability of travelling now in Portugal I feel myself inadequate to; but, so much am I persuaded of it, and so many insurmountable difficulties do I see, that no consideration (were I out of the army) would make me attempt it.

To be short, you will perceive that I am most positively against George, or any other person, coming out to me while I *must remain with the army* in Portugal. If George does notwithstanding come out to me I shall certainly do everything within my power to make him comfortable and happy. But I would urge his bringing (in addition to plain clothes) his uniform as an officer of Volunteers, and it is *indispensable* that he should bring with him a *man-servant*. Money is not to be had out of Lisbon and Oporto. Bills on the English *treasury* even will not pass, and the money for the commissariat and other departments of the army, which does not arrive from England, is obliged to remain at Lisbon and Oporto and from thence sent to the army for use. None however has been raised here for several weeks, and as nearly all that brought out by the *Elide* frigate has been paid away, Lord Wellington does not know what to do for more.

Vizeu
30th March 1810

I have received your letter which confirms that George was to set off for Lisbon (you say on the 9th), and as the letter bears the postmark of Leith 12th I suppose he is now on his voyage. It therefore becomes unnecessary for me to enter more into detail of the unavoidable inconvenience he will experience on his arrival at Lisbon.

Every exertion on my part shall be done to ensure a comfortable reception for him and as soon as I hear of his arrival I shall proceed to Lisbon myself as early and in the most expeditious manner I can, if the Commander-in-Chief will grant me permission. The distance from this is about 200 miles and regulation time of absence when granted is one fortnight – I will ride express to get as soon as possible (which takes three days) and I do not at this moment feel myself quite able for it but I shall try.

You may be well persuaded my dear father that I have great pain in feeling myself compelled to oppose a brother visiting me, and it is with extreme reluctance I have communicated it to you but necessity is [*sic*] no rule and under the circumstances of my situation I feel it proper (and I trust you will think it right) to acquaint you with what may perhaps be the result of George's visit to Portugal. I can assure you, and this from the bottom of my heart, that I should have rejoiced to have seen George at Lisbon and to have travelled with him to the south of Spain had I leave to quit the army on promotion. But situated as I am, it has become me to state to you his visit may well occasion so much perplexity, and I am at this moment very apprehensive that after his arrival at Lisbon there will be nothing for it but for him to return home at an early opportunity.

I feel myself much better today from having taken a strong dose of Physic – but it will be necessary for me to restrict myself to diet for a few days and I shall hereafter drink but little wine. For several weeks past I have been troubled with *cutting teeth* and for five days I was in great pain, but they have now cut the gum and I am quite relieved.

> *Vizeu*
> *2nd April 1810*

In addition to what I have already mentioned to you against George's coming here, I must now state that an order from Sir David Dundas has been given out *to this army* that *during its continuance abroad*, officers promoted shall continue in the *Battalions* the vacancies happen to which they succeed. Thus if a vacancy which gives my Lieutenancy happens here I must remain in the 1st Battalion, and if it happens in the 2nd Battalion I must still remain in this until an officer from that battalion comes to relieve me. The order was issued in consequence of an application from Lord Wellington to that effect. This army is composed almost of 2nd Battalions and it often happened they were much in want of officers from the general regulations being attended to, *viz* that the senior officers of every rank should be in the 1st and the junior officers in the 2nd Battalions. Whenever, therefore, my promotion happens (and I now hear no talk of it) it will be quite uncertain when I shall return home or when I will be at liberty to quit this battalion.

I am much better than when I wrote to you last and I feel quite well but I have left off drinking a drop of wine and I am restricted in diet.

> *Vizeu*
[To his brother William] *6th April 1810*

I received your letter of 13 February with the more pleasure because it contained an assurance that you would write to me again soon and afterwards frequently. For myself – I have already given a similar assurance in some of my former letters, and you will find me punctual; indeed, I am now only apprehensive that in yielding to the pleasure I derive from writing to you, I shall become tiresome.

I wrote to you last on 16 February and I mention having given up all thoughts of my tour for the present, from the rapid advance of the French in the south of Spain, and there being little chance of my promotion taking place soon. In that letter likewise I recall the opinion I have formerly given, *viz* that it might be of use to George to come to me as a Volunteer in this army, while it remained in Portugal.

My opinions in that instance (of course) have been dictated by circumstances, *and they varied accordingly*. But as it may perhaps appear to you odd, I shall therefore explain. When I first thought of George coming to this country I was at Lisbon, and there was at that time little probability of the army being active but in a retreat. There would therefore have been little difficulty in getting him quarters with myself and provisions. The period of our stay here has now, however, become incalculable, and we shall most likely take the field in a month and be actively employed. When in camp and moving about, there is seldom any opportunity of procuring any provisions besides our rations, and there is no possibility of carrying baggage but on animals belonging to ourselves, *which likewise are fed by the commissary. But these would not be allowed to George*, or any other person not in the army, *and without he could not move*.

It was for these reasons I wished you to mount a uniform in accompanying me in a tour, for when away from the army we might oblige the magistrates of the country to get us provisions for payment in the habits of officers, where as individuals money alone would not procure them.

At home you appear to have an idea that travelling in Portugal is arranged as in Britain. There is not, however, any comparison, for in the whole country, except in Lisbon and Oporto, there is not a public house which affords accommodation for sleeping to be put up with but from necessity, and you must be aware trade is carried on by mules without carriages (the roads being too bad to admit any) and in Spain it is very little better.

I regret there has been so little consideration about sending George here, and it places me in a most unpleasant situation, and it gives me ground to apprehend imputations may be laid to my conduct which are impossible for me to arrest, although I feel myself perfectly free from them: and I do this the more because I am fully persuaded that, in sending George to me, my Father wishes to add to my comfort and to make my happiness complete.

In the papers which I have seen to the 14th ult the evidence on the Walcheren business is given at length, but I have read very little of it, and I am not therefore prepared to venture an opinion on it. I agree however, so far with you that in the long succession of failure in our expeditions by land, blame must be attached somewhere, and that it would be of use to the army to try the naval experiment of shooting a commander – as Voltaire makes Candide say – if only '*pour encourager les autres*'.

I observe you have a hit at me and the 'army gentlemen' about their general opposition, but in this instance you have been unfortunate as it was for the very same reason you recommend the *Courier* I ordered out *The Times*.[22] I recollect in England *The Times* used to appear the most impartial paper, and it has always been a supporter of the Spanish cause, but I have seen it for the first time lately – it certainly is much more violent now, and I shall therefore buy the *Courier* to be sent to me. I care very little about politics here, and it is for the foreign and home news I wish a newspaper.

Deserters still continue to come in from the enemy – 45 arrived here last Monday, some of whom are Irish. They report that they belonged to the Irish Brigade, one regiment of which (composed of 900 English and Irish) entered Spain a few months since, and they had not crossed the Pyrenees six weeks before it was reduced by desertion to 500. I suppose by this time you have had the account of the affair at the Bridge on the Agueda. A few days after, the French withdrew from San Felices and that town is now open to us, and our outposts are not molested in any quarter.

General Hill remains yet at Portalegre. Lord Wellington had not talked lately of moving to Cea; it is therefore uncertain when we shall march to the south of the Mondego. I dine at headquarters today and I shall perhaps hear some news. The bracing air of Vizeu[23] has been of great service to the army and our men are now very healthy and stout – our brigade is again respectable in numbers. We are now going on quietly as if at Chatham. The men are remarkably clean and we have field days; indeed, were it not for the convoys of provisions and stores which are continually passing, and detachments of convalescents which often arrive, we might suppose ourselves at peace.

I ride and walk every day when the day is fine – my stud at present consists of a horse, one small mule, a donkey and a goat. The proceedings of the French in Spain are quite incomprehensible – we hear every day of their moving forward and retiring again – this looks as if they were not confident in their strength. For his conduct in Portugal, Lord Wellington certainly deserves the thanks of his country – however much some blame his march and arrangements in Spain, everyone applauds his conduct in Portugal and I think if Portugal can be defended, Lord Wellington of all others is a man most likely to succeed. He possesses the confidence of the natives, has great activity, much courage and his firmness is not shaken by adversity, which for a general on the defensive is a most estimable quality.

I cannot speak fluent Portuguese. It is a most horrible corrupt language and I never intend to learn it. I can speak enough to make myself generally understood and that I think sufficient to know of a base language. French is very useful, I find.

We know of the 3rd Brigade of Guards having gone to Cadiz.[24] By sending so many troops there it must be intended to raise the siege by sorties, as General Stuart gave his opinion that his brigade (with the Spaniards) was sufficient for its defence. If sorties are made one must expect a very great loss.

Vizeu
11th April 1810

Had I known that George certainly was to come out I would have begged him to have brought me stuff for coats etc and shoes, which are not to be had in this country even at Lisbon but at an enormous price and of an inferior quality. In my last letter, I wrote you I had taken steps to ensure George a comfortable reception at Lisbon till I could arrive there, and I have since received a letter from the officer to whom I wrote, couched in the most friendly terms, which professions (from his unvariable gentleman-like behaviour) I have no doubt he will fulfil. But I am now in hopes that I shall be able to set off myself the moment I know of George's arrival at Lisbon, as Lord Wellington has not lately talked of moving to Cea, and he has given two of our officers leave of absence for *three* weeks in Lisbon. The whole of our outpost are now unmolested, and the French having retired from San Felices is supposed to have rendered the removal of headquarters unnecessary for the present, and I suppose the same circumstances has induced the Commander-in-Chief to extend the usual time of one week. From this it would appear it is not expected we shall be so soon engaged in field operations; but Lord Wellington talks of getting up immediately tents for the officers who choose them, and of encamping the army as soon as the weather will permit.

The cause of part of my embarrassment at George's arrival at this time is in some measure removed as, in a fortnight (which three weeks' leave will allow me to spend at Lisbon), I shall have an opportunity in a short tour with my brother of seeing the last positions we are to defend [i.e. the lines of Torres Vedras]. I had not finished this last sentence when an officer of my regiment entered my room and told me Wellington and the heads of departments *are* to move from the day after tomorrow – believed to Cea. I have not heard that this has been occasioned by any movement of the French or what is the cause of it, but it is yet said our information from Spain relative to the enemy continues as incorrect as ever.

On looking over again the two last letters I had the pleasure to receive from you I perceive there are several things which remain unanswered, and I shall now therefore continue.

With respect to the Portuguese, my opinion of them remains what it has always been, *viz* that they hate the French, but I expect little from them as they are completely cowed and they are servile. I should conceive the resources of this country if properly managed sufficient to pay all the troops they can raise, but the government both civil and military from top to bottom is *the very essence of corruption,* and for myself so little confidence have I in their honour that as an enemy there is not one native officer I would hesitate in offering a bribe and I would never doubt of succeeding by it.

Spain is by no means like Scotland; and its situation cannot be compared to the situation of our country in the time of Bruce. But the peasants are certainly a very fine race of people – much might be done with them and to look at them one feels respect so expressive in all their countenances.

By the late papers I have seen, in England, a battle appears to have been expected between the French and us – we have no thoughts here of that yet, but whenever it does take place, I shall write Mr Thomson as well as home.

About the Walcheren business I feel little qualified to give an opinion.

The proportion of officers in the army to men is generally as 1 to 20 and I concur from the superior quarters which they generally have to the soldiers and the means of changing clothes when wet etc. it might in sickness be averaged as 1 to 40. In the Walcheren expedition, from what you state, I observe it has averaged in deaths as 1 to 65, and in sickness as 1 to 52 nearly. This difference may be attributed to the superior care paid to them (the officers) by the medical men who, I must say from what I have seen here, are very ill-qualified for the important appointments that they hold.

In this army there are men in charge of sick now who till they came here never prescribed in their lives, and there are others who have had no practice beyond answering a prescription in an apothecary shop in England. Such are the men entrusted with the lives of soldiers, but it must always be the case in a great degree while the pay remains so small as to induce those only to enter the service who would starve at home. I have myself heard a surgeon say that he had no doubt that *two-thirds* of the deaths in this army were due to the inattention and ignorance of the medical officers.

I do not think there is much chance of my going to Oporto now. The weather continues very rainy and today there was hail. It is very cold – we feel it more because there are no fireplaces in any of the rooms. The thermometer is generally about 48 degrees. Mr Thompson had managed to get me a weekly newspaper sent post free. I have received it regularly to 8 March.

April saw the first British moves in the 1810 campaign in Portugal. Astorga had fallen on 22 April to the French who then started to move against Ciudad Rodrigo. Wellington received news of this forward movement on 26 April but not of the fall of Astorga until the thirtieth. On the twenty-seventh he ordered the 1st Division (Lieutenant-General Sir Brent Spencer had taken over from Sherbrooke as Wellington's second-in-command and Commander 1st Division), which included the Guards and his own headquarters, to move to Celorico, while ordering Hill to dispatch Slade's Cavalry Brigade to Guarda. Other moves followed and by mid-May Wellington had assembled 18,000 British and 14,000 Portugese troops in the area bounded by Pinhel, Almeida, Guarda and Celorico.

Wellington had received cries for help from the governor of Ciudad Rodrigo and from Romana, who had been attacked by Reynier near Badajoz on 21 April. While allowing Craufurd with the Light Division and Hill with the 2nd Division to make some minor demonstrations, Wellington would not let himself be drawn into Spain: 'With an army one fourth inferior in numbers . . . and not more than one third the number of the enemy's cavalry, it would be an operation of some risk . . . to bring on a general action in the plains,'[25] he wrote.

Massena arrived in Salamanca on 15 May to take over from Junot the command of the 80,000-strong Army of Portugal. Instructions from Napoleon were that the full-scale invasion of Portugal would be deferred until September when the extreme heat would have abated and the harvest had been gathered in. Meanwhile two corps (50,000 men) would reduce

Ciudad Rodrigo and Almeida, while Reynier's corps (15,000) would operate around Alcantara and Sera's corps (10,000) would contain the Spanish forces in Galicia and threaten northern Portugal about Braganza.

Meanwhile Robert Craufurd's Light Division, east of the Coa, took every opportunity to harry the French, his advanced posts being in Spanish territory and close to Ciudad Rodrigo. The French opened their batteries against the fortress on 25 June, the day that Wellington advanced his headquarters from Celorico to Alverca. On 4 July Massena sent superior forces to drive in advanced posts of the Light Brigade which retired skilfully and in good order. Ciudad Rodrigo, which was not naturally strong, did not surrender until the evening of 10 July after a heroic defence by its Spanish garrison.

Vizeu
Friday 27th April 1810

In a campaign against an active enemy rapid movements become necessary and they are often very sudden. When I wrote to My Mother yesterday I had very little idea we were about to advance – it has however happened. Lord Wellington received a despatch yesterday evening and at $\frac{1}{2}$ past 12 he gave an order for the Brigade to march this morning at 6 and it has accordingly left Vizeu: for the present it is gone to Celorico and adjacents, but report says it is to move more in advance to San Felices to support the rest of the army in an attack on a French corps in that neighbourhood. The apprehension of the natives, as you may conceive, by this sudden movement has been in no ordinary degree excited for their own safety and ours; but our men are in excellent condition and in high spirits and they have gone with their usual confidence in approaching the enemy. Should an action be brought on I feel they will acquit themselves in the manner that will add to the high reputation that they have already fought for and obtained.

Acquainting you with this sudden movement I regret I am compelled to use the impersonal, for it has been my misfortune to be left behind in charge of the sick of the Brigade with another officer of the Coldstream and I remain at Vizeu. But I am in hopes that the number of sick will soon be so reduced as to make it necessary for only one officer to remain here, and that I shall have it in my power to join the regiment before the first action. While on service I wish to witness every affair – I accepted the Light Company because it is generally more employed than any other and I am much mortified at being left behind, *but in duty there is no choice.*

Lord Wellington has moved forward likewise, with the whole of the officers attached to the headquarters. It would appear from this, the movement is intended to surprise. . . .

PS $\frac{1}{2}$ past 3 since I wrote this, I hear the whole of the sick will most likely be moved to Coimbra, in which case I will have to go with them. I had almost forgot this is my birthday – congratulate my sister for me on it and give my love to all the others.

Condeixa
11th May 1810

When I wrote to you from Vizeu on 27th ult I did not suppose I should have it in my power to write you from this place.

As I mentioned in my last letter I marched from Vizeu with the sick on 30th ult to the hospital at Coimbra. I was to have remained in charge of the sick Guards at that place but I was ordered yesterday to conduct a detachment of sick to Lisbon etc and I have got thus far. I shall arrive at Lisbon about 18th, where I shall probably remain a few days before I return to join the army.

I have heard from headquarters as late as 9th they seem to know little about the movement of the enemy on the frontiers, but report says they are retiring and it is even said that headquarters will return to Vizeu.

Belem
My dear William,   *25th May 1810*

You will see by the date of this letter that I am settled at Belem. I am to remain in charge of the sick at present. There is another officer of the Coldstream here besides, but he is not very well. However, he thinks himself equal to the whole duty and I have written to beg I may be ordered to join the regiment. When abroad the best place to be, and the most comfortable, is with one's regiment.

According to reports, which are relied on in the regiment, I may look for my Lieutenancy in every Gazette. Two Ensigns only are above me. One is promoted by a Lieutenant resigning – the other by a Capt in the Regiment selling out – another Captain is said to have got leave to sell which will promote me. I have heard his name within these 3 days and evidence that cannot be questioned leaves me no doubt that he is going out. But I am not yet at liberty to communicate this even to you. Besides this last opportunity I have been written to by a Lieutenant who has just been taken off the staff to exchange out of the regiment by way of getting a company in a battalion of the line at home and paying him the difference of 200£, if I purchased the company, and 400£ if I get it without purchase, to exchange back into the regiment. I have written him in answer that I considered it next to impossible to get a company at home from the number of 2nd battalions abroad – that I thought his terms exorbitant but to write me a letter stating his ultimate terms and then I would give an answer.

As far as a value of a step goes, a Lieutenancy certainly is not worth near what I must pay for it – but an advance considerably beyond the regulation for every commission (above an Ensign) is always given and I shall not be able to get it without. It should be a matter of indifference to me whether I get promoted in June or August. I would not like a junior Ensign to get over me, which will be done if I do not manage to get a company and exchange. By direct promotion in the regiment the step will cost 800£; if I get it by a company it will cost at least 1,000£. I am anxious to hear from the regiment to know how I stand – when I do hear I will write you again.

I have no news – Massena is reported to have arrived at Salamanca to command the army sent against Portugal. There is no talk of operations beginning yet. Many deserters have come in; they say as soon as there are 30,000 French in Alemtego and 80,000 in front of us North of the Tagus the campaign will be opened by Massena. He has the character of a General but will stick at nothing to accomplish his object. The Portuguese don't seem to relish the idea of so bloody an opponent.

May 25th
½ past 1

I have just received letters from the army of the 23rd. An officer, a *German,* who deserted has come into headquarters – he says Massena, Duke of Rivoli, has been given out Commander-in-Chief (in orders) of the Army of Portugal, which he says now amounts to 60,000 men. Massena is at Salamanca and is making every exertion to get the army ready for commencing operations. At our headquarters they expect a move soon – I hope I shall be up in time for the first affair, though I do not think anything serious will take place before the harvest – provisions are very scarce and as soon as the corn is ripe I think the French will try what they can do.

I begged to be ordered to my regiment in a letter I wrote the day of my arrival in Lisbon – I have received an answer saying the commanding officer of the Brigade was at Vizeu – but an answer would be sent to me as soon as he returned. I expect it every post and I think I shall have to announce my departure from Lisbon before the next mail to England. The commanding officer of the regiment has, I hear, written to the Duke of Gloucester[26] to request the *senior* Ensign may be permitted to purchase a Company in the Line to exchange back into the regiment with the Lieutenant who wishes to go out. So you may probably soon see me Gazetted Captain in the Line. The Ensign next under me has agreed to this and already taken steps to forward the business. Lieutenants terms – so there remains for me no alternative but either to agree to; or allow a junior officer to go over me. This latter I suppose my father will not insist on, although it will cost me so much to prevent it. I hope therefore the necessary direction will be given to Mr Thomson on the event of more money being required than the sum already lodged. I shall write to him on the subject – show this letter to my Father.

Lisbon
1st June 1810

Your letter of 15th ult from London arrived on 26th and it relieved me from much anxiety about my promotion.

I'm sure you will rejoice with me on hearing my application to be recalled to the regiment has been attended to – I received the order yesterday and I shall set off tomorrow.

The enemy it appears have a camp of 80,000 men a short distance from Ciudad Rodrigo and from the reports in circulation at our headquarters there is every probability of the army advancing soon and an action being the consequence. I trust I shall be up in time for the first affair.

The box with the boots and shoes has not yet arrived – it will be very acceptable. I have given directions to forward them the first opportunity after they arrive. I have fitted myself out at Lisbon as well as I could in the short time – everything is very dear – I arrived almost naked and it has cost a great deal.

We hear a great addition to our force will shortly arrive here, *viz* 10 Battalions of infantry and 4 Regiments of Cavalry; of these only 4 battalions are to come from England.[27] These, with the three battalions which arrived about 6 weeks ago, are to form a reserve and are not to be brought into action till we retire to our position in front of Lisbon.

There is not much chance of our being obliged to retire soon, for according to the account of the officer who deserted the other day the French are by no means in a state to undertake the conquest of Portugal yet. Little I think will be attempted before the harvest.

Calorico
13th June 1810

By all the newspapers which have lately arrived from England I perceive your hopes and fears have been erased by the battle in Portugal – it has not yet, however, taken place nor do we expect it. I have often told you not to pay attention to what was mentioned in the newspapers relative to the operations of the army – their information is generally wrong and in this instance what the *Courier* has stated as coming from Lord Wellington is known to be altogether incorrect.

But the reports stated in the paper are very prevalent at Lisbon and in some degree were countenanced by the accounts from the army – I took the alarm and left Lisbon by foot on 3rd inst. The weather was then fine and it was expected the enemy would advance. It did not continue long, for the 4th was as wet as ever and some rivers of water which at home would not be called burns became so swelled as to be impassable – I was stopped at one of them for three hours. It continued to rain and I halted 3 days at Coimbra, but I heard there a movement of the enemy had raised an alarm and the army were ordered to keep one day's provisions always cooked – I left Coimbra on the 6th and I arrived here on the morning of 10th. Till then the weather was extremely cold and wet – it has now become very warm and fine.

Lord Wellington went out yesterday to reconnoitre and returned in the evening. The enemy have been using all their exertions for some time to commence the siege on Ciudad Rodrigo. They've thrown three bridges across the Agueda and they occasionally cross the moor and interrupt our communication. They have destroyed the mills and Ciudad Rodrigo is said already to be in want of provisions. General Craufurd, who commmands at the outposts of the Light Division, I hear was to attempt to throw in supplies last night – the result I have not yet heard.

The result of this attempt will have great effect upon the future operations of the army. Ciudad Rodrigo of itself is not a place of much consequence – its works are by no means formidable and its situation is imperfect, being commanded by a hill within 600 yards' distance, but it will be of the utmost consequence to the enemy for they must have a place to form the magazines necessary to enable them to penetrate Portugal, and they will find in it battering ordnance to besiege Almeida.

Should the fine weather continue, something will take place that will decide to a certain degree the resistance likely to be made by the Portuguese. The whole combined army is within 24 hours' march of the position which we are first to oppose the progress of the French. The post which has always been dispatched at 2 o'clock is deferred – Ciudad Rodrigo is reported to have fallen – this is not believed but *it is completely invested*. A dispatch of importance will be sent off today. The next mail I expect to be able to communicate some news and favourable.

I have just called on Colonel Stopford, who commands the regiment and brigade – he has had letters from Colonel Sir J. Dalrymple saying Colonel West has not been permitted to *sell* out and no step in consequence is now going on – thus disappointment after disappointment has taken place about my promotion. I have yet, however, *one* chance but I fear it is a slight one. A Lieutenant has resigned, which gives the senior Ensign Allan his step. Sir Charles Townsend (who is now in England) report says will resign – if he does I shall then be at the top and there is a Lieutenant who wishes to exchange into the Line for a company, but he demands a difference of 200£ if the Ensign purchases the company and 400£ if he does not. When the steps you heard of in London were expected to take place – it was for the Ensign *junior to me* to arrange with the Lieutenant about the exchange and he *has agreed to the terms, viz* to give a difference of 200£ besides a company of the Line if he purchases and 400£ if he gets the company for nothing. The demand of a difference of 400£ in the event of my obtaining a company without purchase, I consider exorbitant – for I shall be gazetted without purchase, and when I come to resign (if ever it were to happen) I shall have no claim to insist on my successor repaying me any part of it.

Under the same circumstances, however, of the exchange question 500£ has been given and that in *this* regiment two years ago – a precedent for the demand has therefore been established and that demand having been exceeded to by the Ensign *junior* to me. *It is for you to decide whether I shall now agree to it too, or not.* You are well aware how anxious I am to get my promotion and if I do not agree to the terms now proposed I shall stand in the unpleasant light of stopping the promotion of the regiment. But I must repeat I consider the difference of 400£ as very exorbitant and I cannot therefore bring myself to *urge* you to agree to it. While I state this I must at the same time remark appearances at present debar me the hope of obtaining promotion *but* for a sum considerably beyond the regulations.

Whatever may be your decision I must request you to communicate it to Mr Thomson for his guidance in the management of my promotion.

By the post which will bring this to you I shall write to Ensign Ld Charles Townsend to know what he intends to do. It will not do for Mr Thomson to let it be known publicly what sum I must pay for my step. Whatever is given *beyond the regulation* is *only communicated to the parties concerned.* This hint applies to you likewise. Tell my mother I had the pleasure to receive her letter of 19 May on 11th – the one from James has not yet arrived. Remember me to all the family. Adieu.

Celorico
20th June 1810

Things remain in the same state as when I last wrote to you. Ciudad Rodrigo has not yet surrendered nor has it been supplied with stores or provisions. The French have to the number between 22,000 and 25,000 completely surrounded it and cut off all communication with us. They have proceeded in the erection of batteries unmolested but their battering ordnance has yet to come up. Twenty-four hours after its arrival Ciudad Rodrigo is expected to fall.

The fatality which has been so common in Spain attends this place. It has plenty of powder but *no balls.* The disdain the Spaniards have so often manifested for their enemy when at a distance has here been conspicuous. No preparations were made for a siege and before the arrival of the enemy the ammunition was expended.

It is difficult to know who to blame and under a government like that of Spain it would be perhaps wrong to ascribe all to the Governor, but as might be expected reports are not much in his favour; his predecessor was removed on suspicion of disaffection and report now attaches it to him. From Almeida we hear Don Julian (originally a bullfighter but now a Commander of a corps of garrochistas), who had distinguished himself often had been arrested and imprisoned by the Governor of Ciudad Rodrigo, but the populace rose and in turn imprisoned the Governor.[28]

The country between Ciudad Rodrigo and Almeida is open and flat. Lord Wellington says the French are so powerful in cavalry that *we cannot* venture out. You will therefore be prepared to hear of the fall of Ciudad Rodrigo without a movement by us beyond the Coa. This river runs close to Almeida parallel to the frontier into the Douro – behind it we expect to encamp soon.

Notwithstanding the great precautions taken to prevent desertion, the enemy continue to come over to us from all quarters. Lord W. has adopted a policy towards them which without expense to the country encourages desertion. The dragoons who come to us receive the value of their horses and appointments etc, which are disposed of by public sale and the produce paid in dollars. Even *Frenchmen* have deserted to us and some from their distinguished corps – the artillery.

Celorico
4th July 1810

The many disappointments which I have had about promotion had determined me not to write any more on the subject before it actually takes place, but the accounts of its progress which arrived by the mail two days ago flatter so much of my hope of *joining* you soon that I cannot deny myself the pleasure of communicating them.

The two Ensigns above me have been promoted and it appears that had it not been for some omission in the CO of this battalion I should *now* have been Lieutenant by the exchange which I explained to you some weeks ago. The papers, however, wanting, will be forwarded by this day's post and I hope the first answer from London will announce my promotion. The Duke of Gloucester has given his consent to the exchange – a company in the line *is ready to be purchased* – I *am* to be gazetted *to it* and afterwards back into the regiment as Lieutenant by exchange with Captain Canning.

With the company in the Line I am to pay Captain C. 200£. The company is to be had at the regulation 1,500£, which added to 200£ makes 1,700£ from which deducting 900£ (produce of my Ensignary) will leave 800£, the exact sum I should have given for my Lieutenancy by direct promotion in the regiment.

An Ensign to relieve me has been ordered out from London and I have little doubt my expectation will be realised of seeing you in August.

As I am desirous of coming home I shall not, you may be sure, delay unnecessarily. When I get my leave, if a battle be expected I shall wait its result and shall then hasten to bring you the tidings of its success – but if none takes place it may perhaps depend on circumstances. Whether I shall not take a peep into Cadiz before my return but of this the next post will enable me to judge better.

Everything here goes on well – Ciudad Rodrigo has been bombarded but holds out.[29] The Spaniards in it have behaved remarkably well and they have done great execution amongst the enemy. Don Julian with his corps of 'guerrilleros' has cut his way through the French and is now with the Spanish army at the outposts. When I say this much I shall not disguise the appearances, which are formidable and induce everyone here to expect a *hot* engagement very soon. The French in our front have been considerably reinforced. At Plasencia they have assembled about 28,000 men from Merida, Truxillo, etc and General Hill in consequence has abandoned the Alemtejo and moved his corps across the Tagus to Castello Branco and the neighbourhood. Thus the whole British and Portuguese forces are now concentrated on the frontier between the Mondego and Tagus. The Light Division under General Craufurd have retired to Almeida, but five companies of British and a battalion of Portuguese occupy the Fort Concepcion[30] six miles in front of it and the 14th Light Dragoons are in advance of it one league, at Gallegos.

Lord Wellington moved from this on 25th ult to Almeida with the military part of the headquarters, but he retired on Friday to Alverca da Beira where he is now. This town is very centrical [sic] and is about half-way between Celorico and Almeida. The M. de Romana is now there – he arrived two days since. Some regiments of our infantry have been moved from the cantonments in the valleys to the villages on hills and they are now more in advance – everything, though, I think indicates an advance – the Spaniards too with their small corps of 3,000–5,000 are moving up in the direction of Ciudad Rodrigo. Harvest has become general. We are well off for everything but wine is all drunk – no more can be issued to the troops. They are in high health and excellent spirits, and should it be our lot to engage the French on 27 or 28 July we shall celebrate the anniversary of *Talavera* in a victory as brilliant and more complete. Adieu, I never was in better health nor more happy than at this moment, the weather is delightful.

Celorico
11th July 1810

The admirable conduct of the Spaniards at Ciudad Rodrigo has retracted its defence to this day and there is yet no talk of surrendering: on the contrary, the French after being repulsed there three times at two different breaches have judged it necessary to send for more battering cannon to Salamanca, and in the meantime they are carrying on their approaches by mines. These masters in the art of war have thus shown their incapacity to take, without the diabolical means resorted to only in desperate cases, a town defended by a few undisciplined Spaniards, in situation extremely defective and fortified in a manner which according to modern rules is considered indefensible.

Ciudad Rodrigo is surrounded only by a high stone wall and a ditch. Within 800 yards it is commanded by a hill – between this hill and the town there is another hill, which latter is likewise commanded by the works of the town. On the further hill the enemy erected their first batteries and from it they battered a breach – when the breach appeared practicable the enemy came on, but the Spaniards placed howitzers in the breach and repulsed the French, and these then discovered their fire had only had effect to strengthen the wall, for the intervening hill prevented the shots striking the bottom of the wall, and the top part only being demolished, the rubbish fell down and added strength to the under parts. The enemy then battered from the side facing the Portuguese and they soon made a breach, but the ditch here being deep and broad, they were unable to cross and they were repulsed again with great loss.

They suffered severely too in the suburbs which they attacked with cavalry, but the Spaniards from the houses obliged them to retreat. There have been a great number of women and children killed in the town. The place has now only 13 days' provisions and it seems probable it will have to surrender from want.

As to our own army – our outposts have been obliged to retire to Fort

Concepcion. The affair which preceded this was highly creditable to the German hussars; and a few Portuguese light troops which were engaged showed great coolness – Lord Wellington has still his headquarters at Alverca and we remain as before but we can expect an order to march every day – the fall of Ciudad Rodrigo will be the signal for our advance; some regiments have already marched to the banks of the Coa.

The Marquis of Romana has returned to Badajoz – Officers and serjeants for three regiments passed through this [place] a few days since from thence – they are gone to Galicia to organize the peasants.[31]

Harvest goes on briskly – all the corn is nearly cut and *thrashed* out. It is the custom here to do this before they take it from the field. Indian corn, which is the chief support of the poor, will not be ready till September and October.

Celorico
My dear James,   *18th July 1810*

Ciudad Rodrigo has fallen; it surrendered by Capitulation on the morning of 11th inst. The Spaniards in it supported the high character they have acquired in defending towns. The French were repulsed at two different breaches and they failed in producing any effect by mining, but it was evident it could not hold out much longer and after making the admirable defence which they did, the Spaniards acted very wisely in accepting terms.

It was supposed the fall of Ciudad Rodrigo would be the signal for our advance, but contrary to expectations we have not yet moved. We shall, however, most likely in a day or two, for last night orders were issued to keep one day's provisions always ready cooked and the commissaries have been ordered to have *three* days' biscuit ready to carry on mules. When we once break up from our present cantonments there is little chance of our being in houses again till winter.

If the enemy are now in force we shall have hot work immediately, at least we may expect it; the harvest has been general during the last fortnight, they will of course have sufficient supplies to enable them to enter Portugal and it will be their interest to make a push before we can have time to collect all the corn into depots, arrangements for which have been made and directions given.

Since the surrender of Ciudad Rodrigo the French have made several movements – two divisions from thence have been detached to the south, and Reynier with his division has crossed the Tagus at Almaraz and is on the march supposedly to join them.

General Hill in consequence has quitted the Alemtejo and he crossed the Tagus at Villa Velha on 13th and is now about Castello Branco. There was a report that he had done that some time ago but it was incorrect, and only one of his brigade had moved to the north of the Tagus , and he remained at Portalegre – his movement now is known for certain. With his division are all the Portuguese cavalry fit for service and the best regiments of Portuguese infantry. It was by the road thro' Castello Branco that we advanced into Spain, and by it Junot entered Portugal in 1807. By it the French seem determined now to enter again but they will certainly fail, the passes are well defended by heavy ordnance and the roads which in general are very mountainous may easily be rendered impracticable for a long time.

They will not be able to force us in front; by one large force on our right flank in the Alemtejo – another threatening our left either by Chaves or the right bank of the Douro, they might oblige us to withdraw from our present advance position but there is little reason to believe they are yet in sufficient force for this, as it has been found necessary to recall Junot and his corps from the north and now Reynier from the south in order to have a large force opposed to us in front. But we shall see – next mail from here will probably bring you some accounts of our operations that will show the intentions of the enemy.

There was an affair at our outposts near Fort Concepcion a few days since – but by no means a brilliant one. General Craufurd, who commanded, seemed to forget himself – he made dispositions which he never altered and our loss has we believe been equal if not greater than the enemy's without gaining an object – Colonel Talbot of the 14th Dragoons was killed – we took 2 officers, 29 horses and 30 men prisoners.[32]

Macal do Chao
Wednesday 25th July 1810

My dear father,

From the reports published in the London newspapers and what I have lately sent you myself you would I dare say before this expect to hear that we had advanced, but owing it appears to the extreme coolness and good judgment of Lord Wellington it was not till last night we received the order – we marched this morning soon after daybreak and we are now encamped near this village two leagues and a half nearer Almeida.[33]

We shall certainly move again forward from this tomorrow and probably this afternoon or in the night. The French, it appears, after obliging General Craufurd to recross the Coa, crossed themselves to the north of Almeida – I have not heard in what force but it is not I believe very great. It is not expected we shall have much fighting till Almeida falls and this will not take place, if the garrison behave well, under 3 weeks. Then however we shall be much employed. All what I mention in this manner is of course only reports. We know no more than you anything for certain but it is what is generally thought amongst us. It is not thought Lord W. will hazard a general action at this position so advanced.

After trying the Portuguese and feeling the pulse of the French in a few skirmishes we shall probably retire gradually from the frontiers, disputing perhaps the different positions with divisions of the army till we arrive at Villa Franca. By that time Lord W. will have ascertained the reliance he can place on the native troops.[34] In the affair of yesterday one regiment of the Light troops behaved very well and one of the Line we hear ran away – however, they may improve and we must not condemn all from the bad behaviour of any particular corps – several Battalions of infantry and some Brigades of their artillery passed through our quarters yesterday and several days before and in appearance they far outshine any French troops I have yet seen.

As I have not heard every particular of the business of yesterday, I have not pronounced any opinion on it – all reports however blame General Craufurd for having most unnecessarily exposed his men and this said to be in contradiction to orders of Lord W., but as I have no doubt an account of it will be published you will know more than me. Our loss has been excessive considering there was no object in fighting where we did – 22 officers and about 259 men killed and wounded – 5 wounded officers have just passed through our camp – more are coming.

Vinho
30th July 1810

Little did we think when we gained the glorious battle of Talavera that we should commemorate its first anniversary in a *retreat* and that before the very same enemy over whom we had there triumphed.

It has however happened.

The accounts from Lisbon will I have no doubt have acquainted you with the facts but reports from there are always accompanied by such an exaggeration that I feel anxious to moderate the apprehensions which you must naturally feel. It is an event which being long foreseen has not in the least diminished *our* confidence or increased *our* apprehension – our minds are made up for the event and, thus prepared, what have we to fear? The country however has been thrown into a dreadful ferment and the people are deserting their homes and burying their property in every direction.

After the fall of Ciudad Rodrigo our advanced posts have gradually been withdrawn nearer the main body of the army and the rear divisions closed to the front. The result of the attack on the Light Division on the morning of 14th disclosed the intentions of Lord Wellington. From that moment preparations were made for a retreat; the wounded, the sick, the stores and provisions of every description were sent off to the rear and on the morning of 28th the army itself began to retrograde. On that day our division (the 1st) marched from Macal to Chao – headquarters of the Light Division were withdrawn to Celorico and the heavy cavalry and horse artillery were sent to the front – they have now their advance in front of Alverca about 3 leagues from Celorico and our division, which is the rearmost, is cantoned in this and the adjoining villages 5 and 6 leagues from Celorico.

Wednesday morning 1st August

Headquarters remain at Celorico and the position of the army is the same as before. The enemy on the 29th drove out of Freiscedas the picquet of our cavalry, but they retired again and the picquet resumed its station. We are perfectly ignorant of the strength of the enemy on this side of the Coa and it is not known whether the French have broken ground before Almeida. Lord W. of course knows what the enemy are about but I hear they have so many picquets in every direction that it is impossible to reconnoitre. Deserters continue to come in and they say they are yet very badly off for meat.

How long we may remain here seems quite uncertain, but the enemy appear to be more than usually cautious against us and we think they are not yet prepared fully to act. Our retreat will be very slow but everything is prepared to make it rapid if necessary; no cars[35] whatever are allowed to remain with the army, even those attached to regiments for the purpose of carrying the accoutrements of men taken sick on the road were ordered to Lisbon yesterday. And everything now is to be carried on mules – the roads have been cleared of every obstruction and where a lane continues to narrow for a few hundred yards the enclosures next to it are removed and a new road thus opened.

The Brigade of Guards are quartered in Vinho but the Light company are encamped. This has been the case since we left Celorico. And will always be the case while we retreat, but the weather is now fine and I would at any rate prefer it. I am in excellent health. I shall write you very often now as I know you will have numerous reports about us to make you uneasy. I have not yet seen our responding further; indeed, were it not for a little hustle sometimes on the march by the passage of different stores one might fancy ourselves in a state of refined peace.

The minds of everyone being made up, we are as cheerful as we would be at home. I must once more caution you against giving credit to reports from Lisbon. You will easily conceive the defeat of 20 men on picquet or the retreat of a division for a league will be magnified by the terrified natives in travelling 200 miles into a general action and defeat and consequent retreat. You will then not be surprised at the ridiculous reports from the Capital of Portugal.

The Portuguese, superstitious and ignorant in the extreme, are apt to magnify everything. I hope therefore you look to me for every information and you may be assured I shall not lose any opportunity of acquainting you with our situations, however often they may occur. When my promotion takes place I shall feel it my duty to remain here even after the officer who is to relieve me shall arrive, unless I am positively ordered home. You may be sure I am as anxious as anybody can be to enjoy the pleasure of being at home, but opportunities like the present may not again occur to me and it will be but proper therefore that I should see everything practised in my profession that I can. Should this army seem unexpectedly tranquil I will certainly attempt to visit Cadiz before my return.

Moimenta
15th August 1810

The people of this country, who are always easily alarmed, have been in dreadful apprehension for the arrival of this day, for they expected that the French army would celebrate the birthday of Bonaparte by an attack on the British army. No attack, however, has yet taken place and so far from making demonstrations of such intention they have again evacuated Pinhel and withdrawn all their advanced posts from the situations they had occupied after crossing the Coa. The conduct of the French against Portugal is most unaccountable, and should they continue to pursue it the conquest of Portugal will be found an enterprise of extreme difficulty.

Their dilatoriness has already had effect upon the Portuguese and it has infused a spirit into their troops which the most sanguine could not have expected to be shown, even in a branch of the army *viz* the cavalry which in every service is not brought to act till experienced, this spirit has manifested itself as decidedly as amongst the infantry. Not only has the cavalry attached to General Hill faced and attacked superior bodies of the enemy's cavalry, but when routed they have skirmished *individually*. Near Braganza, a town at such a distance as to render support by *British* troops impossible, a squadron of *Portuguese* attacked and defeated *a superior* body of French cavalry, and took a considerable number of prisoners and horses. Near the same town too, Silveira[36] has since surrounded and taken four *hundred infantry,*

The predatory warfare which has been carried on in Spain so successfully has likewise begun in Portugal, and the first effect of a small corps of *Guerrillos* has been the murder of an officer and 25 French soldiers while plundering a mill. The dead bodies of these enemies were left on the spot, but their mules were brought to Marshal Beresford and he has rewarded the leader of the successful band with a commission.

I mention these instances of the good behaviour of the Portuguese because it gives me pleasure, and while it must augment your hopes of their imitating the British troops it will tend to moderate your apprehensions for our safety. I wish I could have it in my power to state that the spirits of resistance to the French was universal but I am sorry to say a contrary disposition has been shown in Lisbon, and the arrival of the account of Ld Wellington's retreat encouraged the partisans of the enemy to give significant hints of their expectations.

In acting as he did, Lord Wellington confirmed and increased the confidence of our men in his judgment and ability. The advanced magazines, the sick and indeed everything that would impede the rapidity of the army were removed to the rear, on the enemy assuming the threatening positions he did on the 27th and the 28th. By a long march of six leagues he placed the infantry behind the Mondego, twenty miles from the enemy and this prepared the *army* for a rapid retreat.

Had it been unavoidable it would have been executed without risk, as new roads were opened where the old were bad, and our left flank was secured by the Mondego. This river, though fordable everywhere from its source to its mouth, is nevertheless an obstacle that would not soon be overcome by an army. It is generally very steep in its banks, and these at almost all points are difficult of approach. On our flank therefore (the left supported by the Mondego and the right by the Tagus) we have nothing to fear, and limited in our defence to the ground between these two rivers we have little to apprehend from an attack in front when protected by the body of cavalry we now possess.

It appears to me our retrograde movement towards Lisbon whenever it is made will be slow. Hill is very strongly posted at Castello Branco, and if forced to retire he can over a difficult country along the Tagus to Thomar where he gets behind the Zezere, while Lord Wellington with the left falls· back to the strong position on the Alva near the Pont de Murcella, from which points if forced we shall retire to Santarem and Leiria and thence to the fortified position of Villa Franca and Torres Vedras. Thus at no time shall we occupy a greater extent of country at twelve or fifteen leagues and at last not more than eight. The French are fully aware of the advantages of ground and we shall see in proceeding against us they will be most circumspect.

Moimenta is a beautiful village about two miles from Vinho (the date of my last letter) into which we have moved, as there is plenty of covering for all the men and the quarters are good.

Celorico
21st August 1810

You did not I dare say expect that I would again have any opportunity to date a letter from this town, but our return here is one of the extraordinary occurrences of this most extraordinary war. Instead of being able to follow up with their usual rapidity the first advantages over an enemy, the French after crossing the Coa were obliged to halt, and they have since found themselves under the necessity of dispersing so much, that not above 16,000 men now remain *immediately* before Almeida.

Reports ascribe various reasons for the dispersion of the enemy – formidable insurrections in their rear and extreme want of forage and provisions, while collected in one body are equally urged as the cause, but the latter has most credit. Lord Wellington seems determined to seize every opportunity to favour the efforts of the Spaniards and he has accordingly pushed on our outposts and closed up the army to the front. Ours is the rear brigade of the army – we are arrived here yesterday, we move forward tomorrow. Headquarters moved from this today to Alverca.

The enemy have opened their batteries against Almeida since the 15th and they found so much difficulty in proceeding with their works from the rocky nature of the ground that many think Lord Wellington will attempt to raise the siege. But this will be an enterprise of so much hazard that I do not think it likely that he will run the˙risk, unless we are superior in numbers to the enemy. The country beyond the Coa and between it and

Almeida is very open and the enemy in cavalry are much more numerous than we are. Our forward movement, however, will be attended with good, for the enemy must either retire, in which case he relieves Almeida, or he must collect all his corps, when the difficulties of provisioning them will return and an opportunity will also be afforded the Spaniards to rise.

In a few days we shall see the effect. Tomorrow is post day and as we expect to march I write today and will leave this here to be forwarded. The telegraph which communicates with Almeida has been at work today – we have heard a heavy firing from there all yesterday and this morning.

The Spanish Genl Ballesteros you will hear has been beat. He imprudently attacked Mortier before the arrival of Romana and the consequence was as might have been expected – he caused some loss to the French but he himself lost about 1,000 men.[37]

Celorico
28th August 1810

After what I wrote to you from this place on 22nd (it was in fact the 21st) inst you would hardly expect I should now date my letter here. In the night of 23rd an order arrived and we marched the next morning to Macal do Chao, where we remained till this morning and returned to Celorico. The French pressed the siege of Almeida so much that they opened on it with eleven batteries within 240 yards on Sunday at daybreak – the cannonade was kept up with little intermission till yesterday afternoon at 2 o'clock when the firing on both sides ceased and it is believed to have surrendered about 5 o'clock in this evening. The particulars (if known to Lord Wellington) are not yet published, but report says the Governor, Colonel Cox, was killed and on this the Portuguese surrendered.

The defence has been most disgraceful. The least sanguine expected the garrison would hold out till Sunday or Monday but as it has surrendered after having been battered only 36 hours it appears probable either that the Governor was killed or that the inhabitants and troops obliged him to surrender. The garrison consists of only one regiment of the Line and three militia and I believe there were not above two or three English officers besides the Governor.[38] The Portuguese have been accustomed to look upon Almeida as almost impregnable and its early surrender will I fear produce much alarm.

We have not yet received any orders to continue the retreat tomorrow but as the order will most likely come very suddenly I think it best to have a letter ready to leave today than to trust to chance tomorrow. We were overtaken by a severe thunderstorm on the march today and a flash of lightning struck the Light company of the Coldstream by which one man was killed and another severely stunned.

Sanquinada
12th September 1810

My last to you is from this (place) on the 5th Inst[39] and there has since occurred nothing of importance either in our army or the enemy's. Lord Wellington has his headquarters still at Gouvea; the Light, 1st, 3rd and 4th divisions of Infantry are cantoned between Celorico and the Ponte de Murcello, in the towns and villages on and near the highroad; and the outposts of the cavalry are at Macal de Chao and Guarda. . . . On the right there has been no movement. General Hill remains with his headquarters at Sarzedas, with his outposts extending in front of Castello Branco, and the right to Villa Veltra and across the Tagus to keep up the communication with a small corps of his cavalry in the Alemtejo. Marshal Massena continues to observe the extreme caution he has adopted since the opening of the campaign – he is forming a complete cordon along the frontier, a circumstance which strongly indicates his incapacity to prosecute the operations against Portugal yet; he has established a large corps of cavalry at Sabugal and he has removed his headquarters to Pinhel. From having removed to a place so near our army it might be inferred Massena feels himself prepared to move forward; accounts however received induce us to believe that this is by no means the case – we have long heard that his army has been much dispersed to collect provisions for which they were in want, and an intercepted letter from Massena to Bertier[40] confirms the reports.

Now it has always been admitted that he will do nothing against this country without a disposable force of 80,000 men, not that so large a force would be necessary to fight us in a battle but in a country so hostile every convoy must be protected by a large escort. There seems at present little chance of the French having so large a force disposable for some weeks, and if they have not I think they will not get us to retire to our fortified position before Christmas. If they come on even in small force, I mean not more than 20,000 or 30,000 men *in front*, we of course shall retire behind the Alva, but with the Ponte de Murcella blown up (which is intended) a show of opposition will be sufficient to arrest the further advance of such a corps.

This country can afford them no supplies – they must therefore bring with them and they have got no magazines large enough.

Granada it is expected will be formed into a depot by the enemy. Its situation is very eligible, being at the meeting of a great number of roads.

Of the Portuguese garrison of Almeida – all the militia who chose were permitted to return to their homes and the regiment of the line, No 24, had the choice of entering the French service or being sent to France – they chose the former and the greater part of the men and 17 officers have effected their escape and rejoined their army.

As usual the *Couriers* I have received today are filled with Private communications from the army in Portugal and the comments of the Editor on them. They are to us (who have had an opportunity to know the position of the army and the *local* of the country) extremely amusing as compared to the *real truth*; they exceed the most ridiculous burlesque I have read – it is quite impossible the letters can be written by officers; they betray too little knowledge for a sergeant of commissary's clerk and the geographical descriptions of towns' positions are worthy only of Portuguese ignorance.

Travossa
25th September 1810

The repose enjoyed by the army after the fall of Almeida was interrupted on 16th by the enemy, who on that day appeared before our outposts in two columns of 30,000 men and obliged them to fall back from Guarda and Celorico almost three leagues to Villa Cortes. The next day the division, both infantry and cavalry, in advance, continued to retrograde upon those in rear, and on the 18th the whole army was in motion towards the Ponte de Murcella, which was crossed by the 1st division of infantry, and it proceeded three leagues to Foz d'Arouce – the cavalry halting near Pinhancos, and the Light and 3rd and 4th divisions of infantry between that place and the Alva. In performing these retrograde movements there were several skirmishes and in one the Royal Dragoons found an opportunity to charge, which they did with such effect as *literally* to upset the dragoons of the enemy.

A small corps of Portuguese, which had been pushed to the left from Celorico, was ordered to retire on the left bank of the Mondego – this was pursued by a column of the enemy which they detached to Vizeu by Mangualde, and they reached it on the 18th with the ordnance of corps of between 20,000 and 30,000 men. On the 19th the first division marched from Foz d'Arouce by a track across the mountains to Coimbra to support the Portuguese retreating from it and the 3rd division fell back behind the Alva and occupied the position of Murcella, where they have since remained.

On the 20th at Coimbra we were under arms before daybreak, joined by two *fresh* regiments of British Infantry and 4 of Portuguese and posted on all the avenues to the town on the left of the Mondego. After daylight we were dismissed and returned to our quarters. We had not, however, been long dismissed when all was bustle – an order arrived and the whole marched to Mealhada and encamped in the woods round about. This unexpected movement, it appears, was caused by the enemy attempting to descend along the left bank of the Mondego in force, but the attempt was defeated by the foresight of lLord Wellington and the rapidity of the troops. The 4th Division, which was on the march to Coimbra, was halted and thrown across the Mondego and the cavalry and Light division passed at Foz Dao – General Leith with his division has been ordered from Thomar and has arrived at Penacova and the artillery of General Hill's division have also arrived, which increases the ordnance in this part to 72 pieces.

The army is now concentrated within a few miles of this village, occupying a position extending about 6 leagues – the right across the Mondego and behind the Alva at the strong pass of Murcella, and the left on the left

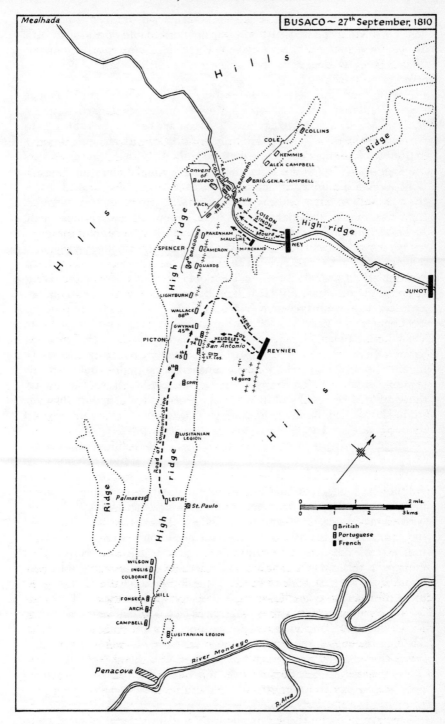

BUSACO ~ 27th September, 1810

of the Mondego on a chain of extremely difficult mountains opposite to where the Mondego and Alva join. In this formidable position we shall dispute the advance of the enemy and everything indicates the determination of Lord Wellington to fight a general action should the enemy feel disposed to attack us here.

Having found his demonstrations on our right insufficient to induce General Hill to quit his position – it is too strong to be attacked in front – Marshal Massena seems to have expected to have been able to oblige us to retire from our position on the left by bearing down with an immense force in front while another corps threatened our flank. With this in view he has recalled all his detached parties and Reynier, who has been opposed to General Hill, has joined the main body of his army and except for Mortier's corps (which is on the march from Seville) there is now no enemy on our right and Mortier has not, I believe, more than 8,000 men. Being prevented also in his attempt to surprise our left by a rapid movement, Marshal Massena will now I think attempt some other manoeuvre – for to attack us in front would be extremely hazardous – the approaches to the position are *difficult* and *neither cavalry or artillery* can be brought to bear upon the important points. He will probably therefore try to turn our left and to do this he must return to Vizeu and with a strong corps descend the right bank of the Vauga, and at the Vauga Colonel Trant is stationed with 10,000 militia men and Genl Silveira is at Lamego with a corps of about the same number. These troops, though unable to withstand half the number of the enemy in battle, would nevertheless in this country throw great impediments to an enemy – between our left and the sea the country though flat is enclosed and intersected by woods and, supported by the troops Lord Wellington could easily afford to detach, the militia will I think protect our left.

I shall now offer no more speculations on the proceedings of the enemy, but I am of the opinion that there will be no general action here for some weeks – as the enemy I think must first be much reinforced and this they will not be soon. I consider it probable that Massena finding his force insufficient to drive us from our positions will content himself this year with taking possession of Oporto and indeed of the country to the north of the Vauga. By doing this he will cut off all our supplies of beef and much of Indian corn. But it is to be hoped the regiments now off the coast (or perhaps at this moment landing) and what are coming will enable us to attack if the French act defensively. At present their advance is within 10 miles of us and they are accumulating fast. They have repaired a bridge which we had destroyed over a small river near Mortago and passed it in force. This brought on a heavy cannonade on 23rd but it has done nothing. The guards, and all the troops in the villages we hold, are within a few hours' march of the position; indeed, they are at the foot of the hill and the rest of the army are encamped – but the artillery in general is either in the position (the Busaco Ridge) or within one hour's drive of it and the 4th and Lt divisions of infantry are in it.

The army assembled here is about 50,000 men without Genl Hill's command of about 10,000. In addition, there are four regiments from England – and the Duke of Brunswick's corps of three regiments which are looked for from Cadiz. The enemy's force is said to be 84,000 men.

4.00 p.m.

There has been firing for the last two hours, the enemy are advancing and our advance gradually retiring[41] – the Militia have moved to their part of the position and we probably shall move tonight.

In preparation for this advance on Lisbon via Coimbra, Massena called in Reynier's corps from between the Tagus and Sierra de Gata. Wellington likewise started to concentrate his forces in readiness for manning a naturally strong delaying position covering Coimbra and keeping open the roads leading south from that town through Leiria and Thomar. These he had already selected and improved.

Wellington was at this time having trouble with the Portuguese Regency Council to which new members had been appointed in August. Following the fall of Almeida they became aware of Wellington's plans to retreat and carry out a scorched earth policy with the help of the local militia and the Ordenanza. To avoid this they tried to get the British government to order Wellington to carry out an offensive strategy, and endeavoured to get their own nominees appointed to Beresford's staff instead of British officers. Wellington would have none of it. He made it clear that any interference in the affairs of the army would lead to his resignation, coupled with his recommendation to the British government to withdraw the forces from Portugal.

Romana was also proving troublesome and might have wrecked Wellington's plans for concentrating his forces on the Mondego, for as soon as Reynier's corps moved north he insisted on advancing, for a second time, on Seville. On 15 September he found himself confronted by a part of Mortier's corps which had been sent on Soult's instructions to fill the gap left by Reynier. Romana fell back but his cavalry was overtaken at Fuente Cantos and routed. His whole force might have been captured had it not been for the brilliant action by the Portuguese Cavalry Brigade, under Madden, referred to by Aitchison on 21 August. As it was, Romana lost 500 men, killed or wounded, and six guns, and withdrew on Badajoz.

Before Massena started his methodical invasion of Portugal on 15 September, Leith's 5th Division (two Portuguese and a recently arrived British brigade) and Hill's 2nd Division were already on the march from the Tagus to Espinhal. Wellington now ordered the 1st, 3rd and 4th Divisions to fall back, covered by the Light Division. Towns and villages were to be cleared of their inhabitants and any stores of use to the French which had not already been removed were to be removed or destroyed. Much of this work was left to the local militia and Ordenanza. Colonel Trant, controlling – more or less – some thousands of militiamen, was to cover the northern flank and raid the French lines of communication.

Wellington's forces were preparing to occupy the positions covering the approaches by the paved road from Celorico, referred to in Aitchison's letter of 2 March when it was reported that Ney had entered Vizeu on the sixteenth. As soon as it became apparent that Massena's main body were advancing via Vizeu and a track north of the Mondego, 'the worst road in Portugal', Wellington changed his plan to one of occupying the Busaco ridge which ran for nine miles north from the village of Pena Corva, on the north bank of the Mondego. Massena's choice of route seems to have been dictated by bad intelligence.

The Busaco ridge was a great natural defence. Long and narrow, it had a steep escarpment to the east, though much of its top was flat. Wellington, with his usual prescience, had had a track constructed along the reverse slope, below and parallel with the crest, to enable him to move his forces unseen by the enemy. The southern end of the ridge rises steeply from the Mondego valley to 1,000 feet. The ridge attains its greatest height of 1,500 feet at Monte Sacro, toward its northern end. On the reverse slope, north of Monte Sacro, stood the high walls of the dilapidated Carmelite convent of Busaco, round whose northern wall and across the ridge snaked the road from Vizeu to Mealhada, on which the French were advancing. Amidst the heather on the western slope of the ridge grew a good many trees and the convent was surrounded by 100 acres of dense wood.

On the twenty-first Wellington established his headquarters in the convent. By the next evening the 3rd, 4th and 5th Divisions were on the Busaco ridge. On the twenty-fifth Craufurd fought a rearguard action at Sula, at the foot of the ridge, and that night the Light Division and the 1st and 2nd Divisions took their places in line with the cavalry in reserve behind them. On the Alva, to cover the Ponte de Murcella, Wellington left 6,691 men (Fane's Cavalry Brigade and Lecor's Portuguese Infantry Brigade).

The Anglo–Portuguese army deployed 52,300 men from left to right in the following order: Colte's 4th Division; Craufurd's Light Division, beside the convent; Pack's Portuguese Brigade in front of it; Spencer's 1st Division on top of Monte Sacro; Picton's 3rd Division; then a long gap only filled by a battalion of the Lusitanian Legion to Leith's 5th Division; and finally Hill's 2nd Division with a forward post overlooking the Mondego from an isolated hill occupied by five companies of the Lusitanian Legion.

Some sixty pieces of artillery were deployed along the position, the horses of the Royal Horse Artillery being kept nearby to enable the light guns to be moved quickly to points of danger.

All the infantry, except for the Light Companies of the brigades, were deployed out of sight on the reverse slope. It was a very strong position, for the French not only had to attack up very steep and broken ground but had great difficulty in positioning their artillery so as to bear on the Allied line. In addition to the road from Vizeu, two other tracks crossed the ridge – one was covered by Picton's divisions, the other by Leith's. By the twenty-sixth Wellington was ready to receive Massena's army of 65,000.

BUSACO

Massena, who had established his headquarters and his mistress at Mortagoa, was convinced that no more than a rearguard, say 20,000 men, of the Allied army was deployed on the Busaco ridge. Moreover, he believed that the Allied centre was their right. After a superficial reconnaisance on the afternoon of 26 September Massena issued his orders. The attack would start at 5 a.m. the following day, when Reynier would advance II Corps (14,000) in one or two columns parallel to the track through the village of San Antonio, which crossed the ridge in a defile south of Monte Sacro. On gaining the ridge he was to wheel right and roll up the Allied line towards the convent. As soon as it was seen that Reynier had gained the ridge Ney's VI Corps (22,000) would advance astride the Mealhada road, clear the convent and open the road to Coimbra. Junot's VIII Corps would remain in reserve.

John Aitchison gives no description of the battle of Busaco because, except for a little shooting by the Light Company to which he belonged, the Guards remained privileged spectators, so far as they were able to see anything through the mist. It is therefore necessary to give a brief account of the events of 27 September which achieved so well Wellington's aims in making this stand before retreating behind the lines of Torres Vedras. These aims were to raise the morale of the politicians in London and Lisbon and of the troops under his command, and, in particular, to give confidence to the inexperienced Portuguese. Except for one militia battalion the Portuguese behaved admirably and from this experience they acquired, in Wellington's words, 'a taste for an amusement to which they were not before accustomed; and which they could not have acquired if I had not put them in a very strong position'.[42]

The fine day of the twenty-sixth gave way to a damp and foggy night. The French lines were etched by the cheerful sparkle of numerous camp fires but the Allied soldiers enjoyed no such comfort for no fires were allowed to disclose their positions to the enemy. Those not on duty lay down with their arms beside them in the heather or under the trees or in the lea of a boulder. One officer of the 3rd Guards who joined the battalion that evening ingratiated himself with a few of his friends by providing them with some cooked poultry and a few bottles of Malmsey Madeira.

Reynier's attack started at 5 a.m. in thick fog: II Corps advanced in two columns in great depth, each on a one-company front. The first to move was Merle's division on the right. The fog, combined with the natural tendency to take a steep hill diagonally, caused them to throw off to the right of their intended line of approach. This brought them up against Lightburne's brigade, which Wellington had ordered Picton to move close to Spencer's 1st Division. Under heavy fire from this brigade and from two guns which Wellington had ordered up, the French column moved to its left. Picton had filled the gap left by the move of Lightburne's brigade with the 88th Connaught Rangers, under Lieut-Col Alexander Wallace, and four companies of the 45th. Merle's column now came up against the 45th and were establishing themselves – though still in some confusion and out of breath – on the ridge when they were tumbled into disarray by a bayonet charge led by Wallace and supported by two guns called up by Wellington. Before the charge Wallace gave orders thus: 'Now Connaught Rangers . . . Pay attention to what I have so often told you – don't give the false touch, but push home to the muzzle!'[43] The French broke before the impetus and were pursued down the slope by British, Irish and Portuguese troops.

On the left Heudelet's division had an easier time in maintaining direction, for they advanced with their left on the St Antonio road. They had the support of fourteen guns playing on the defile where the road crossed the summit. With great gallantry the column fought its way up the steep slope behind a screen of sharpshooters. At the summit the right of Picton's division was ready for them, as were twelve Portuguese guns positioned near the defile. The French were pinned to the ground under intense fire and suffered heavy casualties.

Reynier now sent in his reserve brigade under General Foy to support Heudelet. Seeing that no action was taking place further south, Wellington ordered Leith to move to support Picton. Foy's column sheared off to the right, coming under heavy fire from the Portuguese guns until they had exhausted their ammunition. Foy's men persisted with great gallantry and gained the summit in the midst of Picton's division just as Barnes' Brigade of Leith's 5th Division came up. The fresh troops poured a volley into the massed men of Foy's brigade, who took to their heels carrying their wounded commander with them.

This was the end of Reynier's attack. On the Allied left Ney launched his attack as soon as he thought Reynier had reached the summit of the ridge. Loison's division was destined to come up against the Light Division, which had been most skilfully deployed by Craufurd. Soon the advancing enemy came under heavy fire from a strong skirmishing line of British and Portuguese light troops, supported by the Chestnut Troop, Royal Horse Artillery. These fell back slowly and were reinforced by the 1st Cacadores. Again the French pressed on and the skirmishing line and the Horse Artillery withdrew steadily onto the main position. Behind the crest waited the 1,800 bayonets of the 43rd and 52nd. Solitary upon a rock stood Craufurd, judging the moment. Then, just as the French column was about to breast the crest, there was a lull in the noise of battle. Turning, Craufurd shouted: 'Now, Fifty-second! Avenge the death of Sir John Moore!' and ordered the charge.[44] The men of the two battalions replied with a tremendous 'Huzzah!' and 1,800 bayonets went sparkling over the hill. One French battalion which had escaped the fate of the main column was charged by the 19th Portuguese and the rout was complete. Ney called off the attack of another of his divisions against Pack's brigade of Portuguese.

Massena still had about 20,000 men not yet committed to the battle, but Wellington had Hill's 2nd Division, Cole's 4th and Spencer's 1st Division still uncommitted. Massena's casualties were about 4,500, including one general killed and four wounded. Wellington's were 1,250. Massena withdrew, but within a day found mountain paths by which the position could be turned. Before light on the 29th, Wellington was in retreat again.

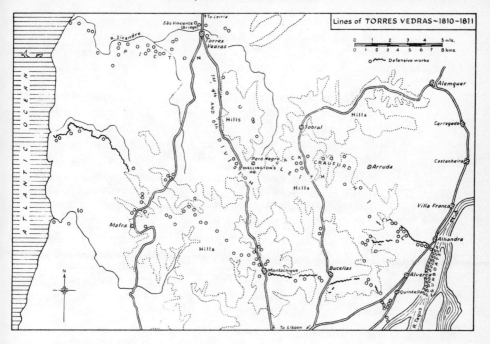

Sobral
9th October 1810

As the *Gazette* will already have acquainted you with the particulars of the action of 27th, I shall make but little mention of it, you will perceive the Guards were not engaged, but an opportunity which every person is envious of having to view a battle was afforded us from the high and commanding situation it was our lot to occupy on the position. The day, however, was much against us, as the fog was so thick that even under the range of musket, one could but indistinctly see what was going on. The 1st Division of infantry, of which we form a part, occupied that part of the position called the *Monte Sacro* which was the highest and was kept in reserve – we made several movements to our right and left to be ready to support the points attacked, but no part of the division was engaged except the Light companies which were positioned in front of their respective brigades, to keep in check the Light troops of the enemy, and they only skirmished a little.

On 28th there was no attack on any part of the line, but on the left of the centre, where the Light brigade and Portuguese Cacadores were posted, there was a sharp skirmish in the afternoon, the enemy having pushed forward a strong body of Chasseurs to mask the movements of his army, which were everywhere retiring under cover of the smoke of villages and heath set on fire for that purpose.

It thus became evident that Massena having despaired of forcing us was endeavouring to turn us and Lord Wellington gave the necessary directions to prevent it. About 10 at night we, the 1st Division, were moved *by torchlight* with all the artillery on the hill, from it to the rear of the left centre, from whence we filed off to the road leading to Mealhada – this operation was very tedious and it was daylight before the rearguard was in motion.

At the same time the 2nd and 3rd divisions of Infantry were ordered to cross the Mondego at Penacova, the 4th and Gen. Leith's division of infantry descended from the position by different ways to the high road to Coimbra and M.G. Craufurd with the Light Division (which forms the rearguard of the army) moved from his station on the position to the higher part *we* had left.

In the morning of the 29th the enemy had no troops in our front except his rearguard, which for a time remained in sight of ours. We have continued ever since to retreat – at Leiria we halted on 4th – our marches have been very fatiguing – as because of the numbers of troops and carriages on the road we could proceed at only a very slow pace – the days were excessively hot and we were generally on the road from daybreak till dusk. All night we slept in the fields. On the evening of the 7th it began to rain and it has continued ever since nor is there any prospect for it stopping for a week. This being the first of the rainy season.

Later near Sobral
13th October

I was interrupted by an order to move to another village – we have been so often called upon and moved about since that I have not been able to proceed – I have just now time to say a few words.

A vacancy has occurred in the regiment by the death of a senior Lieut to which I expect to succeed without purchase if I should not have been gazetted before the account of it is received in England. I have written to the agent and Mr Thomson to stop the purchase of a company. The officer to relieve me is already with the battalion and application has been made to Ld Wellington for leave for me to join the 2nd Battalion to which I now belong – the answer I expect every hour, and ten days at furthest after it comes I shall sail from Lisbon.

Mr Thomson will tell you what I have written him. The enemy are in sight but apparently not yet prepared to attack us. We are in our position before Torres Vedras.

Fear nothing – Massena and his followers will be driven from Portugal – the sooner he attacks the better for us – Colonel Trant I hear entered Coimbra with some Portuguese Militia last Sunday so all the French must be between that town and us.

Comparatively all is quiet opposite us. There was an affair yesterday at the outposts on our right, but it was occasioned by a reconnoitring party of the enemy which after a few cannon shots from them and a sharp fire of musketry were driven back in high style by the 71st Reg.[45] On the night of 13th they attempted to feel our left by pushing on a corp of Light troops *but* these were gallantly repulsed by *a charge* of a Portuguese reg. of the line and the enemy lost 2 officers and some men taken . In every instance in which they have been tried the Portuguese troops have shown themselves worthy of the trouble we have taken in training and instructing them.

The action of Busaco has inspired the natives with a confidence which will not easily be overcome. Invaded by Massena's *present* army Portugal is safe. Opposite us (the 1st division) he has yet only 7,000 Infantry – on our right he is stronger – and in a day or two his whole force will have come up and then if the weather clears up we may expect an attack. Rejoice if he does, for it will prove to us a victory.

My leave has not yet come out and when it does I shall go over all the positions from right to left and then having visited all, the parts of Portugal near Lisbon I have not yet seen I shall set sail. You must excuse my haste at present – at home I shall have time to explain. Adieu.

The check he had delivered at Busaco enabled Wellington to continue his retreat on Lisbon in good order and without undue pressure. On 30 September the last of the Allied troops left Coimbra, preceded by about three-quarters of the city's population. All ages and both sexes took to the road, often in very great distress, their belongings in carts, on horse- and muleback or simply on their heads. All but the rich had ignored Wellington's warning and injunctions, so that quantities of stores of the greatest value to Massena were left in the city. Any pressure which the French might have exerted on the retreating Allies was relieved by their giving over the first two days of October to the sack of the city which included Portugal's only university, an observatory, six monasteries and two nunneries.

Ney crossed the Mondego on 3 October. Massena decided to leave some 4,000 sick and his heavy baggage at Coimbra under the guard of 140 seamen intended for duty on the Tagus. The French were clear of Coimbra on the fourth and in touch with the British rearguard near Pombal on the fifth. Next day Trant at the head of a few dragoons and some 4,000 Portuguese militiamen entered Coimbra, destroyed the bridge and carried off the French garrison, baggage and sick to Oporto.

The Lisbon peninsula is by nature highly defensible. Rugged and inhospitable, it is crossed from east to west by a succession of rolling ridges broken by abrupt protrusions of bare rock and by numerous deep gulleys and ravines. For nearly a year 10,000 Portuguese peasants, relieved weekly, had worked on strengthening two main lines of defence stretching across the peninsula, with their flanks resting on the Tagus and the Atlantic. During this time the hills had been scarped towards the enemy, inundations and artificial obstructions created, and twenty-three new redoubts built, mounting ninety-six guns.

The first line of defence ran along from the coast, along the Zizandre, to Torres Vedras and from there to Pero Negro, where Wellington had his headquarters, and then by Arruda to Alhandra on the Tagus where it was supported by a flotilla of gunboats. The 1st, 4th and newly formed 6th Division were responsible for its defence. Some five miles in the rear was a second and still more formidable line, and finally a defensive system constructed around Sao Julia to cover the embarkation of the army should that become necessary.

To man these defences Wellington had 35,000 British, 24,000 Portuguese and 8,000 Spanish regulars. This was to be no static defence, the strong points would be held by the Portuguese militia while regular troops fought a mobile battle within the system, for which purpose lateral communications and a chain of signal stations had been constructed.

Lisbon

My dear Father,   *27th October 1810*

The Physician has recommended me to proceed to England as soon as I can. I have therefore abandoned the idea I had of making a short tour and shall sail in the packet on 4th November if I can get a passage, and if not, by the first conveyance to be had. There is no news from the army but it appears evident, from the long time Massena has remained before the position without attempting it and the extreme caution he has taken to prevent being attacked, that without reinforcements he will do nothing.

The opinion here and in the army is very prevalent that he will retreat. Though of the two events attack or retreat, retreat may appear the least likely, yet I can hardly bring myself to believe that with Massena's reputation he will fly without fighting – for it would be a retreat as dreadful in its consequences as defeat. I feel rather inclined to think that he looks to some movement in his favour either in the Alemtejo or Estremadura through the Algarve, and I do this because we hear nothing of Mortier who was at Seville. Under the present disposition of combined Armies of Britain, Portugal and Spain there is certainly ground for the conclusion I have made.

Had Lord Wellington apprehended anything from the south of the Tagus he would not of course have united the Marquis Romana's force[46] to his own and he would have had Ballesteros withdraw nearer to Badajoz. He therefore must consider his rear and right flank secure. A week I think will set speculation at rest as, by the time the remainder of Romana's force joins us, Massena will I think either have attempted what he intends to try or Lord W. will have attacked him. The French are building a bridge of boats to throw across the Tagus at Santarem. Lord Cochrane who is now here has offered his devices to destroy them.[47] It will be an enterprise of difficulty and his Lordship of all others is the best qualified for such a task – but it would be such an affront to the naval and military branches already on this station that I should think without direct positive orders from England he will not be employed.

The second division of the Marquis Romana's infantry landed here on 25th. They were very fine-looking men, well-armed, appointed and clothed commanded by Carrera. Two companies of one regiment in their original capes and coats and caps of the 51st regiment of French infantry – the eagle on the front of the cap was reversed. I did not hear where they were taken. My love to all the family.

Massena, knowing nothing of the existence of the lines of Torres Vedras, had difficulty in understanding the cause of Wellington's continual retreat. On 8 October the weather broke, on the tenth the Allies entered the lines in torrential rain, on the eleventh they were reconnoitred by the French cavalry, and on the fourteenth by Massena himself. As a result he decided that he could not attack but was not yet prepared to admit defeat and retire. For four weeks he sat down in front of these formidable defences with his near-starving troops, during which time he took steps towards creating a stronghold around Santaren, further up the Tagus, from where he might cross into Alemtejo.

Trant and the Portuguese partisans had closed in on Massena's lines of communication and had invested Ciudad Rodrigo and Almeida. It now took anything from a battalion to a brigade to provide safe escort for an official French messenger!

Massena had only three things to hope for: firstly, that he could lure Wellington into the open to provide an opportunity to defeat him. But Wellington, though tempted by Massena's need to disperse his troops in search of food, was not to be drawn. Secondly, Massena hoped that Soult would obey Napoleon's orders and come to his assistance, but both the fortresses, Badajoz and Elvas, guarding the southern gateway to Portugal were at that time in the hands of his enemies, and thirdly, he hoped that a change of government in London would bring Britain to terms.

On 2 November, Princess Amelia, George III's favourite daughter, died. This sad event sent the old King into his last period of 'madness'. The Prince of Wales became Regent, though his powers were strictly circumscribed until the passing of the Regency Bill in February 1811. Napoleon had great hopes that the Prince would throw out the Tory government in favour of his former Whig friends, the advocates of a negotiated peace. In the event the Regent confirmed Percival in office.

John Aitchison got his promotion. His new commission was dated 22 November and signed by the Prince Regent in the name of and behalf of His Majesty. Such evidence as exists suggests that he got his Lieutenancy without purchase. His commission reads:

> To our Trusty and Wellbeloved John Aitchison Esq. Greeting.
>
> We do by these Presents, Constitute and Appoint you to be Lieutenant to the Company whereof —— Esq. is Captain in Our Third Regiment of Foot Guards commanded by our Dear Nephew General His Highness William Frederick, Duke of Gloucester K.G. with the rank of Captain[48] in our Army and Pay commencing on the twenty second of November 1810.
>
> You are therefore carefully and diligently to Discharge the Duty of Lieutenant etc.
>
> By Command of His Royal Highness the Prince Regent in the name and on behalf of His Majesty.

CHAPTER THREE

1811–12
Intermission

JOHN Aitchison was to be absent from the Peninsula for eighteen months – a period of consolidation, reorganization, and preparation by Wellington for re-entry into Spain. The 6th Division was formed in October 1810, a weak 7th Division in the following March, and two cavalry divisions in June, bringing the Anglo–Portuguese Army to its final establishment. Standards of equipment and training were raised, and the British commissariat and supply and transport system was expanded and reorganized to increase mobility and the welfare of the troops. Wellington set himself two operational tasks before the opening of the 1812 campaign. First, the French were to be ejected from Portugal, then the frontier fortresses dominating the two gateways into Spain were to be taken – Almeida and Ciudad Rodrigo in the north, Elvas and Badajoz in the south.

Sailing from the Tagus on 31 October, John Aitchison arrived at Portsmouth on 17 November. He was very weak from fever and it was several months before he was fully recovered. After a short visit home he was stationed with the 1st Battalion of his regiment in London.

At home he found widespread distress. The harvests of 1809 and 1810 had failed and Napoleon's embargo on British trade was biting deep. The rate of inflation and the number of unemployed were high and bankruptcies were frequent. Social unrest was widespread – gangs of Luddites were breaking the new-fangled machines that were putting them out of work, and in May Lancashire was on a three-day week. And it was as yet impossible to see how the war might be ended other than by capitulation.

Peace and democratic reform were the policies of the radical opposition, but Percival's government stood firm in the belief that the war must be carried on. Reinforcements for Wellington were limited by the necessity to maintain considerable garrisons in Britain and Ireland to keep law and order, and against the possibility that Napoleon might still attempt an invasion.

The expansion of the Army had increased the problem of manning the Navy, already aggravated by British seamen enlisting in the United States Navy, whose conditions of service were very much better. Financing the Peninsular War imposed a heavy burden, but the problem was less one of overall provision than of finding the gold, with which it was necessary to pay for the import into Portugal of American corn and for the hire of Spanish muleteers and other services, and of which there was a world shortage. By the

summer of 1811 British troops were two months in arrears of pay, and
Spanish muleteers six months, as were British officers' allowances.

Napoleon's attempt to defeat Britain by a trade war was proving a
two-edged weapon. While it weakened Britain, and in 1812, helped to bring
about war with the United States, it also created great distress throughout
Europe and eventually caused Napoleon's alliance with the Tsar to break
down and Marshal Bernadotte, recently elected King of Sweden, to turn
against his old master. But it was not only the repercussions of the trade war
that were turning the tide against Napoleon during John Aitchison's absence
from the Peninsula – the spirit of nationalism was stirring throughout
Europe. Those who had supported the ideals of the French Revolution
against the oppression of the old regimes now demanded Liberty, Equality
and Fraternity from Napoleon. Prussia in particular, so recently humiliated,
was on the road to a remarkable renaissance.

For all the benefits that stemmed from Napoleon's genius as an organizer
and law-giver, he remained incapable of operating any other system than a
centralized dictatorship, one to which Britain and the other states of Europe
would not submit and which, therefore, could only be maintained by the
sword. Before John Aitchison returned to Portugal, Napoleon was already far
advanced in his preparations for invading Russia. By March 1812 he had
concluded treaties with Austria and Prussia, allowing him to cross their
territory and to take contingents from them for his Grande Armée. Napoleon
was now committed to an invasion of Russia with Spain and Portugal still
unsubdued. His march on Moscow proved an utter disaster, yet one from
which he showed remarkable powers of recovery. It was 'the Spanish ulcer'
that ensured his ultimate undoing.

Within the lines of Torres Vedras the Army enjoyed ample and regular
supplies through the port of Lisbon. The harvest had been gathered and so the
problem of feeding Lisbon was lessened – nevertheless, it is claimed that some
50,000 peasant refugees died of starvation within the lines during winter of
1810.

Massena was in a most perilous situation. His army lay at the end of long
lines of communication through country that had been the victim of a
scorched earth policy. Wellington's position in front of him was too strong to
be attacked, while his communications to the rear were cut and harassed by
Portuguese militia and guerrilla forces. By sheer willpower Massena maintained his position for four weeks before pulling back twenty-five miles to a
strong natural position. Here he managed to hold out until 3 March 1811,
when sickness and starvation forced a general retreat.

Meanwhile Napoleon, still determined to control his jealous marshals
from Paris, ordered Soult, commanding the Army of Andalusia, to send
10,000 men to seize the high ground at Almada on the south bank of the
Tagus opposite Lisbon. This was held by Hill with the 2nd Division and some
Spanish forces. It meant bypassing a number of Spanish-held fortresses and
Soult decided it was impractical. Instead he marched against Badajoz with
20,000 men and invited Massena to join him.

Soult withdrew a large part of Victor's corps investing Cadiz, where the

Anglo–Portuguese part of the garrison had been raised to 5,100 men under Lieutenant-General Sir Thomas Graham, enabling the garrison to make a sortie by sea and land behind Victor's remaining forces to cut their lines of communication. Despite the weakness of the Spanish commander of the 15,000 men involved, Graham achieved a remarkable victory, against great odds, at Barrosa on 5 March with his force of Anglo-Portuguese. Subsequent recriminations led to Graham handing over to Lieutenant-General Cooke and joining Wellington, replacing Sir Brent Spencer as Deputy Commander-in-Chief and Commander 1st Division.[1]

On 19 February Soult, having defeated the Spanish Army of Estremadura at Gevora, laid siege to Badajoz. On 8 March he received bad news – Massena had given up the idea of crossing the Tagus to join him and instead had retreated northwards; Victor had been defeated at Barrosa; and the Spanish forces under Ballesteros threatened Seville. On the same day Wellington ordered Beresford to march to the relief of Badajoz. When Soult heard, he realized that he would have to raise the siege but decided first to try an offer of generous terms, since there was a strong pro-French faction in the town. The governor had unfortunately been killed in a sortie and his deputy traitorously accepted the terms. The French installed as governor General Armon Philippon, who was to prove a most resolute and skilful defender.

Massena set out to withdraw his army to north of the Mondego, where he could find supplies. As the French retreated they left behind a twice-devastated country. Only by starving the peasants could the French live off the land and as the Allies advanced sickening atrocities were revealed everywhere, as the starving soldiers had attempted to extract the whereabouts of hidden food supplies by torture.[2] Wellington followed up the retreat with the intention of heading Massena back into Spain. He was helped by the Mondego being in flood and a decisive part was played by the Portuguese militia, under Trant, who held Coimbra and covered the crossing-places along the river.

The retiring French columns were united at Miranda do Corvo on 12 March. Massena decided that he had no choice but to march his remaining 47,000 men eastwards across the Coa, abandoning the greater part of his ammunition and baggage and most of his wheeled vehicles. All worn-out animals were killed or hamstrung. Next day Wellington called a halt. His reorganized commissariat had stood up to the strain of the rapid advance but the two Portuguese brigades were said to have marched and fought for four days without food!

Hearing of the fall of Badajoz, Wellington sent Beresford to command the southern front. He took with him the 4th Division and two cavalry brigades, reducing the Allied force facing Massena to 38,000. Recently arrived reinforcements from home enabled Wellington to form the 7th Division. The Allied advance restarted on the seventeenth in torrential rain. On the twenty-second Massena drew up his army covering Celerico and Guarda while he prepared to cross the hundred miles of barren Sierra de Gata to cantonments in the Tagus valley. Massena's corps commanders were becoming increasingly insubordinate; his soldiers, bootless, exhausted and starving, were near mutiny. Ney, declaring that he would carry out no such plan, was relieved of his command and sent to Salamanca to await the Emperor's pleasure. Reynier, conducting his opposition with greater diplomacy, persuaded Massena to abandon the idea.

At Sabugal, on 3 April, Reynier's corps was saved from destruction by the Light Division by a thick fog and the incapacity of Sir William Erskine who was commanding it. Nevertheless, Colonel Beckwith's brigade, Captain Hopkin's company of the 43rd in particular, greatly distinguished themselves in what Wellington termed 'one of the most glorious actions British troops were ever engaged in'.[3] The French were thrown back across the Coa and on the eighth Massena's army crossed the Agueda into Spain and returned to their base at Salamanca.

Wellington had completed the first part of his programme. On 10 April he issued the following proclamation to the Portuguese people '. . . the cruel enemy . . . have been obliged to evacuate [Portugal], after suffering great losses, and have retired across the Agueda. The inhabitants of the country are therefore at liberty to return to their homes.'[4] He had shown himself more than a match for Massena, probably the best French general after Napoleon, and had done so with most of his best generals – Hill, Cotton, Craufurd and Leith – on home leave. Over the rank and file of his army he had established a remarkable ascendancy, based on trust and respect but devoid of endearment.

The past two years had established Wellington as a master of the defensive battle, and shown the superiority of the thin red line, when deployed in two ranks of trained, disciplined and controlled musketeers, over the dense columns with which Napoleon's army was wont to attack. Now the Allied army was beginning to demonstrate an ability to manoeuvre, something Spanish armies never achieved.[5] Wellington was ready to take the initiative and enter Spain, but first he had to gain control of the frontier fortresses, a process which was to engage the army for the next twelve months.

Wellington's failures and most costly victories were all concerned with siege operations for which the British Army was ill-trained, poorly equipped and badly organized. There was, for instance, no corps of sappers and miners. An investing army is divided between a besieging and a covering force. The great numerical superiority of the French in the Peninsula was such that, given time, they could always muster enough forces to overcome an Allied covering force and raise the siege. Wellington, therefore, had only a short time in which to reduce a fortress. Many of the fortresses he was to besiege lay far inland and he had to bring forward the heavy guns of the battering train and their ammunition over mountainous country and execrable roads by pack mule and bullock cart. This is why Wellington so often stormed fortresses after insufficient preparation, with inadequate and often locally procured siege artillery, and relying on the spirit of his men to carry the defences. Wellington had a siege train but it had remained embarked at Lisbon, as had much of the army's baggage, for he had not ceased to fear that the British government would falter in their determination to continue the war and order a withdrawal. Now, on 18 July, Wellington ordered the ships with the siege train to Oporto from whence it would be carried up the Douro in 160 boats as far as Lamego by water. The train reached its destination at the end of September.

On 22 March the 4th Division had joined Beresford's corps at Portalegre, its soldiers virtually barefoot. Beresford now had under his command the 2nd and 4th Divisions, the Portuguese Division, and a British and a Portuguese cavalry brigade, in all 20,000 men. Mortier then withdrew behind a rearguard strong in cavalry. On the twenty-fifth at Campo Mayor, a cavalry engagement took place which culminated in a remarkable charge by the 13th Light Dragoons. With some Portuguese cavalry, they broke the numerically superior French cavalry whom they pursued until checked by the guns of Badajoz, capturing the French siege train and much baggage.

The main body of the French having retired across the Guadiana, Beresford advanced to Elvas and Juromenha, where he was disappointed at not finding enough pontoons to make a crossing. He improvised a bridge and laid siege to the minor fortress of Olivença, whose garrison of 400 capitulated, after four hours' battering, on 16 April. Latour-Maubourg took over command from Mortier and, leaving garrisons in Olivenza and Badajoz, retired towards Llerena. Beresford arrived with his main body at Santa Marta on the fifteenth. Hearing that some 10,000 Spaniards under Ballesteros were to cooperate with him, he advanced to Zapra. Then, hearing that the French had prevented this, he retired again to Santa Marta, where he was joined by 2,500 Spaniards under Castaños.

On 22 April, Wellington ordered Almeida to be invested and rode south to join Beresford. Having reconnoitred Badajoz, he ordered Beresford to lay siege but, expecting Soult to march to its relief, he left it to Beresford's discretion whether to engage the French at Albuera, which covered the roads to Badajoz and Juromenha, or retire behind the Caia. The only battering cannon available for the siege were forty much-worn seventeenth-century brass guns.

Wellington left Beresford on the twenty-third and four days later, on hearing that Massena had entered Ciudad Rodrigo in force, he hurried north to his headquarters, to the relief of his staff who agreed with Johnny Kincaid that 'they would rather see his long nose in the fight than a reinforcement of ten thousand men any day'.[6] Massena's army had recovered its strength with drafts from France, though they still lacked supplies and artillery horses.

Massena was intent on resupplying Almeida and on 2 May accompanied a supply train with 45,000 men, of whom 4,500 were cavalry, and thirty-six guns. Wellington had 37,000, of whom only 18,500 were British, and forty-eight guns – for the first time his field artillery outnumbered the enemy's. To prevent Almeida being relieved, Wellington had to accept the risk of deploying his army with the Coa behind him – a river which would be most difficult to cross in any sort of order if he were defeated. The army was positioned behind a long ridge running south to north between the Turones and Dos Casas streams. These streams rose in the vicinity of the village of Nave de Haver, on Wellington's right flank, beyond which was a plateau suitable for cavalry action except for some marshy ground. From just south of Fuentes de Oñoro, northwards, the streams had carved out deep valleys.

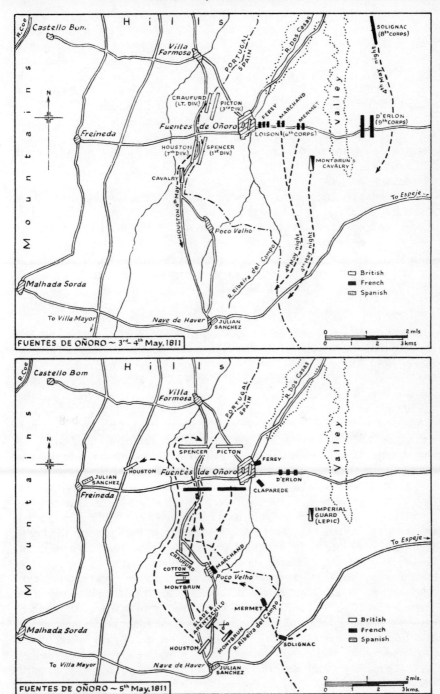

FUENTES DE OÑORO ~ 3rd–4th May, 1811

FUENTES DE OÑORO ~ 5th May, 1811

Wellington deployed his main strength in the rear of the village of Fuentes de Oñoro, whose buildings, intersected by narrow alleys, clung to the steep west bank of the Dos Casas. In the village he stationed the brigaded Light companies of the 1st and 3rd Divisions less those of the Guards. The remainder of these divisions were stationed on the rearward slope of the ridge with the 7th and Light Divisions in support. On their right, towards the village of Poco Velho, was Cotton's cavalry division, and further south still the village of Nave de Haver was occupied by Spanish partisans under Julian Sanchez. On the left flank, five or six miles to the north, the 6th Division occupied a position astride the road from Alameda to San Pedro, with the 5th Division further north still, near Fort Concepcion, covering the approaches to Almeida.

On 2 May Massena advanced in two columns. The weaker one, directed on Almeida via Gallegos, was soon seen to be no threat. The main one he led in person, against the village of Fuentes de Oñoro. There throughout 3 May he tried to drive out the British. With hard fighting the French made some ground but sustained heavy losses. To restore the situation Wellington sent in the 71st and 79th, with the 24th in support, to relieve the Light Companies. The 71st charged and cleared the village.[7]

Massena, as Wellington expected, decided to turn the Allied right where his greater cavalry force could best be exploited. Next day Wellington, having seen the movement to their left of some of Massena's forces, ordered the 7th Division to move into the four-mile gap between the Allied right and Nave de Haver with Cotton's cavalry and Bull's Troop, Royal Horse Artillery. The 7th Division positioned itself north-west of Nave de Haver, with two battalions in Poco Velho, the cavalry providing a screen between them and the Allied right.

Early on the fifth, under cover of fog, Massena started his turning movement. The inexperienced 7th Division (a Portuguese brigade of five battalions, and a brigade of foreign troops in British pay), were very soon deeply involved with the French cavalry, despite the activity of the heavily outnumbered British cavalry. While other units of French cavalry were carrying out a wide turning movement, Massena ordered Loison's corp of three divisions to take Poco Velha. Two divisions formed under cover but Wellington spotted the third and ordered the 1st Division to extend to its right and the Light Division, once more under Craufurd who had returned from leave the night before, and the remainder of the cavalry, under Cotton, to support the hard-pressed 7th Division, which from lack of experience was incapable of manoeuvring in close contact with the enemy. That it had not been over-run was due partly to its own staunchness and partly to many of the French cavalrymen being drunk. While the advance of the Light Division drew the attention of the enemy, the 7th Division withdrew steadily in close columns protected by the cavalry, supported by Bull's troops, who under Norman Ramsey greatly distinguished themselves by having stood to their guns until engulfed by French cavalry, galloping to safety through the ranks of the enemy.

The crisis of the battle had arrived. The Allied line was in danger of being turned and also severed at Poco Velho. Wellington had to shorten his over-stretched position and this meant either abandoning his communications with Sabugal or lifting the blockade of Almeida. He decided on the former, and to reform his line facing south, while retaining a firm grip on Fuentes de Oñoro. Fortunately, at this time, the French cavalry in the turning movement were having trouble in the marshy ground.

Wellington ordered Craufurd to effect the withdrawal of the 7th Division covered by the Light Division and the cavalry. For this manoeuvre the battalions of the Light Division were formed in close column of companies with riflemen thrown out on their flanks to hold off enemy skirmishes. During the three-mile withdrawal across open country, whenever the columns were closely threatened they formed square and although at times as many as 3,000 French cavalry galloped around them, whooping like Red Indians, not once did they dare to charge, and whenever charges by the British cavalry relieved the pressure, the Light Division reformed column and continued their retreat, carrying out their battle drill as immaculately as on a barrack square.

Julian Sanchez's partisans, who had prematurely retired from Nave de Haver, were already in Freineda on the new right flank and the 7th Division was ordered to take post on some high ground, behind the Turones brook, covering the bridge over the Coa at Castello Bom. The Light Division and the cavalry came into reserve, facing south, behind the 1st and 3rd Divisions. As the new line was consolidated an artillery duel took place in which the Allies got the better of the enemy. Discipline had ensured the casualties were surprisingly light.

Interest again centred on Fuentes de Oñoro, where successive attacks were launched by the enemy to drive out the Highlanders of the 71st and 79th. They suffered heavy casualties and were forced back but they never gave way. A battery of Royal Artillery behind the village, firing grape, made swaths through the ranks of the attackers. By noon the French had almost cleared the village and were making ground towards Wellington's command post. Reinforcements had been sent in from the Light Companies and now Mackinnon, who had obtained permission to clear the village with his brigade, sent in the 88th, the Connaught Rangers, with the bayonet, closely followed by the 74th; supported by the 71st and 79th, they consolidated the hold on Fuentes de Oñoro.

By 2 p.m. the battle was over. Wellington had risked an engagement with superior numbers in a position which over-extended his line, had an open flank and was backed by a river with few crossing-places. It had been a near-run thing, and as he afterwards confessed, '. . . if Boney had been there we should have been beaten!'[8]

Massena withdrew across the Agueda, on which line Wellington ordered the cavalry and light divisions to re-establish picquets, and the 6th Division to relieve the brigade blockading Almeida. Since that fortress was of no use to him, Massena had a message smuggled into its enterprising governor, Brennier, ordering him to break out after destroying the guns and fortifications. Having laid mines beneath the principal works and destroyed his guns under

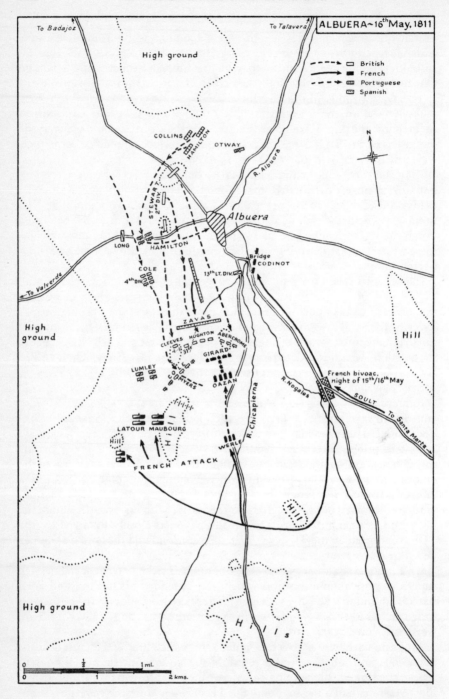

ALBUERA~16th May, 1811

cover of firing at the enemy, Brennier made a silent breakout on the night of 10 May. Leaving delayed action fuses in the mines he set course by the moon and got clear away with his garrison of 1,400, though they later suffered 360 casualties. Wellington was furious at this unnecessary humiliation and asked that no recognition should be given for the battle of Fuentes de Oñoro.

This was Wellington's last encounter with Massena, who on 10 May was relieved by Marmont, a newcomer to Spain. Marmont immediately withdrew the Army of Portugal to Salamanca to refit. On the fourteenth Wellington set out with the 3rd and 7th Divisions to join Beresford in the Alemtejo.

ALBUERA

Badajoz, strongest of the frontier fortresses, had its northern wall washed by the Guadiana, which at this point was nowhere less than 300 yards wide. The town was enclosed with a curtain wall about twenty-five feet high. In its north-east corner, in the angle between the Guadiana and the marshy Rivillas stream, on an eminence 130 feet above the river and precipitous on its northern and eastern sides, stood the ancient castle. From the north-west corner of the curtain wall round to the castle were eight bastions thirty feet high and in good repair. Between the bastions were demi-lunettes and before them ravillons and a wide ditch. To the east of the Rivillas was the San Roque lunette and Fort Picurina. South of and central to the south curtain wall was Fort Pardaleras, and last but most important of all was Fort San Cristobal. On the north bank of the Guadiana, on a rocky eminence rising sheer from the river, the San Cristobal dominated the castle from a range of 350 yards. A fortified bridgehead guarded the bridge, which crossed the Guadiana from the centre of the north wall of the town.

Beresford was laying siege to the San Cristobal, as the key to the castle; the approaches were proving most difficult to construct, as the ground was solid rock. His antiquated Portuguese siege artillery, supplemented by six more twenty-four-pounder museum-pieces from Fort Olivença, made little impression on the thick walls of the San Cristobal. A sortie by the garrison on 10 May was beaten back, but in following it up the Allies suffered 400 casualties from the guns of the fort. The same day reports were received of the approach of Soult with a relieving force.

In these circumstances Wellington had given Beresford the choice of raising the siege and taking up a defensive position at Albuera, or retiring across the Caia. Blake, commanding the Spanish corps, refused to retreat into Portugal, and in any case a sudden storm carried away the bridges and made the former course inevitable. On the thirteenth Beresford abandoned the siege and moved to a position on a ridge running north to south just west of the village of Albuera, and astride the roads to Badajoz and Juromenha. It was not a good one. His dispositions could be seen by the approaching enemy, and the ridge rose from north to south so that the Allied line was overlooked from higher ground on its right flank, which also provided good positions for the enemy artillery.

On the assumption that Soult, in accordance with French practice, would make his main attack against the centre, Beresford had posted the British there with a detachment forward in Albuera. The Portuguese were on the left and Blake's Spaniards, who were very late in coming up, on the right. Soult had 23 – 25,000 men and Beresford 36,000, of whom 12,000 were British. On seeing the Allies' position Soult decided to make a holding attack against the centre and his main attack, with cavalry and infantry, round the Allied right in the hope of cutting off Blake before the Spaniards could get into position. Too late for this, it was nevertheless a dangerous development for it necessitated the Spanish corps changing front to face south, a movement Blake was at first unwilling to carry out because it called for a higher standard of training than that attained by his troops.

There followed a most bloody battle. Cole's 4th Division, in reserve, played a distinguished part in restoring the Allied right and turning defeat into a costly victory. It was a soldier's battle – the slaughter on both sides was terrible, and the suffering of the wounded accentuated by their very numbers. The French suffered 7 – 8,000 casualties and the Allies 6,000, of whom 4,159 were British.

Wellington arrived at Albuera on the twenty-first, five days after the battle, in time to prevent Beresford from sending a defeatist dispatch. Wellington exclaimed: 'This won't do, it will drive the people of England mad – write me down a victory!' His own verdict was that 'another such battle would ruin us'. Beresford's dispatch, no doubt emended by Wellington, pays this tribute: 'It is impossible by any description to do justice to the distinguished gallantry of the troops; but every individual nobly did his duty; and it is observed that our dead, particularly of the 57th regiment, were lying, as they had fought in the ranks, and every wound was in the front.'[9] Visiting the wounded, Wellington spoke of his sorrow at seeing so many of them, to which one man replied who undoubtedly spoke for the army: 'If you had commanded us, my Lord, there wouldn't be so many of us here.'[10] Hill returned from England to relieve Beresford, who reverted to command of the Portuguese Army. He was never again employed by Wellington in independent command, except for the force sent to Bordeaux.

When Wellington had come south he had left Spencer in command of the northern corps with instructions to remain on the defensive and if forced to retire to do so slowly, blowing up Almeida if necessary. He now ordered the siege of Badajoz to be renewed. If it were to be taken it must be done quickly, as Soult was expected to be ready to march again to its relief by the second week in June. The need for speed meant that the San Cristobal must again be the main point of attack and that the same antiquated cannon were used. On 3 June the batteries opened against the San Cristobal and the castle, but the number of unserviceable guns – from blown vents and other causes – mounted daily, and it was decided to send to Lisbon for some British iron guns. On 6 June the breach in the San Cristobal was considered good enough to justify an assault that evening. This failed, as did another made on the ninth, after further battering, with heavy casualties. In neither case were the breaches practicable, and were rendered the less so by the skill of Philippon, the defending governor.

The next day the newly arrived iron guns opened fire and made a practicable breach, but although the garrison was on the verge of starvation Wellington considered it too late to make a fresh assault and so, having suffered 485 casualties, he raised the siege. What had changed his mind was an intercepted letter from Marmont to Soult stating that the former was marching to join Soult and that his advanced corps had already reached Cordova. As Marmont moved south Spencer moved on a parallel course, having, much to Wellington's annoyance, blown up Almeida. On the seventeenth Wellington crossed the Guadiana by fords and deployed his army in the Caia, ready to oppose the advance of the combined 60,000-strong armies of Soult and Marmont. Blake also crossed the Guadiana and after taking on provisions marched south through Portugal to re-enter Spain in Soult's rear and threaten Seville.

The marshals entered Badajoz together on the twentieth but were disappointed to find that Wellington had drawn back into Portugal. They planned to cross the Guadiana and either bring Wellington to battle or failing that lay siege to Elvas. Meanwhile Wellington had taken up and improved a strong line of defence. His right rested on the fortress of Elvas from where it ran by the fortified town of Campo Mayor to Oguella, where a bridge crossed the Gevora. To man this line Wellington had 54,000 men including 37,000 British.

The French threat was less than it appeared. At Busaco they had learnt the risk inherent in attacking Wellington on ground of his choosing. They also believed Blake was still with him and that he was therefore stronger than he in fact was. Moreover, those factors which prevented the French from concentrating numerically superior forces against Wellington for more than a short time were already at work. Immediately Soult had withdrawn his main force from Andalusia there was a surge of guerrilla activity throughout the province, which, encouraged by the Spanish provincial armies, soon spread to Murcia. In the north the French in Galicia and the Asturias were being harassed by Spanish armies, while throughout the area guerrilla bands never ceased to operate and even posed threats to such centres as Santander, Valladolid and Salamanca. This activity was materially supported by the British Mission at Corunna, under General Walker, and by the Royal Navy acting along the Spanish coast.

Guerrilla activity in his rear caused Soult to return to Seville on 28 June. Marmont, having exhausted the supplies of Estremadura, withdrew to the Tagus valley, about Plasencia, on 15 July, while d'Erlon, having provisioned Badajoz for six months, withdrew his corp to Zapra and Merida. Wellington, equally anxious to leave the fever-stricken valley of the Guadiana, moved on 18 July into cantonments in the Tagus valley between Castello Branco and Estremoz.

Wellington was far from satisfied with the Spanish war effort. With all the available enemy forces concentrated in Estremadura he had hoped that 'the French scattered all over the rest of Spain would have had their throats cut . . . . Nothing of the kind!',[11] he complained, 'This is the third time in less than two years that the entire disposable force of the enemy has been united against me, but no one takes advantage of it except the guerrillas', [if only] 'all the Spaniards were like their lower orders'. This was true in general but unfair to some exceptional Spanish generals, such as Santocildes and Ballesteros, whose skill, combined with the ceaseless activity of the guerrillas, had enabled Wellington to march to the Guadiana and back while they prevented any threat to Portugal or the Army developing from the north.

Both sides were now reinforcing the Peninsula. Napoleon, not yet finally committed to the Russian campaign, sent 40,000, bringing the strength of the French forces in Spain to about 360,000. To tie down British forces he again posed the threat of invasion. The camp at Boulogne was re-established and his flotilla of invasion craft reactivated. Many thought that this presaged Napoleon's return to Spain to conduct a final campaign to drive out the British. It might have been better for Napoleon had it been so.

The Anglo–Portuguese Army at this time numbered some 55,000 and a further 5,000 British reinforcements were expected. There were over 14,000 sick, mainly British and young recruits or veterans who still carried the Walcheren fever, such as the those of the 1st Guards Brigade. Moreover, so long as the enemy held Badajoz it was necessary to leave 10–15,000 Allied troops in the Alemtejo watching d'Erlon's corps. Wellington decided that his next task should be the reduction of Ciudad Rodrigo, for which he had ordered the disembarkation of his siege train. Leaving Hill to command on the Caia, Wellington marched north on 1 August and ten days later Ciudad Rodrigo was blockaded by Julian Sanchez's partisans on the north and the 3rd and Light Divisions on the south, but Wellington lacked the necessary superiority of force to lay siege to the fortress or to prevent Marmont from relieving it should he wish to do so. He therefore contented himself with deploying his force over a wide area behind the arc of the Agueda, running north for twenty miles from Fuente Guinaldo, and reconnoitring two naturally strong defensive positions which he could occupy if forced to concentrate. The forward one was at Fuente Guinaldo, where his headquarters were, while the other was west of there at Sabugal on the Coa. The left wing was commanded by Graham who had the 1st and 6th Divisions in the Fuentes de Oñoro area with the 7th Division across the Coa in Portugal. Graham was widely separated from the right wing which consisted of the 5th Division on the Perales Pass and the Light Division on outpost duties east of the Agueda. Between the two wings the 3rd Division was widely scattered and on a six-mile front with brigades covering three roads running south and southwest from Ciudad Rodrigo. The 4th Division was in reserve near Fuente Guinaldo.

In September, Marmont started moving his army northwards over the Sierra de Gata via the Baños Pass. By 21 August, Wellington knew that the French were receiving large reinforcements, but he did not know that Marmont had received two fresh divisions of 13,000 men. A week later he learnt through intercepted letters that Dorsenne, who now commanded the Army of the North, and whose 100,000 men had the primary task of keeping open the lines of communication with France, was planning to join Marmont on the Tormes with 23,000 men. Wellington now reckoned that Marmont might march to relieve Ciudad Rodrigo with 50,000 men. With such a force he believed that after replenishing the fortress he would withdraw. When, therefore, Marmont entered Ciudad Rodrigo on 24 September with 58,000 men Wellington made no attempt to concentrate. Encouraged by this lack of reaction Marmont, instead of withdrawing, decided on making a reconnaissance in strength west and south of the fortress. A strong detachment of cavalry sent to the west forced a brigade of the 3rd Division to cross the Azava. The next day this detachment advanced to Espeja while the greater part of Marmont's cavalry division under Montbrun was directed south along two roads leading to Fuente Guinaldo. Each road was covered by a brigade of the 3rd Division occupying widely separated localities. In the ensuing encounter the Portuguese artillery, British and German cavalry and a company of the 5th Fusiliers under Major Ridge greatly distinguished themselves. The latter, when the French cavalry had over-run a Portuguese battery, counter-attacked with the unusual tactic of advancing in line against dragoons, firing three volleys into them and tumbling them back to the bottom of the hill, whereupon the Portuguese immediately remanned their guns.

Checked in his frontal advance, Montbrun decided to turn the British right with the support of an infantry division sent forward by Marmont. This pause enabled Picton to start organizing his scattered battalions. Wellington ordered the 4th Division to man the Fuente Guinaldo position and the Light Division and Graham's corps to withdraw to it Meantime he rode forward and with great judgment and coolness, actively assisted by Picton, conducted a masterly retreat by the elements of the 3rd Division in contact with the enemy.

It was a smaller-scale repetition of the Light Division's tactics at Fuentes de Oñoro. Over six miles of open country, without artillery support, but under continuous artillery fire and cavalry harassment, the Allied infantry retired in column of companies at half-interval, forming squares, whenever hard pressed, which the enemy dared not charge, then moving on again whenever the pressure was relieved by the repeated charges of their greatly outnumbered cavalry. The retreat continued until the 3rd Division reached their new positions covering Fuente Guinaldo with only eighty casualties – the cavalry suffered sixty. Faced with the new position, Montbrun broke off his action.

While Wellington was conducting the retreat of his right wing, the left under Graham remained isolated twelve miles away around Nave de Haver. Wellington had decided to continue his retreat and concentrate all his forces on the second defensive position covering Sabugal, but first he had to pull in the Light Division from across the Agueda. Craufurd was, however, slow to obey his order, so that Wellington had to remain in position at considerable risk until the twenty-sixth, by which time Marmont had built up a force of at least 40,000 on his front.

All day long the Allies could see division after division of Marmont's force marching up and deploying opposite them. Marmont, however, had no intention of attacking Wellington in a position of his own choosing without a most thorough reconnaissance. Moreover he saw little advantage in doing so and had already used up four of the six months' supplies he had brought forward to replenish Ciudad Rodrigo. During the night of the twenty-sixth, leaving a rearguard to keep the fires burning to deceive the French, Wellington retired on to his rear position covering Sabugal. Marmont likewise withdrew, but counter-marched when it was discovered that Wellington had gone. Graham reached the rear position on the twenty-eighth, and the whole army was now deployed on a very strong position across the great bend in the Coa, from Quadrazaes to Rendo, with the line continued eastwards by the 5th Division.

Marmont decided that this position was too strong to attack and, having replenished Ciudad Rodrigo and destroyed large numbers of Gabions and Frascines which the Allies had prepared for the siege, the French retired into cantonments in Spain. Marmont had missed an excellent opportunity for defeating Wellington in detail. Wellington also went into winter quarters with his main force behind the Coa, leaving three divisions across the Spanish frontier – the Light Division on outpost duties east of the Agueda; the 3rd Division at Fuente Guinaldo; and the 4th west of Rodrigo at Gallegos. Ciudad Rodrigo was kept under observation while preparations for a siege went forward. On 15 October, Julian Sanchez and his partisans carried off 200 head of cattle and Reynard, the Swiss governor, from the glacis!

In the south Hill had remained quiescent, in accordance with Wellington's orders. But on 15 October, hearing that Girard, to enlarge the foraging area of his division, had marched from Merida with some 6,000 men to drive Castaños' Spaniards from Caceres, and was therefore isolated, Hill obtained Wellington's permission to co-operate with Castaños against him. At Portalegre, Hill assembled two brigades of British infantry, a British cavalry brigade and nine Portuguese battalions – some 8,000 men which Castaños undertook to bring up to 10,000.

On the twenty-third Hill entered Spain by Codosera and in foul weather over terrible mountain roads he marched towards Caceres. On the twenty-fifth, hearing that Girard was retreating southward, he followed and two days later received the information which led to the brilliant little affair of Arroyo dos Molinos. On the night of the twenty-seventh, Hill's forces lay at that village within four miles of the unsuspecting Girard. Secrecy was maintained but unfortunately Girard had ordered an early start and one of his brigades had marched towards Merida before daylight. The remainder of his force was filing out when the men of the 71st and 92nd came charging down the village street amongst the rearguard and baggage. Of the 2,600 French troops in Arroyo dos Molines, 1,300 men and three guns were captured and 7–800 killed. Girard was wounded and his force scattered, while Allied casualties were only 100.

Only two events remain to be recorded before John Aitchison's return to Portugal – the reduction of the fortresses of Ciudad Rodrigo and Badajoz. Events in southern and eastern Spain were to provide Wellington with the opportunity for reducing Ciudad Rodrigo. Throughout the war Spanish armies and partisans, supported by the Royal Navy, had continued to tie down French forces in eastern Spain, Here the French were commanded by

Suchet who had recently received his baton on the fall of Tarragona. Here, besides harassment and blockade by the Navy, Britain intervened with small expeditionary forces. Tarifa had been garrisoned from Gibraltar since 1809, and the British provided over half the garrison of Valencia. Following the fall of Tarragona Napoleon ordered the reduction of Valencia, for which purpose Marmont was to send 12,000 men to Suchet and take over responsibility for the protection of his communications. As soon as Wellington heard of these plans he decided to try and reduce Ciudad Rodrigo – even if he failed he would draw off French forces from Valencia.

Wellington's decision was a bold one[12] for although Ciudad Rodrigo was far less strong that Badajoz it was mid-winter and the intense cold made the ground iron-hard and half-froze the rivers. The town stood on a low hill on the northern bank of the Agueda, its medieval curtain wall reinforced by modern defences. The hill on which it stood fell precipitously to the river on its southern side but to the north it sloped down to a rivulet beyond which rose a long, narrow bridge, the Little Teson; beyond this was another stream from whose far bank rose the Great Teson, a plateau thirteen feet higher than the ramparts of the city which it commanded at a range of 600 yards. On the Great Teson the French had built an outwork, supported from the south-east and south-west by batteries at the convents of San Francisco and Santa Cruz. The garrison, commanded by Governor Barrie, a man of no great determination, numbered some 1,800 men.

The fortress was invested on 8 January. Some units, such as the Connaught Rangers, had to march nearly thirty miles in the pouring rain. William Gratton of that regiment records that some soldiers perished from cold and fatigue but an Irishwoman was delivered of a child beside the road and continued to march with the infant in her arms.[13] That night the Light Divison surprised and took the outwork on the Great Teson, and immediately started to reopen the parallel made by the French when besieging Rodrigo in 1810. The difficulties were great: the ground was snow-covered and frozen, the tools sent from England were defective, and the main ammunition depot fifty miles away at Villa da Ponte, but, for the first time, an adequate number of modern battering cannon were available for breaching the walls. Working parties having to wade the Agueda returned to their quarters bruised by floating ice, their clothes frozen stiff upon them.

On the fourteenth, Marmont had met Dorsenne at Vallodolid to discuss the revictualling of Rodrigo. From the size of Wellington's besieging force he concluded that he would need at least 40,000 men for its relief, which he hoped to do by 1 February, a date which, he believed, would give plenty of time before the fortress could be forced to surrender.

Wellington, appreciating the need for speed, pushed forward the operations by all possible means. It had first been intended to construct batteries on the Little Teson but on expert advice he decided to save time by breaching with the batteries on the Great Teson. On the night of the thirteenth the King's German Legion escaladed the convent of Santa Cruz which enabled the second parallel, on the Little Teson, to be opened. The French made a sortie and regained the convent. That afternoon the batteries opened, all but

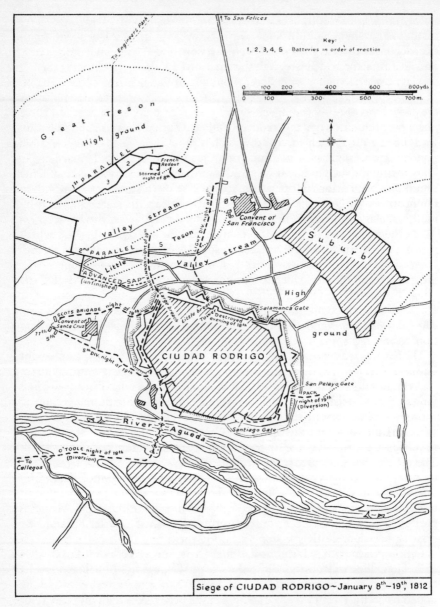

Siege of CIUDAD RODRIGO ~ January 8th–19th, 1812

two of their thirty guns being directed against the north-east salient of the curtain wall, which had been breached by the French in 1810. That night the 40th Regiment retook the Santa Cruz convent, and on the fifteenth a new battery was constructed to make a breach next to the tower opposite the San Francisco convent.

The new battery was completed during the night of the seventeenth and fire from thirty-two guns was opened at day break. By the evening of the nineteenth the two breaches were declared practicable. For the assault the 4th

Division was in the trenches; after some preliminary operations the Light Division would assault the left or little breach, and the 3rd Division the great breach on the right. Pack's independent Portuguese Brigade would create a diversion at the San Pelayo or Eastern Gate.

The Light Division formed up behind the San Francisco convent; James Campbell's brigade of the 3rd Division, which had some preliminary operations to carry out, formed behind the Santa Cruz convent, and Mackinnon's brigade of that division formed behind the Little Teson. At 7 p.m. the signal was given for the advance of the 'Forlorn Hope' at the head of each storming party. The assault was made in silence and the breaches carried by the bayonet in the face of heavy fire from the defenders. Following close on the heels of the 'Forlorn Hope', and two-thirds of the way up the left-hand breach, George Napier of the 52nd was wounded by a grape shot. Seeing him fall his men checked and began snapping their muskets. Napier called out: '"Recollect you are not loaded; push on with the bayonet!" upon which the whole gave a loud Hurrah! and driving all before them carried the breach.'[14]

The assault was successful everywhere, though at some cost. Major-General Henry Mackinnon was mortally wounded when an enemy magazine blew up, and that great warrior and trainer of light infantry, Major-General 'Black Bob' Craufurd, was also badly wounded and died on 22 January. Total Allied casualties were 1,100, those of the French 530, with some 2,000 prisoners.

When the troops entered the town discipline broke down, and soldiers dispersed in all directions in search of drink and loot. The cathedral square was soon filled with a mob of drunken, trigger-happy men discharging their muskets indiscriminately, and it was not until Wellington ordered all the troops to be cleared from the town next day that order was restored. Eleven deserters found in the town were sentenced to be shot.

Wellington had reduced Ciudad Rodrigo in twelve days, ten days before Marmont had thought it might be necessary for him to march to its relief. His achievement was marked by his being advanced to an English Earldom, and the Spanish Cortes created him Duke of Ciudad Rodrigo and a Grandee of Spain. With the fall of Ciudad Rodrigo, Marmont lost his siege train and his forward base for the invasion of Portugal. Wellington, leaving a Spanish garrison to defend the town and repair its defences, immediately turned his attention to reducing Badajoz. This time he would ensure that there was an adequate siege train (at Ciudad Rodrigo there had been insufficient artillery to silence the enemy guns as well as to breach the walls). With the exception of twelve howitzers, it proved too difficult to move to Badajoz the heavy siege train used against Ciudad Rodrigo, so Major Dickson R.A. was put in charge of assembling a fresh one at Elvas. For this he went to Lisbon to arrange the forward carriage of sixteen twenty-four-pounders recently arrived from London and to get a further twenty eighteen-pounders from the Royal Navy. Admiral Berkeley, unfortunately, chose to provide Portuguese guns for which British shot was too small, and considerable effort was expended sorting out Portuguese and Russian ammunition to fit them.

To mislead the enemy as to Wellington's intentions the ships carrying the guns and associated stores from Lisbon were ostensibly directed to Oporto, changing course for Setubal, south of Lisbon, when out to sea. For the same reason he directed that Celorico and other depots in the north should be replenished, and maintained his own headquarters in the north until 6 March. In the meantime the Allied troops returned to their former canton-ments where some at least found compensation for their arduous duties. Surgeon-Major Good of John Aitchison's battalion records dining with a brother officer off soup, boiled neck of mutton, pork cutlets, patties, roast goose, woodcocks and pudding washed down with champagne and madeira.[15] If so far as rank and file were concerned, Wellington, though at times harsh of speech, made the utmost physical exertions in promoting their welfare.

The fall of Valencia on 14 January released French forces for action against the strategically important ports of Cartagena and Alicante, or for action against Wellington. The situation in Andalusia, however, remained such that Soult asked Marmont for 20,000 men to ensure the security of Badajoz. To make this co-operation more difficult, Wellington directed Hill to mount a raid to destroy the pontoon bridge at Almaraz, the only bridge over the Tagus in French hands west of Toledo.

Napoleon, still trying to conduct the war from Paris, had already tied Marmont's hands by ordering him to fortify Salamanca and assemble in its vicinity seven divisions and a siege train (already lost in Ciudad Rodrigo) and to keep Wellington in check by threatening Almeida. 'You must think the English mad', he told Marmont, 'if you suppose them capable of moving on Badajoz while you are at Salamanca, that is to say, in a position to reach Lisbon before them.'[16] Marmont pointed out that he was without transport and could not subsist Salamanca for more than a fortnight.[17] 'To make requisition from even the poorest village we have to send foraging parties two hundred strong.'

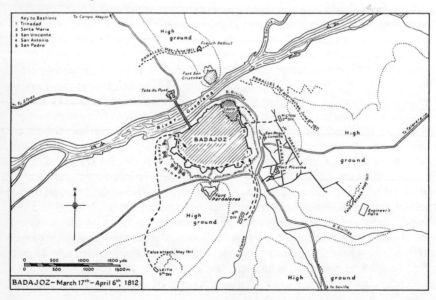

BADAJOZ—March 17th – April 6th, 1812

Wellington understood Marmont's difficulties, even if Napoleon did not, and on 16 February he moved the army southward, but left his headquarters at Portalegre until 6 March. Though the necessary stores for a siege were not yet assembled, Wellington ordered Badajoz to be invested from 16 March. A pontoon bridge was thrown across the Guadiana about ten miles below the fortress and a flying bridge one and a half miles above it. The French had some 12,000 men in Estremadura. Hill with the 2nd Division was ordered to cover the road from Merida, cancelling his raid on the Almaraz bridge, and a covering force under Graham, consisting of the 1st , 6th and 7th Divisions, was sent via Villaba to Zafra. Badajoz was invested by the 3rd, 4th and Light Divisions; the 5th Division had not yet arrived from the north.

The governor of Badajoz was still the staunch and resourceful Philippon who had at his disposal a garrison of about 4,500 effectives and 140 pieces of artillery. He was short of powder and shot, and had five or six weeks' food supply. The defences of Badajoz had been considerably strengthened since the last siege. A strong redoubt had been built north of Fort Cristobal, on the ground where the Allied breaching battery had previously been formed. A covered way had been constructed from San Cristobal to the fortified bridge-head, where the town bridge crossed the Guadiana. Along the western face of the town defences three ravalins had been turned up and sown with mines, the whereabouts of which were fortunately revealed by an engineer sergeant-major who had deserted with his maps. The castle had also been strength-ened, but most important had been the damming of the Rivillas stream to produce an impassable flood on the east of the town and to fill the ditches around the south-east corner.

The strengthening of the San Cristobal was of no moment, since this time Wellington had decided to make the approach from the south-east against the Trinidad Bastion, where a defect in construction had been detected in its southern face. The breaching batteries would have to be constructed on the Sierra de San Miguel, which overlooked the point of attack across the flooded area. The ground to be occupied by the batteries was defended by the outwork of Fort Picurina, the capture of which was a necessary preliminary.

The Park of Engineer stores was assembled in rear of the Sierra and on the stormy night of 17 March working parties opened a 1,300-yard approach trench and marked out the first parallel, about 250 yards from the Picurina redoubt. On the afternoon of the nineteenth the French made a sortie with 1,000 men via San Roque lunette which was connected to the Picurina by a covered way. The sortie was made in fog and the working parties, unarmed and waist-deep in water, were surprised and routed. At the same time the French cavalry raided the Engineers Park. Picton arrived with reinforcements and restored the situation. The French cavalry carried away 500 entrenching tools from the Park and the chief Engineer, Lieutenant-Colonel Richard Fletcher, was wounded by having a dollar piece driven into his groin, hitting him, it was said, where it hurt most – in his purse. Despite this he continued to advise Wellington throughout the siege. The operations were greatly ham-pered by the weather – on the twenty-second the pontoon bridge was swept away and eleven pontoons sank at their moorings. British working parties were much harassed by field guns north of the river, and Wellington ordered the 5th Division on arrival, to deal with these by investing the town from the north.

The next task was to take the Picurina Fort. By the night of the twenty-fourth six batteries were completed and next day thirteen heavy pieces opened against both faces of the salient angle of the Picurina. The day the fort fell Wellington received disturbing news. Massena with 20,000 men and a few cannon was marching towards the Agueda where, as he knew, the Spaniards had done little to put Ciudad Rodrigo into a proper state of defence. Soult had left Cadiz and was marching to the relief of Badajoz with 21,000 men. Wellington ordered Hill to remain at Merida for as long as possible to prevent Soult crossing to the north bank of the Guadiana. The 5th Division was sent to reinforce Graham at Zafra and Villafranca. Should Soult advance to Llerena, Graham was to fall back on Albuera. Meanwhile the siege must be carried on with the utmost vigour. The bastions of Trinidad and Santa Maria were now under continuous fire from thirty heavy cannon.

Soult arrived at Llerena on 4th April. Time was running out for the besiegers. Wellington ordered an assault for the night of the fifth but was persuaded by his chief engineer, Fletcher, to postpone it until the sixth, so as to make a further breach in the curtain wall between the two bastions. This was accomplished by 4 p.m. on the sixth, after which Wellington's artillery was directed against the guns of the defence. Because of the need for speed certain conditions normally considered essential for a successful assault were unfulfilled. For instance, the ditches had not been filled by blowing in the wall of the counter-guard. Moreover Philippon had been tireless in repairing and strengthening his defences. Rubble had been removed nightly from below each breach, which had had a trench dug behind it, its approach mined, and many ingenious obstacles placed in it. Quantities of powder barrels and immense shells were prepared and fused ready to roll down upon the assailants and explode among them.

Written orders for the assault to go in at 10 p.m. were sent out by Wellington.[18] The Light and 4th Divisions were to form up in some quarries and march parallel to each other, the Light Division on the left, close to the west bank of the Rivillas, with a small stream between them, and simultaneously assault the breach between the Santa Maria and Trinadad bastions. Each division kept 1,000 men in reserve. Their advance, the Light Division moving off first, was led by the 'Forlorn Hope' carrying sacks of straw for the assault troops to drop on to in the ditch. They were followed by a party to give covering fire from the glacis and they in turn by the assault parties, each carrying twelve ladders. The 4th Division had also to send a party of the 48th to storm the San Roque lunette, while the 3rd Division was to cross the Rivillas north of San Roque, by a mill dam, take the castle by escalade and attack the defenders of the breach from the rear. Power's Portuguese brigade was to make a demonstration against the bridgehead north of the Guadiana, and the 5th Division against Fort Pardaleras.

A thick mist covered the troops as they moved in silence to their assault positions. At 9.40 p.m. the sharp crackle of musketry away on the right proclaiming that the 48th had started operations against the San Roque lunette.

The main assault by the Light and 4th Divisions went in as planned. The French, fully alerted, held their fire until the storming parties had lowered themselves into the deep ditch, obstacle-strewn and partly filled with water. Then, as the Light Division entered the Santa Maria breach, mines were sprung beneath them, powder barrels and combustibles flew through the air and cannon swept the ditch. The storming parties pressed forward 'under a most dreadful fire of grape and musketry'.[19]

Entering the breaches, they found behind each breastwork '. . . defended by a chevaux de frise, chained to the ground and each containing thirty-six sword blades, each sharp as a razor. The ascent to the top of the breach was covered with planks, hung from the top and resting on the slope. These planks were thickly studded with iron spikes six inches long.'[20] Attempt followed attempt to carry the breaches. The ditch was filled and the ground beyond it deeply covered with dead and dying.

Haggard and drawn, Wellington waited in the quarry as the bad news poured in. When he heard that the last desperate and gallant attempt by the Portuguese Brigade of the 4th Division had failed, he ordered the two divisions to withdraw, reform, and prepare for further operation next day. Little had been heard from the 3rd Division and Wellington sent an appeal to Picton to make a further attempt to carry the castle. In a lull in the firing a clock was heard striking midnight. At that moment a most significant event was happening before the bastion of San Vincente at the north-west corner of the walls. Leith had been ordered to make a demonstration here with the 5th Division against thirty-one-foot-high walls. Not being content with such a role he had persuaded Wellington to let him have a few ladders 'to make the diversion more convincing'. We will return to Leith but must first follow the fortunes of Picton and the 3rd Division.

About 8 p.m. the 3rd Division moved to its forming-up places. At 9 p.m. the order to advance was given, Kemp's brigade leading followed by the Portuguese and Campbell's brigade. Joe Palmer, a subaltern in the 27th Regiment seconded to the Portuguese army,

> . . . had been sent ahead by General Kemp to wade the Rivillas where it flowed under the castle and ascertain whether it was passable for troops. Under cover of our artillery fire most of the division crossed by a narrow mill dam, others waded the river. Discovered by the enemy they were subjected to bombardment while illuminated by numerous rockets. On a signal for our batteries to cease fire the troops advanced to the assault preceded by the 5th Battalion of the 60th Regiment, with bugles sounding, their task to clear the embrasures.[21]

The generally accepted version of what then occurred is that from some confusion Kemp had the ladders placed against the curtain wall between the San Pedro and San Antonio bastions instead of against the castle wall, as Wellington intended. Under a tremendous fire the assailants struggled for an hour to get a foothold on the ramparts without success, during which time first Picton then Kemp were wounded. Palmer told a different story: 'After having gone fifty yards on my hands and knees (the declivity being so great as not to admit walking) I at last got hold of the ladder. We all mounted and got a footing on the ramparts, and we then began shouting – "Viva Ferdinando Septima!" The 45th Regiment entered the Castle, the French flag was instantly torn down and a soldier's redcoat substituted.'

According to the conventional version, Picton, on recovering from the shock of the wound, directed Campbell's brigade against a part of the castle wall that was lower, having been damaged in the previous siege. Here the escalade was led by the grenadiers of the 5th Fusiliers under the intrepid Lt-Col Ridge, who was subsequently killed. The loss of the castle, marked by the bugles of the assailants sounding the rally, was a blow to French morale, even though Picton's men found themselves barricaded within it.

Just as significant was the action of the 5th Division. The operations at the breach had drawn off some of the defenders from the vicinity of the San Vincente bastion; nevertheless when Leith's men attempted an escalade, about midnight, they found the defences well-manned. The assailants met with musketry fire from the ramparts and artillery fire from the flanks. Walker's brigade gained the ramparts and he sent one battalion to clear some houses in the town while the 4th Foot, moving south along the ramparts, cleared three bastions. The French rallied and drove them back but a second brigade was now on the ramparts. Checking the French, they entered the town in two columns and spread out towards the breaches, their bugles blowing, which, answered from the castle, brought about the collapse of the enemy's resistance.

At one o'clock in the morning Philippon led the remainder of the garrison into Fort San Cristobal where five hours later he capitulated. What followed, though less than many of the excesses of the French, left a strain on the character of the British Army. Badajoz was sacked and for three days was in the hands of a drunken mob of British and Portuguese soldiery. Plunder, rape and murder were the order of the day. Some eye-witness accounts tell of old men, women and children being shot and bayoneted. Others say that not many were killed, but that all were left without a rag to cover them or a morsel to eat. Every house was broken into and of the plunderers the women who followed the British camp were the most assiduous.

Against this must be recorded that many officers and men risked their lives in protecting and escorting the innocent to refuge in the church of St John, on which Wellington had had a military guard mounted, or to the British camp, while others found protection by offering accommodation to British officers. Governor Philippon and his two daughters were only saved from outrage through being escorted by two British officers with drawn swords.

The behaviour of the British troops must be judged against the contemporary customs of war. Because of the great casualties which an assailant must expect if forced to carry a place by assault, it had become common practice to summons a place before making an assault. If the summons was accepted terms of surrender were negotiated, which probably included the garrison marching out 'with the honours of war'. If the summons was rejected and the place carried by assault, the garrison was considered to have lost the right to quarter and the place would be sacked unless the inhabitants were considered friendly. Napoleon had complicated the issue by decreeing that any governor who gave up a place before withstanding at least one assault would be executed. Wellington never put a garrison to the sword but sometime later he wrote:

> The consequence of this regulation of Bonaparte's was the loss of the flower of my army, in the assault on Ciudad Rodrigo and Badajoz. I should have thought myself justified in putting both garrisons to the sword and if I had done so at the first, it is probable I should have saved 5,000 men at the second . . . the practice which refuses quarter to a garrison that stands an assault is not a *useless* effusion of blood.[22]

Of those 5,000 men, 3,500 were British. The men were in a savage and vengeful mood, and the inhabitants had shown themselves anything but friendly when British troops were quartered in Badajoz in 1810. The day after the assault Power's Portuguese Brigade was ordered into Badajoz and all British troops were ordered out. The same day Wellington issued an order: 'It is now full time that the plunder of Badajoz should cease.'

At five next morning a party of N.C.O.s from each regiment, under an officer, was to go into the town to pick up stragglers, and the Provost Martial was ordered to erect two gallows in the town to execute any men found in the act of plundering. These orders seem to have had little effect. Next day, Wellington complained that Power's brigade, instead of being a protection to the people, plundered them more than those who stormed the town. The brigade nevertheless remained in Badajoz under arms and the town was put out of bounds to all British soldiers without a pass. This order ended with an appeal to all commanders, staff and regimental officers to assist in putting an end to the disgraceful scenes of drunkenness and plunder that were going on in Badajoz. On the ninth order was finally restored.

The courage and tenacity of the British soldiers had been unsurpassed and when, on the day of surrender, Wellington visited the glacis and saw the piles of dead, he broke down and wept. The regiments of the 4th and Light Divisions had suffered greviously but none so much, proportion to their strength, as the 4th Foot of Leith's division who had 230 killed and wounded out of, at most, 530 all ranks. More serious still were the losses among that rare commodity, the Royal Engineers. Out of twenty-four officers employed as engineers, thirteen were killed or wounded.

Wellington had considered following up the fall of Badajoz with an advance to drive Soult from Andalusia, but the state of the defences of Ciudad Rodrigo was causing him anxiety, so he decided to turn north while leading Soult to believe that his interest lay in advancing into Andalusia. After the fall of Badajoz the French again fell back on Llerena. Cotton, together with three cavalry brigades, was sent in pursuit and on the eleventh occurred a brilliant cavalry affair in which the French were routed and pursued from Villagarcia to Llerena. As part of Wellington's cover plan, Graham was ordered to ask for 40,000 rations in Zafra.

At the end of March, Marmont, with 26,000 men and fifteen days' supplies, started to advance on Ciudad Rodrigo. Though harassed by Wilson's Lusitanian Legion and Trant's Portuguese Militia, he blockaded the fortress while continuing to advance against Alten's independent brigade of the King's German Legion, who fell back before him on Castello Branco. On the fifteenth day after leaving Salamanca, Marmont was within ten miles of that town, but running short of supplies he began to retreat. Wellington started to move his troops northward, leaving Hill, firmly based on Badajoz, to command in the south.

On the twenty-second the British were back at Alfaiates, near the Portuguese frontier. The keys of Spain were firmly in Wellington's hands after a brilliant, though expensive campaign and on 24 April, the day before John Aitchison arrived back in Lisbon, Marmont returned to Salamanca.

CHAPTER FOUR

1812
The Year of
Salamanca and Burgos

———✦———

THE year 1812 was not only the year in which Napoleon was to meet with disaster in Russia, and the United States to declare war against Great Britain, it was also the year in which the initiative in the Peninsula passed to Wellington. His control of the frontier fortresses enabled him to concentrate his forces for a thrust into Spain by the Guadiana valley in the south or via Salamanca in the north without exposing Portugal to counter-invasion. It was not only Wellington's success which gave the Allies the initiative – Napoleon had confirmed it by decreeing a defensive strategy for the French armies in Spain while he was conducting his campaign against Russia.

Organizing and marshalling the Grande Armée for the invasion of Russia had absorbed more and more of Napoleon's energies, and though he continued for a time under the delusion that he could effectively control from Paris the independent French armies in Spain, even he was under no illusion that this could be done once he had entered Poland or Russia. He therefore ordered a reorganization of the French forces in Spain, in particular reducing Marmont's Army of Portugal, and appointed as commander-in-chief his brother Joseph, whom he had taken every opportunity to humiliate and taught his marshals to despise, with Marshal Jourdan as Chief of Staff. Even so the position of Dorsenne, commanding the Army of the North, remained ill-defined, since Napoleon treated Spain north of the Ebro as a part of Metropolitan France and not within Joseph's domain.

Before John Aitchison left England in April, the clubs were already alive with speculation over Napoleon's coming war against Russia, though Napoleon did not leave Paris for Dresden until 9 May nor cross the Niemen with an army of 400,000 men until 22 June. Many people in England expected the campaign in the east to lead to the virtual withdrawal of French forces from Spain and advocated that Britain should do the same – a possibility which caused Wellington, who did not believe in any such French withdrawal, concern. This was accentuated by the murder of Spencer Percival in the House of Commons by a businessman who had been ruined and unhinged by the war. A month of political uncertainty followed which was ended by the Regent appointing Lord Liverpool, who had done very well at the War Office, to the premiership with Castlereagh as Foreign Secretary, much to Wellington's satisfaction.

Wellington's assumption about French intentions in Spain proved correct. The Guard and the Polish units were withdrawn to the Russian front and replaced by less experienced troops. There was also a general post among French commanders; many of those with long experience of Spain were given corps in the Grande Armée – among them Ney, Junot, Reynier, Mortier, Victor and Macdonald.

Aitchison was impressed by the improvements which had taken place in the Peninsular army during his eighteen months' absence, particularly in regard to the administration, yet he often complained of the lack of transport. Some comment therefore is called for, the more so because the future success of that army depended not only on its having been trained to manoeuvre on the battlefield but also on Wellington's having given it sustained strategic mobility by reorganizing the commissariat.

British sea-power provided the firm base for Wellington's supply system and a permanent threat to the enemy's supply lines, a situation which might have been weakened had the war with the United States come earlier. Harassment of the French lines of communication along Spain's eastern seaboard and the support given to the Spaniards in eastern and southern Spain by the Royal Navy has already been referred to, and was now supplemented by an Anglo–Sicilian force under Lord William Bentinck. The British Commissioner in Corunna, Sir Howard Douglas, obtained a small squadron under Commodore Sir Home Popham with a force of marines for similar operations on the Biscay coast. Sea-power also enabled supplies to be landed at many points on the Portuguese coast, an advantage increased by spring 1812 since Wellington had had the navigability of the Douro and Tagus improved so that supplies could be brought as far east as Barca de Alva, on the Spanish frontier, along the former, and to Alcantara by the latter.

For the shortage of land transport that Aitchison complained of, some blamed Wellington, some the government. Neither judgment was fair. The basic land transport in the Peninsula was the pack mule and the bullock cart. The British Army required some 10,000 mules in addition to the baggage mules permanently attached to every unit. For example, a troop of Royal Horse Artillery with six guns required 205 mules for its baggage and supplies. Mules were the life-blood of the Portuguese peasantry so that the number available for the armies was severely limited. The deficiency had to be made good by buying mules in North Africa and by hiring Spanish muleteers, who had to be paid in gold – of which, as already noted, there was a great shortage, while the armies' purchase of mules sent the market rocketing.

Wellington also tackled with vigour the shortage of bullock carts. The Portuguese ones were too slow and cumbersome and he set his new commissary-general, Bisset, to work during winter 1811 having a specially designed cart manufactured in Oporto and Almeida. The limited number of waggons of the waggon train set out from England, being sprung, were reserved for use as ambulances. The target figure was 800 carts, each to be drawn by two bullocks. The bullocks were bought and their drivers hired.

The carts were organized into two echelons of 400 carts each, each echelon being divided into eight divisions, each sub-divided into two brigades of twenty-five carts and fifty-four bullocks, four bullocks being spare.

The commissariat, which came under the Treasury, had in general made great progress over the past three years. At the outset it had been hopelessly inadequate for the Treasury's experience was mainly from wars in the Low Countries, colonial campaigns, or operations within easy reach of the sea and having direct naval support. So frequently had the British fought in Flanders that the commissariat operated there through long-established firms of local contractors! In the Peninsula things were very different. Supplies were scarce and had to be purchased direct from the farmer and transported long distances over atrocious roads and mountain tracks. Wellington was well served by his commissary-generals but it had taken three years before Whitehall had come to understand the conditions.

John Aitchison sailed in convoy from Portsmouth shortly after 10 April. Like so many others, he does not seem to have fully recovered from his illness, almost certainly malaria contracted in the Guadiana valley.

London
9th April 1812

My dear Father,

I am just going to the city to arrange about having a newspaper sent me. I understand the controller of the foreign post will do it – they arrive regularly and cost very little more than in London. When I was in Portugal before I hardly ever got them regularly.

Lisbon
2nd May 1812

My dear Father,

The wind came round to the south 5 days ago and as there is every probability of its continuing I can't expect my pony in any reasonable time. I have determined therefore to buy another in the meantime, and to leave this for the army in the beginning of next week. Animals are incredibly dear just now. For a mule which I would not have given £15 formerly I have paid £27 10/-. They are in great demand at Lisbon – they are scarce and Regiments being constantly landed here and a few days only being allowed officers to provide themselves – the people know it and will not sell but at an exorbitant price.

I should have wished to have remained here several weeks but the movements of the army are so sudden that I feel uncomfortable remaining behind and seeing everybody going to join. In my own opinion and from everything I can hear there will be no action where the Guards are – the opinion here is that they will return almost immediately with Lord Wellington to the south. Having effected the object of the movement to the north (*viz* to raise the blockade of Rodrigo) there would be no reason why they should remain there. Marmont has retired to the Tormes and were Lord W. to advance he would retire further. Commissary General tells me we are throwing in large supplies to Badajoz – from which it seems probable operations will be come active in that quarter – should we proceed to raise the siege of Cadiz it will be necessary to leave a considerable force to check Marmont – the incursion he made into Portugal during the siege of Badajoz was destructive to the part he visited. An order has arrived that all detachments for the 3rd, 4th and 5th divisions are to remain here till further orders, which strengthens the report of Lord Wellington's return to the south, with the greater part of the army leaving General Graham with the 1st Division (ours) to watch Marmont in the north. He did not burn the towns but he destroyed all the standing corn in his power, and every inhabitant who did not flee was brutally murdered.

On Marmont's withdrawal to Salamanca, Wellington put the army into widely dispersed cantonments stretching from north of the Douro almost to the Sierra Morena in the south, with the units as close as possible to supply depots where they were to rest, train and prepare themselves for the coming offensive into Spain. There was, however, one more enterprise to be carried out – the destruction of Marmont's pontoon bridge over the Tagus at Almaraz, which Hill had had to abandon in January. Now, with the capture of Soult's pontoon train in Badajoz, success at Almaraz would deny any communication between Soult and Marmont by bridge west of Toledo.

Heavily fortified works covered the approaches to both ends of the bridge. Hill was again given the task of destruction, and set out with a force of 6,000 including six heavy cannon and some field pieces. He crossed the Sierra between the Guadiana and Tagus by the Pass of Santa Cruz on 15 May and successfully and skilfully accomplished his mission on the nineteenth having to withdraw immediately to avoid being cut off. In support, Wellington moved the 1st and 6th Divisions under Graham to Portalegre, with orders to be ready to advance to Badajoz should the French make a dash for that fortress. Alarmist reports from Erskine, commanding the cavalry, caused the 6th Division to be advanced there.

In fact Soult was greatly alarmed by Hill's audacious march, believing it to herald a major offensive by Wellington into Andalusia – a belief the latter was anxious to sustain and one that was shared by John Aitchison. In fact Wellington had his eyes on the north where he feared that Marmont might act against Ciudad Rodrigo and Almeida whose defence by Don Carlos de España he could not rely on.

The Allies could now put 60,000 men in the field, enough to make a formidable incursion into Spain but because of the forces which, given time, the French could concentrate against Wellington, insufficient to sustain a prolonged and decisive campaign. For this reason he chose to enter Spain by Ciudad Rodrigo, leaving Hill with some 18,000 men firmly based on Badajoz. For by the northern route his advance threatened Madrid and the French main line of communication to Bayonne. This would draw French forces away from Andalusia and eastern Spain and create opportunities for offensive action by the Spanish regular and guerrilla forces. Moreover the French were most mobile just after the harvest, which had already taken place in the south but not yet in the north.

From the time of his return to the end of the war, John Aitchison wrote less frequently to his family but recorded his activities and observation in a diary.

Lisbon

My dear Father,   *7th May 1812*

As the *Impetueux* has sailed [with his brother, Midshipman Robert Aitchison] I have no longer an inducement to remain in Lisbon. My pony is not arrived and I have given up thought of seeing it soon; I have therefore bought a beast in the meantime in its stead, which I have sent off with mules and Lewis today, and tomorrow I follow myself in company of Sir A. Murray, an Ensign in the regiment, with our baggage. We go by water 30 miles (to Villa Franca), and there landing our mules we proceed to Cartaxo that night: which will be making about 50 miles in one day.

General Graham with his division (in which are the Guards) have returned to the south of the Tagus and are now in Niza awaiting the arrival of shoes, shirts, etc., etc., on the receipt of which, it is believed, the army of Alemtejo under Lord Wellington will resume offensive operations. The first movement will be against Seville -- from the preparations it would appear certain that there will be a very active and long campaign in the south. Large magazines are forming and each soldier is being furnished with a small tin pot, to cook his own provisions – the large ones called camp kettles are to be discontinued, and the mules hitherto used for carrying them are now to carry sufficient tents for the men of their respective companies – this arrangement I think will have a salutary effect of ameliorating (if not of preventing) those dreadful complaints which exposure to the dew in the night in Estremadura during the warm season invariably produces.[1]

Lord Wellington still has his headquarters in Fuente Guinaldo (near Rodrigo) and on removing will leave three divisions under General Picton to watch Marmont, who did not in his last excursion muster above 17,000 effective – not leaving his Senior (*Graham*) with a detached army has given rise to many unfavourable reports and from a circumstance which occurred during the siege of Badajoz at Llerena, where it was expected General Graham would surprise and take 1,500 men, the critics now deny him every military virtue but zeal and courage – by the accounts given by those present there certainly appears to have been much blundering – a forced march was made by the first division during the night with every probability of success, and owing to an excess of zeal in the General at one time and also *extreme precaution*, the enterprise miscarried – and in one of those accidents, to which movements in the night are liable, our own men fired on one another and two officers and some of the 7th Division were killed and wounded. As this is a point of extreme delicacy for anyone but an eyewitness to speak of I give this information for yourself solely – I am under no apprehension that you would without this hint have noticed it outside of the family but (as I have heard you say before) it will be perhaps as well to keep it to yourself only.[2]

Diary
Niza
15th May 1812

Arrived and joined the army having left Lisbon on the 8th, during which time we halted 2 days on the road. Great improvement has taken place in Portugal since I was here before. The general appearance of the country is certainly much improved by the cultivation of corn being extended and husbandry has advanced perhaps more during the last two years than in the preceding century. The destruction of the old implements by the enemy has compelled the purchase of new ones and the scarcity of bullocks and labour has induced the farmer to adopt the system which produces the best crops at least expense, and accordingly improved implements have been adopted which but for this necessity the natural aversion to changes in rules and lives would most probably have prevented. From the end of the French invasion, good to the general community has certainly arisen. There remains, however, many sad monuments which cannot fail to excite regret that it should have been purchased so dearly. In every town and on the roads there are standing on former good houses nothing but the bare walls – everywhere the population is scanty and confidence is not yet completely restored – no house is completely furnished and, in most, the roof and the floor are either destroyed or the window shutters and doors have been taken for firewood or in malice destroyed.

Every department of the army is wonderfully improved – the commissariat arrangements particularly now seem admirable. Depots are formed of cattle which are fed on the flats in the valley of the Tagus – each bullock being marked and a driver to every fifty with the superior ones to every 200 – the movable depots are managed in the same way. The mules for the transport of supplies and stores are on the same footing, a superior being answerable for a brigade (equal to 50) with men again under him. These receive a dollar a day for each mule and find food for themselves and animals. Each mule is bound to carry 200 lbs.

The artillery also seem much improved and they now move the 9 pdrs over roads which when we first came into the country would hardly have been considered practicable for 3 pdrs. Two horses have been added to the number usual to each gun at home and they are all in excellent condition. Ld Wellington has arranged for the meadows to be cut for hay in the autumn, so that although the animals following the army (which are at least trebled) are abundantly supplied with forage, there is a great probability of having plenty in the autumn.

Diary
Niza
19th May 1812

General Hill with the 2nd Division of Infantry has advanced (supposed against the bridge at Almaraz). General Drouet in consequence has moved

forward from Llerena to create a diversion – General Graham has therefore advanced the 6th Division to the neighbourhood of Badajoz to be
ready to support General Hill and the 1st Division is ordered to be ready to
move at a moment's warning.

Headquarters still continues at Fuente Guinaldo and the 3rd, 4th and
Light Divisions on the Agueda. All the tents from Lisbon have been
ordered to Abrantes and magazines are forming in Castel Branco, Badajoz
and Elvas. The bridge over the Tagus at Alcantara, which was blown up in
the Spring of 1809, is being repaired – the centre arch, which is the one
destroyed, is of so great a span that no trees can be found long enough to
reach across. It is therefore being made passable by means of cables
stretched by capstans, over which double rows of planks are laid – this
under the direction of Major Sturgeon of the Staff Corps.[3] The repairing of
this bridge will be of the utmost importance in rendering the communication easy between our armies north and south of the Tagus in the ulterior
operations of the campaign. The nearest communication heretofore has
been via Villa Velha, which has thrown the troops out three marches.
These will be avoided by crossing at Alcantara, while by destroying the
bridge at Almaraz the communication of the enemy by the direct route will
be cut off, which must render the situation of any corps requiring support
precarious – their direct communication with the south of the Tagus will
now be by Arzobispo and that road is so bad as to be hardly passable for
artillery. Should Ld Wellington succeed in destroying the bridge at
Almaraz and in re-establishing the one at Alcantara his future operations,
which I suppose will be directed against Seville, are likely to be attended
with success.

Diary
Castello de Vide
Wednesday 20th May 1812

An order arrived during the night and the Guards[4] and the Highland
Brigade moved here, and the German Legion which had arrived yesterday
moved on to make room for us. Castello de Vide is surrounded by a wall
with parapet. It is of an oblong form occupying a valley and two hills from
north-west to south-east. On each of these hills are regular fortifications;
the one on the N. West is a Moorish castle of stone with outworks, but is
now out of repair; no part of the works has cannon and the castle was
blown up by the Spaniards in Don John the 2nd's reign and still is
unrepaired – the walls, however, all round are entire and would make a
good defence against 4 or 5,000 men – and, with only the inhabitants,
would prevent contributions from being raised.[5] As a frontier town therefore it is of importance. About three miles to eastward is Marvao, a very
strong fortress on the summit of a craggy mountain. Its approaches are
difficult and appeared impregnable. The Guards and Wheatley's Highland
Brigade with one battalion, the King's German Legion, are quartered in
Castello de Vide – there's plenty of room and excellent quarters.

Diary
Saturday 23rd May 1812

Went to Marvao – the strength of this fortress is in its situation. The road to it is narrow and remarkably steep and might easily be rendered impracticable. The works are chiefly Moorish and in some places so low as might be escaladed unless defended by a strong garrison of, I think, 2,000 men. The defences have however been improved by some new counter guards which alas flank the old walls, so that in its present state I would deem it impregnable – surprise or starvation are the only ways to obtain possession of it; there are no wells in it but it is well-supplied (particularly the castle) with water from tanks.

Castello de Vide
27th May 1812
(South Eastern Frontier)

Throughout the extent of country which I have yet seen, there is (I am happy to say) an astonishing improvement since I was here before. Increased industry has supplied the want of numbers, and not withstanding the scarcity of labourers, occasioned by the demands of the army, the cultivation of corn is more extensive, and the land in higher order, than it appeared to be during the two former years I was in Portugal. This observation is particularly applicable to the neighbourhood of Lisbon, and the whole of the country within the lines; where every inch is under cultivation – spots which formerly were left untouched, now bear luxuriant crops of corn, and the land is even tilled under the olive trees in such parts as I think would not in my own country defray the expense. This revolution at the hands of the Portuguese shows the great effect of necessity as a stimulus. Bread which formerly cost 1½d and 2d now cost 5d or 6d and every article of necessity of life is up, nearly in the same proportion. The labourer now gains 2/6d and 3/- a day, which to a man with a family is barely sufficient for a livelihood, while formerly he was well paid with 15d.

We came by the valley of the Tagus for about 100 miles – the greater part was quite new to me, and it certainly is by much the best cultivated part of Portugal I have seen. In some places the flat extends for several miles on each side of the Tagus – the whole almost is covered with water during winter – but nevertheless it nearly all becomes dry enough for the plough, and is so enriched by the slime which the water deposits that although they were only sowing wheat and Indian corn the crop will be ready for the sickle in August and September.

At Gallega I had an opportunity of seeing the implements used by a very great farmer and I was surprised to find they have been in the habit of using a harrow, which has only lately been introduced into East Lothian as an improvement. It was not of the same shape as used in Scotland but the teeth are placed so as to act on the same principle, and bullocks being used in place of horses perhaps the large *oblong* is preferable to the *lozenge* on light soil. It was from the valley of the Tagus that Massena drew the provisions which enabled him to remain so long in Portugal, and I am persuaded that the destruction caused by the enemy has been of benefit to the country in exciting the natives to exertions which left to themselves they would never have made.

At Punhete I became melancholy – it was a great station of the enemy and has been almost destroyed. In that town, beautifully situated at the complex of the Zezere and Tagus, we were quartered for a fortnight after driving the French from Oporto, and before we entered Spain. Our regiment in officers was as we had left England – *all known to each other and friends* – of the houses which afforded us quarters there are many without roofs – almost none but one wanting window shutters and doors – the fine olive trees too by the riverside, which afforded us friends a delightful shade in our walks, have been cut down, and there now remains *only the rotten stumps* – enough to draw a tear of sympathy – in bringing to my remembrance some amiable men, and the many happy days I had spent with them.

Such friendship is lasting, and trifles often bring to recollection incidents which at the time passed unnoticed – these often recur now, since joining the Battalion more than formerly – my old friends are almost all gone, so much changed are the officers, than only *one other* and myself are now here who were in action at Talavera.

Little known, however, as I was to some, and stranger to many, my reception by the officers was much more flattering than my most sanguine hope could have anticipated – all have been attentive and I have not yet been supposed to dine at home. I wrote to you (I believe) that I had ordered wings to Portsmouth – I brought them to Lisbon, but notwithstanding, am not in the Light Infantry. . . . I did not write my wish of returning to the Lt company to the Commanding Officer from England – he therefore did not know it. . . in the meantime another company per regiment having been ordered to be formed to act when required as Light Infantry, he has appointed me to the command of the company he had fixed on for that purpose – so that now except wearing the dress (which I might do if I chose) I am still a Light Company. . .[6]

Before this arrives you will have heard of General Hill's success at Almazar and know the particulars better than we do here. The French made an advance with Drouet's corps to distract our attention – in consequence Sir. T. Graham moved forward troops under him to support General Hill in case of need. We marched to this town from Niza on the 20th and were proceeding to Spain (indeed had crossed the boundary) when we were overtaken with an order to return, the object of our move being at an end by General Hill's success. We have been here ever since, but are ordered to return to Niza *tomorrow*; and the whole army in the Alemtejo are to return to their former cantonments. This circumstance has set speculation at work again, and opinions are much divided whether it is preparatory to a march to the north or south. For myself I am quite undecided as to the reasons, [for] either [move], they are equally cogent. It would certainly be a great object to raise the siege of Cadiz, but whether this can be done by our moving to Seville with half our army, leaving Marmont in our rear with 22,000 men, is questionable. Alternatively, having General Hill's corp cut the bridge of Almaraz (i.e. the enemy's direct and certain line of communication), would it not be practicable to overwhelm Marmont with our whole army moving in his front? – while General Hill moves on his flank by Talavera de la Reyna to threaten the Capital and probably oblige the enemy to evacuate it – this appears to me very likely to be attempted if it be true, as I hear, that three regiments which have just arrived at Lisbon are ordered to Cadiz.

Should the capital be threatened by a force superior to what is now near it, and that I believe we have, the enemy must recall part of his troops from Andalusia, and I think the British from Cadiz with the Spaniards ought to be nearly equal to what will remain – the enemy's boats near it being very strong I am not sanguine that we can have a force sufficient to take them. In short everything is so secret here that we argue much in the dark – it appears however certain from every preparation, that we should have a *most active and long campaign.*[7] I take all the valuable precautions recommended by Doctor B. I have a good stock of medicine and shall not fatigue myself with walking as long as I can avoid it – from that I believe originated my bilious fever in 1809 and the effects of it are yet in my constitution.

We have the prospect of being well fed (which we were not then); *our commissariat seems admirably arranged;* we have now always full rations of meat, biscuits and spirits, the men are remarkably healthy – there is an appearance of a better vintage than has been for five years – so say the natives.

Wellington held his cards very close to his chest and it is clear from Aitchison's letters that very few within his command knew or guessed of his intention to advance on Salamanca. Having collected the main body of the army around Ciudad Rodrigo he advanced on 13 June with an Anglo–Portuguese army of 43,000, in three columns, and 4,000 Spaniards in a fourth under Carlos de España. Light dragoons or hussars led all three columns. Aitchison's description of the advance of the 3rd Regiment of Guards with the 1st Division, is taken from his letters and diary.

Diary
Niza
Thursday 28th May 1812

The Brigade returned here, the army having been ordered to re-occupy the cantonments they had before advancing. This retrograde movement when everybody looked to an order to march south has given rise to much speculation, and Castille instead of Andalusia is fixed on as the scene of our first operations. On consideration this one appears to me more probable than the other, holding Ld Wellington's object to be the raising of the siege of Cadiz. We could not move against Seville (which is the apex of the enemy's operations in the south) with a prospect of success in our ulterior operations unless with such a force as to bear down all opposition by Soult's army in the field, and this we could not have while Marmont remains on the frontier of Portugal with his present force, which is estimated at 22,000 men.

It is imperative therefore either to destroy the armies of Soult or Marmont or by driving them to such a distance from each other as to ensure an attack upon one before the other could move to his assistance, and a direct movement against Marmont first appears to be best. Because by getting possession of Salamanca we shall see a fruitful part of Spain, thereby diminishing the enemy's resources and increasing our own, and destroying its defences we shall insure the northern frontier of Portugal as no enemy can move against it with a prospect of success without a secure depot in his rear – our movement on Salamanca will also set the Galician army at liberty to act beyond its own province and force the enemy in the interior to concentrate. The Capital too by this movement will be in imminent danger, and if the enemy adopt the policy which they pursued in 1809 of risking everything for its defence they must diminish their forces in Aragon, Catalonia and at Valencia so much as to paralyse all their efforts in these quarters, and the good which must thus arise to the general cause will be very great.

Diary
Camp near Ciudad Rodrigo
12th June 1812

On the *31st May* the Brigade passed the Tagus by the bridge at Villa Velha and proceeded to Sernadas and the neighbouring villages – it was thus in the afternoon before we ended our march and the way being very bad and the day uncommonly warm. Great numbers of the men were knocked up. The distance 22 miles. 1st June to Castello Branco, 7 miles, the route showed marks of the enemy, the houses being generally damaged and unfurnished – people were returning in considerable numbers to the town and the market was well supplied with butter, cheese, eggs and salad.

9th – halted at Puebla de Azava, where were assembled 4 divisions of Infantry and 3 brigades of cavalry.

Camp
10th June 1812

Since I wrote to James yesterday an order came to march and we crossed the frontier at Alamedilla this morning and are now encamped about 4 miles beyond it – three brigades of cavalry and 4 divisions of infantry with their artillery are assembled here – the whole army will cross the Agueda tomorrow – nothing more is known yet, but there seems every probability of our continuing . . . brilliant as it has commenced.

Diary

11th – by El Bodon to two miles beyond Pastores near the Agueda – bivouac much crowded and very little cover – water at a distance, scarce and bad. 14 miles, 8 hours.

12th – Halted. I went to Ciudad Rodrigo; the breach is still unfinished but it is made secure against surprise by Gabions and the Spaniards have a great number of men employed repairing it. It is being done in a superior style to the old wall, being of fine hewn stone and advanced beyond the salient angle so as to produce an enfilade fire on either face by a gun traversing in barbette. The walls of Rodrigez are very defective, having been built in the time of the Moors; the salient angles are in many points not defended but by their own fire – the flanks in general appear too retired and distant to produce a proper defence to the salient angles but to remedy these defects there appears to have been constructed a sort of Fausse Braye, which in several points opposite the long faces projects towards the country so as to produce flank fire, and this work is advantageously situated. The situation of the town is extremely defective as an enemy could break ground within point-blank range unmolested from the intervention of a rising ground, and from this point the works are overlooked. To remedy this defect the French, when in possession, erected a redoubt on the hill (The Great Teson) but this work was carried by assault on Ld Wellington investing the place in January and converted into a work of attack. It has since been put into a proper state of defence and two more redoubts communicating with this are constructed in advance so as to cover the whole hill, and on rising ground in rear and between it and the town there is also a new 4 sided work constructing so that the approach of an enemy will be very much impeded. Ciudad Rodrigo is at present garrisoned by 3,000 Spaniards who in personal appearance, appointments and clothing are by much the most wretched I ever saw. Bread 1 dollar for four pounds.

Monday 15th June 1812

On passing the frontier on 10th inst I did myself the pleasure to write to you from Puebla de Azava: we continued to march on the following day to the banks of the Agueda, where we halted on 12th (to allow the commissariat arrangements being completed) and on that day the whole army consisting of seven divisions of Infantry and *Three* brigades of Cavalry (British) were assembled in the neighbourhood of Ciudad Rodrigo. [Diary: '. . . with their field artillery and four battering pieces'.]

The army was divided in *Three* corps: and at daybreak on the 13th forded the Agueda in *three* columns. The right corps (commanded by Sir T. Graham) consists of the 1st, 6th and 7th Divisions of Infantry with their artillery and the 14th regiment of the Light Dragoons took the road to Tamames – Ld Wellington himself superintends the centre corps – it consists of the 5th and Light Divisions of British Infantry commanded by

General Leith, and Sir S. Cotton with most of the Cavalry move also with it and the battering train follows the same route.

The left corps is commanded by Gen. Picton and consists of the 3rd and 4th Divisions of British Infantry, General Packs's brigade of Portuguese Lt troops, and one regiment of British cavalry. These three corps are estimated at 40,000 men of whom 3,200 are cavalry. This includes the Portuguese Infantry, one brigade of whom are attached to each division of British except the 1st (ours).

Besides this force, Gen. Hill has the 2nd Division of British and Gen. Hamilton a division of Portuguese Infantry and the Portuguese Cavalry, so that the whole of our force in the field cannot be much under 60,000 men effective. Although on the spot I know nothing for certain of the *general intentions,* it is however known that on moving from Ciudad Rodrigo it was designed the army should be at the end of the 3rd day's march about 4 leagues from Salamanca – we are now encamped within 6 leagues, we have not yet seen any enemy, though they were said to have had a post within a few miles of our camp last night, but we shall probably have an affair with them the day after tomorrow should they have the temerity to remain in Salamanca, and I need not say that the general feeling of the troops at this moment makes us confident it will be glorious.

It seems however likely that they will not so soon make a stand but that Marshal Marmont will unite those forces to cover the Capital which are now cantoned on the extensive line between Talavera de la Reyna and Salamanca. Ld Wellington is prepared for him, act how he may – the columns are in communication with each other and the roads by which they move are not above 4 miles' distant. Should the enemy therefore choose to fight at Salamanca we *are* united, and if not but retires to the *defence* of Madrid, we shall follow him and overtake him – the 1st Corps from its position is likely to have the honour of leading and I hope to have the happiness to write you in a few days the glorious result of our exertions. We have extensive magazines on the Portuguese frontier and the movable depot has 30 days' supplies.

Work on the defences when completed will add much to the strength of that important place but the garrison are such miserable-looking wretches that I fear even with these it will not make so noble a defence in any future attack as it did two years ago against Massena. The country round it has been terribly destroyed – the villages are almost all destroyed – and the inhabitants have returned and *seemly starved* and during the whole of our march yesterday, which was a very long one, we did not see *one* ear of corn – today however the prospect brightened and the country we passed over was well cultivated (altho' houses much destroyed) and covered with luxurious crops of wheat which to every appearance will be ready to cut in under a month.

Diary

17th June appeared on the heights about two miles from Salamanca at 5 o'clock, where we halted till the 6th and Lt Divisions and the Cavalry forded the Tormes – the former at a ford about three miles and the latter about two miles above the town – we then proceeded on our march and forded at the ford of Santa Marta – it is very broad and at the deepest part three and a half feet – bivouacked on the Tormes on the right of the Ford – the enemy, in numbers about 8,000, retired early this morning on the road to Toro and left about 800 men in three small forts lately constructed to cover the bridge. They have burnt or destroyed every house and building within musket shot. These forts were invested by 6th Division, and broke ground at 2 o'clock within 400 yards of the body of the main one.[8]

Went into Salamanca – this town is situated on the right of the Tormes partly on a rising ground and is surrounded by a high wall. The houses in general are very good though much destroyed by the enemy and the public buildings *viz* convent, churches and colleges magnificent. Many of them, however, indeed almost all, are completely destroyed, the roofs being either broken or the floors taken up for the beams. The whole town presents a sad example of the benefit of French visits. Although the town has in a manner been completely in possession of the enemy and indeed almost always occupied by them since the army of Sir John Moore was in it in 1808, it appears as much destroyed as those which were only visited by them in the predatory excursion into Portugal in 1811. There is a good market place well supplied with vegetables and fruit from the Sierra, and the Prado is large and unique – it is remarkably handsome, the houses are exactly alike on each side of the square and it is surrounded by a piazza. In Sir J. Moore's time the town held 22,000 men without being quartered on the inhabitants. I should think it would now hold scarcely half that number quartered in the same manner.

Wednesday 17th June

We are now in Salamanca, by my letter sent yesterday you will see we were near it – at daybreak this morning the army moved to the banks of the Tormes and began to ford – the enemy made no resistance to the passage – they are retired towards Toro, except two weak regiments of Foreigners who they have left in a small fort which covers the bridge – this fort has been but lately constructed and it is not yet finished, altho' the enemy have been working incessantly for the past 12 days at it – the 6th Division are to break ground before it this evening and in two or three days it is expected to be in our possession. . . .

We are encamped about 1½ miles from Salamanca – I have just been in it and I cannot say whether the people are really happy at our entrance – some certainly seem so and expressed themselves but there was great misery . . . on many countenances, which must arise from individual feeling . . . it is all the same to the poor man whether the enemy take by force or the British lay all the provisions under contribution for payment. Everything is very dear and bread particularly so, six shillings on our march have been paid for a *four* pound loaf. The wheat has a good appearance and it will soon be ripe.

There has been no fighting yet – only a little skirmish – yesterday and this morning between our advance and the enemy's rear – the 1st and 7th Divisions are in reserve at present so that *we* are not to attack the fort. We shall have our day yet and it will be a glorious one, as we have some of the best troops in the army in it.

Ld Wellington and M. Beresford have their Head Quarters in the town – the advance is about 6 miles off[9] Marmont had only about 8,000 men here all of them, but 1,200 cavalry and 4 battalions, marched to Toro some days since and these went off this morning – we shall follow but it is said will first halt a day or two for supplies. D. Julian Sanchez corps is about 4 miles off – I saw several in the town today – dressed in every uniform that can be thought of and armed with sword, pistol, carbine and lance with red flag attached to it.

PS Excuse this as it is written on a folded sheet which I had in my pocket – baggage not unpacked and the men have their accoutrements on to be ready.

Camp near Salamanca
25th June 1812

I wrote to you from the day after our arrival and I expected before now to have had the pleasure of having acquainted you with our further success but have been disappointed – we are still in the same place as when I last wrote to you and the difference in our situation, if any, is I fear against us. On the 19th the enemy showed about 16,000 men at the outposts which they gradually increased on 20th. Our advance retired and the whole army on that day moved forward to their support, to a position on a rising ground about 4 miles from this, on the road to Toro – the enemy attacked with a small force supported by their main body but were quickly driven back and they made no further attempt during that day.

On the 21st the armies remained in sight of each other . . . and we began to construct redoubts in the evening to cover our guns and strengthen our position – on 22nd Marshal Marmont having occupied a small height on our right, from which he could see part of our line, Ld Wellington attacked with two battalions and drove the enemy from it. . . . M. Marmont was evidently in great alarm and he withdrew during the night – on the morning of 23rd his rearguard was discovered on the road to Valladolid and our cavalry followed for about 15 miles when they discovered the enemy in position on a range of heights, his left on the Tormes – Marmont that evening pushed a part of his cavalry and a small body of Infantry to the left of the Tormes threatening to advance to Salamanca by that bank – the 1st Division (ours) were therefore moved from the position on the Toro road back to the ford on the Tormes and the next morning at daybreak passed to the left of the river with the 7th Division and a large body of our cavalry – the enemy meantime had passed about 2,600 cavalry and 10,000 infantry – are expected to have attacked but after being marched, counter-marched, marched, counter-marched and marched again, during the whole day, by Gen. Graham, we recrossed the river in the evening where we are now.

The enemy this morning retired about fifteen miles from here, but tomorrow they are expecting 8 or 10,000 men from Madrid and then it is supposed they will advance; we are prepared for them and I have no doubt whatever that even with these we shall beat them. Our force arriving here has about 40,000 and it is now I should think about 38,000, of which 35,000 will be all we can have in the field – the enemy will not be many (if any) more than us.

The fort has proved much stronger than was supposed – it still holds out – we have expended all our ammunition and been repulsed in one attempt to carry it by assault. The operations against it are at present at a stand – waiting the arrival of ammunition. The intention of the French is supposed to be to endeavour to get off the garrison at the fort at Salamanca without a general action – it will appear strange that our chief seems to dread a battle – his reasons must be good I suppose he has ulterior operations in view. We are well fed and will therefore fight well when we come in contact with the enemy – our baggage has been in the rear since the enemy showed themselves and is just come up, so I am much hurried, will write again soon.

SALAMANCA

The Belgian military historian Brialmont, writing in the nineteenth century, described the battle of Salamanca thus:

> The battle of Salamanca was beyond all question the most decisive which the Allies had yet delivered in the Peninsula. It established the reputation of the English army, and brought especially into light the brilliant quality of their general: a sound judgment; *a coup d'oeil*, prompt and unerring, a vigorous execution; and a rare ability on moving troops. Thibaudeau may well say that the battle of the Arapiles settled the question of the French occupation of Spain.[10]

The interest of Aitchison's correspondence about this battle lies in his high tribute to the performance of the German and, particularly, the Portuguese troops. The letter's contribution is often obscured in British histories because most of the independent Portuguese formations were commanded by British officers, the exception being the one Portuguese division, and by all the other Allied divisions being apparently British, whereas, with the exception of the 1st and Light Divisions, they all contained a Portuguese brigade, making up one-third of their establishment. The 1st Division had a brigade of the King's German Legion, and the famous Light Division had a Cacadore (Portuguese light infantry) battalion in each of its two brigades. As a background to Aitchison's description of the campaign a brief outline of it follows. It also draws attention to some important matters which he omits.

Having left Ciudad Rodrigo on 13 June, Wellington and the Allied Army were rapturously welcomed in Salamanca on the seventeeth. On their approach, Marmont, whose forces were short of rations and widely dispersed, withdrew his two divisions from the city, leaving garrisons in the three fortified convents, commanding the bridge over the Tormes, and ordered his forces to concentrate on the line of the Douro. Wellington established a covering force in a naturally strong defensive position on the heights of San Cristobal, five miles beyond the city towards Toro, and set about reducing the forts. Unfortunately, he had underestimated the problem and had too little heavy artillery and ammunition to bring about their capitulation in four days, as he had expected, and it was not until the twenty-seventh, after he had obtained further ammunition, that they succumbed, with little resistance, to assaults.

Marmont, now with a considerable army behind the Douro, came forward on 20 June and confronted Wellington at San Cristobal while attempting to turn his right flank. This caused Wellington to change front and, according to many, including John Aitchison, provided him with a chance to defeat Marmont in detail in the next two days. By the twenty-first Marmont's strength had been brought up to 35,000 and although Wellington admitted to an A.D.C. that it was 'Damn'd tempting! I have a great mind to attack them',[11] he forebore, in the hope that Marmont's manoeuvres meant that he was himself preparing an attack.

On 24 June, Marmont passed two divisions over the Tormes at Huerta. These were checked by Alten's cavalry brigade, already south of the river, and Wellington responded by moving the 1st and 7th Divisions under Graham across the river in support. With the fall of the forts, Marmont, who had been manoeuvring to raise the siege, retired behind the Douro taking up a position between Toro and Simancas, with his centre at Tordesillas where the only remaining bridge was.

Wellington followed up and occupied Pollos, Rueda, Medina del Campo and Nava del Rey, but made no attempt to cross the Douro. He wrote 'It is obvious that we could not cross without sustaining great loss, and could not fight a general action under circumstances of greater disadvantage than those which would attend the attack of the enemy's position on the Douro. The enemy's numbers are equal if not superior to ours; they have in their position twice the amount of artillery. . . .'[12] The opposing armies retained these positions during 3–16 July.

The new French commander-in-chief, King Joseph, wanted to reinforce Marmont, but his orders to Soult to send a corp northwards were ignored, though Soult agreed to maintain d'Erlon's corps to keep Hill in check. When Joseph tried to persuade Suchet to relieve some of the troops under his (Joseph's) direct command in central Spain he was equally unsuccessful. Finally he decided to take the risk of denuding this region and marched at the head of 12,000 men to join Marmont. Though rumours were rife in the Allied Army that Joseph had joined him (see Aitchison's diary), this had not occurred by the time of the battle of Salamanca. Wellington knew of this intention on the sixteenth, through intercepted letters, but Marmont was not to learn of it until later. Wellington by this time also knew that on the seventeenth, the day he laid siege to the forts of Salamanca, the United States had declared war on Britain. Only four regular British battalions garrisoned Canada, and it was clear that this new development might greatly affect the sea and land forces available to support the Peninsular War. His enemy had been similarly affected by Napoleon's invasion of Russia.

Under pressure to take the offensive, Marmont ended the stalemate on 16 July by making a feint at crossing the Douro at Toro while passing his main body over the Tordesillas bridge. Wellington ordered his left and centre to concentrate about Canizal and his right at Castrejon. Marmont first tried to turn Wellington's left and after some confused skirmishing, in which Wellington and his staff had to draw swords and gallop to escape capture, the main bodies of the two armies retreated on parallel courses in close proximity, each endeavouring to outmarch the other.

Marmont now endeavoured to turn the Allied right flank and cut the road to Ciudad Rodrigo. On the night of 22 July, in a great thunderstorm, Marmont crossed the Tormes by the fords of Huerta and Encinos de Abajo, and the Allies went over at Santa Marta and Salamanca. At dawn next day Marmont was on the heights of Calvarrasa de Arriba. All that he could see was a single British division drawn up on some high ground opposite him, and moving south from Santa Marta, and away to the west a large dust cloud. By this time he had persuaded himself that Wellington intended to avoid a general action and was retreating. The cloud, which he thought was made by Allied columns retiring, was in fact made by the baggage train. The troops he saw before him he believed to be the Allied rearguard, from whose destruction he could gain considerable kudos at little risk.

Wellington was as yet by no means certain that Marmont would not pass his main body to the west of Salamanca by the right bank of the Tormes. He therefore left the 3rd Division, commanded by Edward Pakenham, his brother-in-law, who had relieved the invalided Picton, with two cavalry brigades at Cabrerizos, north of the river, to cover his left flank, while his main body lay hidden behind the high ground on which the 7th Division, seen by Marmont, had been deployed. If he remained where he was, Wellington knew that numerically the odds would turn against him, but if he were to retreat on Ciudad Rodrigo his campaign would have ended with nothing gained. He therefore aimed to create a favourable opportunity to inflict a major defeat on Marmont.

Marmont decided to bring forward and deploy three divisions in depth on the heights of Calvarrasa, on 22 July, while sending three more to turn the Allied right and cut the Ciudad Rodrigo road. To secure his flank he ordered two steep and rugged hills to be occupied, the Lesser and Greater Arapil. Seeing his intention Wellington gave similar orders. In the resultant race the Allies secured the nearer, the Lesser Arapil, and the French the Greater, round which the battle was to rage.

As Marmont's manoeuvres had confirmed his intention to turn the Allies right, Wellington ordered the Light Division, with the 1st Division in support, to move forward of the 7th Division facing the Calvarrasa de Arriba heights, and the 4th Division to occupy a prominent hill on the right, the Teson de San Miguel. The 1st Division was moved for an attack on the Greater Arapil which was cancelled, and then returned to its position on the right of the Light

Division, leaving the Light Companies of the Guards to occupy the village of Los Arapiles. Wellington ordered Pakenham to bring the 3rd Division and the two cavalry brigades as quickly as possible from the left wing to form the right at Aldea Tejado on the Bejar-Baños road.

Wellington now built up a new front at right-angles to the old, facing south with the Greater Arapil at the hinge. The 5th Division he deployed on the right of the 4th, with the 6th and 7th Divisions in support and the cavalry on its right. The dust of the 3rd Division confirmed Marmont in his opinion that Wellington was in retreat — it must be remembered that the nature of the ground enabled Wellington's changes of position to remain largely hidden. Marmont's two leading divisions, determined to gain the Ciudad Rodrigo road as quickly as possible, allowed a gap to open up between them and the remainder. Wellington had anticipated and encouraged just such an opportunity. Confirming it through his telescope from the Lesser Arapil at about two o'clock, he turned to his Spanish aide to say: 'Mon cher Alava, Marmont est perdu!'[13] then, galloping to the head of the 3rd Division, he ordered Pakenham to advance at best speed against the head of the French column. Pack's Portuguese made a valiant but unsuccessful attempt to take the Greater Arapil and Wellington launched the 4th and 5th Divisions at the flanks of the French, while Le Marchant's heavy cavalry and the dragoons of the King's German Legion under Cotton, made a devastating charge between the 5th and 3rd Divisions.

Marmont had been severely wounded by a cannonball early in the battle but the French fought bravely though in vain. The leading French division, Thomière's, was shattered by the 3rd Division with D'Urban's cavalry in support, and ceased to be an effective formation. The next division, Macune's, was engaged by Leith's 5th Division and put to flight by a magnificient charge of the heavy dragoons led by Cotton. However, when Le Marchant's brigade carried on against the next French division, though they scattered the leading brigade, they were brought up short and Le Marchant was killed. On seeing the effect of the charge, Wellington exclaimed: 'By God, Cotton, I never saw anything so beautiful in my life, the day is yours!'[14]

Since Marmont and Bonnet were both wounded, command of the French fell to Clausel, who launched a counter-attack against the exposed right of the 4th Division (Cole). The Portuguese under Beresford's direction countered this attack and the 6th Division (Clinton) was now launched and confirmed the Allied victory. The Light Division (Baron von Alten) and 1st Division (Henry Campbell) were now sent in pursuit. Wellington had hoped to destroy the Army of Portugal but the French got away through Alba de Tormes, further up the river, which he fondly imagined was garrisoned by Carlos de España. De España, however, had withdrawn his men when the French advanced, without telling Wellington! The pursuit continued until after midnight but most of the French got clean away.

Next day, 23 July, the pursuit was led by Baron von Bock's cavalry brigade of the King's German Legion. At Garcia Hernandez they came up with the French rearguard, a division which had hardly been engaged. Four squadrons of the King's German Legion (440 men) simultaneously charged an infantry square of 500 men which they broke, and a moving column of more than twice their strength, taking 1,200 prisoners. Their valour and élan coupled with speed of decision and perfect control made this engagement, in the words of Fortescue, 'one of the great achievements of cavalry in the history of the world'.[15]

The Allies brought 46,000 men and sixty guns to the battle, the French 50,000 and seventy-four guns. French casualties were estimated at 14,000, of whom half were prisoners. The Allies had over 5,200 casualties, the proportion of Portuguese to British being two to one, and had captured two Eagles and twenty guns. Wellington's victory had been magnificent in regard to anticipation, timing and leadership on the battlefield. He is, however, open to the criticism of having performed the duties not only of the commander-in-chief but those of his divisional commanders as well. He indeed suffered from a dearth of good, experienced senior officers – the aftermath of the losses at Ciudad Rodrigo and Badajoz, since when Picton and Graham had both gone sick. Salamanca was a turning point. Wellington's army had proved not only that it could fight defensive battles, but that it could outmanoeuvre the French. It also exacerbated the shortage of senior officers, for Le Marchant was killed; Collins, commanding a Portuguese Brigade was mortally wounded; and Leith, Cole, Cotton, Beresford, and Alten were wounded in various degrees of seriousness.

Diary

26th – the supply of ammunition having arrived the battery of 18 pdrs opened in the afternoon with red-hot shot and within a few minutes set fire to the convent in the fort. The governor was yesterday in [sic] terms for surrendering and he had gone so far as talk of private baggage when on a sudden the negotiation was broken off, he says in consequence of communication from the army.

Saturday, 27th June. The fire in the convent continued this morning and was increased by the fire from a battery of hot shot – a battery erected in a new spot during the night which opened against the small forest nearest the town – the salient angle was injured and about eleven A.M., in consequence of a hint being given, the picquets advanced as if to assault when the garrison submitted without offering resistance and our men entered by the breach. Thus has terminated a defence of 9 days. Since the garrison was only expected to defend *four* the event has caused great joy in Salamanca and under every circumstance must be looked on as an event of great importance, and had it been surrendered before the 22nd inst Ld Wellington would most probably have gained a victory over the enemy on the heights of Morisco. There was a fine opening for an attack after the affaire at noon. . . .

The commander-in-chief must have had good reasons for not attacking under circumstances which to us appeared so advantageous – what they were must of course remain a secret for some time, but the ground on which the enemy stood was intersected by bogs and ditches. These would have thrown our men into confusion had we advanced and in case [inde-cipherable] might have been productive of serious loss – under reverse too the Portuguese and Spanish troops could not be relied on and the Tormes being in our rear we would have been exposed to danger in fording it. . . . The enemy retired 5 leagues. King Joseph is said to have joined with 8,000 men. Our baggage which was in the rear (about 10 miles beyond the Tormes) has been brought up to us.

Went over the whole of the forts – they are very strong and most ingeniously constructed, the ditch is very deep – works are in it for its defence and although there are no heavy ordnance mounted on the ram-parts, the light pieces are placed so as to keep a heavy fire on every point and the parapet which is of stone has loop-holes everywhere. There are no outworks, but the convent is surrounded by palisades and a breastwork of earth so as to be completely within itself. An enemy therefore having gained the works has still it to attack. The breach at the end fort [?] is so impracticable that I could not get up in open day, assisted as I was by taking hold of the Fraises.

There was plenty of every kind of supplies, both ammunition and provisions of every sort, and the only reason for surrendering therefore must have been the dread of an explosion; this is the one assigned whatever may have been the real one. The garrison marched out at 6.20 – they were composed of companies of different regiments – in the hospitals there were 60 wounded, and 11 officers and 2 men killed. The surrender of these forts has caused the enemy a loss of about 800 men and we have lost about 200. In its construction, its resistance, and finally its fall there appears something peculiar in this fort that well merits serious consideration. It is said to have been begun two years since by the enemy and to have been worked at ever since, but it is evident that no great exertions could have been made, as the defences were not near completed and the houses within range of the guns were not destroyed until the British army appeared. Thus far therefore it was imperfect but its situation is also defective, as at every point it can be approached by the assailants unperceived, and the ordnance for its defence were *all light*. Nevertheless, with a garrison of under 800, it has arrested the operations of an army of 40,000 men from 17 June (i.e. 10 days). Whether the means employed to reduce it were inadequate? Ld Wellington must not have thought so or his information must have been bad. I believe the latter but he is said to have been disappointed at its not falling the third day with the means used! He has then committed an error in undertaking an enterprise with inadequate means, or his judgment deceived him! Whichever supposition be true it has been much to the advantage of the enemy the sacrificing of these 800 men (delay was everything to them and should similar sacrifices produce or be likely to produce similar effects it will evidently be the interest of Marshal Marmont to make them). Accord-ingly I am persuaded that we shall find him acting on this system and leaving garrisons in Toro and those places on our line of operations where he has small forts. His interest (even with a superiority) appears to me to be to manoeuvre so as to maintain a strictly defensive covering of the Capital

– ours I should conceive to bring matters to issue as speedily as possible by a general attack – Ld W., however, seems to think otherwise and to look to the liberation of Spain not by one brilliant but by a series of campaigns – it must be recollected however that a general action must be fought and then the question is whether an attack in the Val de Morisco or the position near the Douro be the most in our favour? In that case the conclusion appears to me evident; but I shall pursue the argument no further because the conclusion to which I should come would be against what I really suppose right (*viz* the judgement of Ld Wellington).

Sunday, 28th June – Te Deum was celebrated this morning in the Cathedral, at which the Duke of Ciudad Rodrigo, Wellington, and all the general officers assisted. Last evening there was a general illumination, a most interesting sight. The men let off fireworks, the women in their transports kindled bonfires in the streets with baskets and chairs, and the little children in groups of six and eight danced the Bolero to a favourite national air, and accompanied themselves very prettily with castanets. This evening the inhabitants gave a ball to the Commander-in-Chief to which the officers of the Guards were invited – under all circumstances it must be allowed to be magnificent and it was a pleasant sight to witness British, Portuguese and Spanish officers joining in the same dance with the most perfect cordiality.

The natives have begun again to bring in corn. On our first arrival they did well in this respect but the resistance of the fort diminished their confidence and this left off till its fall. There is every prospect, however, now of being supplied as far as their means will allow, but corn is scarce and the bread is made chiefly from American flour and consequently very dear. Six shillings for 4 pounds. The country round Salamanca, as far as can be seen, is very open and covered with corn, chiefly wheat–agriculture here seems well-understood – the ground is highly cultivated and the crops luxuriant. Since we left Rodrigo the whole country after passing the Agueda, with the exception of that between Tenebron and Tamames, has been almost entirely covered with corn and the crops generally are bearded wheat mixed in many places with rye.

Diary

Medina del Campo

Thursday 2nd July 1812

Arrived here this morning in four very easy marches from Salamanca. The whole army moved by two parallel roads, not above a mile distance. . . . The enemy 20,000, had been in this town the night before. Momentos of which were everywhere visible – many doors and shutters destroyed – the town is famous for wine – but all the cellars (and they are many and excellent) were broken open by the enemy and the wine spilt which they couldn't use or carry off – on the 1st July . . . a mile beyond Alajos – there was so much difficulty in procuring sufficient wood to cook with that vines were obliged to be cut. The country is quite open but covered with corn and vines. Barley harvest has generally begun.

Today there has been a good deal of firing heard to our left, it was the enemy firing on the Guerrillos attempting to destroy a bridge over the Douro. Marshal Marmont has passed the whole of his army to the right of the Douro at Tordesillas, except a rearguard.

4th July – the 1st and 7th Divisions moved from marshy ground the west of Medina del Campo to the north of it – this marsh is reported so unhealthy by the natives that although the shepherds attend their flocks in the daytime they never sleep there.

Medina de Campo
6th July 1812

The second day after the fall of the fort at Salamanca we continued our offensive movement. We reached this place in three easy marches. The enemy had previously withdrawn from the threatening position which hc occupied in our front at Salamanca, and he retired by the road to Valladolid on the 30th ult. There was an affair between the cavalry of each army, and the 11th Lt Dragoons gained by it a seasonable supply of a *1,000 rations* of bread (500 loaves), the next day our advance and his rear were engaged, but we made a few prisoners – he began to pass to the right of the Douro (and defeated a corps of Guerrillos in their attempt to destroy a bridge near Tordesillas) and, with the exception of the rearguard, the whole were across this river by the evening of 2nd – on the 3rd inst Marshal Marmont attempted a reconnaissance, in which he was defeated by the 3rd and Lt Divisions, and the affair terminated in his being driven across the river, with a loss of about 100 men in the ford (which was above the *middle*).

Our advance crossed, and both armies have remained stationary since. What is next to be done is not known, but our operations seem cramped from the want of supplies. We have not yet wanted bread any day, but we get very little besides the biscuit from our magazines in Portugal and there is no probability of getting fully supplied in Spain till the harvest, which will not be general for a fortnight yet, and till then I apprehend we shall of necessity remain quiet. Our headquarters at *Rueda* (between the Douro and us, three miles from here) – the 1st, 4th and 7th Divisions are encamped near Medina del Campo, the remainder of the infantry between Hd Qrs and there and (indecipherable) to its left, and the cavalry are in that neighbourhood except one regiment, which is on the Madrid road at the rear of our right.

Our brigade was under orders last night to make a march to intercept a convoy, but we did not move and this morning parties were sent for branches of trees to build huts, the ground which we have been on for the past week not affording the least shade – from this circumstance it is pretty evident that there is little chance of moving soon.

The enemy's force in the Peninsula must be very weak, as from all his endeavours Marshal Marmont has not yet more than 32,000 men and all the garrisons in *his* rear have been reduced to furnish this number – With these, however, he will be able to defend his position at Valladolid, but I have no doubt that he will be forced from it by Ld Wellington – we have about 36,000 including all the Portuguese and Spaniards troops with us – General D'Urban is moving upon Toro with a corps of Portuguese (partly militia) of about 8,000, and the Spanish army of Galicia which is also moving in the same direction under *Castaños* is said to be about 12,000; when we are united to these, we shall still have a numerical superiority even after Marmont has been reinforced by K. Joseph and Gen. Bonnet; the former of whom cannot bring more than 8,000 and the latter has not more than 10,000 men.

Nevertheless, it would not be prudent in Lord W. to attack until we have several days' consumption on hand, as without supplies we could not follow up any victory and besides, whilst we maintain ourselves where we are, we compel the enemy to remain collected – which in the meantime distresses him for provisions, and gives an opportunity to those parts which he has evacuated to recover. The people here exalted beyond measure at our arrival, much more even than the natives of Salamanca – their houses are a good deal destroyed but not near so much as at Salamanca – we are the first British troops who have been in Medina and in consequence have been much canvassed by the people – last night they gave a public ball. There is to be another tonight.

Diary

7th July – the men ordered to build huts.

13th – moved this morning unexpectedly back to Villa Velde, one league, in consequence of Marshal Marmont having moved a large body to his right and threatening to pass the Douro.

14th and 15th – remained in Villa Velde. Turned out every morning at 3 o'clock and stood to arms and one hour after daybreak moved into the village, where we remained during the heat of the day for shade; at night moved to some high situation which we slept on.

16th – the enemy having shown a decided determination to pass the Douro we marched this evening to La Nava del Rey and occupied a rising ground about a mile from it.

17th – moved into La Nava during the heat and at 7 returned to the spot we occupied last night with intention to remain there till morning, but at 10 o'clock ordered to march right in front and made a long night march by Alaegos to Canizal, where we arrived on the 17th about 9 o'clock.

18th – we were ordered to march at 3 o'clock this morning back to La Nava but this order was soon countermanded and we were kept under arms with our baggage on the animals till 11 o'clock , when an order was given for us to march right in front to La Orden [Torrecilla de la Orden] – we arrived there near 2 and began preparations for cooking but before the meat could be delivered to the companies we were ordered to our arms and to march immediately back to Vallesa. Here we met the 6th Division, which had in the morning made a movement to its right and was on the road back to Canizal – we followed it and on arriving there at 8 o'clock took ground for the night. This morning there was a severe affair at the outpost near Alajos – Marmont attempted a reconnaissance but was repulsed by the Cavalry and 4th Division. Their men afterwards retired to near Castelhcira, where they are now.

19th – our baggage kept in the rear at La Orden but we had permission today to send for a canteen – excessively hot. The whole army assembled near this village, occupying ground in its front on both sides of the rivulet in close columns of regiments – the Lt Division on a range of hills about two miles in front and the enemy on another range of hills about a mile further off – all quiet till almost 4 when the enemy got under arms and commenced moving to his left – we did the same and moved over the high ground through the village of Vallesa.

20th July – at daybreak we moved forward to the bank of the ravine but the enemy having during the night made a movement to his left which was followed by the 6th and 7th Divisions, to correspond we moved down to our right and formed upon their left – on our front Marshal Marmont had formed his lines with his left occupying the summit of a ridge of hills which run at right-angles to his front.

Ld Wellington drew out his army in two lines and offered battle – the ground was perfectly level at every point but our right, where was the same range of hills as occupied by the enemy's left; and was passable for every arm – the heavy 18 pdrs brought up – Seeing Ld Wellington thus determined to fight Marmont thought proper to refuse, and he soon moved up to the summit of the hills on his left and advanced. Ld Wellington made a corresponding movement with the 7th and the Light Divisions and part of the Cavalry, and moved the remainder of the Infantry and Cavalry by a road which ran at the foot of these hills.

As the enemy continued to advance on the high ground the British army moved forward by the road in a parallel direction, and for the space of three hours there was the most beautiful movements perhaps ever witnessed of two armies of 40,000 men each trying to arrive at a certain point first. The skirmishes close on the flank of the column engaged – on reaching the village Babila Fuente the advance of the enemy halted and began to cannonade from the hill above it – they threw a great number of shot and shells at the column in passing but with almost no effect.

The enemy during the night had gained with a small force the road on the Tormes direct to Salamanca and the advance of the main body was now in communication with it, and it therefore became necessary for Lord W. to move towards Salamanca – we struck off to our right and continued to march till 4 o'clock, when we took up ground for the night in the village of Cabeza Vellosa. This day was excessively hot, two or three mules with baggage were taken and about 100 stragglers by the enemy.

21st July – moved off our ground before daybreak and arrived on the Tormes near Salamanca at noon – formed in column and cooked at six in evening. The whole across the Tormes by the ford of Santa Marta

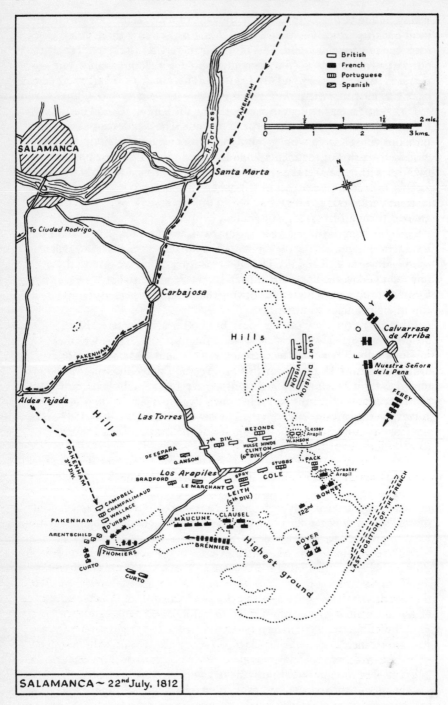

SALAMANCA ~ 22nd July, 1812

corresponding to the enemy who crossed at a ford about 6 miles further up. We at first took up ground for the night close to the river, but before we could pitch our tents we were ordered to our arms and the whole commenced moving up to the high ground – the enemy having advanced as if decided to attack. As we crossed the river the sky became very dark. There was every appearance of a great storm. The lightning began as we ascended the heights. The flashes, which were very frequent, served to guide us to our proper position and it seemed as if the fire was sent by heaven to assist our righteous cause – here was a grand and imposing spectacle that ever was witnessed – upwards of 20,000 men formed in line and close columns of brigades within musket shot, only seen by the flashes of lightning , and nothing heard but the occasional report of a gun at a distance fired upon the enemy from our advance – we halted on the crest of heights – the storm continued and increased, and near daybreak was accompanied with remarkably heavy rain, soon after which it ceased and began to clear away. In such circumstances it is surprising how the mind turns every appearance to our advantage. This night we were confident of victory – the day dawned and discovered the hostile armies close to each other – the sun rose sublimely and with it the carnage began, but did not terminate with the setting. Even her sister luminary, the moon, hardly closed the feats of this memorable day.

About seven o'clock the enemy attacked with his light troops those of the 7th Division which formed the advance on the right of our First line. and they skirmished for several hours. The position at first occupied by us extended for nearly two miles on a range of heights at right-angles to the river: the enemy endeavoured to turn this and moved to his left during the skirmish which seemed to have been begun for this purpose. They made a push for two prominent hills, the Arapiles, considerably to our right but on the same line of heights we occupied – on this indication the cavalry, which had been chiefly posted on the left in the plain by the river, were brought round to the right and moved at the head of the first line which inclined to its right, and had succeeded in occupying one of these hills but did not arrive at the other till the enemy were in possession of it – these two hills became a prominent in the proceedings of the day and appeared the *point d'appuie* of each army.

The line was now formed with its right thrown back nearly at right-angles to its original front, and the 1st Division were moved up immediately to the village of Arapiles, the cavalry were formed in its rear and afterwards the 7th Division – On occupying the village the enemy manifested an intention to attack but he soon continued moving to our right and Ld Wellington immediately issued orders for the 1st Division to attack – we moved therefore into the village of Arapiles, but had hardly entered it when the order was countermanded and we returned and formed in columns of regiments to the ground we had previously occupied.[16] It was now noon and the enemy were seen moving large bodies under cover of a distant wood upon our right and he occupied with artillery (supported) all the eminences on our front.

A small body of our Cavalry were sent to the summit of a hill on the right to look out – Ld Wellington soon went to it, and *it* became in a short time the bone of contention and led to the general action. On this hill was the most beautiful and *stage*-like skirmishing for several hours. A party of our Hussars who at first occupied it were soon driven from it by the enemy, but being supported the enemy in turn were driven back – supports were brought up by both sides. Marshal Marmont seemed resolved to gain it and with this view moved a large body forward. His centre became exposed and his line from its extent was weak – Ld Wellington had waited for such an opportunity to attack and he embraced it – In a position such as [that] occupied by the Allies the advantage is evidently great; while the enemy were compelled to move round the projecting angle our men were moved across it under cover of the heights – our support therefore never appeared and in fact did not arrive at the threatened point until the moment wanted – like the angler who humours the trout.

Till fairly hooked, Ld Wellington by *appearing* to dread seemed to forward M. Marmont's intention – when baited he attacked!

The enemy's right and centre were attacked about 5 o'clock and soon driven from all the heights which they occupied. The 1st line of 6th Division attacked an eminence near the centre on which was posted a heavy battery and carried it – but the enemy rallied and re-took it and our 1st line was driven down the hill in confusion on the second – it stood firm and advanced and the 61st Regiment[17] here made one of the most brilliant charges ever recorded. While things went on thus in the centre our right was not less successful. The French were everywhere driven from the ground and Le Marchant's brigade of heavy cavalry aided by the heavy dragoons, the K.G.L. having got in the rear of the enemy, charged and made 1,200 prisoners.

Gen. Pack, who was posted with his brigade of Portuguese on the height at the angle, attacked that occupied by the enemy but this attack unfortunately failed and his regiment suffered severely. It had however, the effect of diverting the attention of the enemy from the 6th Division, which otherwise it would have taken in flank during its advance.

In little more than an hour the enemy left was completely beaten and in retreat. . . . It was now dusk and this favoured the enemy's escape. Ld Wellington continued to pursue with the 1st and Lt Divisions while the enemy remained in a body and afterwards directed the march upon the fords of the Tormes. About Alba, at 12 o'clock we halted and there remained for the night.

23rd – The 1st and Lt Division with the Cavalry in front moved in pursuit of the enemy at daybreak, whose Corps had reunited and crossed the Tormes at Alba by the bridge and the fords in the neighbourhood. His rearguard was overtaken at La Sorna (near Garcia Hernandez) and attacked – the Cavalry took to flight and the heavy dragoons of the K.G.L. immediately charged the infantry, broke the square and took the whole 1,200 prisoners. The body of their rearguard manifested an intention to resist on a range of heights above Villa Alba and the advance of our

Cavalry were therefore compelled to halt for the Infantry – on the arrival, however, of the 1st and Lt Divisions, who advanced in columns of regiments at forming distance on their right flank and front, the enemy evacuated the heights and retreated – it was pursued as far as Penaranda and great numbers of prisoners made. To this day the loss of the enemy in prisoners alone is estimated at 6 or 7 thousand, the killed in battle is immense and the road is strewed with dead bodies or sick and wounded, so that on the whole their loss cannot be estimated under 10,000 men and we have besides taken 5 Eagles and Standards and 21[18] pieces of ordnance, but it is not from the numerical loss of the enemy that we are to prize the victory of Salamanca. Its moral effects in the cause of Spain are incalculable – the circumstances under which it was gained, chiefly by Foreign troops, with two entire divisions not engaged [1st and Light] and these the two finest divisions of the army – at a time too when the enemy relied on victory. These considerations must have great affect in stimulating the Spaniards to resistance, and if the physical energy of these people is to be called into action by anything it will be by the battle of Salamanca.

There was one division of Spanish troops present under Don Carlos de España but they were kept in reserve and took no part in the action, during the morning of the 22nd. However, a small body of them (about 300) were sent to Alba de Tormes to occupy the fort and they succeeded in getting it. Don Carlos, however, became alarmed for them (being thus in rear of the French army) and he recalled them without our Chief's knowledge, which turned out the most unfortunate circumstance that could have occurred; for, the fort commanded the bridge and by it the enemy crossed the Tormes after he was beaten – had therefore the Spaniards defended it the annihilation of the enemy would almost have been certain – pressed as he was by us after defeat.

Having thus noticed the *battle of Salamanca* I must not pass over the behaviour of its inhabitants, who in every respect have showed themselves as sincerely attached to us as from the behaviour of the French to them and their own professions we had reason to expect. During the three days that we were on the heights of Villanes, where there was no water and we were so much exposed that not a bush could be got to make a fire, they cheerfully obeyed Ld Wellington's order and men and women, young and old, visited us, bringing with them loads of fresh water and dry wood; after we returned to Salamanca on the 21st, apparently being driven back by the enemy, our hospital, stores of every description being removed to the rear – they manifested no desire to upbraid us with deserting them; on the contrary, most seemed to place full reliance that we would do our utmost to protect them, and all those who had little hope of our exertions being successful yet were resigned to their fate and treated us to the last moment with as much civility as when we first entered. After driving off their enemy after the Battle, when their assistance was most wanted, they came forward both high and low as became them, and even ladies of birth went to the field of battle and lent all their delicate assistance at removing the wounded *into their houses* and administering every comfort in their power

– this lasted the whole night and they have since assisted at the hospital. But let the rest of Spain follow the example of Salamanca and they shall be equally protected!

30th July 1812. Arrived on the banks of the Douro near Boecillo – our Cavalry are now in Valladolid, the Lt (division) are across the Douro and the 1st on the left bank close by. The other divisions of Infantry have made a movement to the right in the direction of Cuellar, with a view it is supposed of preventing the junction of King Joseph's army with the remains of Marmont's. The reports from Valladolid make the French acknowledge to have 20,000 men *hors de combat* and all prisoners and deserters agree in 21 pieces of cannon lost – though we have only found eleven, and eleven generals are killed and wounded – including Marmont and Bonnet.

Contaracilla
25th July 1812

My dear father

We have fought a battle with Marshal Marmont's army and gained the most glorious complete victory which has been achieved in the Peninsula.

Having collected all the men which he could from the different garrisons in his rear, joined to the army of the Asturias under Bonnet and 6,000 from Aragon under Caffarelli, Marmont crossed the Douro with his whole force on 16th and advanced – we collected at first at La Nava del Rey on 17th and retired from it in the evening of the same day in consequence of the movement of the enemy and made a forced march during the night to Cañizal, in the neighbourhood of which there was a brilliant affair of posts on the 18th. We offered battle on 20th but Marshal Marmont refused and obliged us to move to our right. Having gained the direct road to Salamanca on the Tormes, we continued to move to our right as the enemy moved to *his* left and on the night of the 21st we forded the Tormes and moved into position on the heights covering Salamanca on the left of that river.

Marmont on 22nd continued his endeavours to turn our right, which caused us some fatiguing manoeuvres, but Lord Wellington observing his intention determined to attack, and accordingly moved against his centre in the afternoon – in two hours it was penetrated and the wings were separated and by dark he was in full retreat – we followed till midnight, making great numbers of prisoners – we pursued till yesterday; and today we have halted to allow stragglers to come up – our loss I believe does not exceed 3,000 while that of the enemy is estimated at 12,000, of whom about 6,000 are prisoners. The action was fought chiefly by the Portuguese and they behaved in a manner which could not be excelled. Two divisions of our army, about 10,000, were not engaged, the Light and 1st Division, and they have been employed in advance to pursue – only the companies of the Guards were engaged.[19]

On the last day of July, John Aitchison wrote a long letter to his father incorporating nearly all the material concerning the battle of Salamanca which has already been taken from his diary. He added, however, a number of matters which are of importance and interest in understanding the battle and Wellington. These are set out below as extracts from letters.

> The banks of the Douro, from Valladolid
> 31st July 1812
> Six miles south-east

After remaining some days on the ground near Medina and the neighbourhood the army was ordered to hut, and from that circumstance it became evident that Lord Wellington's offensive movements must be at an end, while the enemy maintained the position which they have occupied. In this determination it would be presumption in me to say he was right, but I may observe that while he could have maintained himself in so advanced a situation in Spain in a manner separating the main army of the French from their other forces and its direct communication with the Capital, he gained in a material degree the object of his quitting Portugal.

Distress must always be produced to an army when obliged to remain collected in an enemy's country – the French felt this – to reinforce Marmont on the Douro they diminished their forces in other quarters so much that they could barely defend their fortified places; the country between them was in possession of the natives and the Guerillos assembled in such formidable numbers round Marshal Marmont as nearly to isolate him and his army during this time. No inconvenience arose to the Allies – we remained in small bodies at different places well-supplied with everything, and our retreat was secure should events have rendered it necessary – the enemy however ascribed Lord Wellington's conduct to a different cause. That policy and the army which he had viewed and dreaded on the heights of Morisco Marshal Marmont began to under-rate and *despise* – accordingly he assumed unusual boldness, he manoeuvred large masses very suddenly and with great rapidity and his extreme arrogance in attempting to turn both our flanks was checked, and he sustained on the 22nd instant the most single defeat which any army has experienced since the revolution.

From his manoeuvres Marshal Marmont seemed to calculate much good effect from rapidity. He would first threaten one point and then another, and sometimes when from every appearance he had taken up his quarters for the night he would move in a direction which seemed the least to be expected. Ld Wellington however was aware of him – but the troops were much harassed and from the 16th until after the battle we were not certain of being in one place three hours together – some days we were on the move from before daybreak till dark and we had two long night marches.

In proportion as the enemy crossed the Douro and advanced Lord Wellington assembled his forces, and retired to Cañizal on the 18th. . . .

Throughout the whole of Spain which we have been in, and particularly

in the country round Salamanca, the ground is in no manner sub-divided –
it is passable at all points for every arm of an army and there are even few
ditches which oppose any difficulty to the passage of artillery. In such
country it is difficult to find a position which will increase the strength of
an army – Ld Wellington however found one about 2 miles from
Salamanca (East) on the left of the Tormes – the advance was in an oak
wood with the first line and extended from the Tormes about a mile. The
second line occupied a range of heights, with its left also on the Tormes.
The Cavalry were on the plain near the Tormes and to the rear of our right,
and Don Carlos de España occupied the bridge of Salamanca with his
corps of Spanish Infantry.

In this position Marshal Marmont did not choose to attack us; he made
a strong reconnaissance soon after daybreak which caused a severe skirmish till 7 o'clock and he then, as on the two preceding days, moved rapidly
large bodies to his left endeavouring thus to force us to quit it. . . .

The British army was now to be placed in a different situation to what
they had been accustomed – they had been tried in defensive positions and
had proved themselves the best in the world, but they had not been
accustomed to *attack*, and acting as they were with raw troops (who
indeed were the majority) against veterans . . . the most sanguine could not
be free from apprehension for the results. The two senior officers next to
Ld Wellington were decidedly averse to attack, but he remained firm in his
resolution and the merit of victory in consequence all his own.

Except the Light and 1st Divisions the whole army was employed, and I
was consequently a spectator and saw everything that occurred as far as
the dust and smoke and some inequalities of ground would allow. The
Infantry advanced with great rapidity and regularity and carried everything before them after obstinate resistance. At one point the first line was
attacked after gaining the summit of a hill and driven back, but the second
line moved up into its support and the 61st Regiment made one of the most
brilliant charges which has ever been recorded. The Portuguese generally
acted equally well as the British – on the right of all the Infantry and nobly
supported by the Cavalry – they got in rear of the enemy and Gen Le
Marchant's brigade made a charge and took many prisoners, by 5 o'clock
the victory was decided to be ours and the enemy were on the retreat – their
manoeuvres here were equally fine, as before the battle they threw back
their left in the most perfect order on the hill (before noticed) which had
unfortunately been attacked unsuccessfully by General Pack, and as soon
as it came in line with their right the hill was evacuated and the whole
retreated into the woods. . . . We continued the pursuit at daybreak and
next day and soon after fording the Tormes the cavalry came up with the
rear of the enemy and in one charge took 1,200 men – they were checked
by the enemy's Infantry and compelled to wait our arrival – we made all
haste to come up but from excessive heat we could not arrive before they
had reached a considerable distance and taken up the position on a hill
apparently determined to resist – our columns of attack were immediately
formed, but on seeing us they began to retreat and we were only able to

throw a few shells into them at a great distance. With the exception of one halting day we have followed till yesterday making many prisoners every day, besides those by the peasants, and the loss must be very great, though I believe we are not certain of more than 6,000 prisoners besides the wounded and these with the killed will not I suppose exceed 10,000 men – they calculate their loss much greater from 15–21,000 and I can easily believe it much beyond what we know for certain from the number lying dead on the roadside in fields, and straggling as they are all over the country many will be murdered which will not be accounted for. Their loss in Generals has been severe and they are now commanded by a young man little known – they have retreated from Valladolid upon Aranda de Duero – supposed with view to forming a junction with King Joseph, who is near Segovia with about 15,00 men. They are in very low spirits – very badly off for everything and will not I think make such resistance again. 800 sick men taken at Valladolid – What has become of the Galician army no one seems to know – it was to have been upon the Esla about the same time that we were on the Tormes but it does not seem certain that it has got so far up.

Wellington's victory at Salamanca brought him fame throughout Europe. He had already taught the French to beware of attacking him on his own ground and now, by his mastery of manoeuvre on the battlefield, he had established a moral ascendency over Napoleon's marshals. Yet his handling of the Army during the rest of the campaigning season was to be the least satisfactory and most controversial period of his command and led to the army's faith in his leadership being badly shaken.

He freely admitted making serious miscalculations and errors of judgment in the siege of Burgos but the disillusionment of the army following their triumph at Salamanca was more broadly based and seems to have been born of unfulfilled and unrealistic expectations – for instance there was talk of an advance on Paris! Such expectations showed a lack of understanding of the political and military constraints under which Wellington laboured. Some reference to these is necessary if John Aitchison's views are to be seen in perspective.

The balance of forces in the Peninsula remained unfavourable to the Allies, the British Army in Spain was irreplaceable, and with the United States at war with Britain from 17 July it might not even be kept up to strength. The cost of the Peninsular War to Britain, too, was onerous, and there was a strong body of political opinion in favour of withdrawal.

Wellington was convinced that Spain was where Britain could make the greatest contribution to Napoleon's downfall but the time was not yet ripe for grandiose strategic aims like driving the French out. His aim was the more limited one of preventing the French establishing effective control over any part of the Peninsula and to tilt the balance of power, without taking undue risks, until the time was right to reject them altogether.

Throughout 1812 the French maintained 340,000 troops in Spain. The Anglo-Portuguese Army numbered 60,000 and had to be split to secure the Portuguese base, so that Wellington could never command more than 45,000 in the field. His strategy was to tear the French between their need to concentrate whenever the Allied Army penetrated into Spain and their need to disperse in order to live off the country and keep in check the Spanish provincial armies and guerrilla forces supported by British maritime power. The latter, by tying down the French forces, denying them supplies and harassing their lines of communication, reduced the size of the forces the French could concentrate against Wellington, prolonged the time required for them to do so, and limited that for which they could remain so. On the other hand, by forcing the French to concentrate Wellington created opportunities for the Spaniards to deprive the French of such degree of control as they had managed to create.

We must now return to the battlefield with a reminder that the day before his great victory Wellington had decided that he would almost certainly have to retire to Ciudad Rodrigo and had already ordered away his baggage train. That day Major Alexander Dickson R.A., in charge of the siege train, ordered Sergeant D. McLaren to take the artillery stores there and 'to have the most particular care of the Government bullocks to see none of them desert or are lost, and also that they have good pasture'. After the battle he wrote:

> I really believe Lord Wellington fought against his inclination, and that if Marmont by his manoeuvering had not pushed him so hard he would quickly have fallen back and relinquished Salamanca to the French. The audacity of the enemy was such however that British honour required it should be checked, and most severely M. Marmont has been punished for playing tricks with such a leader as Lord Wellington.[20]

Clausel, having been saved from destruction by nightfall and de España's evacuation of Alba, took his shattered forces to Arevalo where he arrived on 24 July and turned north to Valladolid. On the same day, but unknown to each other, Joseph arrived with 14,000 men at Blasco Sancho, fifteen miles further south. Wellington, following up, did not reach Aravela until the twenty-seventh. He then followed Clausel to Valladolid where he found that the French had fallen back on Burgos, abandoning a number of garrisons on the Douro. Wellington entered Valladolid where the French had left seventeen guns, a large quantity of stores, and 800 wounded. Instead of continuing to follow up Clausel Wellington decided to march on Madrid. Leaving Clinton with the 6th Division and some cavalry at Cueller, to keep watch on the Douro, on 12 August, after a sharp skirmish on the outskirts, he entered Madrid amid tremendous public acclaim.

When Wellington turned south Joseph fell back on Madrid and then led the Army of the Centre out along the road to Valencia with a convoy of 2,000 vehicles and some 10,000 refugees, who, having collaborated with the French, feared vengeance. In intense heat, without food or water and harassed by guerrilla bands, it was a nightmare march from which many men, women and children never awoke.

Wellington is criticized for not having exploited his brilliant victory with the élan all had come to expect of Napoleon, and for choosing to enter Madrid rather than pursuing Clausel to Burgos which, in all probability, would at that time have been easy to occupy. That he was slow to follow up is in large part explained by the fact that his administrative services were in process of redeployment for a general retreat at the time of the victory, and the baggage train was already within a short distance of Ciudad Rodrigo. That he chose Madrid rather than Burgos was due to a number of factors. If he occupied Burgos he risked exposing his communications to attack from Joseph's army, which could have been substantially reinforced by Soult or Suchet. On the other hand, entry into Madrid would have a favourable political effect not only in Spain but also at home, where grave news of Napoleon's advance into Russia was coming through. Moreover, it was not thought that Clausel could pose any serious threat for some time to come.

Portillo
2nd August 1812

We came here yesterday, where we have halted supposed to await the results of a movement against Segovia by Ld Wellington with the 3rd, 6th and 7th Divisions – if the enemy will but wait till these come up to them the result is certain, but it is more likely Joseph will find it most prudent to retreat to Madrid – in which case I dare say Ld Wellington will follow with part of the army and leave the remainder on the Douro to prevent reinforcements. Our sick, I am sorry to say, are becoming very numerous but a few days' halt will recover many of them – my liver has been threatening me but I am now better and will be quite free from it in a day or two more.

On the same day as Aitchison's letter, Wellington wrote to General Castaños to say that Marmont's army must be driven off without loss of time, to enable the whole of his forces to be turned against Soult. He would press forward as far as possible and might even undertake the siege of Burgos. The Army of Galicia under Santocildes was to move eastwards to join him. On 8 September, on receiving information of the situation in Andalusia, he ordered Hill with the 2nd Division and the 18,000 troops under his command to cross the Tagus and advance to Toledo, to stop Joseph from recrossing the Tagus.

The board was set up for an advance on Burgos. Success depended upon Wellington having sufficient means for its rapid reduction. His security depended upon the Tagus rising to create an obstacle to an advance against him from the south, and to diversions being created by the garrisons of Cadiz, Alicante and by the most active Spanish general in the south, Ballesteros. Unfortunately, the means for reducing Burgos were in every way inadequate, the rains did not start until Wellington was on the verge of retreat, and Ballesteros mutinied on hearing that the Cortes had, on 22 September, made Wellington commander-in-chief of the Spanish Army, while Maitland and those who succeeded him in rapid succession proved to be no better than broken reeds.

Joseph's attempts to obtain reinforcements for Marmont had been ignored by Soult and Suchet. Now he ordered Soult to evacuate Andalusia and march to join his forces with those of Suchet and the Army of the Centre in Valencia, by which means Joseph hoped to put an army of 80,000 to 100,000 in the field against Wellington. Soult at first declined, for he had already proposed an alternative plan based on his belief in the importance of retaining control of Andalusia. By this plan Joseph's Army of the Centre and part of the Army of Portugal would join him in clearing southern Spain and by threatening Portugal with a field force of 60,000 men, hopefully bringing about the withdrawal of Wellington from Spain.

Under threat of dismissal Soult complied, and raised the siege of Cadiz leaving 281 damaged, but mostly repairable, guns in Allied hands. Meanwhile, in response to Wellington's orders to keep Soult's forces pinned down, Brigadier-General Skerrett with an Anglo–Portuguese force of 1,800 from Cadiz had been landed at Huerta. There he defeated a French force twice the size and advanced on Seville to find it evacuated, but with large quantities of military stores and 242 pieces of ordnance in good condition. On 9 August the promised Anglo–Sicilian force of 7,000 at long last landed at Alicante under Major-General Maitland.

As soon as it was known that Wellington had gone to Madrid, Clausel brought his forces forward to Valladolid to relieve the garrisons left behind at Zamora, Toro, Tordesillas and Astorga. This Foy accomplished, except Astorga which had just fallen to Santocilde's Spaniards. When Clausel entered Valladolid Clinton fell back on Arevalo. While this was going on Wellington, leaving the 3rd and Light Divisions at Madrid and the 4th at Escorial, moved the 1st, 5th and 7th Divisions, two Portuguese infantry brigades and a light and heavy cavalry brigade to Arevalo, from where, on 4 September, he led them towards Valladolid.

Camp
11th August 1812

Two days more and we shall be in Madrid! – if we continue to march. We have just crossed the Guadarrama Pass, and we are now within 28 miles of it.

I can now assure you of the perfect re-establishment of my health – every symptom of the liver complaint has left me and I feel so much better than usual from enjoying the keen and salubrious air of these mountains for these four days, and I hope I shall continue well during the rest of the warm season.

I wrote to you from Portillo on 2nd inst. Since then we have made gradual progress towards the Capital. Marshal Marmont, with the remains of his army, after leaving Valladolid moved towards Aranda as if with the intention to form a junction with the King, but he suddenly turned off towards Burgos where he is now – Joseph didn't wait the effects of Ld Wellington's demonstration against him but quitted Segovia and retired to the neighbourhood of Aranjuez where are some reinforcements. Ld Wellington has therefore left a considerable corps at Cuellar under Maj-Gen. Clinton to watch Marmont, and he has proceeded himself towards the

Capital with the main body of the army, and if all goes on as there is every prospect of it he will date a dispatch from Madrid tomorrow – the Prince Regent's birthday.

I wasn't sufficiently well when we were on the Douro to think it prudent to go to Valladolid, but I have made up for the want of seeing it by visiting every place of note since – Segovia – San Ildefonso and the palace of Rio Trio and I shall go to the Escurial tomorrow. You must not expect a description of these places or you will be disappointed. I feel my inability, and the impression made on my own ideas if described to you would be very different from the flattering accounts which you may read of them in every history of Spain. I regret that such enormous sums of money should have been expended to so little account and with so little taste – San Ildefonso has certainly its merits, though out of the immense pile of building which strikes an observer at a distance only two suites of apart-ments are used – the King's and the Queen's. The gardens are laid out in the old formal style; they are provided with waterworks which from the specimen I saw must be most magnificent – like every other great Spanish undertaking, however, they have not been finished.

The high road is remarkably well made and carried by bridges and causeways over many hollows and marsh, and for 30 miles they are very numerous. The enemy had all the indirect communications by this road and in consequence had troops stationed in all the posts and villages near it, but they were so much harassed by the Guerrillos as to be under the necessity of fortifying some place in each which still remains. I am now in command of the Light Company – the officer who had it in the battle was wounded[21] and I was appointed to it the next day – I did not mention this before from fear of alarming you. My pony has come up in the last four weeks; it is very fat and in her paces as good as I could wish.

Diary

12th – which halted I employed in visiting the far-famed Escorial, which after viewing with attention I can only denominate an immense mass of building without taste as to situation or execution and chiefly occupied by monk's cells and paltry Royal apartments. The Palace of the Infantas however is of quite a different nature and claims pre-eminence from its furnishings in every respect – many of the paintings on the walls and ceilings if on canvas might be suffered and would grace a collection of pictures. The staircase is of beautifully variegated marble, both the steps and walls, and there are two rooms in the upper storey with highly polished floors of inlaid wood. The whole is in admirable order and too much cannot be said in its praise.

The sepulchre of the church of the Escorial is magnificent. You descend to it by a flight of about 50 steps made of variegated marble – the sides and ceiling of the staircase are of the same and polished in the highest style – the sepulchre itself is octagonal, one side being occupied by the door and the opposite by an Altar. The coffins are of fine marble beautifully gilt and each has an inscription on who it contains – there are already 7 Kings and 7 Queens in it.

13th August 1812. Moved forward to the Puente de Ratamar on the Guadarrama river, where we bivouacked in an open space without the least shelter from the sun.

This march was called only 3 leagues but the latter part of the road near the river is very hilly and more fatiguing than 4 ordinary leagues. In all the villages which we have passed through on the high road since we came near Segovia the enemy have had fortified posts for about 150 or 200 men. The Guerrillos, it seems, were so active that it became necessary to have these for escorting couriers.

There was an unfortunate affair at the outpost in the evening of the 11th in which we lost three guns and Horse Artillery owing to the misconduct of the Portuguese Cavalry. It appears that Brig-Gen. D'Urban, who commanded the Portuguese Cavalry, being in advance at the village Majadahonda, judged a favourable opportunity to charge the leading squadron of the enemy and directed the Portuguese to attack. They moved forward briskly into the charge but before coming into contact with the enemy they were panic struck and ran away; they were pursued with great rapidity by the enemy and these three guns, which were supporting, fell into the enemy's hands. In their terror they ran through the heavy German dragoons who were near the village unbridled, and before these could form they were captured by the enemy and suffered severely but it was owing to their steadiness that the Portuguese escaped. The advance of the army and headquarters moved into Madrid in the evening of the 12 inst.

14th August – The remainder of the army arrived at Madrid, King Joseph having withdrawn with his army except about 2,000 men left to garrison the Retiro. The joy of the inhabitants at our appearance has been excessive, and they have given vent to their feelings with all that extravaganza which could be imagined of a people on finding themselves free after a bondage of four years.

Lord Wellington is regarded as a Demi-God and the army under him looked upon as invincible. The governor of the Retiro this day sent to propose a capitulation and it has been granted him on condition of surrendering the prisoners of war – the officers and men keeping all their private baggage – thus have 2,500 men been made prisoner without loss on our part. . . . They marched out in the afternoon. The surrender of the immense Retiro had been of much consequence to us in gaining seasonable supply of necessaries for the army, and it will allow us to have some repose since our operations have been forwarded by it beyond calculation. It appears to have been bad policy in the French having a garrison in the Retiro, since from the defective state of the fortifications and the situation of the magazines they could not make a defence – hence they submitted without resistance.

The constitution framed by the Cortes has been proclaimed and a new government in the name of Ferdinand VII has been appointed. The whole town was illuminated last evening and this in a most splendid style, and the effect was rendered more grand from the window curtains of silk hangings used on processions on Saints' days being displayed on the outside – 'all the world' was in the streets and it was most gratifying to see and receive the cordial embraces of the Spaniards to all the British officers, who in return did themselves the pleasure to give their arms to the Spanish ladies and protect them in the crowd in the public walks by the Manzanares.

The division continue to bivouac – the 4th and 5th Divisions in the gardens of the Casa del Campo and the 8th and 7th Divisions, which were to have besieged the Retiro, are in Madrid – the cavalry are a little in advance towards Toledo. The municipality gave last night a very superb ball to Ld Wellington, to which all the officers of the Guard being invited, I attended. Nearly 600 persons were there and the display of beauty rivalled London but the affability of the Spanish ladies is not less conspicuous than their beauty, and at every town where we have been they have shown such marks of attention without the formality of being introduced as has made a deep impression. Already is the French language abolished and in compliment to the British no lady, although they all speak it well, will acknowledge that she understands it!

Lord Wellington is lodged in the new Palace – a most magnificent building and though not near finished it is already said to have cost a million Sterling. I have been all over it and it exceeds in magnificence so much what I could have imagined that I shall not attempt to describe it – no idea of mine could do it justice. Every room appears to outshine the other – in its symmetry, the splendour of the furniture and in its decorations and notwithstanding the spoilation of the French it is still filled with valuable originals of all the first masters of Spain and Italy. The audience hall is very grand – 90 feet by 50 – hung all round with rich crimson velvet bordered with broad gold lace – 5 windows in front and between every two a large mirror from the ceiling to the floor – the throne is of the style surmounted by the handsome canopy.

It is the fashion to walk every evening until dark in the Prado – a long broad space with six rows of trees each side enclosing a walk – the middle space is for carriages and has some handsome fountains at certain distances which supply water for the trees, and it is conducted to their roots every morning and evening by channels cut and kept in order for the purpose. This space on one side is supplied with a great number of cane chairs where any person may sit down when tired. Lord Wellington regularly attends the Prado and it is very flattering to see the attention with which he is treated. The museum and other public institutions are open and every person in uniform is admitted without fee.

Madrid
15th August 1812

We have gained the object of our march – Madrid is in our possession and the enemy who were left in the strongly fortified post of the Retiro surrendered yesterday morning at discretion; without a cannon shot having been fired against them. Such seems the effect which Ld Wellington's fame has upon the French.

The Commander-in-Chief with the advance of the army entered the Capital on the evening of the 12th; two more divisions entered on the 13th, and the Light and 1st Divisions yesterday – our heavy ordnance were not up, but the Governor of El Retiro, from the dread of red-hot shot being fired against him, surrendered at discretion, and we have thus got without loss 2,200 prisoners (chiefly French) 15,000 stand of small arms – and the stores of every description *viz* powder and ball, shoes, shirts, clothing, biscuit, etc, are so immense that I am afraid of committing myself by spreading what I have heard.

Ld Wellington, who was received by the people of Madrid with the distinction due to his merit, on his arrival was conducted to the King's Palace in state amidst the Vivas and embraces of all ranks, and now he cannot make an appearance in public without being in danger of suffocation from the embraces of the ladies – this expression of esteem for the British nation has not been confined to the Commander-in-Chief, but has been shown in a less degree to all ranks and departments of the army – in short, since we passed the frontier we have been treated with such officious attention and marked respect by the Spaniards that I fear (if it continues much longer) we shall be spoiled, and take very ill with the cold civility of our own country people.

The feeling of attachment to the British here appears as general as their rejoicing at being relieved from the French is sincere. All seem anxious to fight against the enemy and the Juramentados who were taken in the fort yesterday have already entered El Medico's corps of Guerrillos – they have been for several days blockading the fort of Guadalajara, and the 800 Frenchmen who compose its garrison were expected to lay down their arms yesterday on hearing of the surrender of El Retiro. After the fall of the Retiro the City presented the appearance of a Saint's day – the doors and windows of every house were ornamented with silk damask hanging on the *outside*. The portrait of Ferdinand the 7th was displayed under a crimson velvet canopy at all the public buildings, which everybody saluted by uncovering his head in passing – in the evening there were brilliant illuminations – all the world were in the streets and the houses continuing ornamented as during the day – the appearance of the whole was more gratifying and splendid than any description can make you conceive. The Theatre was open and Ld Wellington was greeted in a most marked manner on entering and on leaving it.

The effect of our possessing the Capital I should think will be shown instantly throughout Spain, and I have little doubt that the ranks will be filled by it, and I am led to augur favourably from the superiority which all (even their soldiers) appear to allow the British army. To a people who have in a manner been excluded from the rest of the world so long, the appearance must be very striking. The height and bodily strength of our men (which is considerably greater than the generality of [indecipherable] and Spaniards, the splendour of our clothing and our appointments, the style in which they are kept, the horses and their harness – all must lead to impress such a people as the Spaniards with romantic ideas of our importance.

An officer, I hear, is to go home with dispatches and I think this is the hope of getting it sent at the same time – I have not seen the sights of Madrid – there are so many that I shall take several days – these we expect we shall have – we are now encamped in a shady walk close to the gates of the town and we expect to remain here several days, particularly since our request seems to have outstripped calculation – the army requires a halt and there is no reason for its moving – King Joseph has retired towards Toledo. It is not of course know in what direction we shall move next, but as this campaign seems to be from a matured plan calculating on the effects of co-operation I should think His Majesty will find it prudent to give up Toledo without waiting for Ld Wellington's arrival there, if as is said here that General Maitland has landed in Catalonia.

Diary

18th August – The garrison of Guadalajara, consisting of 700 men, has surrendered to the Empecinado[22] on the same terms as the garrison of the Retiro. The army of King Joseph has abandoned Toledo and continued to march towards Valencia. The 7th Division have marched to the Escorial and the 1st is ordered there also.

The weather since we came to Madrid has been oppressively hot but every sort of refreshing drink is to be had iced and there are delightful baths on the river. These are formed by digging in the river bed and built on every side with wood so it excludes all dirt, and the rain and the sun are kept out by mats laid over framework – the river is divided into regular streams, two for baths and the water constantly running and filtering itself through the sand is always clean and cool – two streams on each side of the baths are for washing and here you may see all the washerwomen of Madrid at work, while they are protected from being wetted by wooden boxes which they sit in and from the heat of the air by canopies erected for the purpose.

Madrid
My dear William,   *22nd August 1812*

The date of this letter will be sufficient to excite your curiosity as you will no doubt expect a description of this Capital, but I fear you will be disappointed. The City itself is so handsome, the sights are so numerous and superb – the Inhabitants so civil – particularly the ladies so beautiful and affable, that I feel myself quite incapable of doing justice to either; and were I qualified, the partiality which I have taken for Madrid would allow me to point out only beauties – defects it has none (unless a little want of accommodation to foot passengers can be called so) and were I ever disposed to find fault I know nothing by which to gratify such disposition

– it approaches perfection as nearly as in my idea any town can do. You will perhaps give me credit for sincerity in this Phillipic when I tell you that I am now returned to Madrid from about 30 miles' distance, and this at a time when but for the assistance of my friends I could not remain in it two days (from the want of money). After remaining under the walls three days the army broke up and four divisions of Infantry marched back to the Escorial – Shiffner[23] and myself found it particularly stupid remaining there without anything to do amongst a crowd of men whom we see every day, and got leave of absence for three days – these we took care to precede and, setting forth even before our leave began, arrived here about 10 o'clock – yesterday we showed ourselves in the Prado and one theatre – today we dine with Ld Wellington and go to another theatre and tomorrow we return home.

These three days I think you will consider well spent, at least I am sure I feel them so. Notwithstanding the very warm weather I have had no symptom of bile for the last fortnight.

You will at least look for political news but be not surprised if I give little. All here is going on as in peace and but for the Guards and sentries of British troops in different parts of the town we might fancy ourselves here during a time of peace. King Joseph has given up Toledo (which is now possessed by the Guerrillos) and they say marching to join Suchet. Marmont, who went to Burgos with the remains of his army, has returned to the line of the Douro and reoccupied the country between Burgos and Valladolid, which latter place he has also entered – as he is not in a state to undertake any serious offensive operation this movement of Marmont's must have been made with a view to favour the garrison of El Retiro, but they having surrendered he will, I think, again retire, especially as General Clinton has been ordered to move against him. The Galician army (Santocildes) is on the Douro also, so that if they are good for anything there can be no doubt of Marmont being forced to retrograde.

23rd August – Deputations from all the Cities and towns now freed from the enemy have been waiting with addresses on Ld Wellington – the deputation from Toledo dined with him yesterday – Don Carlos de España has been appointed Governor of Madrid and is busy raising recruits, who are drilled twice a day – El Medico and El Empecinado (Guerrillo leaders) are both here and their Corps have much increased; the latter's come to thousands. There is no appearance of our moving soon, so little so that the artillery of all the divisions at El Escorial but one are still here – we are all at a loss to conceive our next operation – we stood much in need of rest and this halt will do much in recovering the men, as they are now all lodged in houses which has not been the case before, since we left Portugal.

Should we remain stationary a week or so longer I shall endeavour to make an excursion to Aranjuez. It is not above seventy miles from the Escurial and the Gardens etc there are very well worth seeing – My pony which has turned out very well will carry me there in three days with great ease – you will think nothing of such a journey, but what with the heat etc it is very good work in this country.

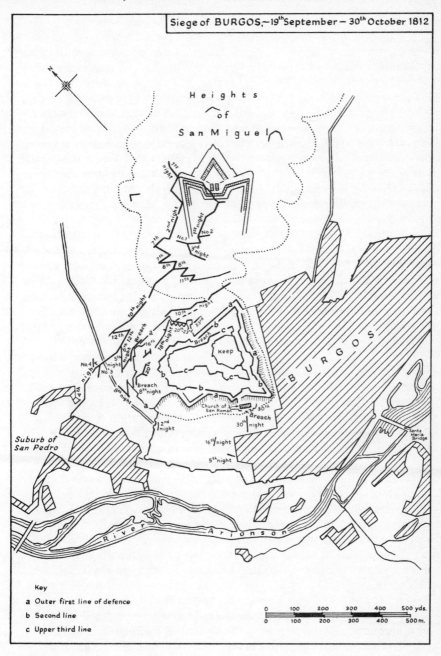

Siege of BURGOS,—19th September — 30th October 1812

Heights of San Miguel

BURGOS

Suburb of San Pedro

River Arlonson

Key
a Outer first line of defence
b Second line
c Upper third line

BURGOS

Wellington crossed the Douro on 6 September and next day missed an opportunity to destroy Clausel's rearguard through lack of clear instructions by Pringle, temporarily in command of the 5th Division, and inefficiency in the quartermaster-general's department. Wellington did not press the retiring French as he was still waiting the arrival of Santocilde's Army of Galicia with 11,000 men, so he proceeded slowly toward Burgos and was joined by Santocildes on the sixteenth, a week later than he had ordered. Clausel was by then deployed to cover Burgos, so Wellington planned to attack the French position on the eighteenth but the enemy slipped away during the night and Clausel, having thrown 2,000 men into the fortress of Burgos under an intrepid and enterprising commander, General Dubreton, marched the Army of Portugal back to the Ebro.

Burgos was invested on 19 September, the 6th Division taking ground on the left bank of the Arlanzon river, which the remainder of the army crossed. The 1st and 6th Divisions and two independent Portuguese brigades were to undertake the reduction of the fortress, while the 5th and 7th Divisions took up a covering position astride the road to Bayonne, at Monastero de Rodilla, some nine miles north-east of Burgos. A Spanish infantry division was quartered in Burgos town.

Wellington's preconception of the fortress was that 'it was not unlike a hill fort in India',[24] and these had given him little trouble. Consequently, when he first examined the fortifications he was unpleasantly surprised – not that the works were a formidable obstacle to a force properly equipped and trained in siege warfare, but against the means at his disposal they were indeed formidable for he had only five Royal Engineer officers and eight Royal Military Artificers, and his siege train consisted of three twenty-four-pounder guns with 1,306 rounds of ammunition between them, and five twenty-four-pounder, much worn, brass howitzers. Although he had the 5th Division, which had distinguished itself at Badajoz, he preferred to carry on the siege using two divisions with no previous experience of such operations.

Aitchison's description of the siege is detailed, his views on questions of morale of lasting interest and his criticisms of Wellington shrewd. The background material here is therefore restricted mainly to quoting Wellington's views expressed during and after the siege, and to drawing attention to passages where Aitchison's account differs markedly from that of accepted authorities.

No time was lost in assaulting the outworks, which was successfully accomplished on the night of the nineteenth, mainly through the leadership and valour of Major Edward Somers-Cocks, of the 79th, lately of the 16th Light Dragoons, but at considerable loss. (Fortescue's account differs materially from Aitchison's.)[25]

On 21 September, Wellington wrote to Lord Bathurst, Secretary for War: 'I am apprehensive that the means I have are not sufficient to enable me to take the Castle. I am informed, however, that the enemy are ill provided with water; and that their magazines are in a place exposed to be set on fire. I think it possible, therefore, that I may have it in my power to force them to surrender, though I may not be able to lay the place open to assault.'[26] An attempt was made to take the castle by escalade on the next day. This miscarried and the troops engaged suffered considerable casualties. This failure depressed the besiegers while raising the morale of the garrison. Wellington now decided to breach the place by sap and mine. This meant getting close to the walls, for which the expertise and tools available were barely adequate, a situation that was not helped by heavy rain on the twenty-third. Moreover, all kinds of ammunition and powder soon ran short, since musketry fire had had to substitute for lack of artillery to keep down the heads of the garrison while the work went forward. That day Wellington sent to Santander to ask Commodore Home Popham, for two twenty-four-pounder guns with ammunition, and powder.

On 27 September, Wellington wrote: 'It is not easy however to take a strong place well garrisoned, when one has not a sufficient quantity of cannon; when one is obliged to save ammunition on account of the distance of our magazines; and when one is desirous of saving the lives of soldiers.'[27] It is sometimes contended that Wellington could have got more guns from Home Popham at Santander or from Madrid – indeed Edward Pakenham had offered to see that these reached him. He did seek some from the nearer source, but too late in Aitchison's view, and these were still fifty miles from Burgos when he was forced to raise the siege. Writing to the Prime Minister in November and taking the entire blame for the failure upon himself, he had this to say:

In regards to means, there were ample means both at Madrid and at Santander for the siege of the strongest fortress. That which was wanting at both places was the means of transporting ordnance and military stores to the place where it was desirable to use them. The people of England, so happy as they are in every respect, so rich in resources of every description, having the use of such excellent roads etc will not readily believe that important results here frequently depend upon 50 or 60 mules more or less, or a few bundles of straw to feed them; but the fact is so . . .[28]

The argument about the lack of transport is met by Wellington's critics by pointing to what had been accomplished elsewhere; they argue that, had the guns from Santander been asked for on 20 September, as suggested by Sir Howard Douglas, British Commissioner in Corunna, they would have arrived in good time. This overlooks the fact that Wellington had no intention nor expectation of carrying on a long siege, eleven days longer than that of Badajoz! So that even with the greatest exertions he would not have expected the guns to arrive in time, an error of judgment as we now know.

Many critics also contend, and with good reason, that had Wellington been prepared to commit more men to the assault, as in previous sieges, he would not only have taken the fortress but would have done so with fewer casualties. Aitchison is very interesting on the effects on morale of pitting small numbers of men from a variety of units and nationalities against superior numbers of enemy behind walls. The reason for Wellington doing so was the memory of

Badajoz, which caused him to revert to the eighteenth-century practice of spreading potential losses between regiments in hazardous operations.

On 2 October, Wellington wrote to Hill: 'Although I have not given up all hopes, I am afraid we shall not succeed in taking the castle. It is very strong, well garrisoned, and well provided with artillery. I had only three guns; one of which was destroyed, and another much damaged last night.'[29] Such pessimism in a commander is bound to be reflected in his troops, and it showed in the lack of effort and growing absenteeism among working parties. None had taken part in previous sieges, all were war-weary, and only the Guards fully maintained their morale.

On 29 September a mine was exploded under the west face of the outer wall of the castle, but again the assault failed. This breach was reopened by cannon fire on 4 October and a gallant assault by the 24th Regiment gained a lodgement between the outer and second walls. Preparations for breaching the second wall went forward but at 2 a.m. on 8 October the garrison made a sortie, the second of its kind. They destroyed the sap and approach works and carried off the entrenching tools before being beaten back. It caused the death of a very promising officer, Major Somers-Cocks, to Wellington's deep sorrow.

Following the arrival of forty barrels of powder from Santander, ammunition from Ciudad Rodrigo and 462 French shot, which soldiers had been paid to collect, a final assault was attempted on the eighteenth which again failed. Of it Wellington wrote: 'It is impossible to represent in adequate terms my sense of the conduct of the Guards and German Legion upon this occasion, and I am quite satisfied that if it had been possible to maintain the posts gained with so much gallantry, those troops must have maintained them.'[30] Full credit for the failure of the Allies at Burgos must be given to the gallantry, enterprise and skill with which it was defended by General Dubreton and the garrison. Not only had they held a position of strategic importance for a month but they had, for the time being, broken the spell which Wellington had cast over his troops.

Why did Wellington persist so long in the siege of Burgos after recognizing the inadequacy of his means to reduce it? Was it, as Aitchison suggests, from stubbornness and overestimation of his own abilities? Wellington believed that the political and military advantages that might follow from the reduction of Burgos could be very great. To Lord Liverpool on 23 November he wrote: 'We should have retained still greater advantages, I think, and should have remained in possession of Castile and Madrid during the winter; if I could have taken Burgos, as I ought, early in October.'[31] An examination of all the military factors suggest that this was an optimistic appreciation, but the alternative – another retreat into Portugal – was from every point of view unattractive.

Diary
Escorial
30th August 1812

Four divisions of Infantry, *viz* the 1st, 4th, 5th and 7th, are now collected at this place and well-lodged in large buildings and barracks – no part of the Royal suite of rooms is occupied. These troops, it is reported, are to march to join General Clinton, who with the 6th Division was left at Cuellar to keep the enemy in check during our advance to the capital – he has since, it seems, found it necessary to retire all his posts to the left of the Douro in consequence of the advance of General Foy with the remains of the 'Army of Portugal'. He entered Valladolid on the 14th inst, having previously obliged the Galician army under Santocildes to retire; he has since continued to advance towards Astorga with about 12,000 Infantry and 1,200 Cavalry and he arrived with the latter at La Baneza within 5 leagues of Astorga on the 21st, but the garrison of that place had fortunately been obliged to capitulate on the 19th to the Spaniards and the whole (1,200) were sent off towards Corunna just as the enemy appeared for the relief. On finding this, General Foy returned towards Valladolid, bringing with him the garrison of Zamora (which had been blockaded by the Portuguese Militia under General Silveira) and of Toro, but that of Tordesillas, consisting of 250 men, had surrendered and been carried off by General Santocildes.

The army at Alicante, which has so long been inactive, has at last moved forward and General Maitland, who commands it, was at Montforte on the 17th. It consists of about 8,000 men from Sicily, of whom half are British. Suchet had retired from San Felipe with intention it was supposed of crossing the Xucar, and a division of Spaniards under General Roche had occupied Cadiz in consequence. We marched this day to Guadarrama.

Adaja
5th September 1812

As soon as he found that the forces which Wellington left at Cuellar, on marching to Madrid, were only equal to act defensively, the enemy advanced on the line of the Douro with the whole of his disposable force in the North. These were the remains of Marmont's army, and augmented (as they have been lately) by part of the cavalry from Joseph's army, they only now amount to about 16,000 infantry and 2,500 cavalry, which circumstance says more for the brilliant result of the battle of 22 July than I can otherwise have credited. Wellington no doubt foresaw this movement of the French, and there is reason to believe that he wished to entice them to it; and for this purpose General Clinton, who commanded the force left at Cuellar, was to move from thence back to Olmedo on their advancing and he subsequently retired to Arevalo. The enemy advanced in the first instance to Valladolid from which the Spaniards retired, and they then proceeded towards Astorga with a view to relieving its garrison, but they had luckily capitulated and been marched away prisoners the day before the enemy's cavalry reached it, and the enemy therefore retraced his steps to Valladolid (withdrawing in his retreat a small garrison left in the forts at Zamora and Toro) and in the course of tomorrow he will find it prudent to retire from it also.

The force was assembled with so much expedition that two days ago the enemy did not know that we had more in Arevalo than one division, but we had then 3 divisions of Infantry besides one unattached brigade of 3 regiments, and this evening or tomorrow morning it will be increased by another division of Infantry and we shall then be as numerous as the enemy in Infantry, and be within ten miles of them – our cavalry here are three brigades. Wellington joined us the day before yesterday to direct our movement, and (they say) in less than three weeks he will have left *us* in *Burgos* and returned to Madrid. We have in *it* and the neighbourhood 3 divisions of Infantry and some cavalry.

By that time it is supposed the South of Spain will be free from an enemy's arms in the field – Soult says he is going to join Suchet near *Valencia* – in that case we shall be joined by General Hill, and then another battle in that quarter will I think cause the enemy left as well as his right to be behind the Ebro: Soult is the most experienced and by much the most able of the French Generals in Spain and he may therefore give Wellington a little more trouble than the others, but some of his men have already felt a British attack and *our* men, both British and Portuguese in this army, are now so confident that a battle and victory are synonymous. While we carry on operations against the enemy in the field, General Maitland's army will undertake the siege of those places possessed by them in our rear – such at least is reported to be the plan, and none certainly ever offered brighter propects.

We may expect something from the Galician army – reports speak very favourably of it, and it will have no excuse for not leaving its own province. We had last night a mail with newspapers to 12 August and a messenger arrived in the morning by whom we have news from London of the 17th. The *Gazette* I hear was then published and all your apprehensions allayed. It is said that packets are to go from Corunna now, which will shorten very much the time of your getting our letters.

Hitherto the 1st Division have had little to do, but we shall have our day yet; the companies of the Guards were the only part of our division engaged on the 22nd and they conducted themselves in such a manner as will prove what will be done when our day comes. One officer who was severely wounded there has already joined us, by which I am not now with the Light company. In my last to you I mentioned the great scarcity of money with the army – it still continues to be felt though in less degree, as they have issued a fortnight's pay as being to 24 April. I have not yet drawn on Coutts since I wrote to you but I shall probably have occasion to do so in a few days – the bill will not exceed 30£ so I hope there will be no difficulty in its being honoured.

You will now be so busy that I can hardly expect you will write me yourself just now – but harvest will be over ere you get this and then I hope you will do me that pleasure. The corn is all cut and housed here, the country is one colour throughout, all the grass there having being burnt up. You are before us with your vintage – it will not be general here until the end of this month and we had no grapes before the middle of August. Remember to to my Mother, Robert and all the rest. Adieu.

Diary
Valladolid
7th September 1812

We had yesterday the good fortune to reach the Douro before noon and we crossed the river by the fords of Herrera and Arroyo, and the object of the expedition was nearly being crowned by the most complete success. The enemy we had every reason to expect had no notice of our approach. Indeed, we took them so completely by surprise that their cavalry and artillery were out of camp foraging, and several were taken prisoner by our advanced guards. I spoke to these men and they represented the number of their troops encamped on the heights of La Cisterniga and its neighbourhood at about 6,000 men with 6 pieces in position. They certainly did not seem more, and notwithstanding the nature of their position, which was strong, we had no doubt of success – three strong divisions of Infantry and two brigades of cavalry were up but from some mistake the guns of the 5th Division, which was to have led, missed their way and the attack in consequence was delayed – before they arrived and the other divisions had taken their stations, the enemy had assembled and encircled themselves with vedettes – they also had strong bodies of Infantry on the heights flanking the roads to their position. It was then so late, nearly 5 in the evening, and Wellington then judged it advisable not to attack – we returned to the river and began cooking.

This morning about 11 o'clock we moved forward, the enemy having withdrawn during the night, and we arrived on their late position of La Cisterniga just in time to see their rearguard of cavalry retire through Valladolid across the Pisuerga and blow up the bridge. They were pursued through the town by the cavalry but sustained no loss – it was 11 o'clock before the infantry quitted their bivouac and they afterwards halted for a considerable time on the ground where the French had been posted.

This unhappy result to our expedition, which had every prospect of succeeding, has caused great disappointment in the whole army and an inquiry, it is said, has been ordered into the cause of it, at present it appears to have been originated with Maj.-Gen. Pringle, who commanded the 5th Division (in the absence through illness of General Hulse) in not sending *explicit orders* and a guide to the Artillery attached to it. We bivouacked on the 5th in a wood near the Fresma and shame be it said we were delayed nearly 3 hours in the morning from ignorance or neglect in the QMG's department – nobody could conduct the columns to the proper road – and it was most ludicrous and melancholy to see three different Divisions attempting to get out of the wood – their leaders becoming so confused – changing the direction of march and returning to whence they had set out from – till at length it was thought best to halt till a guide could be procured.[32]

I shall suffer myself to make no more remarks on the person to whom blame was attached but in the failure of the enterprise itself, I cannot say too much – it is too glaring an instance of *incapacity* to be easily forgotten, and when it is considered that the connection which every expedition of a campaign has with another it may be attended with very bad consequences to our further operations.

I have no doubt of success had the attack been made when we first came in sight of the enemy with our Infantry – they were then not more than 6,000 (say 7 or 8,000) and an isolated body, the remainder being at Tordesillas a distance of 15 miles – we had 3 divisions of Infantry up – and although the majority of these were Portuguese and foreigners, yet they had acquired too great an ascendancy by the battle of Salamanca to make it a consideration. Just as we have since seen the position could be turned by its right. For this, however, there was not sufficient time after the arrival of the artillery and it is for their non-arrival that we have to account for the attack not being made. The anxiety which Lord Wellington evinced for the success of the enterprise and the expression of mortification which escaped him sufficiently prove it.

Valladolid 14th September 1812. The inhabitants last night gave a ball for Lord Wellington and the town was illuminated for that night. The garrison of Cuenca quitted it on hearing of the surrender of the Retiro but they were entirely surrounded by Villacampa[33] and were made prisoners. They amount to 1,000 men.

The French who were here under General Clausel – their rearguard is now at Dueñas. It is reported that Soult is making preparations – to evacuate Andalusia – he has published a proclamation at Seville indicative of such intention and holding the Spaniards responsible for the Magazine there till his return.

Heights 3 miles from Burgos 17th September 1812. We broke up from Valladolid on the 15th and followed the enemy by short marches till the evening of the 16th, when we were joined at *Pampliza* by three divisions of infantry of the army of Galicia. There was this day an affair at the outpost and the enemy afterwards took up a position on the heights at about four miles' distance near Celeda del Camino, which they seemed determined to maintain. Wellington on returning from reconnoitring issued the order and it was communicated to the troops at midnight that he intended to attack the enemy at daybreak should they remain in their strong position – we were accordingly under arms and formed at 4 o'clock when we moved forward – but the enemy had withdrawn his main body during the night and their rearguard retired on our approach and were pursued close to Burgos but without loss.

This retreat, before a powerful enemy, of the French has been the slowest perhaps ever known; we seldom marched more than 6 miles a day and the enemy were never passed. The whole country between Valladolid and Burgos by the valley of the Pisuerga is extremely favourable for cavalry and the road is excellent. . . . The valley of the Pisuerga at its greatest breadth does not exceed three miles and is bounded on both sides by a range of high hills – the high road is on the left of the river and by it the British advanced – the Guerrillos of Martinez were on the hills on their left and Don Julian Sanchez with his corps was on the hills on the right of the river, protecting our right, and he was supported by a corps of Spanish Infantry which advanced by the valley. The banks of the Pisuerga generally are very steep though not high, and the bottom is generally so muddy as to be impassable for an army.

Camp
20th September 1812

We are at Burgos – the fort was invested the day after our arrival and the operations against it have been carried on with the rapidity and success which was looked for from the 1st Division. Yesterday morning we made a long detour to get to the N.W. side of the place – we marched left in front and before the rear of our column had halted, the light companies of *Colonel Stirling's* brigade (which formed the advance) gained possession of the outworks on the hill – the Hornwork was assaulted at night by the 42nd Regiment and General Pack's brigade of Portuguese, and after half an hour's resistance was carried in the most brilliant manner.

In this assault we lost nearly 300 men – the Hornwork was defended by 500 of the enemy but they all escaped, except 1 Captain and 62 men who were made prisoner, and we also took 3 pieces of cannon. The gallantry of the 42nd Regiment was conspicuous and they unfortunately suffered severely from a party consisting of 2 companies being ordered to advance slowly in front (firing) so as to draw off the attention of the garrison, while the other troops advanced to the assault. A working party of the Guards were up and began a trench across the Hornwork as soon as it was carried – 3 of these men belonging to the 3rd Regiment very gallantly volunteered their services and *carried the scaling ladders before the forlorn hope.*[34] Tonight ground will be broken with half a musket shot of the body of the place, and 6 days more and I hope to be able to acquaint you with its fall.

On the 16th the Galician army under Santocildes (Don José) completed his junction with us, when Wellington resumed that activity which they had caused being suspended. The enemy to the number of 18,000 were within 3 miles of us in position on advantageous ground, and at midnight he issued an order that it was his intention to attack them should they remain there at daybreak. The enemy, however, did not give us an opportunity – we were under arms two hours before day, but before we could complete the dispositions for attack he withdrew from his position and retreated towards Burgos. Wellington followed with the whole Allied army before onwards of 10 miles, and then halted for the night: during this movement there was only a little skirmishing, their rearguard having fallen back on their main body. As our advance came up on the 18th he withdrew to Burgos and our cavalry passed by it at about two leagues.

The whole of our army are now around Burgos with two divisions of Infantry and a brigade of Light Cavalry advanced on the road towards Vitoria, in which direction the enemy retreated and are now about 20 miles distance from us. The garrison in the castle and works around it, are reported from 1,200–1,800 men and a general officer (said to be chief of the Staff) has undertaken its defence – it is an old Moorish building situated on the summit of a hill immediately above the town, which the French have strengthened by all such modern fortifications as their long experience in Spain have taught them to be best suited for similar defences. Connected with works on a rising hill near, they had constructed a fort, and it was this . . . which the Portuguese and 42nd Regiments stormed last night.

The castle itself is of arched masonry and has been much increased by the enemy. It is so solid as to have a battery of 8 heavy pieces on the top, and these are so elevated as to command all the out-works and every eminence within shot. The works, however, which have been taken are being converted into works of attack and they already offer cover to our working parties, and the reverse side of the hill, which is shelved, protects the men as they approach to relieve so that our loss in the attack has yet been very small – the 42nd suffered severely in the storm; two officers were killed, and amongst the wounded poor Menzies is the worst – his leg was broken at the commencement and in carrying him off another ball entered the thigh, ran down the bone and lodged in the groin. Our division is besieging. It is not yet come to my turn. Before it does the works will be so near completed as comparatively to put me in safety.

The Galician army amounts to 11,000 men – the Infantry are not promising in their appearance – the cavalry (3 Regiments) are tolerable, the artillery are the best; those which I had the best opportunity of seeing are in the *highest order* and well appointed. The whole force of the enemy in this part of Spain are called under 30,000 in the field and round these there are perhaps as many Guerrillas but these show themselves of very little use when united. Our army including the Spaniards I suppose 28,000 in the field, so that if they will but fight there is no doubt we shall beat the French. Mina (a Guerrillo leader of boundless activity) has undertaken to break up the roads to France to prevent their escape.

Diary
23rd September 1812

Our works have been carried on with the rapidity which was to be expected of the 1st Division but not with the success which they merit. The hornwork has a considerable command over some parts of the body of the place – a battery of three pieces has been constructed in its gorge behind the palisades and the trenches have been carried down to the right and another battery of 4 pieces already made, which has a commanding direct fire on the second line and is so well placed as to have only an oblique fire upon itself. The batteries have not yet opened, but in consequence of their being so forward it was attempted last night to make a lodgement within the first line. For this purpose 400 men were employed – half British and half Portuguese – the Portuguese were destined to escalade from near the Gate and running along the covert way to clear it, while the British attempted to escalade in front of the old wall, but the night unfortunately being very light and the Portuguese so strongly opposed, they were compelled to desist, so that the British found it impossible to drive back the enemy in the front attack. . . . There was this day a truce for two hours to bury the dead and the Governor of the Castle, General Dubreton, most handsomely gave up all the men who were wounded and left in the ditch.

The failure of this attempt has produced a strong sensation in the troops and very unfavourable reports to success are in circulation. In fact the place is very considerable and our means of attack very limited – we have no battering guns but three 18-pdrs (known as Thunder, Lightning and one with a damaged trunnion, Nelson, and five 24-pdr howitzers), and the place is so much greater an obstacle in consequence than was Ciudad Rodrigo that it is said the Engineers have given their opinion that it will be doing an injustice to the Artillery to make them open their fire. The Castle itself is a high square building of masonry and so solid as to have five 24-pdrs on the top and it is fortified so as to form a sort of Citadel; and this again is surrounded by all such works as the French in their great experience of such situations in Spain have found best calculated for its defence. The work is irregular but approaching in form a four-sided figure – the first line is of earth towards the hornwork but in some places with a stone revetment and a small Convent at one of the angles is dextrously taken into it so as to add greatly to its strength – the parapet is fraised throughout its extent and all the guns have embrasures. The second line is a fauss-bray, being lower than the rampart and at about 10 feet from it, which space is intersected by palisades. In front of this again, there is a shallow ditch and covertway with palisades. The hill of St Michael is at the distance of about 250 yards and is directed, on the body of the place there is a high stone wall running down the hill on which the Castle stands about 100 yards to an old wall, which appears to have been erected merely to support the earth which is scarped – this however is angled and coming round nearly parallel to the second line, opposite the Convent, forms a third line – it has a parapet fraised throughout, and at the point of the wall a covered way and small glacis. This is separated next the town by a covered communication and palisades, so as to form a flank defence with musketry on the approaches from the hornwork. It was this point which was last night attacked and at the lowest point. Mines are now talked of as being the only sure method of gaining it and a week after having made a lodgement in it the place ought to be taken.

In noticing the failure of the attack it is but proper to note also that the force employed was composed of many different corps – Portuguese, British and Germans, and the men were not appraised of the nature of the service for which they were required until the moment of attack. They were thus unprepared for the desperate enterprise, and instead of having made up their minds they were taken in the moment of irresolution – they knew that the garrison of the place far outnumbered themselves – they had no personal knowledge of the officer who commanded and they could have but little reliance on those supported because they were unacquainted with each other. Nor was the honour of any particular corps pledged. Hence the want of that confidence so necessary on such occasions, and under these circumstances it would have been more wonderful to have had success than it has been in being defeated. Instead of following with the characteristic boldness of British soldiers they went on as if to execution, and on reaching the walls when decision was wanted they appeared seized with a stupor and stood exposed to a disastrous fire without having the power of returning it. This is an unhappy omen at the beginning of a siege; in such operations prodigies are required of men and they are realized through confidence – but let not the spirits be depressed – where much is required let every assistance, real or imaginary, be brought forward and on such occasions employ whole regiments or detachments from one corps – their honour then becomes pledged and from a reciprocity of confidence in the Officer and Soldier and Soldier and Officer, even seeming impossibilities are overcome. I shall now say no more as I trust that this instance will be the last of employing a body of men from different corps.

Burgos
26th September 1812

The operations of the siege have been carried on with much activity, although there is a prospect of their being prolonged considerably beyond the time which I stated that the fort was likely to fall. The guns are in our batteries but they have not yet opened, as it is though our ordnance are not sufficiently heavy and *numerous* to effect the reduction of the Castle by a breech – the trenches have therefore been carried *close* to the outer walls and mines are being made – an attempt was made to carry the lower defences by assault a few nights since, but it unfortunately failed – Major Lawrie of the 79th, who commanded, was killed and our loss otherwise severe – two officers of our brigade were wounded – our whole loss however has not been very great – as our covering parties fire so much musketry at the enemy as to prevent their artillery-men taking steady aim – we are in some places so near that the guns cannot be pointed low enough to hit us, and the ground is so soft and free of stones as to diminish the effects of shells bursting – but it has been by these that we have principally suffered – the attempt to storm the other night was made by detachments; it would have been much better to have employed whole regiments – the men would then have known who to rely on for support – had this been done I am certain we should have succeeded within possibility.

Diary
30th September 1812

After the failure on the 22nd a mine was begun under the lower wall and it was exploded last night. A party from the 6th Division was destined to enter by the breach and make a lodgement. The advance of this party (a corporal and three) gained the breach but the Field Officer with his party lost their way and the advance were driven back and no lodgement was made. Thus again has another failure taken place – I shall not say from employing detachments of different regiments, but in this as in the former instance such were employed. The three 18-pdrs are in the battery in the hornwork and howitzers in the other battery, but neither have opened yet – nay, it is said that from the superior fire from the works that our fire will have no effect and that we are to attempt to take the place by musketry and mining 'veramus' – The walls indeed are not thick – they are of a sort of medium between field and permanent fortifications – I think about 10 feet thick – but they are well provided with ordnance and the garrison is strong – said to amount to 2,500 men.

They are considerably annoyed by the fire of our musketry and in consequence the fire of their guns is ill directed and does little execution – their shells are not well thrown, in general falling either much too short or going too far – they do not appear to understand mortar practice by shortening the fuse, and hence they are compelled to fire with a great elevation from which some of their shells have burst in their own works after a nearly perpendicular flight – they have now however improved in securing their marksman and everyone has an embrasure made on the top of the parapet by two wooden boxes filled with earth and so placed as to fire from between them.

The breach made last night does not seem practicable and the enemy are being employed securing it – they are cutting a trench across it and defending this with a parapet of gabions.

5th October The trenches leading from the hornwork have been completed so as to join those carried on by the 6th Division from the town, and some of our firing parties are so close to the outer wall to be seen from it only. On the 3rd the howitzer battery opened and fired 24-pdr shot from them on the old breach and rendered it pretty good by yesterday afternoon. At 5 in the evening a new breach was sprung close to it and the 24th Regiment, which had been ordered into the trenches for the purpose (at 2 o'clock), immediately stormed both breaches in the most gallant style and effected a lodgement with small loss.

The enemy were taken by surprise at first but they soon assembled and then opened a tremendous fire from every gun which could be brought to bear – all was unavailing. They made a sortie at night but were speedily driven back with loss. The approach to the lower works is much favoured by the nature of the ground, which is broken and being considerably lower than the foot of the wall is not seen from it. In this low situation two attempts were made to construct batteries with a view to improve the first breach and the guns (three 18-pdrs) for that purpose were brought there, but the enemy brought so many to bear upon this battery that it was unable to open – the parapet was both times knocked to pieces and left barely sufficient shelter for the artillery – men who were compelled to *lie* down close to the parapet – two out of three guns were wounded, one severely in the muzzle, and the other having a wheel broken and after being moved from about 50 yards from the battery was left exposed to the enemy for the whole day. They have since been brought to their old places, two in the hornwork and one in the howitzer battery.

During the storming by the 24th the enemy were fired upon apparently with effect by several howitzers and 9-pdrs with Shrapnel shot[35] from different situations at a distance, and they were also fired upon by all the guns and howitzers in the battery. These consisted of: one/18-pdr, one/9-pdr and three/24-pdrs howitzers.

This success has improved the spirits of the army, though those likely to know are not yet sanguine of taking the place – the garrison however are said to be suffering much from a scarcity of water and the enemy are reported to have made a movement to their left towards Logroño in the design, it is said, of bringing off the Garrison. This perhaps would be the best thing that could happen to us, though they hold different language at H.Q. – there they talk only of preventing the *escape* of the garrison.

I went into the town today and was very happy to find a woman at almost every door busily employed in tearing rags to pieces to make lint for the hospitals – they seem all in great spirits and the prospect of soon being freed from the enemy, who ever since the commencement of the siege have kept them in dreadful alarm – the castle completely commands the whole town and looks particularly into the market-place – into this they constantly fire and several of the inhabitants have been wantonly wounded from no other course than appearing. While noting this cruel behaviour of the enemy I cannot help noting an instance of want of *gallantry* shown myself today. On returning to camp with another officer we overtook a party of Spaniards consisting of Father, Mother and two daughters – we accosted them and invited them to our tents, which the ladies with the affability peculiar to their country women immediately accepted – for a considerable part of the way we were hid by the garden walls and trees from the castle but we came to a part where the road ran so exposed to it that to avoid being fired at one went across the fields. I mounted the elder daughter behind me to cross a ditch and proceeded in full view of the Castle when, near a second ditch, they (unlike the politeness which the French have so much credit) threw a shell at us, but luckily we were at such a distance that we received no injury from the explosion which took place.

Burgos on the whole is a very handsome town, though at present in great disorder. Many (nearly half) of the houses are shut up, but there is nevertheless a most excellent market which is well supplied with mutton equal in fat and flavour to English and as great a profusion (good quality) of fruit and vegetables as I ever saw. There is also great quantities of fresh butter made from cow's milk and brought on women's backs from the province of Santander – chiefly from the hills of Reynsa at a distance of 28 leagues. These women are very extraordinary-looking beings – they are remarkably stout and from their dress very difficult to know whether men or women (this is Basque country).

There are large barracks for both Infantry and Cavalry on the flat by the riverside and one row of very handsome houses between the two ridges of Segovia, and the river here, as in Madrid, is separated into two channels. Between them there are fine walks between rows of trees which appear to have been planted within 30 years. The high road too is ornamented on both sides with trees from Celada de Camino and these continue beyond Burgos. The country about Burgos generally is very flat and there are many very small runs of water and ditches, all of which are very difficult to pass from the nature of the soil, which is a deep and stiff clay.

The enemy have raised the siege of Cadiz and retired and Colonel Skerrett with one brigade of British and some Spanish troops have carried the defences of Seville by assault and obliged the enemy to retreat from the town. There now remains no doubt of their quitting Andalusia. The troops here have hutted, the weather has become very cold and there is much damp in the night, but the troops on the whole are healthy. The 'Armies of the North' and of Portugal still continue quiet on the Ebro, where they retired to on our approaching Burgos.

7th October Since we established ourselves in the outer work, our parties have been at work in improving the breaches made by the mines and in throwing down the fraises and walls so that it is now easy of ascent in every point, and the parapet which was formerly a defence for the enemy now affords good protection to us – along the whole extent we have parties to fire which is not above 100 yards from the second line, and on our right our men are within a few yards of the enemy – so close indeed as almost to reach each other with their bayonets – we are now proceeding by sap towards the second line and another mine under it is in a considerable state of preparation.

The enemy yesterday attempted to drive us out of the works, and at about 4 in the afternoon they made a sortie with a great part of the garrison – they drove in all our men and regained both breaches, but a party of about 30 of the Guards were well protected behind the parapet near the stone wall on the left and they maintained themselves in it till the troops which had been driven out of the breaches rallied when, animated by the example of the Guards, they cheered and stormed again and afterwards drove the enemy into their works. Captain C. particularly distinguished himself and it was chiefly owing to his conduct [and] of two Sergeants of the Guards that we regained our situation – the enemy used all in their power to drive out the small party of the Guards – they rolled down shells, grenades, etc and they had even the audacity to approach to their side of the parapet and stab at our men with their bayonets, but they suffered for their temerity and the ground was strewn with their dead. The ardour of our men after the enemy gave way was not to be restrained and they jumped over the parapet and pursued them to the second line, from which circumstance our loss was severe, not less than 120 in all. The enemy effected their purpose too far in destroying our gabions and levelling the sap and they carried off all the working tools. There has been a considerable fall of rain which has tended to impede our progress.

Camp before Burgos
7th October 1812

Since we came here the time of despatching a mail had been very uncertain and we have not been told of it as we used to be formerly, but I hear that one will be sent off this evening and I wrote on the chance of it – knowing how anxious you'll be to hear from me.

The siege of the fort has been prosecuted with much assiduity since I last wrote to you and considerable success, but the weather for the last week has been very wet and consequently unfavourable to our operations. It has retarded our approaches and rendered the soil, of which the enemy's works are constructed, so adhesive greatly to diminish the effect of our shot: we have, however, succeeded in making a small breach in the second wall – and although the enemy in two different sorties effected their purpose (destroying our works) we have re-established our sap and prolonged it to the glacis – the siege is therefore drawing to a close – and we may calculate on the place being in our possession in two or three days after we have made a lodgement in the second wall – and this I presume will be affected in the course of today or tomorrow.

The storm of another work I told you took place in open day and the enemy attempted to regain the work during the night but were repulsed – next day at 4 in the afternoon they renewed this attempt with their whole garrison and aided by the most tremendous fire, which I ever saw of cannon, they succeeded in driving us out of both breaches and they levelled our works and carried off the intrenching tools – but a small party of about 30 of our men maintained themselves behind a breastwork (the enemy being on the near side and stabbing at each other with bayonets) and from their spirited conduct the work was regained and we were completely re-established in it before dark. An officer of our regiment (the only one present) was wounded and our whole loss was, I believe, about 120. They made a sortie again about midnight on the 6th and levelled our sap but they were soon driven back – Major Cocks, 79th Regiment, was unfortunately killed, and the army in him has lost one of its most promising officers.

The breach in the second wall was practicable on the 9th and the enemy supposing we would storm came out at night to prevent us – no attempt was however made but the Coldstream Guards, who were in the trenches, drove back the enemy losing one Ensign, 12 men killed and about 30 wounded – my regiment was on duty this morning for 12 hours. It has not been my turn again since I wrote my sister. I think it will very likely not again come to me before the place is taken.

A deserter came out yesterday and reports that the garrison have 700 sick and wounded – that they are extremely dissatisfied and have made application to the Governor to surrender but he is determined to resist until the last and has shot two men for remonstrating – there is certainly no reason why he should give in yet – indeed, by the laws of war he ought to suffer death if he did, but it is probable that as soon as we have established ourselves in the second wall that he will capitulate.

The enemy in our front have collected and a new general Souham (took over 3rd October) has assumed the command, but they have not advanced and their outposts I believe are fifteen miles off.

It is reported that our division and a brigade of cavalry are to go to the South with Wellington after this place is taken – I hope it will be so, as I have suffered sufficient wet and cold to make me wish myself away from this – the winter here is very severe and there is no comfort of a fire in the houses. We have built a kitchen of turf and thatched with reeds which we find a luxury in these cold nights. Adieu.

Diary
14th October 1812

Notwithstanding the wetness of the weather the works of the siege have been carried on, but we have not renewed our sap – the firing parties are established between the exterior and interior lines within a hundred yards of the body of the place. Our hopes of taking the place are very low – indeed, it is quite evident that our means are inadequate and it is now said that our operations are to be suspended until the guns arrive from Santander. The sailors have run them up to Reinosa and an engineer and the horses of the reserve are gone from here to bring them. Musket ammunition is uncommonly scarce from the great expenditure against the castle. The enemy are approaching – yesterday there was an affair between the Cavalry at the outposts.

19th October For several days lately the howitzers have been used in throwing red-hot shot into the church in the inner line, but although they have destroyed the roof they have not been able to set it on fire. On the night of the 17th the 3rd Regiment, being in the trenches, attempted to remove some boxes which formed a parapet for the enemy but two officers were wounded (Lts. Holbom and Knox) severely and we were obliged to desist. A mine which was carried on, on the 18th was reported ready and it was determined to storm the breach – escalade the line at the moment of the explosion, for which purpose 350 of the K.G.L. were ordered into the trenches at 3 in the afternoon to reinforce the 450 of the Coldstream Guards already there. The mine was accordingly sprung at 5 in the afternoon and the breach caused by it was instantly attacked by a detachment of Portuguese and Spaniards. The breach made by the gun was at the same time attacked by the German Legion and the line was escaladed in a most gallant manner by the Guards; all these attacks succeeded and the Portuguese maintained themselves, but the enemy soon brought so tremendous a fire upon the Germans and Guards that they were both obliged to retire suffering great loss – Major Warren of the K.G.L. was killed and 1 Ensign killed and 2 Lts. wounded. Nothing could exceed the gallantry of the German Legion and Guards – they advanced with the greatest intrepidity, and after carrying the second line, planted the ladders against the inner wall, which some of the men even stormed and it was evident that had the breach been larger and those appointed to attack it more numerous, then the place would have been taken.

The whole of the men employed in the storm did certainly not exceed 700. The *breach* was not above 10 feet wide and the garrison were at least 2,000. In stating the great superiority of the garrison to the numbers by which they were attacked, I cannot but remark the impolicy of it. It appears to me that to ensure success men should have confidence in themselves, which in all desperate cases is only to be acquired by numerical superiority – in this instance it will be answered perhaps that the numbers would not have been of use, as from the smallness of the front attack no more could have been employed advantageously, but it must be recollected that they might have been in the trenches ready to support and I am persuaded from what I have seen that a soldier knowing that whatever may happen *his party is the stronger* will go on to attack a large body with a confidence which will ensure success, whereas when his own party is inferior to that which opposes him both in numbers and situation, he is, in a measure, beaten before he begins and the least difficulty leading him to expect defeat he ceases at once to persevere.

In every instance therefore where the individual courage of the common Soldier is to be exercised, I hold it as a general rule that it must be strengthened by showing him that he is the strongest party – few vulgar minds can estimate the rate of advantages of situation, but *all can count heads*. If this principle be admitted, its application is particularly strong in the instance in question, where the garrison had it in their power to *count* every man singularly as he entered the trenches. At night it is different and a small body attacking a greater has a good chance of success from the alarm and confusion and the ignorance of the assailed in the number of their enemies.

With the failure of this attack the siege at Burgos may be considered terminated, for the enemy have assembled and are advancing to its relief and it is beyond a doubt our inability to take it without a great addition to our means. Thus after the exertions of a long month has this victorious army been defeated by a petty *fortress* with the loss of 2,500 men – merely I may say from self-sufficiency in its Commander – for it is the most lenient term which my imagination suggests in excuse for him. As it is now beyond correction it will be of little use to vent reproach on the author of this defeat, but it may be an instructive lesson to examine the causes of it. It will show that the most noble minds and greatest heroes are liable to over-rate their own talents or by being intoxicated with success to commit themselves from inconsideration.

I will be perhaps wrong to go so far back, but since 6 September a strange fatality has attended the operations of this army, which there is little doubt might have been avoided had the attack of that date been as successful as it should have been. Clausel's force, however augmented, would never have made head against us, much less have acted offensively and whence failure – over-confidence and the same thing or presumption has now caused our defeat at Burgos. Before he undertook the expedition Wellington must have been fully aware of the obstacles which he had to overcome and he should have provided accordingly at all events after he himself saw Burgos. He knew the nature of its defences and consequently could estimate the means proper for its reduction.

Whichever assumption be correct his conduct will be condemnable. If the first, it is in vain to throw the blame on the British Ministry for not supplying a battering train – the victory of Salamanca supplied us with that – as at Madrid we found a battering train equal to reduce a Fortress of the third order and it will augur an incredible poverty in Spain to deny the possibility of her transporting it. But heavy guns were moved from Segovia to Ciudad Rodrigo, a distance a little short of that from Madrid to Burgos. In the second his discretion is only to be defended at the expense of his good judgement.

If he saw that his means were inadequate to take the place, why did he persevere after carrying the hornwork – it would have been proper then to have waited till guns were brought from the ships at Santander (a measure which was resorted to when too late). The distance is only 14 leagues and at the beginning of the siege everybody said they were necessary. In every point of view this failure is most unfortunate – it has undeceived the French of our invincibility – it has dampened the ardour of our own men – it has diminished their confidence in our Chief – as he betrayed unsteadiness in frequently changing his plan of attack and in resolution of carrying it into execution when fixed upon, and lastly it has excited apprehension in the Spaniards and in some places matured their passiveness into indirect hostility.

In short it has blasted our prospects in the present campaign and damaged our plans for the next.

We have remained all day ready to march, since yesterday morning the enemy have shown a determination to advance – Wellington has been out all day reconnoitring – uncommon rain. No work going on – hornwork mined at the salient angles – tools given into store.

Camp before Burgos
Monday morning 19th October 1812

Another week has passed and we have not brought our operations against the Castle nearer a close than when I last wrote to you. The weather has certainly been very miserable (almost incessant rain and very cold) which in a slight degree has impeded us, but our Chief I fear has presumed a great deal too much on his name and attacked with very inadequate means. On first seeing it, we were prepared to find it a more serious obstacle than was Ciudad Rodrigo, but no one imagined that it would last 11 days more than the siege of Badajoz, and *at the end of that time* to be as unable as at the beginning to calculate when it would fall – at present I shall say no more – it would but serve to alarm my own apprehensions without quieting yours.

I have been in the trenches since I last wrote to you but I do not think it will come to my turn again (for a week anyway) unless some extraordinary duties should be required, and in less than that time it is to be hoped that we shall either have reduced the place, or have converted our siege into a blockade, until the arrival of additional means. We began with only three heavy guns; two of these were rendered useless *before the batterys opened* – Wellington confessed in his public despatch *these* inadequate to the reduction of the *temporary* forts at Salamanca – however much more then ought he to have judged them inadequate for the destruction of the *permanent defences here*? I have not been in the habit much of questioning the *conduct* of our Chief, even when it differed from what I expected, but it is as proper to speak sometimes as it is fit at other times to be silent and I own it appears in this instant to be *extremely impolitic* not to say *most wantonly reprehensible*.

10 o'clock – The working parties in the trenches have been discontinued this morning and our division (which is the only one before Burgos) – have been ordered to be ready to march at a moment's notice – we are yet ignorant of the cause – weather today is worse than ever – it blows excessively hard and rains in torrents – I hope we are only moving into cantonments, as although the enemy have collected and been joined by M. Massena[36] they are not reported to be advancing. Our whole loss in the siege at this stage must be 2,000. Adieu.

Throughout the siege there had been considerable skirmishing between the covering troops and the enemy. On 3 October, Souham relieved Clausel in command of the Army of Portugal pending the return of Massena (Marmont having been invalided) – an event that never took place. From the thirteenth onwards activity greatly increased and on the twentieth Wellington pulled back the covering force to a naturally strong position nearer Burgos, adding the 1st Division, less Stirling's brigade, to the 5th and 7th Divisons, and the Spanish forces. In the last days of the siege Sir Edward Paget arrived to take command of the 1st Division, bringing with him Colonel James Stanhope, who wrote in his journal: 'The 1st Division is halted or rather bogged down between the Castle and Villa Toro. . . . I visited the trenches. They are the very devil, for if one is not drowned or choked with mud at the first Boyau, one is nearly sure of being shot in the first line if above five feet high. I never saw anything like it. If you held up a cap, you had two or three balls through it at once.'[37]

Souham advanced against the Spanish part of this line with 15,000 men, so exposing his flank to the Allies. Seeing this Wellington galloped up to Paget, saying: 'By God! I never saw so impudent a thing in my life; do move down and attack them.'[38] Thereupon the 1st Division, supported by the 5th, drove the French back, but it was too late in the day to exploit this success.

The Army of Portugal had had its morale restored, and reinforcements from France and a detachment from Caffarelli's Army of the North enabled Souham to put about 51,000 men into the field. This was unknown to Wellington when he planned to give battle on the anniversary of Trafalgar with an Allied army of 21,000 plus 12,000 Spanish troops of dubious value. However, that afternoon Wellington heard from Hill, who had been left to contain the Army of Andalusia, that he had had to retire before the combined forces of Joseph and Soult. The planned diversion in the south had not been effective nor had the rains come, so that the Tagus remained fordable. The French with some 61,000 men, faced Hill's Allied army of 34,000 plus 12,000 Spaniards.

Wellington stood on the Pisuerga and Carrion during 23–25 October, when, owing to the bad behaviour of some Spaniards, he found both his flanks turned and had to race Macune for the bridge at Cabezon. From Cabezon he wrote to Lord Bathurst:

> I felt severely the sacrifice I was obliged to make. Your Lordship is well aware that I never was very sanguine in my expectations of success in the siege of Burgos, notwithstanding that I considered that success was attainable, even with the means in my power, within a reasonably limited period. If the attack on the first line on 22nd or 29th had succeeded, I believe we should have taken the place [he attributed failure to mistakes made by the troops through inexperience], notwithstanding the ability with which the Governor conducted the defence, and the gallantry with which it was executed by the garrison.[39]

By now Wellington had learnt the strength of the forces against him and realized that his intention of holding the line of the Douro was no longer practicable. To Hill, separated from him by 150 miles, he wrote that if he, Wellington, were able to delay the enemy sufficiently, Hill was to retire to Arevalo, where he would join him, but if not Hill must retire by the Tagus valley.

By the end of October Souham had crossed the Douro at Tordesillas and reached Toro, and on 30 October Hill evacuated Madrid. Wellington, who had taken up a position behind the Douro with headquarters at Rueda, had 'got clear away in a handsome manner, of the worst scrape I ever was in'. Here he remained until 6 November. 'I fairly bullied the French into remaining quiet on the Douro for seven days,'[40] he claimed. This achievement was much assisted by Caffarelli withdrawing his forces from Souham's command, making the two sides approximately equal.

Wellington now decided that the forces threatening his lines of communication necessitated joining Hill not at Arevalo but further west at Salamanca, and issued orders accordingly. On 8 November the two Allied armies met in the Salamanca area. Wellington, including his Spanish forces, had about 65,000 men, which he at first deployed covering both sides of the Tormes, but later on when Soult, Joseph had put in overall command of all these armies, started to turn his left flank, he withdrew to the right bank on to the old Arapil position. These preparations for battle on the ground of their former triumph greatly raised British morale. But the longed-for trial by combat was not to be. Soult, despite having 80,000 men, was shy of attacking Wellington in his chosen position and, learning from the mistakes of Marmont, he moved wide on the Allied right flank to manoeuvre them out of the position. Unfortunately the Tormes was still fordable – had the rains come Wellington believed he could have gone into winter quarters on that river.

The climax came on 15 November when the soldiers on both sides looked forward to a trial of strength in what might have proved to be the decisive battle of the war. Wellington had determined, if the French refused battle, to retire on Rodrigo; the sick and the baggage had already been sent off. At two o'clock, when there were still no signs of a French attack, Wellington gave orders for the plan of retreat (in three columns with the Light Division forming the rear guard) to be put into effect. The hazardous process of disengaging in the face of a numerically superior enemy was greatly helped by heavy rain, which was to continue for most of the retreat, 'at 4 o'clock it was as dark as night'.[41]

The most terrible part of the retreat was about to begin. Morale, which has been high when battle seemed imminent, collapsed into sullen resentment as soon as further retreat, in pouring rain and deep mud, was ordered. The armies of Wellington and Hill had already exhibited many breaches of discipline during their retreat to Salamanca, and many stragglers had been taken by the French. From now on things were to get progressively worse and the scenes of misery engendered by cold, wet and hunger are vividly depicted in John Aitchison's letters. There are, however, two matters on which he does not touch but which deserve mention.

Among the retreating columns were hundreds of wives, camp followers and soldiers' children. They enjoyed no privileges but shared to the full the miseries of the men. Some were tough old campaigners whose whole lives had been a struggle for survival, but others, the wives of officers, were the product of gentle homes. Notable among these were the lovely young Juanita Smith and Susanna Dalbiac, wife of Lieutenant-Colonel Charles Dalbiac, commanding the 4th Dragoons, and daughter of a former commanding officer of that regiment. Married in 1804, this girl, who had been a delicate child, had followed her husband everywhere. In Spain she rode with him at the head of the regiment and more than once found herself on the field of battle. At Salamanca she watched from a flank, but within range of the enemy artillery, her husband lead the 4th Dragoons in the magnificent charge by Le Marchant's brigade. Believing him to be wounded, she spent the night alone upon the battlefield searching for him among the dead and dying. Before the final retreat she spent much of her time in Salamanca looking after the wounded. Throughout it she slept on the ground each night, sharing a sodden blanket with her husband. Not all were such admirable characters, but characters many of them were, tough and indomitable, who were as likely to get drunk as their men and often proved the greater plunderers.

British field commanders in the Napoleonic Wars had endeavoured to cut down the horde of camp followers and baggage which the army attracted, but with scant success. Some idea of the problems these presented to an army on active service, even in good times, can be gleaned from this extract from Colonel Lejeune's[42] journal of the Peninsular War, recording how he had been passed by

> . . . an English Captain riding on a very fine horse and warding off the sun with a parasol: behind him came his wife very prettily dressed, with a small straw hat, riding on a mule and carrying not only a parasol, but a little black and tan dog on her knee, while she led by a cord a she-goat, to supply her with milk. Beside Madame walked her Irish nurse, carrying in a green silk rapper a baby, the hope of the family. A grenadier, the Captain's servant, came behind and occasionally poked up the long-eared steed of his mistress with a staff. Last in the procession came a donkey loaded with much miscellaneous baggage, which included a tea-kettle and a cage of canaries; it was guarded by an English servant in livery, mounted on a sturdy cob and carrying a long posting-whip, with which he occasionally made the donkey mend its pace.[43]

Much of the misery of the retreat was inevitable, but the inefficiency of Colonel Willoughby Gordon, who had been sent out to be quartermaster general, and the insubordination of some senior officers and the collapse of discipline, accounted for that which was not. That many units were reduced to eating acorns and making forays into the woods to shoot pig, for which two men were hung, and that the British were short of Spanish supply wagons, was largely due to Gordon having sent the supplies to the rear by the wrong route. Aitchison complains frequently about the lack of transport. This was caused in no small measure by the bad conduct during the retreat of officers in charge of convoys towards the Spanish muleteers and waggoners, which caused them to desert in large numbers.

On 18 November, Wellington ordered the retreat to continue on three routes. That allotted to the Spanish army crossed a flooded stream by a bridge, while the two columns of the Allies were given more circuitous routes which crossed the stream at fords. General William Stewart, who had taken command of the 1st Division when Sir Edward Paget was captured by the French on the previous day, got together with two other divisional commanders and decided to disregard orders and cross by the bridge. It is easy to imagine the delay and chaos this insubordination entailed. When the troops did not appear on their expected route, Wellington set off to find them. On the way, it is said, he encountered an officer in charge of a convoy. When he asked what he was doing, Wellington was told: 'I've lost my baggage,' to which he replied: 'Well! I can't be surprised . . . for I can't find any army.'[44] Arriving at the bridge Wellington for once was speechless, for 'By God! it was too serious to say anything.' Fortunately Soult made no attempt to take advantage of this opportunity to inflict a most serious defeat on the Allies. It is surprising that John Aitchison makes no mention of the incident since his own division was involved. It highlights the degree to which Wellington had temporarily lost the confidence of his subordinate commanders. The indiscipline shown during the siege of Burgos, which increased as the retreat progressed, and accounted for the loss of 7,000 men by the time Ciudad Rodrigo was reached, was mainly the result of war-weariness. Wellington, with his usual understatement, wrote: 'They have been in the field and almost continually marching since January last; their clothes and equipment are much worn, and a short period in cantonments would be useful to them.'[45]

Late on 19 November the army reached the vicinity of Ciudad Rodrigo. The 3rd Division halted in the dark and Sergeant Joe Donaldson of the 94th recorded: 'We heard at last the well-known summons of "Turn out for biscuit" ring in our ears. We had got to food at last. Instead of the orderly division each man seized what he could get, and began to allay the dreadful gnawing pain which had tormented us for four days of unexampled cold and fatigue.'[46] Last of all came the exhausted rearguard, the Light Division, who had been without rations longer than any other formation.

The campaign of 1812, which had started with such bright hopes, had in the eyes of the rank and file ended in failure. They blamed Wellington for not trusting them to beat the enemy at a second Salamanca, and their faith in their leader had been badly shaken. Those not prepared to blame Wellington blamed the government. Wellington, who above all wanted to see the government supported, publicly accepted responsibility for any failure. On the credit side he could claim that since January nearly 20,000 prisoners had been sent to England and that the arsenals at Ciudad Rodrigo, Badajoz, Salamanca, Valladolid, Astorga, Madrid and Seville had had their contents taken or destroyed, including some 30,000 cannon.

From the other side of the hill the campaign of 1812 appeared to be a considerable success for the Allies. General Maximilian Foy, who had formed a high opinion of Wellington and who was to meet him finally on the field of Waterloo, wrote: 'Lord Wellington has retired unconquered with glory of the Arapiles (Salamanca), having restored to the Spaniards the country south of the Tagus, and made us destroy our magazines and fortifications – in a word all that we have gained by our conquest, and all that could assure the maintenance of it.'[47]

Diary
21st October 1812

We moved forward yesterday morning before daybreak and took up a position covering the road from Vitoria. The enemy presented himself at about 5 in the afternoon. The 1st and 5th Divisions immediately moved down to the plain upon him and drove him back and we afterwards returned to our position on the heights. . . . General Pack's Portuguese brigade – some Spaniards – the 58th and 24th Regiments are left in the trenches.

There is one circumstance I find that I have not mentioned of the siege of Burgos. We were so short of ammunition after two of the 18-pdrs were rendered unserviceable (which be it remembered was the case before they opened) that a reward was offered in General Orders for every shot brought to the depot of 8-pdrs and 16-pdrs which correspond to our

9-pdrs and 18-pdrs from this precarious source a considerable supply was obtained but the expenditure of our single 18-pdr was so great that for this it was not sufficient.

22nd October. At sunset last night every preparation was made for retreat and we began to move as soon as it was dark. The baggage having been sent off about two in the afternoon the troops began to move off about 5 in the evening. The Artillery and all carriages of the army and the cavalry moved round by Villa Toro to avoid being annoyed by the fire of the Castle[48] but the 1st Division of Infantry passed through the town of Burgos, and for a considerable distance along the riverside within musket shot of the Castle, and although it was very clear moonlight they were not discovered and consequently not fired upon. . . .

Tordesillas 31st October. Our army is now encamped on some rising ground without any shelter – the water is very bad and wood nearly a mile off.

What we are to do a few days more will determine – it is to be hoped we shall be able to maintain the line of the Douro but unfortunately for us all the towns are on the right bank, which is occupied by the enemy, and it will therefore be very difficult. Could we have occupied Tordesillas with 10 or 15,000 men as a *tête-de-pont* there might have been some chance, as in all probability the enemy will not be able to remain long collected from the operation of the Guerrillos in their rear. But this not having been done, the thing, I fear, is impossible. On the night of the 29th and the greater part of yesterday there was a great fall of rain which has swollen the river tremendously but it is now fine.

Camp
31st October 1812

Since I wrote to you on the 19th instant most important events to this army and the cause of Spain have taken place, but I am sorry to say that they have not been of that promising nature as those which occurred in the early part of the campaign. We have returned to the Douro where our offensive operations, I fear, may be considered as already terminated for the present year. As it would only add to the melancholy which their non-accomplishment has created, I shall not now revert to the brilliant prospects of this army opened by the victory of Salamanca and increased by the surrender of Madrid – it would be enough to content myself at present with relating what has occurred since my last letter.

On first seeing Burgos officers competent to decide judged our means inadequate to its reduction within the period which defences of its class ought to be taken, but there was *hope in time*, and we all expected that the good fortune of our Chief would succeed and the place be taken: but this has proved to be (what you have often said) IMAGINERY and the happy results of his former enterprises must now be ascribed only to good arrangement – different conduct has been followed by a different result, and after 31 days' perseverance he has been compelled to relinquish the siege of Burgos.

The enemy had collected towards the beginning of this month a very considerable force in our front, and they gradually advanced towards Burgos as they found our inability to take it; on the 19th they were within one day's march of it in force and Wellington then judged it proper to raise the siege and move forward to meet them. Accordingly on the 20th, soon after daybreak, the whole allied army was assembled in position about 7 miles from Burgos, on a range of hills covering the high road from Vitoria; in the afternoon the enemy came down upon us with a large body of Cavalry and about 15,000 Infantry, but being uncertain of the points occupied by us, they exposed their own right flank in their advance upon our right, and this error was instantly taken advantage of by Wellington – he quitted the heights with the left of the army, and advanced on the plain and gained considerably towards the rear of their right – but night came on and they effected their retreat, and we returned to our position about 9 o'clock.

We remained looking at each other throughout the whole of 21st, the enemy bringing up fresh troops and we making preparations for a retreat. As soon as the sun set we began to move, and notwithstanding it was fine moonlight we passed under the guns of the Castle within range of grape shot without being discovered, and before daybreak on the 22nd the whole of our army was three leagues in rear of Burgos. The next day we made a short march of a league and a half but we were compelled to quicken our pace on the 23rd, but the enemy pressed us with cavalry and ours who were covering our rear behaved (as usual) *very ill* – they were completely overthrown by the enemy and suffered severely, and but for the steadiness of the Light Battalions of the German Legion who were supporting *would have been destroyed.*

We reached Dueñas on the 24th and from the long fatiguing marches and their own intemperance the enemy made prisoner a considerable number of our stragglers. On the 25th we occupied a position behind the Pisuerga, having blown up the bridges, but the enemy turned our left by Palancia – they did not however come down in great force and they were driven across the river after a severe skirmish by the 5th Division and some Spanish Infantry who behaved well. On the 26th we re-crossed the Pisuerga by the bridge at Cabezon and occupied a position – the river runs in front and was only passable by the bridges at Cabezon and Valladolid and three deep fords which were well defended, and our right was covered by impracticable hills. We remained in it during the whole of the 27th and 28th – which the enemy employed in bringing up fresh forces – on the 29th we continued to retreat and after destroying the bridges we crossed the Douro at the Puente de Douro the same day and [indecipherable] extended to Tordesillas to destroy the bridge.

The Pisuerga is a river very difficult for an army to pass, from its banks generally being steep and the bottom of it stiff clay. The weather had been quite fair from the evening of the 19th to the 29th and in that time the water fell very much, so that the fords were becoming easy, which I presume caused us to give up a position which otherwise would have been impregnable. The weather changed the same day that we gave it up and during the night of the 29th and all yesterday till afternoon there was a very heavy fall of rain which has again swelled the rivers. We are now behind the Douro, which I hope we shall be able to defend.

The enemy are repairing the bridge at Tordesillas and they have a picquet on this side of the river – our division, with another of British, one division of Spaniards and some Portuguese are opposite to it and I think will be enough to prevent the enemy passing by it. We are throwing up batteries to destroy their repairs – they have unluckily the town on their side and the banks are the highest. The Douro throughout its course is very rapid and deep. The enemy have moved towards Toro, where I have no doubt they will find the bridge destroyed.

In short, the enemy in all are called 45,000 men, of whom 5,000 are cavalry – I cannot credit it, from what I have seen, there being more than 30,000 Infantry, but they say that they have certainly 8 divisions. Our force is certainly not above 30,000, a greater part of whom are Spaniards. We are reduced prodigiously since we moved from Valladolid in September. In the siege of Burgos and on the retreat we must have lost 3,000 – the sickness is great, having been constantly out.

The Guerrillos are reported to be about Burgos – Mina and Longa have joined – if so Caffarelli who was employed against them cannot remain here long, and without his force the army will be unequal to continue the offensive. Soult is reported to be moving to his right so as to pass the Tagus without coming to Toledo and then advance upon General Hill; if he accomplishes this we shall then I fear lose Madrid – for the want of 8 guns what has been lost? Instead of establishing ourselves in Burgos with our advance on the Ebro we shall do very well if we can maintain ourselves between the Tagus and Douro till Spring. By that time we shall have such a park and battering train of Artillery as an army ought to have, and then I hope we shall always employ too great instead of too small means against enemy places. Our policy I conceive ought to be to beat down all attempts at resistance and to reduce a place if possible in one day what we might be sure of in three by ordinary means. We lost all our heavy guns at Burgos.

Mesquitello
10th December 1812

My dear Father,

If I have not written to you since the 31 October, it is not because I cease to the attention of your desire of having *my* account of our proceedings.

The retreat from the Douro to the Agueda is already known; my communication of it therefore is for yourself: to you it may be acceptable, and it affords me pleasure writing it – to anyone else it would be tiresome. I may relate circumstances which are not perhaps generally known, the feelings of horror excited by some no longer exist, and my description therefore might be inanimate and prolix, but you will excuse me – I shall endeavour to relate what I have seen, and shall not hesitate to make remarks where opportunity and inclination prompt me.

While we remained encamped opposite Tordesillas, the most contradictory reports were circulated of our future operations; they generally breathed anything but despondency, and as they had credit for originating in a quarter which shall be nameless, we were far from expecting retreat. The truth however at last became known, and we heard that General Hill was expected with his army at Arevalo on 4 November. Marshal Soult had completed his junction with Suchet and the King, and with these united forces had *turned* General Hill's defensive line on the Tagus – Madrid was then left open and the pass of Guadarrama being also abandoned, it was evident that we were unable to maintain ourselves on the Douro. We retrograded on the 6th and effected our junction with General Hill, and three days after, Wellington had arrived with his whole army on the scene of his former glory, and took up a position on both banks of the Tormes covering Salamanca. This we hoped we should be able to maintain, notwithstanding our disproportion to the enemy, which was now represented as very great.

The army which had driven us from Burgos, including 12,000 new troops from France and the division of Caffarelli, is now estimated at 45,000, of whom 4,000 are cavalry, and Soult's army was called 40,000 infantry and 4,500 cavalry. Our effective force in the field, including all the Spaniards, was 60,000 infantry and our regular cavalry of every description did not exceed 5,000. To remedy this inferiority we constructed field works on the weak points of the position, and we had unbroken spirits and former success in our favour.

The rains which had fallen at the end of October still affected the Tormes and there was every appearance that there would be more; *unfortunately*, however, it kept fair until the 13th, and in the meantime a ford was discovered above Alba. Marshal Soult, with that judgement of spirit of enterprise which has distinguished him above all the other French Generals, passed a great part of his force by it *at night,* and by noon of the day following, in spite of a cannonade from 14 of our pieces, his whole army was on the left of the Tormes. Wellington's fate was now decided; (and little as the elements may be supposed to affect a General, 15 November affords a memorable instance of their influence). He assumed his former position on the Arapiles, but here he had everything to hope – the ground was already consecrated by the blood of Heroes on 22 July, he still fought in the same righteous cause – the troops who that day had signalised themselves were still with him – *impatient* to repeat their former deeds – their brethren from the Alemtejo glowed with emulation, and the newly raised Spaniards were desirous of equalling their allies and rivals the Portuguese – the army was confident of Victory. We are safe, said the Salamancans – it is enough that you are here.

The night passed thus, and at dawn on the 15th the fires of the enemy were discovered, but unhappily at a distance. It was our game to fight – not Marshal Soult's his object was the same as his predecessor Marmont's – to surround and destroy us – but profiting by his error he kept far beyond reach of shot in marching to gain our rear, and we had no hope in attacking him. Thus, by two in the afternoon, our bright prospects were at an end, and we saw ourselves compelled to abandon to a remorseless enemy the faithful unsuspecting inhabitants of Salamanca.

We retired over the open country in three columns, and scarcely had we ascended those heights from which we first saw the devoted City, when it began *to rain in torrents* and continued all that and part of the following day. 48 hours sooner, Salamanca would have been *saved* and we should still have been on the Tormes in *quarters* while the enemy would have been compelled to have dispersed themselves.

Oh fortune how fickle is thy favour – History perhaps cannot match *this* instance of thy instability!!! When quiet we prayed for rain – we were now in retreat, it came down and was a nuisance, what we courted as an Ally *now* became a formidable enemy – we found streams where before had been none, brooks were swollen to considerable rivers, and the whole surface of the flat country which we passed over became so much swamp, as to be nearly impassable for loaded animals off the roads, which were very narrow. We retreated by three, our cavalry on the right by the high road (which was the only good one); to avoid the enemy's overwhelming force of cavalry, the infantry were compelled to keep in *the woods*, the roads through them being given up to the Artillery and waggons. Many men and baggage animals *thus* became worn out, and by the end of the 3rd day's march the scene was indescribable melancholy. I never saw so many dead animals in so short a distance – independent of these, however, our route was sufficiently marked by the bodies of men who had died from wounds or sickness and others left to become prisoners, perhaps a worse fate *from want of means to bring them off*.

The above is no exaggerated statement, written to excite compassion or impose on credulity, it is the unstudied statement of an eyewitness.

We slept on the bare *wet* ground for 6 nights following the middle of November (sometimes after marching from daybreak till dark) and in that time there was but one night and one day without rain or hail. November when there is no sun, I think fully as severe in this country as at home, so listen to the rain and hail battering your windows while you sit by the fire in winter, and think of a soldier in Spain!

I have marked with particular emphasis the want of transport for the sick in this army, because it appears to me to be so shamefully deficient that nothing can palliate, much less excuse, it. After passing the Agueda when an enemy pressing the rear could no longer be urged in *extenuation*, I have seen sick soldiers rolled up in their blankets, lying by the roadside, left for want of conveyance, perhaps to die: and within a few miles of Ciudad Rodrigo, I had one from my own company *left to his fate (having lost the use of his limbs from cold in the retreat)* and this after exhausting my own means, by carrying on my private mules another in the same state – I shall also mention while on this subject that from the same deficiency of transport, *wounded Soldiers* were abandoned on the field, and this too at a time when by their valour they had so far driven back the enemy as to render their comrades safe from being molested. Will such enormities as these be believed in Britain? In that country so renowned for the devotion of her Sons – held up to the world as a honourable example of pious charity with riches!!

What must be thought of a government so stinting in comfort – nay *bare justice* – to the defenders of their country, as to deny a General the means of easing the suffering of the Soldier when *worn out,* probably of restoring him to the service; and this the government of a country which compelled to adopt *every plan* which human ingenuity can suggest could keep *full* the ranks of her army? I do not hesitate to say that such Governors ought to be dismissed; for if such conduct can be freed from the charge of parsimony – what can be urged in defence of their judgment since, on the simple question of cost (not in a political view as expenditure of human life, but cost as applied to the replacing of a horse), I find on a very moderate computation of the recruiting and equipping each man for *this army,* it will be more for those lost between Salamanca and Ciudad Rodrigo than would have covered the expense of keeping animals to carry them for 6 *months;* instead of five days, which is all that would have been required; and I have taken for data the simple rate of hire paid by government for animals in the Peninsula, *viz* 5 shillings a day for each mule. Such economy!!

The means of carrying sick attached to this army in the field is only six waggons to a division; a division consists of 5,000 men and a waggon will hold 7 men – conveyance is thus provided for 42 men, which is quite enough for casualties on ordinary marches, but on extraordinary occasions (such as a skirmish) what *of necessity* is resorted to? – why, that men who are unfit to march by sickness only, are turned out to make room for the wounded!! What becomes of these men? – they make exertions to follow till nature at last is exhausted, and they fall down and die; or perhaps are *picked up singly by the enemy,* who in pursuit have neither the power or inclination to give comfort.

Is the Soldier rendered unfit for service by sickness not equally entitled to be taken of as the one who has had the misfortune to be wounded? Nobody one would think would deny this? Yet Ministers by their conduct do! Do they then really suppose the moral feeling of a Soldier so entirely calloused by service as to be indifferent at seeing his Comrade abandoned to a miserable end, when no longer equal to his arduous duty. No. he argues thus, what is your *fate* today my comrade, may be mine tomorrow, and with that before his eyes, with what spirit can he go into action? Our enemies can answer well these questions, they found the impolicy of such a system and remedied it.

The French now have means for carrying sick in the field for ordinary and extraordinary occasions, and when *both* are insufficient, they collect their sick and leave Medical men with them – they are then well taken care of, as in war; it is a law to respect Hospitals, and the attendants are not prisoners. Hence in several instances we have returned considerable numbers of sick taken in hospitals, while it has never appeared by our returns whether any of our own fell into the enemy's hands, and yet the loss on both sides I believe at least equal *in similar circumstances;* may I assert in confidence of its truth that we have lost twice the number of our sick and wounded in this retreat than we took of the enemy's in *the pursuit* after the battle of Salamanca.

Pardon this digression – it is longer than I intended, but when the feelings are so intimately concerned the ideas follow in quick succession, and it is not easy to stop – to resume – I proceed to a consideration of the Campaign which appears to me as a whole to have been as brilliant as ever made. You will perhaps not think so, and I have no doubt it will be represented otherwise by almost all the public prints – because its results have not equalled their predictions, and it is a failing of nature that we are generally much readier to defend our erroneous opinions than to retract them.

Our ideas I have found as unreasonable under disappointment as in success – in both, our opinions are decided by the feeling of the moment – but few can divest themselves of it sufficiently to reason – and hence seeing but one side, our conclusions are unjust. Now, however, when the mind has suffered to subside into its ordinary course, we may discuss dispassionately the merits of those high expectations which were universally held out after the battle of Salamanca and surrender of Madrid. I think they were unreasonable – though I cannot condemn them – nay, I myself anticipated so much in the exultation of my Countrymen that I encouraged expectations and propagated them, which a little reflection on what was known to everyone of this would have taught me to have considered distant and uncertain.

At the opening of the Campaign our army in the field was equal to any one army of the enemy, but it was not equal to any two. Our plan therefore is to attack and defeat before they could unite. The plan being thus fixed and so much forwarded by the destruction of the bridge of Almaraz, which cut off the best and most direct communication of the armies of the south and north of Spain, it remains only to determine whether the first operation should be on the south or north of the Tagus. For reasons best known to himself Wellington determined on the latter – it disappointed many of his army, and it was in opposition to the opinions (of I believe) every public writer in England who presumed to give an opinion.

The result of the plan followed is now well-known and it can be only from a belief that had the other been followed it would have been more successful and anyone can find fault now. I contend that there is no grounds for such expectation – for had we moved against Soult instead of Marmont, leaving a force to watch him (who it is conceded would have remained on the defensive), what would have happened? – we might have taken Seville, *perhaps* raised the siege of Cadiz – fought a general action (gaining a victory) by the Autumn, entered Madrid, whence we might have remained till the junction of the armies *as now* would have compelled us to have retired.

This I presume is as much of the zealous advocates of the plan *before it was tried* could have expected from it – but it is not so brilliant as that which followed from the other – since in addition to gaining all these advantages we have increased the Spanish forces from a quarter which we would not then have possessed – we subsisted 5 months on the resources of that part of the country – and we have still in reserve the recruits which may be expected from the South and the subsistence required for the army in the winter months. A reference to the map will at once show you the superiority of the first over the second plan – as we moved on the *string* while the enemy moved on the *bow*. It was from this that after leaving Madrid we were 60 days in advance of the enemy's movements to form a junction. These were unhappily lost in moving towards Burgos and besieging it – a feature in the campaign which, notwithstanding my approval of the whole, I must call a great *error*. I have already said much on this point in my previous letters and as my paper is now near finished I shall not say more. The responsibility of its failure – I ascribe solely to Wellington but Ministers have much to be blamed for too – in not sending reinforcements after the battle of Salamanca when they had heaps at home which might have embarked at a moment's notice and that would have repaired our loss on that occasion. Adieu for the present – I shall perhaps say more of this hereafter – my last letter was to Jas on 1 December but there have been no arrivals. Give my love to my Mother, George, Robert and all, and in my name wish all a happy new year and many returns etc.

Mesquitello
24th December 1812

My dear Father,

Since my letter of yesterday the mail has arrived and I have had the pleasure of your letter of 26 November – as it requires an immediate answer I write now, otherwise it was not my intention to have written to you so soon after my *very* long letter of the 10th.

There is nothing going on and consequently no news; but it is amusing to read in the London newspapers (which have come to the 4th inst) the opinions on the late campaign – so like our countrymen they are now as unreasonably *desponding* and abusive at our retreat as they were after our victory at Salamanca – unreasonable in their expectations of uninterrupted success!! I am glad however to notice that the blame is generally thrown upon the *Ministry,* not on the general and the army, although the latter appears to me by no means exculpated from undertaking the siege of Burgos with so inadequate means, and it is upon this enterprise that the whole hinges. I have already expressed myself on this point so often that it will perhaps be tiresome to say more; however, I will still venture. The Ministry are accused of impolicy in not providing sufficient means of transport – the accusation *is just,* as I have noted in my former letter, and I trust exposed its prodigality. They are accused too of unnecessary delay in sending reinforcements after the battle of Salamanca – this is so clearly just, as I think must damn their capacity for conducting a vigorous (which in the end is the most economical) war – they have forfeited the confidence of the world by it and I only hope will receive its *reward* in being dismissed.

In saying this much, however, I do not clear our Commander who remains responsible for the siege of Burgos. The Ministry did not provide him with a battering train, it is true, or what is the same thing sent the guns to Lisbon *but kept at home* the means of moving them. But fortune supplied the want of foresight and at Madrid we found sufficient ordnance to have reduced the Castle of Burgos in four *days*. These, it is believed here, might have been carried to Burgos or, if not, it argues a greater want of assistance from Spain than anybody would imagine – but several *heavy* pieces *were sent* from the interior of Spain to Ciudad Rodrigo – sufficient evidence of *possibility!!!* Admitting, however, the impracticability of transporting a battering train from Madrid in 60 days – why not bring 24-pounders from the ships at Santander, a distance of 70 miles? For this the most ingenious advocate of his *Lordship* cannot defend, *but* at the expense of *his* judgment and prudence – since the Engineer and Artillery officers at first sight said that they could not calculate on the reduction of the Castle without battering, and at the end of nearly a month's operations his Lordship was so convinced of this that he sent off his *cattle* to bring guns from the ships – (*vide* dispatch – they were absent when the siege was raised). I condemn Lord Wellington for attempting to take Burgos *after* he had himself seen it, when he must have known his means were inadequate – he ought either to have blockaded it, till he could get proper means, or at once have relinquished the idea of besieging it – thus he is responsible for the 2,000 men lost in the siege.

On the whole I am still of the opinion that the campaign was as brilliant as ever made – brilliant as it was, however, it is evident that had the resources actually at the command of the Ministry been applied, it would have been more so, and we might now have been in possession of Madrid with our left on the Ebro. 6,000 British Infantry and 2,000 Cavalry *additional* after the battle of Salamanca would have ensured this, while the points cannot now be calculated upon in the next campaign with *double these numbers* – under proper management, too, the Spanish army of Galicia might have taken the field in June with an effective force of 30,000 men instead of remaining merely inactive until September when it could bring forward barely 12,000 *very ineffective*.

It thus results that no good can be expected from that quarter until great alteration is made in the Spanish Government. You will hardly believe, *but it is a fact,* that a great part of the shoes and clothing which were issued to the Galician army at Salamanca in November, *new from Britain,* have already been sold by the soldiers. They get very little pay from their own government and no regular issue of provisions, and the poor men are thus compelled to turn everything into money to satisfy the cravings of nature. The want of money which was so severely felt in our army all last summer still exists, and although two months' pay have been issued since coming here, we are yet in arrears from 24 July.

I have sent to another village to inquire after Richardson – the messenger has just returned bringing notice that he only joined with a draft from England about 10 days ago and he is now with the Grenadier

Company and quite well – for myself I was never better. I take a good deal of exercise on my pony whenever the weather will allow me to quit the house. We have a report here of another frigate being taken by the Americans – the navy of that station do not keep up their character as their army has done – I hope our friend Captain M.[49] will be sent there soon – I would not like to be the American who may meet him.

Adieu – tomorrow is Christmas and I wish you all a happy one and merry Adieu.

Your very affectionate son.

The circumstances of the retreat were to have widespread, though temporary, repercussions within the Army and among the general public at home. From Freneda on 28 November, Wellington wrote a long letter of instructions on matters of discipline, administration and training while the troops remained in winter quarters. It was addressed to divisional and brigade commanders and was not intended for publication. Unfortunately this was not made clear and a number of formations placed it in the Order Book. As a result it soon found its way into the London papers, raising a general storm. Its tenor was set at the beginning:

> The discipline of every army after a long and active campaign becomes in some degree relaxed. . . . But I am concerned to observe that the army under my command has fallen off in this respect in the late campaign to a greater degree than any army with which I have ever been, or which I have ever read . . . yet this army has met with no disaster, it has suffered no privations which by trifling attention on the part of officers could not have been prevented . . . nor . . . and hardship excepting . . . the inclemencies of the weather when they were severe . . . from the moment the troops commenced their retreat from the neighbourhood of Burgos on one hand and from Madrid on the other, the officers lost all command over their men. Irregularities and outrages of all descriptions were committed with impunity, and losses have been sustained which ought never to have occurred.[50]

He pointed out that marches had been short, halts long, and that they had not been pressed by the enemy. He went on:

> I have no hesitation in attributing these evils to the habitual inattention of the officers of the regiments to their duty as prescribed by the regulations of the service and by the orders of the Army. . . . I am far from questioning the zeal, still less the gallantry and spirit of the officers of the Army. . . .

Looked at today, the constructive parts of the letter seem admirable and the censorious ones in general well deserved. But there can be doubt that Wellington played down the very real hardship which had been endured – hardships largely resulting from the breakdown of administration; officers not impressed at being compared unfavourably with the French for the time taken to provide hot meals when they were forbidden to remove doors for firewood and had nothing to cook! The greatest mistake was in apportioning blanket blame in an army whose pride and *esprit de corps* is bound up with the honour of the regiment – a situation which was hardly improved when Wellington publicly exonerated the Guards and the Light Division from his strictures. John Aitchison's letters no doubt express the views of most of the young officers.

At home much political capital was made of it. Among those who condemned Wellington were a number of naval officers – the Royal Navy was feeling the loss of its previous monopoly of public esteem to the Army.

Early in the New Year John Aitchison wrote home:

Mesquitello
21st January 1813

My dear Father,

It is already twelve days since I received your letter of 18 December with the accounts of the brilliant success of the Russians – the same mail brought me details of the destruction of the corps of Davout and Ney. For the last four days we have had reports of another with news to the 1st inst, but it has not yet arrived and we still look forward to further accounts from Russia which I assure you we are as fully as anxious to receive as you all appear to be at home. She has really performed prodigies – but much is yet to be done before we can gain the object of our war – a favourable peace.

It will be a miracle if Bonaparte be in such a state in the spring as to resume the offensive – here we are preparing for it, but I fear with less prospect of success than last year but we shall see – while there is life there is hope, and I am far from desponding.

At this moment we have an uncommon number of sick, and from my means of information we are reduced to *half* the *effective* strength at which the army was at the beginning of the campaign. . . . While the army is in motion sickness to a great extent seldom prevails, but within a limited time after halting, diseases break out which most certainly have excited during the period of exertion and evidently caused by it.

Thus in the Campaigns of 1809 and '10, when the active part was over by the end of August and October, the most sickly seasons were October and December and the January and February following were the most healthy – in this campaign where the active part was not over till December we were not very sickly till now. It is unluckily increasing every day and we have many *deaths* – these happen in greater proportions among the men last arrived in the country – the old campaigners I find generally pretty well, and those who have been once ill invariably the most healthy after. How strongly does this then argue in favour of the government using extraordinary means to recover those men now in this country rather than (as I told you in my letter of 10 December) by want of additional means rendering it necessary to supply their place!!! But to judge by all the information which I have been able to collect, our Medical establishment is as inferior to the French in quarters as I have shown it to be in the field. This is a lamentable fact, and I presume arises from a system of ill-judged (and consequently *extravagant*) economy, which has frequently distinguished Ministers in their conduct towards the Army. I am not writing for the sake of finding fault – I may deceive myself but I am not discontented, and I may notice what I conceive defects and to you it is only proper. In the field after the first month of exertion and during its continuance I found our non-effectives in the proportion generally of about 1 in 5 to 1 in 7 and, after the first fortnight, tailed off and decrease to 1 in 3. We take a good deal of exercise now and have regular parades every day and twice a week we assemble in fighting order and manoeuvre for about 10 or 12 miles a day.

I notice what you say of many people grumbling about the result of the campaign – grumbling seems one of the privileges enjoyed by our free constitution, and to judge by the frequency in which it is indulged it is one of the most valued. But it is in the nature of our countrymen to find fault. I cannot, however, comprehend by what the principle almost everyone fancies himself qualified to judge military matters, many of whom I am confident are ignorant in their own profession and not one in 500 of whom has a proper idea of the requisites of an army in the field.

Mesquitello

My dear Father,   *1st February 1813*

Since I wrote to you on 2 January we have had two English mails bringing news to the 9th ult. By the first I had the pleasure of Helen's letter of 25 December which informed me that you are all very well and had spent a most happy Christmas together, and I would indeed have been delighted to have *completed* the number, and I now hope that I shall *before the next*. Your public prints and particularly the Ministerial breathe a continuation of the war, but here we have great hopes the extraordinary success of the Russians will lead to a general peace. Had our successes in this quarter been as complete as they might have been, we should certainly, I think, have returned home early in the Summer, but as it is, it seems impossible to assign a period to our stay here, but it will not I think exceed another year. In that time peace will either be made or our exertions on the Peninsula on the large scale will be abandoned; in either case is it likely that the 2nd Brigade of Guards will remain in Portugal?

It is evident that France is not equal to an offensive war at the same time in Russia and Spain; that she will abandon one, therefore, is most probable: and Russia as being of the smallest moment, after the efforts of last year, it is clear that without a very great increase, this army will be unequal to oppose the comparatively small number of French now in the field; if France can maintain a defensive with Russia (and I think she can) her forces here will of course be much increased, when our operations as in

1810 will of necessity be confined to a defence of Portugal. For this object only, our present force is greater than would be required, and our *means*, say the Ministers, are not capable of sufficient extension to drive the present diminished numbers of French beyond the Pyrenees, *which* I presume would be our only view in extending our services again to Spain.

Thus we have every prospect of little to do during the present year – but a change of Ministry, if not a peace, may upset all my speculations and I suppose there will be some alterations, if not a total change – the Wellesley party are the most likely to come in, and then we shall have those measures which ought to have been adopted last year – no Ministry would have wished for a better opportunity of doing great things – yet none ever did so little – Without a subsidy to any foreign powers, with an extraordinary note of credit – the army – the only army which they had to pay – was in arrears 5 months – its operations were cramped for want of money – nay, victory itself could not be turned to account for that want of means.

There is no system so expensive as that which undertakes objects with inadequate means, yet this was the system pursued after the experience of 3 years had shown its folly. Had our losses only at the battle of Salamanca been replaced when they might have been – we should have followed up the fugitives to Burgos, *and provided as we ought to have been* with a battering train, *then* that petty fortress would not have cost us 500 men, instead *as was the fact* a greater loss than the battle of Salamanca. But it is not in the numerical loss only that the army has suffered by it, *as* you will see by the '*Courier of the 9th January*'. The letter of Ld Wellington to the army in it, in my opinion ought not to have been published. What it states is in a great measure true, but I have no hesitation in saying that the picture is overdrawn, and what I admit to be correct I think may in great part be ascribed to other causes than what his Lordship does. As you would alarm a man with a belief of great danger, to make him provide the *better* for his security, so Ld W. seems to have overstated the want of discipline in his army to encourage it being increased.

When censure is general, no one will take it to himself, and it would have been better therefore of his Lordship to have marked those regiments in which 'outrages and irregularity of every description were committed' than to have stigmatised the whole as he has done. I was not ignorant of the contents of this letter before it was published, nor of the irregularities to which it alludes, but I never mentioned them to you, because I think it better at all times to keep 'defects' in the background, and more particularly when an exposition of them to the world may serve to initiate but cannot cure them in those people in whom they are supposed to exist. In reasoning thus, I take no blame whatever to myself nor to the corps to which I belong – nay, I am happy at being able to say of the Guards (what Ld W. has said in his General Order) that 'their *conduct has ever been most exemplary*' and luckily in proof of the superiority of *our* system there was a Battalion of Guards with Genl Hill when he retreated from Madrid, and they maintained the high character which Ld W. has given *those* who had so long been under himself.

I shall not now attempt to answer Lord W.'s letter paragraph by paragraph but I have in a former letter duly stated what happened in the retreat. I related what happened in the corps which I had the best opportunity of seeing *viz* my own and the others of the division and I am quite certain that I stated nothing but what I knew to be true and indeed what I had myself in great part *felt*. Ld W. says that 'the army met with no disaster, it suffered no privation, but what a little attention by the officers would have prevented and no hardship but occasioned by the weather.' He says, moreover, that the marches were short, the halts long and frequent!!! Is it then no disaster to be obliged to fight for existence and then to leave on the field to die or be eaten by birds of prey those who were wounded? Yet this happened on the retreat at Dueñas!! And what could have tended more to impair the zeal of the soldier for the service, may spread the spirit of disobedience and disaffection!! Is it then no privation to be without food – absolutely for 24 to 36 hours? Yet this was the case on the retreat (I don't say that it was not oftener and not longer in many corps but it was once in every corps in the army that for twenty-four hours neither bread nor meat was issued *when due*). It often happened that the men had no bread, as it was issued 3, 4 or 5 days in advance which they could not keep so long, and could regimental officers have 'prevented' it? – no – they could not, or they would, as they themselves suffered also. Is it no hardship to march fourteen hours without food, on the worst of roads in bad weather? Yet this happened on the retreat!! And who could have prevented it? I know not what are long marches but I do know we marched eight Spanish leagues – that it was nearly 3 hours after dark before we arrived on our ground – it was then a wine country surrounded by cellars – the men broke into them and irregularities were the consequence of the drunkeness. Nor do I consider the crime so great when the system of destroying everything to prevent falling into the hands of the enemy had been enforced *by these same soldiers by order* when retreating in Portugal who now *for the first time since* were retreating in Spain.

It was not from starting late that we were late at ending our march – as the first long march we were all night on the move, the second we marched as soon as all the columns would march off, and the third and fourth, hours before daybreak, and on the two latter it was dark or nearly so before we got on our ground, and on these days the most irregularities were committed. But to end these remarks – there has been but one complaint against a soldier of my regiment since we came into quarters and in the *army* there has been only *one* order for a General Court Martial in the same time – sufficient proof that the relaxation of discipline of this army could not have arrived at that height which a perusal of Wellington's letter only might make you imagine.

I cannot now say more and when I began I had no intention of saying so much. My love to all the family.

CHAPTER FIVE

1813
The Advance to the Pyrenees

ON 19 October 1812, two days before Wellington started to retreat from Burgos, Napoleon had left Moscow on one of the most momentous and, for him, disastrous retreats in history. The total casualties of the Grande Armée will never be known but can be taken as between 350,000 and 450,000, of whom more than half were dead, killed in battle or died of wounds, cold or starvation. The remainder were prisoners of war. Without Ney's courage and indomitable spirit, the whole army would probably have been annihilated – as it was, under his leadership some 20,000 miserable wretches staggered back across the Niemen on 13 December.

Napoleon, who had abandoned his stricken army on 5 December, arrived back in Paris on the nineteenth. Here, with astonishing vigour and ability, he immediately set about raising fresh armies to stem the Russian tide. He called up 100,000 old conscripts, ordered 100,000 National Guardsmen to 'volunteer' for foreign service and anticipated the 1814 call-up with a further 150,000 men. From Spain he brought back more than 20,000 men including the remainder of the Guard, the Hessians and a number of experienced units at low strength to act as cadres.

The Russians entered Warsaw on 8 February. Britain and Russia had been Allies since July 1812 and at the end of February Prussia joined the Alliance. Berlin was entered on 4 March and Hamburg on the eighteenth. Bernadotte's Sweden now intimated her readiness to join the Alliance. By mid-April Napoleon was nearly ready for a counter-stroke. He concentrated his armies near Jena and at the end of May retook Hamburg. Although the call-up met with considerable resistance in France, such was still the magic of his name that about half the German states, including Saxony, joined him. He won two bloody battles at Lutzen and Bautzen but could not follow up his victories and the Allied armies, though discomforted, kept the field. Fearing that these victories would destroy his plan for a Fourth Coalition, Castlereagh, the Foreign Secretary, entered into fresh negotiations with Russia and Prussia at Reichenbach where Britain offered £2 million for Russia to keep 150,000 and Prussia 80,000 in the field.

It was of the greatest importance to bring Austria into the coalition, but Metternich was playing a subtle and evasive game. Ignoring Britain, he offered to mediate between Russia and Prussia on the one hand and Napoleon on the other. He negotiated an armistice to last from 4 June to the end of July, later extended to 19 August. When news of Wellington's victory at Vitoria was brought to him, Metternich was profoundly impressed and decided to join the Fourth Coalition as soon as he had prepared Austria for war. Having presented Napoleon with a list of demands which were certain to be rejected, Austria declared war on 11 August.

These events in Europe and the war with the United States had important repercussions on the war in Spain. To rebuild his forces for the defence of central Europe, Napoleon withdrew 20,000 men from Spain and gave Joseph to understand that he could expect no more reinforcements. For the first time for years French strength in Spain fell to below 200,000.

The British government, fully supported by the Duke of York who was again the head of the Army, was determined to reinforce Wellington by every means possible, and like him saw the possibility of ejecting the French altogether from Spain in the coming campaign. Finding reinforcements was not easy. At war with the United States the needs of Canada could not be ignored and Britain might, for political reasons, have to make at least a token contribution to the land forces of northern Europe. Wellington was sent two additional cavalry brigades, bringing his cavalry numerically nearer that of the enemy. These were the Household Cavalry Brigade (two regiments of Life Guards and the Blues) and a brigade of hussars (10th, 15th and 18th Hussars). In addition he received the 2nd/59th Foot, a troop of Royal Horse Artillery. Numerous drafts were also dispatched to bring units up to establishment.

For Wellington events in Europe, while promising great opportunities, were also a source of considerable anxiety for, should the armistice end in a peace treaty, Britain would once more be isolated and Napoleon able to send massive reinforcements to Spain. A further worry was the effect of the American war on the support he could expect from the Royal Navy. The war in the Peninsula could only be sustained so long as the Navy could protect his sea lines of communication, and he was to rely on the ability to shift those lines of communication to the Biscay ports to maintain the momentum of his campaign to throw the French out of Spain.

American frigates, though few, were first-class ships, manned in part by British seamen, they had inflicted some humiliating defeats on ships of the Royal Navy. In spring 1813 American privateers destroyed and captured British ships off Oporto, including a transport with a detachment of the 18th Hussars; other ships, with stores destined for the Allied army, were also captured. The Royal Navy was suffering, as indeed it had throughout the war, from a shortage of frigates and small vessels for escort duties. The expansion of the Army had meant that the Navy was less well-manned than it had been; moreover, since Trafalgar, some parts of the Navy had suffered from complacency and a loss of purpose. Whereas formerly the Navy had been the unquestioned darling of the people and had tended to look down on the Army, Hood and Nelson being notable examples, the boot was now on the other foot and it must be admitted that some members of the Army did not find the Navy's humiliation entirely unwelcome. Such attitudes were not conducive to co-operation.

Wellington's 1812 campaign had liberated all southern Spain, and on November the Cortes had appointed him commander-in-chief of the Spanish armies. By forcing the French to concentrate their armies against him, he had created opportunities everywhere for the Spanish guerrilla forces, most notably in the crucial areas of French communications in the valley of the Ebro and between that river and the Pyrenees. At the beginning of 1813 the French had 95,000 men between the Tagus and the Douro, twice as many as the year before.

As soon as Napoleon was back in Paris he reverted to his former practice of trying to run the war in Spain by remote control. He approved Joseph's concentration north of the Tagus, recommended that the Army of Portugal should shift its headquarters and base to Valladolid. As soon as he realized that it took months rather than weeks to get orders to Joseph, owing to the activities of the Spanish guerrillas, he ordered him to send six divisions from the Army of Portugal to join the Army of the North, now under Clausel who had orders to suppress the guerrillas and restore safe lines of communication. This was a formidable task, for the bands, under the leadership of such able and enterprising men as Mina, Longa, Diaz Martin ('Empecinado'), Mendizabal, Duran and 'The Pastor', had grown greatly in strength and efficiency. Mina, for instance, had over 8,000 men and his own artillery.

On the other side of the hill Wellington's army was enjoying its longest respite of the war. The Allied infantry went into cantonments along the Douro and, the cavalry further south, in the valley of the Mondego, where forage was available. The Guards were back in Vizeu where they had been in 1809. The 1812 campaign had played havoc with unit strengths – for instance John Aitchison's battalion, which had mustered 1,052 all ranks present and fit for duty on May 1812, mustered only 604 on 1 December. At Christmas there were some 20,000 sick. Despite new drafts, Wellington was obliged to reduce the establishment of some units to six companies, instead of ten, and the weakest to four. The latter he paired, creating 'Provisional Battalions'. During the winter more Portuguese battalions were raised and when the army marched in May Wellington had at his command 52,000 British and 28,000 Portuguese troops 'a larger and more efficient army than I have yet had'[1] and 25,000 Spaniards.

In preparation for the coming campaign, Wellington set out to improve the system of transport, the living conditions of the troops in the field, their health and discipline. Some of these reforms are mentioned by John Aitchison. For examples of how health and discipline might be improved, Wellington turned to the Guards who had always run their own hospitals and achieved better results than did the general hospitals at the base. On the advice of Dr McGrigor, head of the medical department, he ordered the medical administration to be decentralized and regimental hospitals set up. By doing away with the necessity for sick men to make the long and tedious journey to the base, and incidentally spreading contagion, most favourable results were produced. The army of malingerers at Lisbon, whose occasionally atrocious behaviour earned them the name of 'The Belem Rangers', was also reduced.

To Wellington it seemed that half the secret of the Guards' high standard of discipline lay in the responsibility they allowed their senior N.C.O.s Sergeants in the Guards performed all the duties normally falling to subalterns in regiments of the line. He wanted to see their system adopted throughout the army, and to encourage the acceptance of greater responsibility recommended that the pay of all sergeants be increased to restore their pay differentials which had been eroded during the war. Because of the shortage of specie this was turned down but as a compromise it was decided that one sergeant in every troop of cavalry should be made a troop sergeant-major, and one in every infantry company a colour sergeant, having the regimental colours embroidered beneath his chevrons; these two new ranks would carry additional pay. To look after the discipline of the army as a whole, the Royal Military Police was created on the joint initiatives of that great army reformer, the Duke of York, and Wellington. A special unit of the Staff Corps was formed from carefully selected officers and men. They were all volunteers, received extra pay and were organized into four mounted troops operating directly under command of Wellington's headquarters. A year earlier York had laid the foundations of the Royal Army Educational Corps by placing an educational sergeant on the establishment of every infantry battalion for the instruction of young soldiers and the children of soldiers.

For what he hoped would be his last campaign in Spain, Wellington tactfully got rid of the worst of his senior officers. Graham and Picton returned, their health restored, the former to his previous appointment of deputy commander-in-chief and Commander 1st Division, the latter to resume command of the 3rd Division. Major-General Sir George Murray replaced the ineffectual Colonel James Gordon in his old appointment of quartermaster-general, and Sir Robert Kennedy returned as commissary-general.

In May, Wellington appointed a young captain in the Royal Artillery, Acting Lieutenant Colonel Alexander Dickson from command of the siege train to overall command of the artillery, British and Portuguese, in succession to Lieutenant-Colonel G.B. Fisher. Fisher, described as 'a very pleasant man, a great artist, connoisseur, traveller etc', did not get on with Wellington, who drove him to resign. It is recorded that at their last meeting Wellington told Fisher to 'Go to hell!', and was much amused when the latter coolly replied, 'Then I'll go, Sir, to the Quarter Master General for a route!'[2] Dickson was twelve years younger than Fisher and had four Royal Artillery officers in the Peninsula senior to him, so, having come out to serve with the Portuguese artillery, he discreetly wore the uniform of that corps.

Another important addition to Wellington's staff was a Judge Advocate General, Francis Larpent. Larpent, who kept one of the best Peninsular diaries, joined during the retreat from Burgos. By doing everything possible to make the system work and by dealing with the accumulated backlog of court-martial cases as quickly as possible, he played an important part in improving discipline. By mid-March 1813, he could report 'We have flogged and hung people into better order I think. . . .' By the end of the month he presented Wellington with a report on courts-martial with the statement 'that we are mending and that we have not tried fifty cases (hung eight, transported eight or ten, flogged about sixty severely and broke several officers) for nothing'.[3]

Wellington's strategy for the campaign was to use the mountainous country along Spain's northern coast to turn the right of successive French positions and threaten their communications with Bayonne. His forward movement would be sustained through the Biscay ports and a siege train of artillery would be kept embarked at Corunna ready to be.called forward.

At the start of the campaign Joseph had some 42,000 men on the Portuguese frontier, including 9,000 cavalry, and with 100 guns. He was concerned about the growing strength of the Allied Army, a concern which was not shared in Paris where Wellington's strength was greatly underestimated. There was considerable disagreement among the French commanders on the strategy to be followed. Joseph referred the matter to Napoleon who told him that his first priority must be to protect and keep open communications with France.

Throughout the winter the right of the Allied Army, under Hill, maintained an advanced post at Bejar, near the Baños Pass and due south of Salamanca. Wellington intended to keep Joseph in doubt as to whether he intended to advance on Madrid by the Tagus or by Salamanca or, if he advanced on Salamanca, whether he intended to turn aside to Madrid or advance on Burgos. He expected Joseph to react to an advance on Salamanca by withdrawing to the line of the Douro. He therefore planned to deceive Joseph into believing that he intended to repeat his campaign of 1812 by advancing on Salamanca in person at the head of about a third of his force while the main body, under Graham, crossed the Douro in Portugal and struggled through the mountains to the line of Esla.

Graham, with 50,000 men, was given a few days' start across the Douro into Tras os Montes. Wellington and Hill with 32,000 men, and with a Spanish force of 10,000 men on their right, advanced on 22 May; Wellington was in command of the two centre columns directed on Salamanca, Hill to cross the Tormes further up. Graham, in touch with the Army of Galicia, of 20,000 men under Castaños, on his left, crossed into Spain on the twenty-fourth with the main body. Joseph fell back on the Douro only to find himself already outflanked.

By 4 June the Allies had concentrated some 100,000 men north of the Douro in the vicinity of Toro. The French fell back to the Ebro, taking up a series of positions along the Pisuerga and blowing up the defences of Burgos. They saw little of the Allied forces, for instead of advancing along the high road Wellington turned north into the mountains, aiming to get between the French and Santander, a port he wanted for bringing forward supplies, and to turn the naturally strong defensive position afforded by the Ebro by crossing it near its head waters and threatening to cut off the French from Bayonne. In this he succeeded and thus brought on the battle of Vitoria.

Napier's poetic description of the difficulties of this part of the campaign happily complements Aitchison's narrative:

Neither the winter gullies, nor the ravines, nor the precipitate passes amongst the rocks retarded even the march of the artillery. Where horses could not draw man hauled; when the wheels would not roll, the guns were let down or lifted up with ropes – six days they toiled unceasingly and on the seventh they burst like raging streams from every defile into the basin of Vitoria.[4]

Mesquitello
22nd March 1813

We are still as quiet as when I last wrote you, nor does there appear any symptoms of moving soon – the fact is one cannot move any distance from our magazines till there is sufficient green forage on the ground for the cavalry, which will not be for a month yet, at least; and the longer we wait the more likely are we to take the field strong, and the new levies to be effective, and it will be the more difficult for the enemy to supply themselves when collected.

There is a report (on the authority of a letter form Genl Hill's army) that Soult has withdrawn 8,000 men from Toledo and gone towards Valladolid and by the accounts from Headquarters there seems little doubt that he has himself been recalled to France – there is no reason to suppose that any part of the army is to accompany him, and it is supposed that he is going to confer with Bonaparte on the best plan for his campaign and, this being settled, that he will return to Spain. In the meantime the enemy are indicating their apprehensions of soon being obliged to concentrate. In Salamanca and all the towns on the Tormes they have imposed extraordinary contributions and they are exacting payment with unusual severity.

We are getting rather more healthy than we were – we have not many fever-sick but there are not many deaths as were some time ago and there are not near so many bad cases – I hope that in the course of another month we shall not have above 200 on the sick list which will reduce the proportion to about 2 in 9. Three of the regts of cavalry which served in the last campaign have just been ordered home, their horses being drafted into the other regts here.

The 1st Brigade of Guards has been, I believe, the most sickly in the army – they have lost upwards of 600 men dead – and they have still above 800 in hospital which is supposed to arise from both battalions having been in Walcheren[5] – I never saw two finer-looking battalions than they were 5 months ago but now they are not so strong as we are – they have just marched to Oporto to try the effects of a change of air.

I direct this to London where I hope it will arrive before you leave it.

Mesquitello
20th April 1813

My dear father,

The busy season here is coming on, and after we once begin moving I think there will be sufficient rapidity in our operations to afford me at all times a variety of news, which I shall of course take frequent opportunities to communicate; indeed, there are many reports in circulation of our being about to march, but they appear to have little more foundation than the probability of our army being assembled as soon as the country is sufficiently forward to enable us to keep the field – at present, things are unusually backward and from a very opposite cause from what is often complained of in our country at this season – the want of rain – we have had a remarkably fine winter, and so dry that there has hardly been a shower since January – the soil is generally very light and there is consequently a great deficiency in the crops – the grass is everywhere very scarce and the late warm weather has nearly ruined the early crops of barley and rye – they are both in full ear, but very small and thin. It is from this cause, I believe, that the Cavalry did not begin to come up from Lisbon sooner – the last division only left it on the 7th and it will yet be a month before they can reach headquarters in good order.

Our animals are now beginning to get into good order, as we have begun to cut green forage. Grass though is very limited, but it is produced in great quantities from their system of irrigation, which appears to me excellent tho' undoubtedly very expensive. The Portuguese dig into the sides of the hills for water, and they conduct it by regular cut channels to a considerable distance to their *patches* of grass (I cannot call them fields – they are so small). When it is scarce they shut up the mouth of the cut to answer for a reservoir, and being emptied every morning and evening, the grass grows very fast during the day. . . .

Turnips lately have been generally introduced here but they do not understand the cultivation of them, and they are generally planted in wet situations, and not being thinned they run all to top – which is the only part which the Portuguese use. I have endeavoured to explain their proper use, but they are here so bigoted to their own customs that I do not think they will benefit by my advice.

Sheep are very lean and of so wretched a breed that a whole one seldom weighs more than 30 pounds. The Black Cattle are better but so scarce that it has been found advisable to raise the contract price to 15 pence the pound (17 oz), which from the Bullocks falling off before being killed and the weight being completed when the animal is *alive* will cost the government at least 2 shillings. No division has been able to keep a supply of more than 12 days' meat and the Commissaries have been even then obliged to go to the market with ready money. . . . We have only yet been paid to November. Our sick are wonderfully diminished – we have only about 70 in hospital and of these not one is in bed.

Mesquitello
27th April 1813

My dear father,

I do not think that there is much chance of our coming home soon, though there can be little doubt that the extraordinary successes of the Russians will in the end lead to a Peace – all parties stand much in need of repose and Bonaparte's policy certainly is to accept fair terms, which I should think will be offered to him.

In this quarter there is not much appearance of repose – the French, tho' certainly diminished by drafts to organise the new levies, are still formidable in Spain, and they seem determined not to give up any part of it until we compel them – we have yet heard nothing of moving but we are making every preparation for an active campaign, and from the arrangements made there is every expectation of it also being a long one. I believe I told you that we are now to carry tents for the men on mules which were formerly in use to carry camp kettles – these have been replaced by light tin ones, which are to be carried by the men – I do not think this is a good plan, from the many chances of the man whose turn it is to carry the kettle for the mess not arriving at the end of the march. To render each man, however, with a certain degree independent, I have got it made a regulation in the regiment that every man shall have a small kettle of his own[6] (in lieu of a soup dish which they used to carry) – I began this with my own company a year ago, but as it is a little more expensive to the men, it was not then much adopted, but the benefits of it are now so obvious to all that most requested to have them this year, which has made therefore a regulation. I mention this of myself in consequence of your request. I have always commanded a company since my return to the Battn without anyone being above me in it. I have today only 7 sick out of 87 men present, so that you see we are now pretty healthy. I am also responsible for the mule to carry the tent – £10 was allowed to get a better one, which you will perhaps think a great deal but you will be astonished when I tell you that none are to be got under £30 and good ones are worth £50 and £60 and those fit for carriage are worth near £100. In short everything is much dearer than in England and treble what it used to be here. Since the allowance of *beef* a considerable supply of cattle has been obtained, but the consequence is that many young ones are killed and I have seen them working at eighteen months old.

We have kept out of our pay from the necessity of the Commissaries paying for them in hard cash – and we have just been paid up to December and they talk of another issue soon. We have been paid in *Guineas* ever since we arrived in these quarters and the last were quite new and coined in 1799. They are not worth so much here as what they sell for in England by 2/3d but they come cheaper to the government than Dollars – it is against the law to expend them but for the purpose of paying the troops, and the supplies are therefore still paid for in dollars.

Mesquitello
9th May 1813

My dear father,

Since I wrote to you on the 27th ulto we have remained quiet, but we are about to commence operations and it is at this moment been intimated to us that we shall move tomorrow – at present we know nothing, as the route has yet to be given us, but a few hours more will let us know in what direction we are to march. It has been reported for some time that the enemy were concentrating on the Douro. And it is now said that to enable us the better to drive them from it we shall at once cross that river at Lamego (Portugal) and thence moving north enter Spain and form our conjunction with the Galician army about Benavente. Toro is reported the central point of the enemy, so that it is most probable that some part of the British army will move by the north of Portugal – I hope it will not be our division, as the roads there are very bad and mountainous and that by Salamanca is in the country flat and good.

Villa Mea

15th May 1813

My dear father,

As I mentioned in my letter to you of the 9th we marched the next morning and we are now halted here within a few miles of Lamego for want of a sufficient number of large boats upon the Douro. We are, however, to cross that river early tomorrow at Peso da Regao, ours being one of the divisions destined to turn the enemy's position on the Douro. The 5th Division have already crossed in the quarter also, the 3rd Division are crossing higher up at San Joao de Pesqueira, and two brigades of Cavalry which are to accompany these three divisions are now marching north by Braga and Chaves – the whole of this force (under Sir T. Graham) are to assemble at Breganza, Outeiro and Vimioso, where it will arrive about the 24th inst, and then the combined army will approach the Douro from every quarter. We shall at once enter Spain and form a conjunction with the Galician army. Ld Wellington with the 4th, 6th, 7th and Light Divisions and the greater part of the cavalry will move by Salamanca upon Zamora, and Genl Hill with his own corps will move from Plasencia upon Madrid to support the Alicante army in driving the enemy from the Tagus, should they attempt to maintain themselves there.[7] They have re-occupied Toledo, which would show as if it was their intention to do so, but this is rather supposed here to have been done to deceive, and it is expected that they will abandon the line of the Tagus as soon as our whole army is in motion and concentrate on the Douro, which is of the utmost importance for them to maintain as covering their communications with France. They have thrown up some new works at Zamora which they occupy at present with 5,000 men and Toro is at a central point – and they appear at present to be determined to keep both these places as long as they possibly can – the former is not very strong but the latter is formidable from the Spaniards having neglected to destroy its defences effectively, while we were at Burgos. Our first operations, then, will be against these places and we shall certainly not move further until we have taken one of them – both command passages of the Douro and it is indispensable that we should have one secure passage of that river for a ready communication with our forces one each side of it.

I have not lately heard any estimate of the enemy's numbers, but since the select men quitted Spain with Soult only two regiments of Hessians have entered it and the loss of Soult himself may be considered as equal (to us) to a great diminution of their numbers. We shall have, I think, about 60,000 British and Portuguese infantry and 7,000 cavalry and what the Spaniards may be I have not heard, but I cannot believe that of those who will act in combination with us their numbers will equal 40,000 effectives in the whole, and I have no means of judging from their description, though I own that I am not sanguine that they have much improved, notwithstanding the evident necessity for it, which has been allowed by all their best generals.

There has been a very great fall of rain these three weeks and it is not over – our men however are tolerably healthy and I think that battalions of infantry will average about 500 men and the regiments of cavalry about 300 each. We are well supplied with everything and I have no doubt that we shall be well supplied during the whole summer, as the river Douro has been made navigable under the direction of our Engineers as high up as Miranda de Douro. I continue in very good health and so does Pincher and Lewis. My pony also is very fat and in excellent spirits. They all join in love to my mother, etc.

Villa de Fraes

My dear father,   *4th June 1813*

Since I wrote to you from Villa Mea on the 15th ult we have been so constantly marching that I have not had any opportunity to send letters.

We did not cross the Douro so soon as was expected but we nevertheless reached Braganza on the 25th, and the next day we moved forward in one body and encamped on the frontier of Spain.

Ld Wellington had crossed the Douro by different routes with the whole of the army except the Light division and Genl Hill's corps, and he assembled them upon the river Esla on the 30th, but it was so much swelled by the rains as to be quite impassable without bridges, and there was not one on it below Benavente. This circumstance occasioned some delay but a part of the 15th Hussars boldly *swam* across that river on the morning of the 31st and made two of the enemy picquets prisoners, and this enabled a pontoon bridge to be established soon afterwards. Ld Wellington the same day pushed forward with three brigades of cavalry and three divisions of infantry and the rest of the army with six battering guns followed the next day – the Spanish army of Galicia under Castaños at the same time crossed by the bridge of Benavente and pushed on. The enemy, seeing us thus so formidable, retired and our headquarters were in Zamora on 1 June – they have since continued to retreat as we advance, affording some oppor-tunities to our Cavalry to distinguish themselves – the Hussars have maintained the high reputation which they acquired under Sir John Moore and the day before yesterday the 10th *annihilated* the 16th Regiment of French Light Dragoons – of 300 men, 250 being taken prisoner or killed; the officers (except two) and a few men escaped, *only* from being mounted on English horses (say the 10th) which were taken from our other Dragoons in this country. This brilliant affair took place in the presence of about 5,000 Infantry of the enemy and some squadrons of cavalry after a chase on a plain of about 4 miles. The whole of this part of Spain is admirably suited for the operations of the Cavalry, and the Hussar brigade are already felt the acquisition to this army which was expected of them. They show themselves exactly what Dragoons should be, extremely active and ever anxious to meet the enemy, and it is to be hoped that from their brilliant example a spirit will be infused into our other British cavalry which no superiority of the enemy will get the better of, but at present I believe we are rather superior in that arm to them and if not in actual numbers to their Infantry also. Our morale strength is certainly equal – every branch of the Army is in most perfect state of equipment and the men look more healthy and much better than I have ever seen them before. The battering train in the field, I fear, is the only defective. I don't know of any guns but six 18-pdrs, but Burgos now is the first place we shall have to attack and these it is supposed will be sufficient till others are brought from Santander. We are now marching in four corps – the Galician army will form a 5th on the left of all – on the left of the British Genl Graham commands the 1st and 5th Divisions, two brigades of Portuguese infantry and 2 brigades of British cavalry – Genl Picton is next with the 3rd and 6th Divisions. Lord Wellington is with the 4th and 7th Divisions and most of the Cavalry, and Genl Hill is on the right with his own corps (2nd Division) and the Light Division – he was yesterday at Morales in front of Toro on the Douro. The bridges at the latter place and Zamora have been repaired. You will hear of the success which we had at Salamanca – Lord W., they say, was disappointed as from what has since been known – had he had information of their situation two French divisions might have been cut off.

PS *Villerias – 6 June.* We have continued to move forward without seeing the enemy; he continues to retire. Valladolid has been abandoned by him and he quitted Dueñas this morning – Headquarters are in Ampudia about 4 miles off and the whole army is within a few miles. On looking to the map you will perceive that we are marching to the westward of Palencia (we are now within 10 miles of it). By this route we shall turn the only position which the enemy could take up on this side of Burgos – so that we expect that they will make no stand on this side of the Ebro – they are 60,000 strong – we are more. We have reports that the French were defeated at Dresden on 7 May, which I hope will turn out true.[8]

Sotresqudo
12th June 1813

Hitherto our operations have been eminently successful and we have freed without loss, nay, almost without firing a shot, the whole kingdom of Leon and part of both the Castilles – in short from the happy appearances at present I begin to be sanguine that this will be *our* last active campaign in the Peninsula.

We have continued to move with great rapidity and ever since my last letter on 4 June you will perceive we have gained an immense tract of country – we entered Palencia on the 8th a few hours after the enemy quitted it and our column having marched nearly north ever since we are now within thirty miles of the source of the Ebro. The enemy are retiring behind that river and it is probable that they will make no attempt at resistance till we try to cross it; they have already retired their rearguard from Burgos. Genl Hill with the right of the army is near it and it is reported will be entrusted with its reductions should that measure be judged proper – but this under existing circumstances is what we do scarcely think indispensable.

It was so last year when from our limited force our line of operations was of necessity confined to one road, but our means now are so much more powerful that we have but a small proportion in that direction and the possession of it by the enemy, while it will cause them a certain loss of upwards of 2,000 men, will be of small importance to us, as our supplies will come north of it through Léon and from the ports in the Bay of Biscay. It is indeed reported that the enemy have already blown up Burgos and abandoned it[9] but I do not myself credit it, as the flattering hope of such a defence as it made last [year] will, I think make them attempt it again, and they may suppose that we shall not proceed beyond it till it falls.

They are said to have no idea of this force on our left, which including the Spaniards is estimated at 46,000 men, and they have not yet retired from Santander. It would appear to me that Ld Wellington intends to bring the enemy to a general action as soon as possible and if so, which certainly is our policy and not the enemy's, will push on at once to the left of the Ebro and blockade Burgos. If successful the French will be ruined, if beaten we shall still be safe, as they cannot be strong enough to pursue us.

The Ebro, you will perceive, runs nearly across Spain and is very formidable but it is to be turned above its source by the bank of Reinosa and we are evidently to attempt it. Longa, Mendizabal and Mina are said to be united in Biscay to 36,000 men and in possession of one bridge of the Ebro for us to pass by – we were at one time marching direct upon Reinosa but yesterday we suddenly turned to our right and made a short march towards Frias – we are halted today and if we move tomorrow 3 days more will enable us to judge for certain.

This part of Spain is very poor and much laid waste, so that being so far from our magazine we have already suffered the want of bread in the last 6 days – sometimes we have had none and other days $\frac{1}{2}$ or $\frac{1}{4}$ allowance – however, as we shall not now move so rapidly we shall soon be well off again. The men are wonderfully healthy – money very scarce – 6 months in arrears of pay. For myself I am very well, having great hopes of seeing you again soon.

Zuesa
19th June 1813

We have been so late reaching our camp and I have had so little notice of a mail from England that I have barely time to write you – I am well. We are now within 30 miles of Vitoria, which I hope we shall reach in a day or two but probably not without much opposition. As yet the enemy have given us little fighting – we passed the Ebro unmolested on the 15th by the bridge of San Martin and have been very much harassed ever since – yesterday our column had an affair with them out at the pass of Osma, which we gained in about 4 hours, but Ld Wellington with the Light Division had an affair also near Espeja – they made 250 prisoners and took much baggage – *we took neither* – the fact is we do not manage well – our country man Genl G. [Graham] who commands us has shown himself a good deal too old – he is as far as concerns himself extremely active but he harasses the troops beyond conception and in the field he displays little science and still less decision.[10]

We came today about 12 miles only, yet we were on the march from ½ past 3 am till past 5 pm and the day on which we crossed the Ebro (15th) we went only 22 miles but were under arms from 4 in the morning till ½ *past 12 at night*. In short we have had a most fatiguing time of it. Only one day's halt since 28 May, bread *very, very* scarce. Things look well and in one or two days we hope to be either in Vitoria or to have gained a battle. The enemy are reported to be about 80,000 and determined to oppose us – the country is most favourable to them; indeed, it exceeds so much in strength any which I have ever seen that I cannot convey a proper idea of it – the passes generally are very narrow roads through mountains, everywhere else is inaccessible. I conceive them impregnable by direct attack – our column is one which acts on the flank of our main body and destined to turn them. Burgos you will hear has been destroyed; the French blew up the Castle on our approach.

We have had some very bad weather – it has rained all day and is so very cold we might fancy ourselves in the north of Scotland in January instead of the province of Biscay in June. The roads are much broken by the rain. I wrote to you on the 12th from Sotresquado and will continue to do so every opportunity – excuse great fatigue and bad accommodation for writing no more now.

Adieu

VITORIA

Some of Wellington's officers advised him to stand on the Ebro; however, he believed it easier to stand on the Pyrenees. There was, then, no intention of carrying the war into southern France, for discouraging reports of Napoleon's recovery from his Russian disaster were reaching Spain. So the advance continued and by 20 June the army had closed up to the river Bayas on a wide front and the 3rd and 7th Divisions had crossed it. Before them lay Vitoria, nestling on a plain extending some twenty miles from east to west and ten from north to south, hemmed in on every side by rugged offshoots of the Pyrenees. The southern half of the plain was covered by low, partially isolated hills. Through the plain ran the Zadorra, a lively trout stream about forty yards wide and crossed by many bridges, none of which had been destroyed. Fordable in many parts, it had deep pools where a number of mill dams had been built. Its banks were steep in most places. The course of the

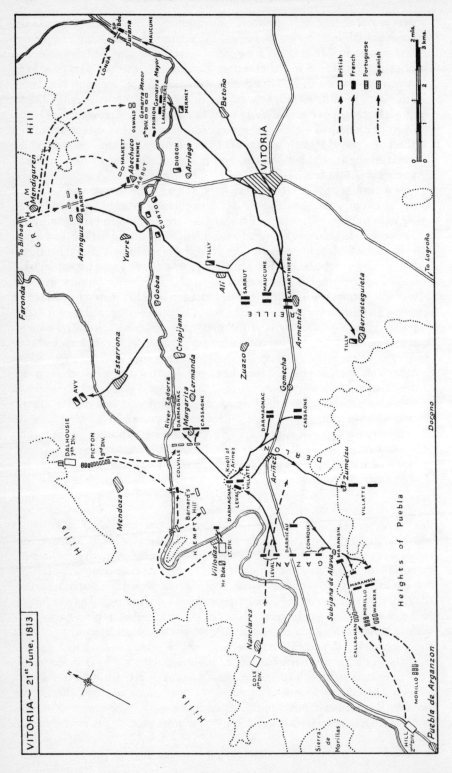

VITORIA ~ 21st June, 1813

Zadorra ran east to west, north of Vitoria, until it struck the Monte Arrato when it bent sharply to the south-east. In the bend the bank was precipitious. After making two further great bends, the stream settled down to flow in a south-westerly direction, leaving the Vitoria plain by the narrow Puebla Gorge, between the heights of Puebla and those of Morillas.

Vitoria did not offer a position of natural defensive strength but it was an important centre of communications on the main road from Madrid and Burgos to Bayonne – that road entered the plain by the Puebla Pass and left Vitoria in a north-easterly direction. The main road from the port of Bilbao entered the town from the north, and that to Pamplona left it in a south-easterly direction. It was a position to which Suchet could send reinforcements from his 32,000-strong army in Catalonia.

At Vitoria, Joseph had some 60,000 men under arms, of whom 11,000 were cavalry, and about 140 field guns. He also had his siege train, his military chest, estimated to have contained £500,000, and all the baggage, functionaries and paraphernalia from his Court at Madrid. There were also thousands of Spanish refugees who had supported the French as well as great quantities of military stores. Joseph had sent away one large convoy on the nineteenth under escort of a division from the Army of Portugal, and intended sending another on the twenty-first.

Though there is evidence that Joseph considered withdrawing to a better defensive position, he felt himself under no immediate threat and, according to Private Wheeler of the 51st, 'Such was King Joseph's confidence that he had caused scaffolding to be erected for the people to see him beat the English. The tops of all the lofty churches and buildings were crowded with spectators to witness our disgrace. Grand dinners were provided with wine in abundance to drink to the health of the conquering French.'[11]

It is frequently stated that Joseph expected Wellington, as usual, to turn the right of the French position. A skirmish on the twentieth between a French brigade, sent up the Bilbao road to occupy the fortified town of Murguia, and Longa's guerrilla forces, causing the French to withdraw, seemed to confirm this. Nevertheless, Joseph deployed his army facing west and laid back in depth from the Puebla Pass to Vitoria. Gazan's Army of the South was forward covering the pass, with a picquet on the heights of Puebla; d'Erlon's Army of the Centre to their right rear, on the high ground between Arinez and Gomecha; behind them was stationed the reserve, Reille's Army of Portugal, which had recovered only half the divisions detached to Clausel's Army of the North. When a deserter came in with information strengthening the view that Wellington intended to act against the right, Reille sent a division across the Zadorra to occupy some high ground covering the Bilbao road and faced his corps in that direction. This manoeuvre left a gap of some six miles between the two halves of Joseph's army.

Wellington had the advantage of being able to overlook the French position from the heights of Morillas. He had decided to carry out one of the most difficult of battlefield manoeuvres, a converging attack by a number of columns through difficult country. Against a more active enemy, splitting his forces like this might have been highly dangerous, but he believed he could rely on the passivity of his foe. On the right, Hill, with the 2nd Division (Stewart), the Portuguese Division (Silveira), Spanish Division (Morillo) and Alten's and Fane's cavalry brigades – say 20,000 men – was to cross the Zadorra by Puebla de Arganzon and force the pass. In the centre Wellington was personally to control two columns comprising 30,000 troops. The right centre column, with whom he advanced, composed of the 4th Division (Cole), Light Division (Baron von Alten) and four brigades of cavalry, was to cross the Bayas at Subijana and move to Nanclares on the Zadorra to await orders. The left centre column under Dalhousie – the 3rd (Picton) and 7th (Dalhousie) Divisions – was to cross the Bayas at Anda and converge on the right centre column at Tres Puentes. The left column under Graham, comprising the 1st Division (Howard), the 5th Division (Oswald), Longa's partisans, and Pack's and Bradford's independent Portuguese brigades, some 23,000 men, followed up by Giron's Spanish corps of 12,000, were to occupy Murguia and advance on Vitoria from the north by the Bilbao road. Graham was instructed to keep in touch on his right and act according to circumstances. If the other columns were making little progress, he was to help them; if, however, they were doing well, he was to turn the French right and cut the road to Bayonne.

The first shots in the battle were fired about 9 am as Morillo's Spaniards scaled the precipitous heights of Puebla, driving in the French picquet, and enabled Hill to pass the 2nd Division through the pass. Fierce fighting took place and Hill sent Cadogan's brigade to support the Spaniards. Cadogan was struck but had himself carried to the edge of the escarpment from where he could witness the progress of his Highlanders, and there he died.

By this time Jourdan, Joseph's chief of staff, had decided that Wellington intended to turn not the right but the left flank. He announced that all movements against the right were feints, and Joseph gave orders for d'Erlon to send a division to the left to cover the road from Logroño, thus weakening the French centre. At the same time, Gazan reinforced the Puebla heights leaving Subijana unoccupied, which did not prevent Hill from passing his force through the defile and occupying that village, which he retained against counter-attacks by two French divisions.

There was now a pause while Wellington waited for his other columns to close up to the Zadorra. The Light Division and Hussar Brigade, under Wellington's own guidance, had advanced unseen to within a hundred yards of the bridge at Villodas which he intended to assault. On their right, the 4th Division was in position behind Nanclares. On their left, round the hairpin bend, Picton's division had reached Mendoza but Dalhousie and two-thirds of the 7th Division had lost their way and were not at Tres Puentes. Not only were these bridges intact but their approaches were not covered by guns. A few French skirmishers crossed the river near Wellington and were driven back. A peasant brought information that the bridge at Tres Puentes was unguarded. Kemp's brigade, led by the 95th, quickly crossed without loss, except for their peasant guide who was decapitated by a stray cannonball. The Tres Puentes bridge secured, Wellington sent orders for Dalhousie to take the bridge at Mendoza with the 7th Division. Picton whose temper was never far off the boil, seethed with frustration at the absence of Dalhousie. Intercepting Wellington's orders and finding that the 7th, supported by the 4th and Light Divisions, were to take what he considered to be his bridge, he bawled at the A.D.C.: 'You may tell Lord Wellington from me, sir, that the 3rd Division under my command shall in less than ten minutes attack the bridge and carry it, and the 4th and Light Divisions may support it if they choose.'[12] Whereupon, led by Picton with his usual string of expletives, the 3rd Division swept over the river, followed by the 4th at Nanclares.

Wellington now had four divisions across the river supported by ample artillery. Gazan began bringing his divisions back on to and around the high ground behind Arinez, from where Joseph and his staff had been viewing the battle. Now gunfire could be heard away to the north heralding the approach of Graham by the Bilbao road. This had taken longer than expected, but now the Army of Portugal was driven back on to the line of the river. The efforts of the 1st and 5th Divisions to take the bridges at Ariaga and Gamarra Mayor were hotly contested but Longa's men, bypassing the French positions on the high ground east of the Bilbao road, crossed the Zadorra higher up by the Durana bridge, so cutting the road to Bayonne east of Vitoria.

On the western front the French, driven from the Ariñez position, fell back on the Zuarzo ridge but made little attempt to consolidate it and Jourdan ordered a withdrawal to a final position in front of Vitoria, along a feature between Ali and Armentia. Beyond the city 'thousands of carriages, animals and non-combatants; men, women and children were huddled together'.[13]

The 3rd Division was held in front of Ali but the 4th Division, on their right, stormed and carried the positions on their front, while the 7th division passed between Ali and the river and fell on the flank of Sarrut's division, facing Graham. Joseph now passed the order to retreat by the Salvatierra road and French resistance collapsed. Only Reille seems to have kept his head, rallying two of his divisions at Betore, east of Vitoria. He led them on the Salvatierra road to act as rearguard to the rest of the army which, having abandoned practically all its equipment and ordnance, was fleeing in disorder towards Pamplona.

Wellington found his selection of so junior an officer as Alexander Dickson for overall command of the Allied artillery more than justified on the battlefield and during the pursuit. It was largely due to the artillery that the French were driven from successive ridges in their centre, at Arinez, Zuaco and immediately in front of Vitoria. Unlike Napoleon, Wellington normally fought his artillery dispersed, but on this occasion, to Dickson's joy, 'the nature of the country and the want of roads, was the means of throwing a large proportion of our Artillery together away from their divisions, which I availed myself of, and by employing them in masses it had a famous effect'.[14]

Salvatierra
23rd June 1813

My dear father,

   Lord Wellington has nobly confirmed his claim to his foreign title of Duke of Vitoria[15] by a most splendid victory over the French at that place on the 21st instant. In instances of prodigies of individuals and regiments in hard fighting, it has not equalled his first *offensive* battle – Salamanca – but it surpasses in its immediate results. It has firmly established the many qualities of the British soldier to those more immediately tutored, nay fostered by his own care (the Portuguese); it has offered them an opportunity to prove a claim to excellence in *attack* which cannot be surpassed even by the British. You will see the public account that they were chiefly employed and how they repaid the confidence reposed in them.

The whole disposable force of Spain with the exception of Suchet[16] was assembled and in position with 170 pieces of Artillery commanded (nominally) by their King. They had no particular wish to fight but were fully prepared for it, and so confident of success that nearly 3 hours after the battle began (about ½ past 4 in the afternoon) they were surprised to hear that we were gaining ground. Their position throughout its front, in the whole extent, was very formidable, being protected by the Zadorra, a river only *passable* by two *bridges* which they possessed and from locality suited for the best resistance – this obstacle, however, was got the better of by our chief with his usual care; and Genl Hill with his own and other strong corps, having passed the river below the enemy's position, attacked his left flank (which was thrown back on some high ground) and notwithstanding a tremendous fire of cannon he successfully carried four positions, almost without a discharge of musketry. His right and centre were at the same time threatened by Genl *Graham* with his own corps, and soon as he saw the success of *our* right he attacked both bridges and carried them – the enemy immediately retreated in confusion with much precipitation – all his artillery in position was taken, and he was soon compelled to abandon the greater part of those which he had got some way off – in short the victory was most complete. The generals, about 500 of their *ladies*, the military chest (with much treasure) and the whole baggage of the army fell into our hands and Joseph himself was obliged to escape with only the clothes on his back – his valet with his carriages and wardrobe being with the baggage.

The plain by which they retreated was very woody and much intersected by ditches – these favoured their escape and, as everyone threw away whatever impeded his flight, but few prisoners were taken. The Artillery and stores taken are immense – I fear saying how many guns because from the difficulty of counting – many different reports of their number are given. I believe from all that I hear that there are at least 110 pieces besides ammunition wagons and were I myself to form an estimate from what I saw in one place about 4 miles from Vitoria, I would call them more.

The French army in Spain may now be considered ruined, having lost its chief material, and we shall probably have little fighting till we reach the Pyrenees. I have not time now to expatiate on the magnificence of the sight – the whole French and Allied armies in columns in a plain within 3 miles – perhaps in all 180,000 men, but I hope soon to have the pleasure of relating to you by *our own fireside* many stories which will never reach you through the published prints.

Toloso
26th June 1813

Genl Graham with our division and the Galician Army was detached the day after the battle in the hope of intercepting the garrison from Bilbao and the neighbourhood which were also escorting a large convoy, but from the unfortunate state of the weather we were a day too late in cutting the high road and the convoy which consists chiefly of sick and *Renegades* has escaped. We came up with their rear near Villa Franca on the 24th and there was a sharp skirmish – it was late in the day and they got the town. Yesterday we found them posted so strongly round the town that we could not attack them till just before dark – they defended themselves on the heights and in the town with much obstinacy but [we] carried it and were quartered in it at night. Genl Graham was wounded slightly – the Spanish troops behaved magnificently. You will perhaps think me very lazy in not writing to you oftener and longer letters, but I am sure if you saw how we are harassed you would not expect me to do more. I have hitherto kept my health pretty weak but not my temper, which I must say is much ruffled. We are only 6 leagues from France.

It was late in the day when the pursuit began. The infantry were tired and hungry, though not too tired to join an orgy of looting followed by night-long celebrations by the light of bonfires. The country astride the Salvatierra road down which the French had fled was not well suited to cavalry and afforded many good positions for delaying action. Pursuit on the twenty-first, such as it was, was mainly accomplished by Ponsonby's brigade of heavy cavalry and by the Household Cavalry brigade. Had Cotton or some equally competent cavalry leader been present and in overall command something more might have been accomplished. It was not, however, the terrain or Reille's rear-guard that imposed the greatest delay on Wellington's forces in pressing the pursuit, but the golden apples dropped by Joseph in inadvertent imitation of Atalanta.

In and around Vitoria the ground was strewn with cannon, overturned carriages, tumbrils, wounded and dead soldiers and countless civilians – men, women and children, live and dead horses and mules, and other farm and domestic animals, including monkeys and parrots. Innumerable carriages and carts, some said as many as 3,000 blocked the road to Salvatierra about a mile from the city. They contained the families of generals and courtiers and the followers of Joseph's Court and army. So numerous were the women that a French officer called this company *'un bordel ambulant'*. With them were trunks laden with jewels, money and art treasures looted from Madrid, as well as their personal belongings. There were carts loaded with every kind of military store, ammunition, wine and food. But by far the most attractive prize was The Caja Real, Joseph's military chest, estimated to contain £500,000, of which, to Wellington's fury, only £30,000 found its way into the public coffer.

As soon as the general retreat had been ordered the French gunners, who had been firing to the last, cut the traces of those guns which had already limbered-up and been hooked-in to their teams of horses and galloped into the mêlée on the Salvatierra road, while the drivers of carriages and carts, seeing a better chance of getting away on foot than on wheels, abandoned them, though a few light vehicles attempted to bypass the jam by driving across country. The hussar brigade, galloping into the city ahead of the army, added to the confusion. Finding themselves amongst the baggage, to which the populace and camp followers were already helping themselves, they joined in the free-for-all.

King Joseph escaped from his carriage by a hair's breadth by jumping on a horse just as Captain Wymondham, 14th Light Dragoons, and Lieutenant Lord Worcester, 10th Hussars, broke in on the other side. Amongst Joseph's wardrobe Wymondham found his silver chamber pot and the 14th thereafter became known as 'The Emperor's Chambermaids'. Joseph's state and private papers passed into Wellington's hands as did a number of rolled oil canvases. Two soldiers dismantled Jourdan's marshal's baton to share between them but it was recovered and presented by Wellington to the Prince Regent.

As soon as the Allies entered Vitoria, Giron's Spanish division was sent in pursuit of Macune, who was escorting a convoy of great value along the Vitoria to Bayonne road. The 6th Division, which had taken no part in the battle, was ordered forward to Vitoria where with the 5th it was to defend the city against the possible advance of 15,000 French troops under Clausel from Logroño. Every battalion was also directed to leave a small detachment in the city to help maintain order, look after the wounded and sort out the trophies. Unfortunately they behaved disgracefully and Wellington had to send an assistant provost marshal with powers to hang marauders and anyone resisting authority.

In Vitoria the scene in the hospital was appalling: '. . . seventeen or eighteen hundred men without legs or arms etc, or with dreadful wounds and, having nothing to eat for two or three days, the misery extreme, and not nearly hands sufficient to dress and take care of the men, English, Portuguese, Spaniards and French altogether, though the Spaniards and Portuguese had at first no provision at all for their people'.[17]

The rest of the army followed up the French along the road to Pamplona. Joseph had got his army on the road to Pamplona at 10 pm on the twenty-first and it was not until the twenty-third that British cavalry caught up with his rearguard. Clausel heard of Joseph's defeat when he had advanced to Trevino, within twelve miles of Vitoria. He then retired to Logroño on the road to Zaragoza. After some skirmishes Joseph reached Pamplona on the twenty-fourth. He reinforced the garrison to 4,000 men and deprived of all his artillery, turned north for the French frontier – Gazan, with the Army of the South, used the Orthez road up the Carlos valley, and Joseph the Bayonne road through the valley of Baztan. By 8 July, after a fight with Hill's 2nd Division for the Maya Pass, all the main passes through the Pyrenees were in Wellington's hands and his left flank on the banks of the Bidassoa.

On reaching Pamplona, Wellington left Hill to blockade it and turned south with four divisions to try and intercept Clausel. He now heard of

Murray's failure at Tarragona and the loss of his siege train. With nothing to distract Suchet, other than the Spanish forces in Aragon and Catalonia, Wellington did not want to drive Clausel and Suchet together, for the latter's field armies numbered about 23,000. Wellington therefore returned to Pamplona, relieved Hill of blockading the city and directed him to drive the French from the Baztan valley and secure the Maya Pass. Owing to the mountainous terrain, lateral communication between the Allied forces occupying this wide front was very difficult and Graham's corps was separated from the main body of the Army by the rugged Sierra de Aralar, the bridge between the Pyrenees and the mountains of Cantabria.

We must now consider the state of the Army following the victory at Vitoria and the progress of Graham's corps, to which John Aitchison belonged. Wellington left Vitoria about ten o'clock on the night of 21 June to go to bed, announcing his intention to pursue Joseph early next day. Up early, he found that his Army had scarcely slept after an all-night carousal following a twenty-mile fighting advance. As a result, orders to form the advance guard were not received by the Light Division until mid-day, and the main body only started to move off at 2-30 p.m.

Although the French were also demoralized they got away quickly. Larpent observed:

> The 23rd and 11th Portuguese regiments, who behaved in the field on the 21st as well as any British did, or could, . . . on the march, though smaller animals, were most superior. They were cheerful, orderly and steady. The English troops were fagged, half tipsy, weak, disorderly and unsoldierlike; yet the Portuguese suffer greater real hardships, as they have no tents, only bivouacs, and have a worse commissariat.[18]

To Bathurst, Wellington wrote:

> We started with the army in the highest order, and up to the very day of the battle nothing could get on better, but that event has, as usual, annihilated all order and discipline. . . . We have in the service the scum of the earth as common soldiers; and of late years we have been doing everything in our power both by law and publications to relax the discipline by which alone such men can be kept in order.[19]

Graham's corps, less the 5th Division, marched with the rest of the army but late on the twenty-second they received orders to turn north from Salvatierra and march on to Villafranca in an attempt to cut off Macune and the convoy. Owing to a misunderstanding over the orders they did not take this route until the following day, and in the confusion captain Norman Ramsay R.H.A., the hero of Fuentes de Oñoro, was put under arrest by Wellington for disobedience to orders. Such was his reputation that the incident became something of a *cause célèbre* in the army.

On 22 June, Foy marched down the San Sebastian road to Mondragon to cover Macune and his convoy by checking Giron's and Longa's Spaniards who were following him up. During the night Foy heard of Graham's advance over the San Adrian Pass and when Graham advanced early on the twenty-fourth he found Macune strongly posted at Beasain, where his route joined the main Vitoria–San Sebastian road. By turning the right flank of Macune and then of Foy, who was in a supporting position, Graham was in Villafranca that night. The French continued their withdrawal harassed by Spanish guerrillas, and took up a naturally strong defensive position covering the town and pass of Tolosa. The Spanish forces had now joined Graham. On the twenty-fifth Graham detached Giron to turn the left of the French position and Mendizabal to turn the right. This achieved, at six in the evening Graham launched an assault with his two Portuguese brigades and the Light battalions of the King's German Legion, belonging to the 1st Division, and entered Tolosa.

Foy's strength had by this time risen to about 16,000. Contact was now made with Reille and the remnant of his Army of Portugal, which was about Santesteban, south of Irun and halfway to Pamplona. Reille ordered Foy to withdraw to the north bank of the Bidassoa, leaving a bridgehead at Behobi. Graham continued his advance on the twenty-ninth, leaving the bulk of his troops at San Sebastian, including the 5th Division which had been sent to join him. The Spanish divisions advanced to the Bidassoa with the 1st Division in support at Oyarzun.

Herpani
3rd July 1813

My dear father,

After remaining at Tolosa till the 29th we came on here only I believe from want of knowing what to do with us, for the same confusion and indecision which has been manifest throughout this year, when we were separated from Ld Wellington, have been shown here. After remaining encamped in the worst weather I ever saw at this season, some of us have been put into quarters and the rest it is supposed will be soon; that is, I suppose, when a heavy sick list shall have confirmed our Commander in an opinion which he is said to have entertained the day after our arrival here 'that there was no necessity for removing us from Tolosa'. Arrangements were made to send us back there where we would have been well off, but for appearance sake I suppose we have been kept out in very wet weather.

You will I dare say think me very ill-natured in writing thus but it is not without cause, and were you to see how things are managed you would allow that there is sufficient to provoke less irritable tempers than mine – it would try those of the greatest stoic. In short [indecipherable, but obviously meant to be Graham] is anything but a General – always galloping – constantly deciding yet ever undecided, he creates confusion and fatigue to all under him.

The enemy have passed the frontier – the Spaniards are at Irun and some are making a show of besieging San Sebastian, where the French have left a garrison of 1,600 men – they have no chance of taking the place without great means, which they do not now possess. It is very strong – Burgos a

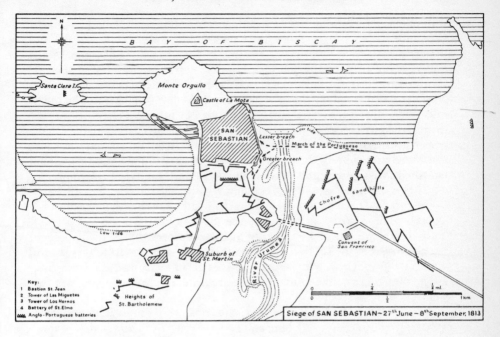

Key:
1 Bastion St. Jean
2 Tower of Les Miguetas
3 Tower of Los Hornos
4 Battery of St. Elmo
⚔ Anglo-Portuguese batteries

⚔ Heights of
    St. Bartholemew

Siege of SAN SEBASTIAN ~ 27ᵗʰ June – 8ᵗʰ September, 1813

joke to it. Ld Wellington has passed Pamplona where there is a garrison of 4,000 – Genl Hill is blockading it, but whether he means to attack or not we do not know. . . .

The importance of the port of San Sebastian for an advance by the Allies into southern France was similar to that of Antwerp for the invasion of Germany in 1944. Before undertaking the invasion of France, Wellington needed San Sebastian as an advanced base. It took six weeks and cost much money to move supplies on muleback from Lisbon and, though Santander and Corunna were available, San Sebastian would be much more convenient; besides, he needed to clear his lines of communication by reducing it and Pamplona.

Without the means to besiege two places at once, he decided to lay siege to San Sebastian while starving out Pamplona. The harbour of Passages, just east of San Sebastian, provided a convenient place for landing the siege train and stores. This picturesque inlet soon became the scene of great activity, twenty-four-pounders were landed from Commodore Sir George Collier's ship, with ammunition, other great guns and all the military equipment for the siege. Other commodities such as biscuit and rum were brought ashore from the transports. Collier commanded the blockading squadron.

The siege train was landed under the supervision of Lieutenant-Colonel Augustus Fraser, who had got his brevet promotion only the week before and was to command the Royal Horse Artillery at Waterloo. On 30 June, one of the few fine days, Fraser sat on the sands at Passages 'surrounded by a dozen little girls; one, he wrote, 'is mending my foraging cap, the rest singing: "Viva

Wellington!"".[20] Soon the scene on shore was as animated as that afloat. Two Portuguese regiments were employed, some making gabions and fascines for the siege, others moving stores and seeing them loaded on to 300 mules. Oxen were used for drawing the guns.

San Sebastian was a small place and Wellington did not expect it to resist for more than a few days after the batteries had opened against it. The town walls were, however, very difficult to approach. Immediately north of the town a precipitous rock crowned by the Castle of La Mota marked the end of the narrow sandy peninsula on which the town rested. On the west the town walls were lapped by the sea, on the east the estuary of the Urumea came to the foot of the walls at high tide but left a rocky foreshore at low tide, at which time the estuary itself was easily fordable. Against the south wall of the town a hornwork had been built out, covering the width of the low-lying peninsula. Beyond the hornwork had sprung up the suburb of San Martin and beyond that again the heights and convent of San Bartolomeo marked the approach to the town from the south-west. The other approach was from the Chofre sandhills, due east across the estuary. The Castle of La Mota could bring fire, though plunging and therefore not very accurate, to bear on any part of the peninsula.

The French governor, Emanuel Rey, had come from Burgos bringing some of that intrepid garrison with him, and Foy had reinforced him so that he now had a garrison of about 2,700. At the time of the battle of Vitoria the defences of San Sebastian were not in good order. Rey set about restoring them with energy. In particular, he fortified the convent of San Bartolomeo and burnt and cleared from the peninsula all the buildings which masked the fire of the hornwork.

On 3 July a British frigate with nineteen smaller vessels arrived to blockade the port, but proved unable to prevent an occasional small boat from St Jean de Luz getting in at night. After Wellington had reconnoitred the place on 12 July, he left the conduct of the siege to Graham who kept the Spanish forces on the Bidassoa supported by the 1st Division at Oyarzun as his covering force, and proceeded to lay siege with the 5th Division and two Portuguese brigades, making use of both approaches. As a preliminary, the heights of San Bartolomeo had to be secured. Batteries were raised against the convent and opened a heavy cannonade on the fourteenth which was kept up until the seventeenth when the convent, now in ruins, was easily taken by assault. The assailants, the 9th Regiment, three companies of Royal Scots, and some Portuguese, then moved down on to the peninsula to repulse a sortie from the hornwork, coming under the guns, they were driven back with considerable loss. On the twentieth two batteries on the left and four on the right of the Urumea, in all thirty pieces of ordnance, opened fire on the works. From the sandhills a breaching battery of eleven twenty-four-pounders played for three days against the town walls, between the towers of Los Hornos and Las Miguetas, at a range of six hundred yards. By the twenty-third they had made a 'practicable' breach and were then turned on to the wall south of the Los Hornos tower where, by the evening, they had made a breach thirty yards wide.

The assault should have gone in on the twenty-fifth, but unfortunately some shells had set on fire immediately in the rear of the breach a number of houses which burnt so fiercely that the assault was postponed. Rey spent the night retrenching in the rear of the breaches and sowing every sort of obstacle, as well as placing artillery to flank each breach and loopholing houses for the same purpose. The assault was timed to go in at 4 a.m., while still too dark for the British guns to have any observation, and contrary to Wellington's advice, that it should be made in daylight. The choice of time was, however, limited by there being only sufficient foreshore from two hours before to two hours after low water. The British had shown themselves inept and untrained in all their sieges, relying for success on the sheer courage of their men, but of all the plans for assault this was undoubtedly the least likely to succeed. Despite strong hints from Wellington, the point of attack was prematurely disclosed by opening the batteries before the approach trenches had been completed.

The assault was to be mounted from the trenches on the isthmus. The assailants had to advance for 300 yards under the fire of the fortress, so close as to be assailed by hand grenades and other missiles thrown from the parapet. It was, moreover, difficult to advance in good order since the foreshore, uncovered by the tide, was covered in large pools and slippery rocks. The Royal Scots, supported by the 9th Foot, were assigned to the nearer breach, the 38th Foot to the further. To ensure still greater confusion, the 38th were at the back of the column. The signal for the advance was the firing of a mine in an aqueduct under the eastern wall of the hornwork close to the town. It was also the signal for the British artillery to cease fire.

The mine went off with great effect, causing many French to leave the hornwork and blowing down much of the counter-scarp. Those who tried to take advantage of this situation were, however, mowed down by musketry fire from their flank. The Royal Scots were allowed to reach the breach without interference but then encountered a tempest of fire from in front and from both flanks as they attempted to enter the breach. Those who succeeded were faced with a drop of fifteen feet and rows of still burning houses. The Royal Scots recoiled and in doing so ran into the 9th and 38th Regiments, who for a time persisted in advancing against this tide of men. Then, discouraged by coming under British Artillery fire (from those who had not heard the mine explode), they broke and ran for the trenches, leaving behind 425 officers and men killed, wounded or taken. Of these, the Royal Scots lost 86 killed and 245 wounded.

On hearing of the failure of the assault, Wellington returned to San Sebastian and was there when the French launched the battle of the Pyrenees. After the major part of Joseph's army had crossed into France, Jourdan had proposed a counter-offensive in conjunction with Clausel and Suchet, directed round Wellington's right flank. This proposal met with considerable support among the marshals, but Joseph's army was in low spirits and badly in need of re-equipment and reorganization, and nothing came of it.

Joseph had lost his kingdom and Napoleon was determined to remove him from all command. On 1 July he appointed Soult to command all the armies in Spain and the Pyrenees. Immediately Soult set about reorganizing his forces, which by mid-July numbered some 80,000 men, into a single army. He greatly raised morale and was now ready to put his plan for a counter-offensive into effect. His intention was to raise the blockade of Pamplona, which was running short of food, and by turning Wellington's right flank to force him to raise the siege of San Sebastian and retire to the Ebro. His method was to make preparations for a feint attack on the Bidassoa, as if to raise the siege of San Sebastian, while shifting the weight of his forces to his left flank.

San Sebastian and Pamplona are more than forty miles apart. To cover the sieges of both cities in depth, Wellington had to disperse his forces over a wide area. Their positions and responsibilities, from right to left, were: Cole, with a reinforced 4th Division and Morillo's Spanish Division, covered the approaches to Pamplona from St Jean Pied de Port via the Roncesvalles Pass; Hill, with the 2nd and Portuguese Divisions, guarded the approaches via the valley of Baztan and the Maya Pass; Dalhousie's 7th Division was at Vera guarding the crossing of the Bidassoa and the Col de Vera, with Alten's Light Division forming a reserve; Pack's 6th Division was back at Santesteban, well placed to support Hill, Dalhousie or Alten. Still greater depth to the defence of the approaches to Pamplona, which was blockaded by Spanish forces under O'Donnell, was given by Picton's 3rd Division at Olague, from where he could support Cole or Hill.

West of the Sierra de Aralar the dispositions remained unaltered except that the siege operations were broken off and a blockade maintained instead. In any case, after the failure of the assault there was a shortage of ammunition and a number of guns needed replacing.

Oyarzun
My dear father,   *13th July 1813*

I have never since I have been in the Army experienced so much mental irritation as in this Campaign and it has I do think increased illness . . . the imbecility and indecision of [left blank, but obviously meant to be Graham] is only to be equalled by the ignorance and indolence of his Staff.

Our Division is now encamped on hills in front of this town covering the higher road, and to support the Spaniards who are in our front occupying Fuenterrabia and Irun on the Bidassoa river (which forms the boundary), and on the other side of it are the French. It is only 5 miles from this but I have not been able to go to see, although we have been here since the 8th, the weather having been so bad – such very heavy rain for a continuance and so cold I never felt at home in April. It is now I hope over for 3 months, the wind having changed last night to the north and it is now fine though cold.

I need say little of the stations of our different corps as a dispatch went off to England this morning from Ld Wellington, which with the present wind I dare say will be read in London in 8 days. Everything however goes on remarkably well with him as he has in his press at this moment orders for the conduct to be observed by the troops entering *France*; indeed, some have already crossed the frontier, and the whole I suppose will as soon as San Sebastian is taken. Ld Wellington came to this quarter two days ago to look at it and the siege is being carried on by the 5th British Division, 2 Portuguese brigades and some Spaniards. A good battering train is in part landed, and tomorrow morning a battery will open against the Convent, which when taken (the work of a day) will facilitate our approach to the town; this it is not expected will be difficult to take either, and then 2,600 men shut up within a Castle and its works, which have few bomb proofs, must surrender within a short time after we shall have bombarded it.

San Sebastian has a port [and] will be of great importance to us for receiving supplies from home, and to the Spaniards as a fortress. The Castle stands on a high rock of considerable extent bounded on three sides by the sea, and there are I believe but one or two landing places for boats. The ground behind this work is quite flat (here stands the town) and this again is formed into a Peninsula by fresh water and is strongly fortified. In advance of it, again on the mainland, the French have fortified a Convent and have covered communications from it with the town – this convent is to be attacked tomorrow.

Sir T. Graham is to have the direction of the siege, for which reason I am glad that we are to have nothing more to do with it than making Gabions, etc, for it at a distance in our covering position – Lord W quits this (place) tomorrow but returns in a few days to Ernani. Pancorbo has surrendered on favourable terms.[21] It is of great importance and very difficult (indeed called impracticable) of attack and the 600 men who were in it might have annoyed us for a long time.

The most unhappy occurrence in the Peninsular War is what has just been done by that fool Sir J. Murray. You know after what he called his defeat of Suchet that he embarked at Alicante and besieged Tarragona, and landed twenty-four 24 pdrs and ammunition, but a report being brought him that Suchet was coming to attack – he re-embarked his army (without seeing the enemy) leaving every gun and store to their fate, although Admiral Hallowell offered to bring them off. The army returned to Alicante and Lord W. Bentinck has now got the command. Sir John has gone to Sicily.[22] How such a man could ever get the command of an army was a surprise to everybody, for when only a young M-G here he was *recommended the benefit of English air,* for losing his brigade for two days *when pursuing Soult after his defeat at Oporto,* but it was an accident as being on his way to Sicily from home he was desired to call at Alicante to see Lord W. Bentinck, who was supposed to be there – he however had not arrived and Sir John finding himself his senior general remained and was confirmed in command by Ministers – NB Sir John has three seats in Parliament and strong interests in four more. This failure is said to have prevented Lord Wellington laying siege to Pamplona – it is however closely watched by two divisions.

The Spanish troops in this neighbourhood altogether I believe to amount to about 25,000 men, and they have improved so much since we saw them before at Burgos that it is hardly credible. They appear to be kept in good order and are very well clothed, appointed and armed and they have behaved very well in every affair in which they have been employed.

A Messenger has arrived with Lord W.'s new title of Field Marshal and a paper of 3 July – so you know of the Victory at Vitoria – now is the time for Ministers to exert themselves to send out reinforcements to repair the losses, and to enable us to keep the principal passes of the Pyrenees under control until *we have got them*. If it is done, nothing I can conceive, certainly not a greater success in the north than Bonaparte has had, would ever make the French formidable in Spain again. He must now look to his own country, for Lord W. I have no doubt means to enter it as soon as he can, and even if he advances only a few leagues it will cause such an alarm as to prevent any men being sent to act against the Russians – I do not suppose we shall advance far yet, but it will be a great point to feed our own army and the Spanish from it, of course for nothing.

Now we get very well supplied. We have in this part of the country got a good deal of salt pork and we are now to have it twice a week from England – it has been landed about 4 miles off. The country is very rich and well cultivated but very uneven, the hills are high and very rugged, though compared to what we have been accustomed to can hardly be called mountains – the valleys are consequently narrow, but produce very excellent crops of wheat and Indian corn, and the sides of the hills are planted with chestnut and apple trees. The latter very numerous and they make great quantities of cyder now selling for about 1½ pence a pint. We are badly off for forage and as there is no grass and from the wetness of the season the harvest has hardly begun, so that we have no straw. I don't understand their system of husbandry here – one sees no fallow fields and no crops *but wheat and Indian corn* – they are very careful in weeding the latter which is planted in the same as you do beans, so must I suppose count as a preparative to the wheat crop. The soil is a deep clay and after much rain impassable.

THE PYRENEES

Having expressed his displeasure at the failure to take San Sebastian, Wellington left on 26 July for his headquarters at Lesaca. On the way he learnt that the troops at the Maya Pass had been in action. During his absence George Murray, the O.M.G. had received these reports, had ordered the Light and 7th Divisons to be prepared to move. Wellington ordered the Light Division to fall back on Sumbilla and Dalhousie to be ready to support Hill. Early on the twenty-sixth it was learnt that the French were in possession of the Maya Pass. None of the intelligence so far received had changed Wellington's belief that Soult's objective was to raise the siege of San Sebastian, for he had heard nothing from Cole.

The battle of the Pyrenees was fought over a large area of mountainous country and was very much a soldier's battle. The courage of the Allied soldiers compensated for some inept generalship and enabled Wellington, with his quick comprehension, genius for being in the right place at the crucial time, and personal leadership, to turn possible defeat into certain victory.

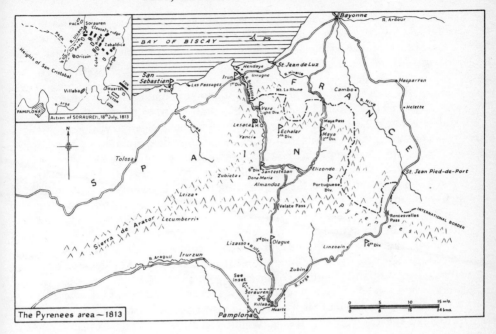

The Pyrenees area — 1813

Soult's last counter-offensive on Spanish soil was launched early on 25 July. On his right d'Erlon attacked the Maya Pass held by Pringle's and John Cameron's brigades. For ten hours these weak brigades fought off 15,000 Frenchmen, inflicting heavy casualties. Their own losses were also heavy, totalling about 1,500.

The main attack was made by Clausel and Reille, operating directly under Soult, against the Roncevalles Pass, on Cole's sector of the front. The intention was to relieve Pamplona and turn Wellington's right. Reille was to attack down the western side of the Val Carlos salient towards the Col de Lindux, while Clausel on the eastern side of the salient attacked Altobiscar. National Guards were to threaten Spanish forces guarding Cole's flank at Orbaiceta and exaggerate the size and scope of the French offensive by lighting fires and making other demonstrations.

Clausel's advance was strongly opposed by Byng's brigade, and Reille's by Ross's supported by Anson's, while Campbell's Portuguese Brigade operated most effectually on their left. The French lost much of the advantage of superior numbers through the mountain terrain confining them to very narrow fronts. Fog put an end to operations in the afternoon and during the night Cole withdrew to some high ground south of Linzoain.

Next day Clausel renewed his attack and Cole carried out a withdrawal to a position between Erro and Zubiri, where he was in touch with Picton who had brought the 3rd Division across from Olague. Picton, the senior, then decided to retire their combined force of 16,000 on Pamplona, Soult followed up Clausel along the main road on the right bank of the Arga, Reille by mountain tracks on its left bank. To avoid giving up the Arga and Ulzana valleys Picton decided to make a stand with the 3rd Division near Arleta to cover Huarte and also Cole's 4th Division about Oricain. Cole took up a very strong position on a ridge, in rear and east of Sorauren, with Picton echeloned back on his right.

From the morning of the twenty-sixth Wellington had been kept informed of events of Hill's front, but from Cole he had heard nothing. Hill having stabilized the position around Elizondo, Wellington decided to visit Cole. En route he intercepted a report from Cole, defeatist in tone, announcing that he was retreating on Pamplona and that should he have to fall back further, he would take the road to Vitoria. Wellington ordered the 6th Division to Olague and set out to find Picton. Hearing that Cole was near Sorauren he galloped on to meet him. While sitting on the bridge at Sorauren waiting for orders for the 7th and 2nd Divisons to follow the 6th, he was nearly taken by a French Cavalry patrol.

Coming on Cole's position from the left Wellington rode his horse on to the ridge, arriving amid the blue uniforms of Campbell's Portuguese, who recognized him and shouted 'Douro! Douro!', a cry taken up all along the Allied line, so immediately declaring his presence to Soult on the hill opposite. Soult with half his force, 15,000 men (for Reille had not yet come up), had the choice of attacking Wellington in a position stronger than Busaco, or waiting for reinforcements with the knowledge that Wellington was also likely to be reinforced and that his own supplies were running out. He decided to wait.

Wellington had put the 6th Division in motion towards Pamplona and pulled back the Light to cover San Sebastian from the east in case Pamplona was relieved. By the twenty-eighth, when Soult attacked Wellington's left and centre with 30,000 men, the Allies had some 20,000, as the 6th Division had come up on Cole's left. The fighting was fierce. The 27th and 48th Regiments particularly distinguished themselves in successive bayonet charges by which they hurled the enemy back into the valley, as did the 40th in defending Spanish Hill in the centre. By 4.30 p.m. Soult, his men weak from starvation and having suffered 3,000 casualties, had given up his attempt to relieve Pamplona.

The French retired on the night of the twenty-ninth. Wellington followed up and ordered the Light Division to march north and cut off the French retreat through Sumbilla, and for Graham to cut them off from the Yanci bridge. Fierce fighting took place between Cole and Clausel's troops near Sumbilla on 1 August, but Graham failed to take the necessary action. The Light Division, after a forced march of forty miles, took up a position on the banks of the Bidassoa from which, while the light lasted, they had some excellent shooting at the retreating enemy.

Soult's offensive had cost him 13,000 killed, wounded and taken. He had failed to relieve either Pamplona or San Sebastian and he had lost a great quantity of equipment. His army was back in France as demoralized as it had been under Joseph. Why then did Wellington not follow up his victory instead of ordering his army to dig in on their present line? The principal reason was the continuing uncertainty over the future situation in central Europe. The truce between Russia and Prussia and France continued, and Austria remained neutral. If the truce were to end in a peace treaty, Britain would once more be faced with the whole of Napoleon's military might. San Sebastian and Pamplona still held out and Wellington's men needed rest and to be re-equipped. Memories of the way in which the defeated and demoralized revolutionary armies had rallied in 1793, once the soil of France had been invaded, were held by some as an argument against invasion. That it was unfounded will be seen, for the French were sick of war, and their own army on re-entering France had pillaged and raped as freely as any foreign invader would have done, and the peoples of the south-west districts, like those across the Spanish border, were neither French nor Spanish but Basques.

In the same period Allied losses, excluding the Spaniards, were about 7,100, the 4th Division and Barnes's brigade of the 7th providing the most notable examples. Of the former Wellington wrote, 'It is impossible to describe the enthusiastic bravery of the Fourth Division . . . ', and of the latter: 'In my life I never saw such an attack as was made by Genl Barnes's Brigade upon the enemy above Echalar . . . it is impossible that I can extol too highly . . . these brave troops, which was the admiration of all who were witnesses of it.'[23]

Having once more ejected the French field armies from Spain (Suchet was still active in Catalonia, which had been made a part of Metropolitan France by Napoleon's decree in mid-1811), Wellington ordered his army to dig in and was again free to concentrate his attention on reducing San Sebastian. Meanwhile Rey, the governor was greatly strengthening the defences and because of delay in landing new siege artillery and replenishing stocks of ammunition, the siege could not be resumed until 22 August.

The 1st Division had been reinforced by the arrival of the 1st Guards Brigade under Maitland. John Aitchison had a recurrence of malaria and to give him a change he was posted as commandant of Passages, which, with the delay in the reduction of San Sebastian, had become increasingly important as an advanced base. Not only were all kinds of military stores, equipment and supplies being landed there but it was also used as a depot for the infantry where drafts were landed and embarked for England. At the same time it was developed as a convalesence area and was to become the site of a large hospital.

Soult was also busy reorganizing his demoralized forces. On 12 August Austria, Russia, Prussia and Sweden joined Britain in the Fourth Coalition against Napoleon, and Soult knew he could expect few if any reinforcements. He made the sensible suggestion to Suchet that they should join forces but Suchet preferred independent command and Napoleon appears to have been too busy elsewhere to support Soult, though the latter was directed to relieve San Sebastian as soon as possible.

Apart from the renewal of the siege of San Sebastian and fatigue parties improving the frontier defences, this was a quiet time for the Allied Army. After all their successes over the French, it seems strange that there should have been a serious rise in desertion. Many attributed this mainly to those whose seven-year term of service had expired and were surprised to find that they could be held for another three. A contributory factor was the hard living conditions in the barren mountains. The desertions influenced Wellington's decision to advance so as to canton his men for the winter in the plains of France. This hardly accounts for their fighting for the French but many joined the Chasseurs Britanniques and caused confusion by appearing on the battle-field in British uniform. It is probable that many of these were Irish.

Though officers shared with their men the lack of opportunity for recreation in the mountains, they were far better placed to make themselves comfortable, and although Wellington had done much to cut down the British Army's baggage, the amount that travelled with them still astonished the Spaniards. Wellington personally lived hard but was expected to entertain widely. What this meant in terms of transport can be gauged by Larpent's description after having a meal at 4th Divisional Headquarters:

General Cole lives very comfortably to do this even in his way, he has now travelling with him about ten or twelve goats for milk, a cow and about 36 sheep at least, with a shepherd, who always march, feed on the roadside, on the mountains and camp with him. When you think of this, that wine and everything that is to be carried about, from salt and pepper and tea-cups to saucepans, boilers, dishes, chairs and tables, on mules, you may guess the trouble and expense of a good establishment here.[24]

Val de Oyarzun
12th August 1813

My dear Father,

There is little going on here just now; since the defeat of Soult the Army in general has been quiet but the siege of San Sebastian has been re-commenced, though it proceeds very slowly — I do not know from what cause, but somehow or other we do not manage sieges well. We have made batteries to attack a new point, from that which we failed in before, and the guns are landing and being put into them, but I do not hear when they will begin their fire, although a good supply of shot has arrived. The reduction of San Sebastian by force will now be a more serious business, as the enemy have entrenched all the streets of the town — however, if once taken the Castle I think will not hold out long. Pamplona is said to be much straightened for provisions; indeed, there can be no doubt of it from the efforts which the enemy made to relieve it — their loss in all is now estimated at 18,000 men. If it falls, Ld Wellington I should think will move into France, as the possession of the Pyrenees will then be secure. The enemy, afraid of this, are fortifying themselves along their whole line, although the ground is almost impregnable by nature. However, when we have the Fortresses we shall move by Pau, which will render all their present positions of no consequence.

We too are fortifying all the heights by which the enemy would pass in entering Spain again, a precaution which is only proper. There is a great deal to do here in reducing the Fortresses of Catalonia and that coast, which are in general supplied for a long time. It is a pity therefore that any men have been sent to Germany,[25] as from the small numbers they can be of very little use, and here they would be of greatest service. We have received no reinforcements but a few hundred drafts for different regts. But we hear that some entire regiments are coming out – not more I fear than will replace our loss this Campaign. Infantry we want most, this country is not suited for Cavalry, and they are of no use in sieges. In France they will however be much required as the country is flat at a short distance from the frontier. . . .

The Castle at Zaragosa has been taken by Mina with upwards of 400 men, and Tarragona has been abandoned by the enemy after being blown up.[26] General Castaños has left the Army to go to Cadiz to be at the head of the Army – this change I fear is a political trick of the Regency to diminish his and Ld W.'s influence – I cannot help thinking that there is still much jealousy in the Spanish government which will cause great dissension. Castaños is now at Tolosa having assembled a sort of board or Parliament to raise taxes in this Province – the King of Spain being only Lord of Biscay and the people are taxed by themselves only – so far it is right to *seem* to humour their privileges[27] – for seeming *it only is*. Genl Giron, who commanded the Galician army here, has gone to Catalonia and is succeeded by Lacy, a good officer and very enterprising – the former is nephew to Castaños and of course he is promoted if the latter is advanced. We hear that there is no chance of the Allies making peace – the armistice must have been very useful to them. If they only go on as they have done Bonaparte must be driven into terms, if he is not dethroned.

We had an alarm this morning of marching, from the enemy having increased their force opposite us – they are supposed to have come from their own left, I suppose with a view to retard our progress in the siege of San Sebastian by threatening an attack – there is no fear, if they do make the attempt – but of this there seems to be no chance. I do not yet attend parade or take duty but am very well, only not quite so strong as formerly – the weather is now very warm but changeable, which is against me.

Private   *Passages*
My dear Father,   *19th August 1813*

Instead of going to Camp, I have arrived here in an Official capacity as *Commandant*. This fine-sounding title may at first strike you as an appointment of high authority and consequence – it is so in effect to the service (thought it may not be so to me immediately) as to it belongs the superintendance of all sick and wounded Officers and soldiers of the army sent here for the benefit of the health or passing to Hospital stations – and it is so completely independent of every authority that no Officer, however high his rank, can interfere with my arrangements but by orders from the C-in-Chief.

I am not certain whether any emolument be attached to it, nor do I much care – my chief object in accepting it being for the benefit of my own health and as likely also of making myself known – it was given to me in a way which you will think as flattering as I do – Genl Stopford, whose good opinion I believe I have retained since he commanded our regiment, wrote a private note to me to say that the division had been ordered to find an Officer for that duty and as he heard that sea bathing would be good for my health he would get me appointed if I chose – he had a good deal (at least used to have) to say with Ld W. and it flattered his appearance of patronage my accepting his offer, which I did immediately (every man has his weakness). . . .

I do not wish you to talk of this to anybody (but my Mother) yet some members even of our own family might be apt to mention this inadvertently and people might make unpleasant remarks should the offer not turn out to be equal to *their* extravagant ideas; I will write again to you about it soon – my own ideas are exactly what I have stated above and I do it now to show you how well I am and that I am not unworthy of your good opinion of me.

My dear Father,

Passages
25th August 1813

Since I wrote to you on the 20th I have been very much occupied by the business here, which from the want of a resident to make arrangements had got into a state of great confusion – my duty is not confined to the charge of the sick and wounded only but is connected with every department of the Army; all attachments of Soldiers are, while they remain, under my orders and every officer; from the number daily arriving and going away must receive their instructions from me, you may judge of my business; I have had very numerous levies every day, and having much correspondence and no clerk yet I have been employed from morning till night – this continual change of scene with the sea air and constant bustle have had a happy effect on my health and strength, which are materially improved. Things will get into a regular course in a few days more and then I shall have more time. The situation of Commandant at stations generally is filled by old Officers who prefer remaining quiet to marching with their regiment and they have much to do with paying convalescents from the Hospitals – here I hope to have nothing of that sort to do as this is not a Hospital situation, and I shall of course endeavour to get relieved from it as soon as there shall appear any chance of its becoming more of a Civil situation than Military. I hardly think that it will ever be so, as I am in communication with the heads of departments and of the Navy and of Hd Qrs of the army, and it is for this reason that I prefer it to common regimental duty in camp.

Every preparation is making to open the batteries against San Sebastian in a day or two – a new battering train landed the other day and . . . it is said a good supply of ammunition and the guns are all expected to be in the batteries by the night of the 27th. Many of the guns, altho' new, which were used in the former attack were rendered useless from the touch hole melting by the quick fire. The town probably will be destroyed, as the enemy have intersected the streets so with different defences that this measure will be indispensable to communication. Three attacks are to be made and the breaches once practicable, there can be no doubt of the success if *properly directed* – of the assault.

My servant Lewis met with an accident the other day in a boat which has obliged him to keep in bed and I am afraid he will be confined for some time – this puts me to great inconvenience.

On 26 August seventy-three pieces of artillery opened fire on San Sebastian, and forty-eight from the Chofre sandhills. By the thirtieth the bastion of the hornwork had been much reduced and that of St Jean swept away, with the breach extending for 250 yards to a point between the towers of Las Miguetas and Los Hornos. Further north was a smaller breach eighty yards wide. As before, the 5th Division was to make the assault.

At 2 a.m. on 31 August the sea wall along the eastern bastion of the hornwork was overthrown by the springing of three mines. The fog lifted at 8 a.m. and from then until the start of the assault the batteries poured their fire into the place. At the larger breach, the 'Forlorn Hope' was led by Lieutenant Macguire of the 4th and followed by a sergeant and eleven men whose task was to sever the connections of a French mine, under the sea wall of the eastern demi-bastion. The French, however, fired the mine, bringing down the wall and burying the heroic party.

Macguire and a few men got to the top of the breach but were killed. The assault was made by Robinson's Brigade in two columns. On getting to the top they found themselves facing a sixteen-foot drop, beyond which were loopholed walls from which they were shot down in heaps, and between the two every sort of obstacle. The breaches were also flanked by artillery. Recoiling to the foot of the breach, they found themselves sheltered from all but sniper fire.

Graham ordered both attacks to be renewed by Hay's Brigade and then by the Volunteers of the 1st and Light Divisions. All failed. After consulting Alexander Dickson, Graham ordered all the available artillery to be trained on the hornwork. The cannonade, a few feet above the heads of the troops on the breach, lasted for half an hour, enabling some of the Light Division to get into some houses to the right of the larger breach. Meanwhile, the 13th and 24th Portuguese forded the waist-deep Urema near its mouth, while a party of the 85th in boats made a demonstration of landing behind Monte Orgullo. The Portuguese, who had advanced under intense fire, were assaulting both breaches when at the critical moment a large quantity of ammunition which the defenders had collected behind the southern end of the larger breach blew up in a series of explosions. This took the French aback and enabled Hay's brigade and the Portuguese to carry both breaches and gain access to the city.

Rey withdrew to Monte Orgullo. It was 8 September before batteries were ready to reduce the Castle. After enduring the fire of sixty pieces for two hours Rey surrendered. It had taken fifty days to reduce the town, and cost the Allies 3,700 in killed and wounded. Following the assault, the town witnessed more disgraceful scenes of rape, pillage and murder than had been seen even at Badajoz. For two days the troops ran amok and were only brought under control when driven out by the burning of the town. The Portuguese, who had no love of the Spaniards, did their best to emulate their British comrades.

My dear Father,

Passages
31st August 1813

Whatever may have been the discredit which the British Army suffered by the defeat at San Sebastian, it has been most fully recompensed by the success there today – in no instance since the commencement of the Peninsular War has it had more obstacles to encounter and in no instance – not even in the capture of Badajoz – have they been more gloriously overcome. The conduct of every man engaged was so truly admirable, that no words in our language can do them justice – it required to be seen to be conceived; and when history should give to future ages the simple narrative of this day's deeds – they will excite admiration rather than belief. Portuguese troops acted their part excellently, and they are well entitled to participate in all the praises that can be bestowed.

I should be most happy to give a narrative of what occurred, but the details of a siege are always confused and it would require more talents than I am now possessed of to make them understood. I was not up in time to see the advance party move forward – when I arrived they had already gained the breach, but were halted on the top of it by the obstacles which had been erected in the night behind it, and they were suffering severely from a destructive fire of musketry from the houses and of cannon from the castle and other parts of the works; in this situation they were detained at least an hour and a half; all the while however they were being reinforced, and at length the bugles sounding 'the advance' and a hearty 'hurrah' announced to the spectators that we had gained an advantage. The fire of our batteries became more sustained and a column of Portuguese from the sandhills rushed through a part of the sea, which had not sufficiently receded (being waist high), and fording the river at its mouth arrived at the breach without regarding grape and shot and shells which literally showered. From this time our men gained ground gradually but the enemy fought desperately in the town and there was still a tremendous fire of musketry at three o'clock when I left it – the whole town, however, was taken and I hope we shall be able to keep it. It was hardly done, when a thunderstorm came on with rain and it has continued ever since – this we may consider an act of providence in our favour for Marshal Soult this morning crossed the Bidassoa with a considerable body and attacked our men, and we may hope that it will swell so as to assist in his destruction. He is very strong but we shall I have no doubt beat him – every man has been sent forward to support the 1st Division.

The storm of San Sebastian began about half-past ten o'clock and was witnessed by many thousands of people assembled on the hills around it. In it were employed the 5th Divison, one Portuguese brigade and an attachment of the 1st, 4th and Light Divisions.[28] We furnished from the two brigades of Guards 200 men, of which my regiment sent an Ensigns' party – I have not heard whether they were employed. The harbour here is very crowded with transports, there have arrived great numbers of sick – should any orders be given to abandon the place I shall have much to do, but I do not apprehend it. Our loss at San Sebastian has been very severe. I have not heard the circumstance but Sir. R. Fletcher, chief engineer, is killed and Generals Sir John Leith, Oswald and Robinson are wounded.

Passages
13th September 1813

My dear Father,

... The Castle of San Sebastian has at length surrendered and the garrisons been embarked for England. They did not hold out above three hours after our new batteries had opened; they are the finest men I have ever seen of their numbers from the French army. The consequences of surrender of that place are already felt as Soult, although he had pledged himself to make one more effort to relieve Pamplona, has now given it up and is himself very apprehesive of an attack from us; it is generally believed in the army that Ld Wellington means to attack one part of the French position soon. It is near Lesaca and was occupied by us when we first came to the Pyrenees but during the battle of Pamplona has remained in the enemy's possession. I think it very likely therefore that Ld. W. will attack that part to add strength to the other parts of his position but there is little chance, in my opinion, of his attempting a general attack until Pamplona has fallen or his defences of the Pyrenees shall have been completed.

We are constructing works on every part of our line similar in plan to those of Lisbon but they are not quite of so permanent a nature, as the urgency of time here is greater and the risk will afterwards will be less. Suchet, you will know by our last accounts, has become so formidable that Ld Wm Bentinck had found it necessary to retire to the Col de Balaguer. Probably, therefore, he will attract Ld Wellington's notice soon and should the hostilities in Germany render it impossible, as I have little [doubt] they will, to send reinforcements to Soult, he may send off from this army one or two British Divisions even now. Pamplona, it is expected, will not hold out much beyond the end of this month but if it does fewer troops will be required to cover the blockading army, as the state of the country at that time becomes generally so bad as to be impassable but by the roads.

You see by the date of this letter that I am still Military Commandant here. When I first accepted the appointment I explained my motives and views to you which you would think satisfactory. As I expected my duty has increased and become chequered and instead, as at first, being confined to finding quarters for the sick and wounded and seeing them forwarded to a hospital station, I have now almost unlimited authority over the town and part in every thing which relates to the Army. The

Adjt-General, Sir Ed Pakenham, has been frequently here and I have had three interviews with him, and my orders come from him only as the agent of Ld W. and no one else can interfere with my arrangements. He has ordered every assistance I require and offers more if necessary so that now, besides about 150 British, I have 100 Portuguese troops who are to remain permanently to assist in the duties of the station.

I have had [responsibility for] the embarkation of the French garrison of San Sebastian and the distribution of the Guards – in short every body of men who arrive here are subject to my orders although the officer commanding [them may] be superior to myself. . . .

I know that I have gained great weight with the Spanish people and authorities – the Commander of their troops here orders instantly whatever I desire and has in one instance been necessary for me to add my signature to an order of the Civil magistrates to assure its obedience. The latter is much under my will, as I ask nothing but what it is just for the public service: but have whatever I do require done immediately – I avoid all interference in his internal government and save him being annoyed by the British Military and Civil department, so that he is as zealous in forwarding my orders as his predecessor who, when I first came here, I found most reluctant in assisting all departments of the army and was complained of by everybody who had dealings with him; so much that a General who was stationed here told me he believed he was attached to the French cause, and recommended me to report any instances of his neglect which he had no doubt would soon occur. . . .

I have written this to go with the fleet which takes the French prisoners – I have still upwards of 500 to be sent and great number of ladies and families from San Sebastian to forward to France.

Passages
27th September 1813

My dear Father,

. . . The duties of my office are certainly important and they increase. I believe I told you when I first came here what I thought was likely to occur – I thought (and I was right that this place from its situation must increase in importance and consequently that whoever was in command here must be known. I am now known to the Adjutant General both by personal interview and by my correspondence with him – nevertheless my office is not exactly what I wish and you must not be surprised to hear that I have hinted at a desire to be relieved. I have not addressed myself directly to the Adjutant General officially but I have had my views and feelings conveyed to him by a friend of his and he has agreed with me.

On hearing that it was determined by Ld Wellington to make permanent establishment of hospitals for 1,200 men in the neighbourhood, I wrote to say that the commandant of a hospital station did not suit my ideas and however desirable it might be (and I know is) to many old officers, yet it was a line of service which I would rather forgo if I had any choice. I received for answer that a Commandant would be appointed for the hospitals only, and that though my services might be required in getting them established, my Command would remain separate, as before, and a compliment was at the same time paid to my manner of conducting it. A Provost was sent to superintend the police of my Command, and an Adjutant was promised and will be sent as soon as a judicious selection can be made. Thus was I indirectly asked to continue here and I of course answered that my services should always be freely given where they could best be used, for the public service.

My opinion continues the same on the line of service and certainly I should prefer active duty in the field to remaining quiet here. However, I shall not be precipitate in anything which I may do, my great object being to ensure my promotion in the quickest manner. There is pay attached to my office here – I am not yet certain of the amount. Excuse this long account of myself but I know you wish to know how I am situated.

We have received London news to the 16th which brings us, methinks, very favourable news from Germany.[29] It requires only the *people* to take a decided part to make the contest there certain. Everything here has the appearance of a move – supplies have for some days and are still being forwarded to the army with extraordinary dispatch – new pontoons have been landed and sent up and the troops, both Portuguese and British, have been marched from before San Sebastian and a Spanish garrison has been put into San Sebastian. I went there the other day and have seldom seen a more melancholy spectacle – the prettiest and most regularly built town in Spain a heap of smoking ruins and the poor inhabitants, destitute of everything, trying to pick up some trifling remains of their property!! As a fortress it will have to be armed afresh – some of our battering train have been put into it and the remainder embarked. The breach is I think as strong as any part of the defences – it is still so difficult that I could hardly get in at it even now.

The belief here is very general that the army is about to enter France but I cannot think that Ld W. will make a general move into it till after Pamplona falls, tho' it appears not improbable that he will move forward the right of the Army and attack one of their divisions to assist Lord W. Bentinck in disposing of Suchet. At any rate I think our part of the Army will not have much to do just yet – the river Bidassoa being in this front so formidable that its defence will certainly be turned by crossing higher up and moving in the rear of the enemy, which necessarily will compel them to quit our front – however, should Bayonne be besieged this year our corps will probably be employed on it. It is quite certain that the army cannot remain where it is at present. Snow is already on the mountainous part and there are not sufficient cantonments but a great way in rear of our present line. We shall probably therefore take up our winter quarters in front of the passes in French villages. The weather is already very unsettled and cold. I am glad to hear so favourably of the harvest – I wish I had a few loads of your straw here – it is not to be had for love or money within 20 miles and our poor animals are suffering much. The corn we get is chiefly mixed *barley* from England, which is bad feeding.

Passages
My dear father,   *25th October 1813*

Since the left of the army crossed the Bidassoa there has been no occurrence of consequence – the enemy have worked incessantly at their several defences and we have been busy throughout our position line. There has been no attempt at a forward movement on our part although every preparation is indicative of such intention of Ld Wellington as soon as Pamplona falls. This is the day fixed upon from the information of an intercepted letter which was deciphered, but it appears that there is yet sufficient provisions in the place to allow the garrison 6 ounces each daily till the 30th. It is rather supposed, however, that the Garrison will blow up the defences of the Citadel and attempt to escape; in that case they will lose all claim to mercy and it is given out as the intention to put all to the sword who may be caught.

Be that as it may it is very evident that until it does surrender no general movement will take place. It is so close to the frontier and situated in so important a point on the high road that great danger might result from moving the army at a distance from the blockading force, but as soon as the place falls these dangers will cease and the advantages now felt from it by the French will in a much greater degree revert to us.

There seems now no strong reason against our invasion of France – the principle of reaction which was so much dwelt upon against it has been found to be more in idea than reality, and you who have so strong feelings of the obligation which every native owes to his country will hardly believe it less felt by the French – yet it is the case and instead of the Invasion of France being the signal for every man uniting for her defence they are deserting to the rear and to us, not for the sake of joining our service but to avoid being pressed into their own. I have within the last two months had opportunities of conversation with many French officers and men from different quarters and have been truly surprised to find so general a disgust at the War – all are for peace – they lament the blind policy of their Emperor tho' they seldom abuse him – but the feeling amongst the common Soldier is to prefer an English prison to being sent back in exchange to France.

We have news from London of the 9th which appears to me so good as to remove all doubts of Bonaparte being brought to reason in the winter. Our battering train has been sent to Santander so that no more sieges will be undertaken by us this year. This coast is becoming very unsafe[30] and we must somehow or other increase our magazines, or our supplies in the winter will be very precarious.

Passages
My dear father,   *30th October 1813*

It was not my intention to have written to you again from this until I could send you a long letter explaining everything, but having a very good opportunity by private hand I cannot delay letting you know that I have been replaced in my charge here in consequence chiefly of my own application, which I told you of some time since, and am on the point of joining my companions 'in arms' with the Army. I shall probably leave this tomorrow or the day after and the first opportunity I have of writing I mean to enclose you the Adjutant General's authority of my quitting this, which I hope will prove gratifying to you. . . .

There seems no doubt that we shall all advance into France the moment we can after Pamplona falls. The Cavalry and Artillery have been moving up for these three days but the roads may probably be found so impracticable [from] the tremendous rain which has fallen for four days that the movement may be delayed. It will, however, certainly take place as soon as the weather will permit, which I am happy in saying appears to give hope of being soon. . . .

On the day San Sebastian fell, Soult launched a further attempt to relieve it. In anticipation of this Wellington had had three lines of defences constructed behind the Bidassoa. The first embraced the San Marcial feature, which tactically dominated the area; the second ran from the northern end of the Jaizquibal ridge through Fuenterrabia and Irun to the ridge of Monte Aya; the third ran through Oyarzun occupied by the 1st Division.

Reille was to make a direct assault across the Bidassoa and take the San Marcial feature while Clausel would protect his flank by a limited advance between Vera and the Aya feature.

The San Marcial feature and Irun were held by three divisions of the Spanish corps under General Don Manuel Freyre, with Howard's and Aylmer's brigades under the 1st Division in support on their left and Longa's Spanish Division behind their right. The Light Division to their right was to be ready to threaten any attempt by Clausel to march on Vera. The 3rd and 7th Divisions were ordered to make demonstrations along their fronts without getting deeply involved.

Soult launched his attack under cover of fog. Leaving two divisions to protect his left flank from interference by the Light Division, he forded the river on a two divisional front driving back Inglis's Brigade. He then halted, considering it imprudent to proceed while San Marcial remained in Allied hands.

Reille, having three divisions under his command, crossed the Bidassoa above Biriatou, shortly after daylight. The French advance against the Spaniards holding San Marcial was over steep ground broken by brushwood. When two-thirds towards the summit they were charged by the Spaniards and thrown back to the foot of the hill. Rallying and with fresh troops they made a second assault, reaching the ridge next below the summit. Seeing the Spaniards waver, the 85th from Aylmer's Brigade were sent to their support.

Freyre sent a request to Wellington for the support of the 4th Division. As his aide reached Wellington, the Spaniards could be seen launching their second charge which again hurled back the French to the bottom of the hill where they panicked, rushing headlong into the river. The French engineers broke up their pontoons to go to their rescue, and a number of boats sank under the weight of the fugitives. Seeing this Wellington turned to his aide, saying, 'Go tell your General that as he has already won his victory he should keep the honour of it for his countrymen alone'.[31]

The diversions ordered by Wellington further east had been successful. Beaten everywhere, Soult had decided to call off the offensive, when the fighting was terminated by a violent storm which broke about 4 p.m., turning the Bidassoa into an impassable flood and cutting off Clausel's direct retreat, forcing him to retire on Vera.

French casualties over the two days were 3,808, with a very high proportion of officers who had had to expose themselves urging on their reluctant soldiers. Freyre's Spaniards were the heroes of the battle. For the first time since Spanish regular troops had stood in line with the Allies they had borne the brunt of the fighting and they had overthrown an enemy who had triumphed over the regular Spanish troops on nearly every occasion. Their successs was the more honourable since from the usual neglect of the Spanish government they were near starvation. Allied casualties were Spaniards 1,679, Portuguese 529 and British 417.

The remainder of Wellington's Peninsular campaign was to be conducted on French soil. Essentially it consisted of a series of river crossings: the Bidassoa, 7 October; The Nivelle, 10 November; the Nive, 9 December; the Ardour in February 1814 and, finally, after a number of minor crossings, the Garonne near Toulouse in April. John Aitchison returned to regimental duty on 4 November, participating in the operations for crossing the Nivelle, Nive and Ardour.

At the end of September, Pamplona still held out and the situation in central Europe had not yet been clarified, but the situation in Catalonia had stabilized since Bentinck's setback at Ordal. Wellington, while as yet unready to make an unlimited invasion of France, recognized the political advantage of being the first Allied force to set foot on French soil. Besides, in his own words, 'The heights on the right of the Bidassoa command such a view of us that the sooner we get them the better.'[32] If he possessed those heights he considered he could hold his ground even if Russia and Prussia were to make peace. Additionally, they provided a valuable base line for a further advance.

Since Soult's abortive attempt to relieve San Sebastian, both sides had been digging in. Soult's defences were considerable and included an armed camp covering St Jean de Luz, called Bordagain. His first line stretched from St Jean Pied de Port to the sea, some thirty miles of broken country, whose defence overstretched his 47,000-man army. These he had organized into three corps: d'Erlon's on the left, Clausel's in the centre and Reille's on the right. The Allies held the Maya and the Roncesvalles Passes and Soult believed that from these Wellington would attack his left so as to penetrate along the grain of the country and turn his position on the Nive and Nivelle. Wellington encouraged this belief by inspecting the Maya Pass sector and launching from there on 1 October a reconnaissance in force by a Portuguese brigade which captured seventy enemy and 2,000 sheep, while moving his formations successively westward to increase his forces facing the French centre and

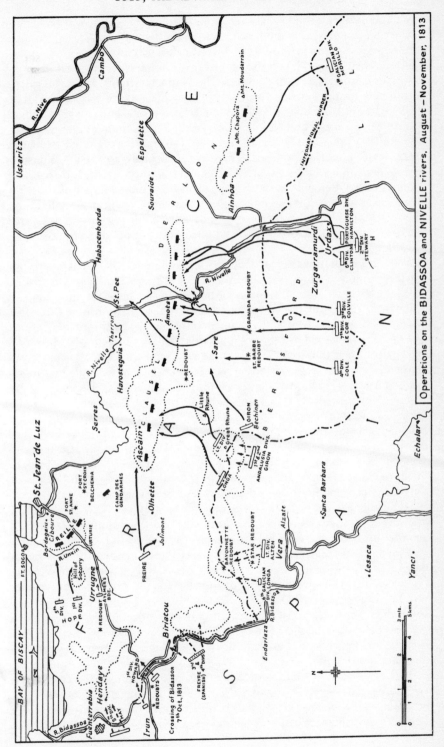

Operations on the BIDASSOA and NIVELLE rivers, August — November, 1813

right. The estuary of the Bidassoa, on Soult's extreme right, was to be the crucial point of attack, and when it came nearly two-thirds of Soult's forces were deployed on or in support of the French left flank.

In the centre, Clausel held the rugged ridge running east to west from its dominant feature, the Great Rhune, to the Mandela heights. From this ridge, a prominent spur ran down towards the Bidassoa, west of Vera. To the east of it a detached hill, the Boar's Back, covered the approaches to the main ridge. Beyond Mandela the French line followed the Bidassoa in a north-westerly direction, with the occupation of a series of features, the main one being the Croix des Bouquets, to the sea. There were no bridges over the Bidassoa below Vera – that which had carried the main Irun to St Jean de Luz road had been destroyed. Below Irun the Bidassoa was tidal and while it was fordable in places at low water, it could be as much as twenty feet deep at high tide or when in flood. Like John Aitchison, Soult believed the estuary to be operationally impassable and Reille had stationed only one battalion opposite the Allied left.

Wellington's plan was for Colville, commanding the 3rd Division, to pin down d'Erlon by demonstrations from north of the Maya Pass. Alten, with the Light Division and with Giron's Andalusians on his right, and Longa's Galician Division on his left, was to assault the Great Rhune–Mandela heights feature, with Cole's 4th Division in support. The front from Mount Aya to the sea was held by Freyre's Spaniards, Aylmer's brigade and Howard's 1st Division. All these were to ford the river and attack the enemy posts on their immediate front, but the crucial crossing was to be made by Major-General Andrew Hay's 5th Division, now held in reserve, at the mouth of the estuary. Having crossed they would take the town of Hendaye and turn the enemy's right flank opposite the 1st Division's front, so ensuring Howard a quick advance to a position to cover the construction of a bridge of boats at Behobie over which the artillery would pass. Lack of forage had induced Wellington to send most of the cavalry and much of his field artillery back to the Ebro valley. To give additional support for the crossing of the Bidassoa, thirty eighteen-pounders from the Navy had been emplaced.

To locate fordable places near the mouth of the Bidassoa, Wellington had had surveys carried out in co-operation with the local shrimp fishermen. To achieve surprise it was necessary to bring forward the 5th Division, the guns and the bridging material under cover of darkness, making the crossing at dawn. On 7 October low tide would be at 7 a.m. and on 5 October Wellington decided that this would be the day for the assault, provided the weather was favourable.

On the night of the sixth the assaulting troops moved into position along the riverbank, leaving their tents standing. A violent storm with continuous thunder and lightning did much to drown the sound of the forward move of guns and pontoons.

At 7.30, led by the Light companies, the 5th Division started crossing by two fords. The water was bitterly cold, but, holding their muskets and ammunition above their heads, they waded through the swift-flowing water, in places chest-high. When they had reached a sandbank, mid-stream of the

1,000-yard-wide estuary, a rocket was fired from the church tower at Fuenterrabia as the signal for the 1st Division and Freyre's Spaniards to begin fording.

The 5th Division took Hendaye with little opposition. They then turned the French right flank on the front of the 1st Division and soon the Croix des Boutiques and all other objectives were in Allied hands. Further advance on this front was stopped and the construction of two floating bridges begun. Wellington had obtained complete surprise, bringing against the 5,000 men in Reille's first line four times that number, while Soult was just where he wanted him, carrying out an inspection on his eastern flank. Allied casualties on this front were about 400, mostly borne by Freyre's Spaniards, who had had to ascend the steep and wooded slope of Mount Calvaire under fire.

Fighting on Clausel's front was stiffer, for a deserter had warned him of the imminent attack at 4 a.m. The area was mountainous and the ground over which the Allies had to attack was very steep, rocky and in places covered with brushwood and briars. Alten, commanding the Light Division, was in general charge of the operations. On the right Giron's Andalusians were to attack the Great Rhune, while on the left the Light Division with Longa's Galicians were to take La Bayonette, a masonry star redoubt crowning the centre of the ridge between the Great Rhune and Mandela heights.

The attack on La Bayonette was made by Kempt's brigade on the right and Colborne's brigade on the left, the enemy having first been cleared from the Boar's Back, an isolated foothill. Kempt's and Longa's men were more inconvenienced by the steep, rugged ground than by the enemy, but eventually reached the main ridge, sweating, breathless and in some disorder. Colborne had a more arduous task as he had first to take a star redoubt, built on a small plateau, and three redoubts before his men could reach a position from which to assault La Bayonette. They carried these works advancing up the steep mountain spurs against strong French resistance.

Before them lay the great redoubt, La Bayonette, a much tougher proposition because it had the support of a mountain battery of three guns, and from it the defenders could roll down great boulders on to their assailants, upon whom they also poured a heavy fire. For a time the boulders held up Colborne's advance, but the enemy fire was not so effective since it had to be directed downhill and most of it went high. With the promise of support from Cole's 4th Division, on the left, the 52nd, their bayonets sharp and glistening in the sun, advanced steadily. The enemy abandoned the redoubt when they realized they were in danger of being cut off by Giron's Spaniards advancing round their right from the Mandela feature, and by Kempt's brigade working round their left. The enemy lost three guns while Colborne's brigade sustained 184 British casualties and the Portuguese rather fewer.

On Alten's right Giron, after some stiff fighting, established his men on the west shoulder of the Great Rhune. When Soult arrived at last on the central front he promptly built up the troops on the Great Rhune itself to six or eight regiments and no further progress was made that day. On 8 October the Great Rhune was enveloped in fog until the afternoon, when Giron renewed his attack, the French to his right being pinned down by holding attacks by the 7th Division against their positions south of Sare and by the 6th Division towards Amots. During the night the French abandoned the Great Rhune, withdrawing to a lower but formidable position on the Little Rhune.

In three days' fighting the French had lost some 1,600 men and ten guns. Allied casualties were about the same. If the battles of the Pyrenees were soldiers' battles, the crossing of the Bidassoa was a general's. Wellington had deceived a surprised Soult, turning him out of an immensely strong natural position. He now held that position, from which he was able to watch Soult set about building an extensive network of defences on the Nivelle to cover the approaches to Bayonne.

Wellington's directions for the conduct of the Allied troops when on French soil had already been circulated to all ranks. Wellington was determined to avoid a guerrilla war against the Basque peasantry, such as the French had had to contend with in Spain. Looting and pillage were forbidden and all supplies were to be paid for. By these measures he hoped to induce the local peasantry at least to tolerate the invasion. However, following the crossing of the Bidassoa outrages did occur, though the peasants were no more plundered by the Allies than by the French Army which had been expected to live off the country. For this behaviour Wellington recognized that the Spanish and Portuguese troops had some excuse, for they had many atrocities committed against their own people to avenge. Moreover, their own governments failed to provide them with regular pay and rations – the British Army had received no pay since April and the staff since March.

Both sides took steps to enforce discipline. Wellington had a number of British soldiers hung and Soult went so far as to have a captain, and Chevalier of the Légion d'Honneur, shot. The Spaniards he could not control, and after the crossing of the Nivelle he reluctantly had them all withdrawn into Spain except for their best-disciplined troops commanded by Major-General Pablo Morillo.

Pakenham, who as Adjutant General controlled the newly organized Military Police, went about 'like a raging lion' instilling discipline. The day after crossing the Bidassoa, Wellington issued a further General Order in which, *inter alia*, he threatened to bring the names of officers who misbehaved to the attention of the Prince Regent, and a number he sent back to England. That day he wrote to Lieutenant-General Sir John Hope, who had relieved Graham in command of the Allied left, that after the action on the seventh he 'saw many men coming in drunk and loaded with plunder. . . . If we were five times stronger than we are we could not venture to enter France if we cannot prevent our soldiers from plundering.'[33]

At this time Wellington was having great trouble with the Spanish and Portuguese Regencies. In 1812 Spain had adopted universal suffrage and a liberal constitution, the exception being that the only legal worship was that of the Roman Catholic Church. The Spanish Regency, filled with jealousy and incensed by the destruction of San Sebastian, which they claimed had been done deliberately to promote British commerce, announced that they were to terminate Wellington's appointment as commander-in-chief of the Spanish armies. The Portuguese Regency claimed that their troops were not getting the credit they deserved in the English press, and demanded a separate Portuguese Army. There was substance in their complaint. The Portuguese soldiers, under British leadership and training, had improved remarkably and were now regarded as reliable fighting men. Their contribution to the Allied victories was, unfortunately, too easily overlooked, since apart from one Portuguese division the remainder were either in a Portuguese brigade, which formed a part of every British division except the 1st Division which had a brigade of the King's German Legion, or were in independent brigades, nearly all of which were commanded by British officers. A further complaint by Portugal was that Britain's use of the northern Spanish ports was ruining Lisbon's trade. At the same time the Portuguese government was little better than the Spanish in providing for their army – the Portuguese muleteers were two years in arrears of pay! Wellington's response was to announce his intention of resigning and leaving the Peninsula should either of these proposals be pursued.

John Aitchison had applied to General Sir Edward Pakenham, Adjutant General, to be allowed to rejoin his regiment. On 20 October, Pakenham arranged for his relief by Captain Stewart of the 74th and to Lieutenant-General Sir John Hope, who had relieved Graham who was ill, he wrote, '. . . I cannot resist expressing to you the satisfaction derived from your Captain Aitchison's assistance. . . .'

Pamplona capitulated at last on 30 October, and the 4,200 men of the garrison were allowed to march out with the honours of war. They were embarked at Passages on 5 November, the day after Aitchison rejoined his regiment. Wellington's anxiety about his rear was now at an end but the situation in Europe was still unclear. News that the Bavarians had turned against Napoleon, bringing about the dissolution of the Confederation of the Rhine, reached Spain but it was still possible that the central European allies might reach an agreement with Napoleon, leaving Wellington to face the French alone. On the other hand, his troops could not winter in the high Pyrenees. They must either withdraw into Spain or find winter quarters in the fertile plains of France. Wellington planned to accomplish the latter.

Camp near Andaye, France
8th November 1813

My dear father,

Having already in my former letter explained to you my views on first accepting the Command at Passages – the nature of my duty while there and my reasons for wishing to quit it – I can have but few remarks to make on enclosing to you the letter which I received on being recalled [from the Adjutant General, Sir Edward Pakenham]. But I hope you will derive as much satisfaction from it as I have done and the more so as I can assure you that the thanks in it are not mere official expressions of approbation. This I have learnt by private communication from an Officer under him at Headquarters and the General who first recommended me for the situation.

You know by a former letter that I had my feelings explained by a friend to General Pakenham on requesting to be recalled, which he most fully agreed with and applauded; and as soon therefore as arrangements were made which would remove any inconvenience likely to result to the service from a change, I had permission to join my Regiment. I accordingly arrived here on the 4th and my reception from the General and Commanding officer[34] has been as gratifying as I could have wished – I have dined twice with the former and once with the latter; which trifling I mention to *yourself* to show the terms on which I am with both. My situation at Passages was not what is usually called a *staff* appointment, although I am not without hope that it may be the means of leading to one when an opportunity may offer hereafter.

I have just come off picquet where I was close to the enemy in our front. They appear pretty numerous, tho' not more than we shall manage. They were in great alarm all yesterday of an attack and they were not so without grounds, for the plan was all arranged in the course of the day and we had orders to attack early this morning, but the roads on our right having been found quite impassable for carriages the order was countermanded. There was a fall of rain yesterday morning and probably as soon as the effects of it shall be at an end we shall attack. In our front, on this side the Nive, the enemy occupy in position a range of heights which they have crowned with fieldworks well-armed – these may be occasion of some loss, but as *our* attack will be combined with others on our right I am of opinion that the enemy will soon abandon them, as in the event of remaining in them till we carry them by assault the whole would be probably either put to the sword or made prisoners as the river in their rear has few bridges over it.

We have so many opinions as to the future intentions of Lord Wellington that I shall give you few, but it appears to me that his operations altogether will depend on the weather – In the Pyrenees the roads are already choked with *snow* and several divisions have been obliged to move into lower situations in consequence. It is evident, therefore, that without settled and fine weather we cannot move on our right and as the positions of the enemy and all the rivers are to be turned by it, it would be a very precarious movement, an advance of the centre or left, and even in the event of success the gains would not be equivalent to the cost.

The great object of our advance, I think, will be – quarters for the troops – under all circumstances I should not conceive Ld Wellington intended to act offensively (these being gained), though it would be absurd to suppose that if an opportunity offered he would not improve it to bring Soult to a decisive general action and establish himself on the Garonne – the Ardour I believe does not afford a very formidable defensive line, and as we shall be able to blockade Bayonne we shall probably pass it; but I do not suppose we shall attempt to besiege till we are firmly established in France – but if we do there is already at Santander a large battering train in addition to what was left after San Sebastian.

We are very badly off for long forage – there is plenty of corn but nothing else but *grass* – nearly one half of the animals of the Army in the Pyrenees had died – the French in the same position in '93 (or '95) lost nearly 36,000.[35] Our cavalry generally are in tolerable condition and they have been on the Ebro river during our advance. I am quite well and so are Lewis and Pincher and my mare is nearly so again.

THE NIVELLE

The crossing of the Bidassoa was followed by a month of comparative quiet. Soult devoted this time to strengthening a naturally strong defensive position, turning it into a veritable lines of Torres Vedras, by constructing redoubts, erecting batteries, creating inundations, obstructing fords and improving his communications. Convinced that Wellington would again try to turn his right he paid particular attention to the defences of the fortified port of St Jean de Luz, and strengthened his right under Reille at the expense of his left under d'Erlon. His weakness was that with not more than 74,000 men and about 100 guns he was unable to man his extensive defences and keep in hand a reserve.

From the western slopes of the Great Rhune to the sea, Reille had 23,000 men. Clausel, in the centre, faced the Great Rhune with 15,000 men, for his forward defences being on the Little Rhune and around Sare, and his second line south of the Nivelle between Ascain and Amots. To his left d'Erlon had deployed 11,000 men north of the Nivelle with his left on Mount Mondarrain. The bridge at Amots provided the only link between Clausel and d'Erlon. Away to the east Foy with a division at St Jean Pied de Port kept an eye on the Roncesvalles Pass from which the fall of Pamplona had enabled Wellington to transfer most of Hill's divisions westward to the Maya Pass, relieving them with Spanish troops.

Wellington held the initiative; moreover, the heights of the Great Rhune enabled him to overlook all the enemy's positions. From his observation post on the Great Rhune, Wellington overlooked most of the enemy defences. Immediately below him to the north-east and separated by a deep declivity lay the Little Rhune, which Clausel had fortified and garrisoned with three battalions. Beyond it could be seen Amots, whose bridge formed the link between Clausel's and d'Erlon's corps, and beyond that again, across the Nivelle, the high ground on each side of St Pee. Junction points between formations are points of tactical weakness: it was against Amots and St Pee that he would direct his main thrust. The attack must soon be made, for winter was setting in and troops and guns had already had to be dug out from under four feet of snow on the Roncesvalles Pass. He must either find winter quarters in the fertile plains of France or retire into Spain.

Having completed his survey, Wellington turned to the senior officers, Alten, Kempt, Colborne and Napier (commander of the 43rd and author of the classic history of the Peninsular War) of the Light Division, who accompanied him, and remarked: 'These fellows think themselves invulnerable but I shall beat them out, and with ease.'[36] Observing their scepticism, he explained that though only slightly superior to the enemy in numbers, he had 90,000 of whom 26,000 were Spaniards, he could concentrate overwhelming force at his chosen point of attack and penetrate the French line before Soult could move reserves to stop him. The French were to be attacked all along the line.

Hope on the left was to make a strong holding attack towards St Jean de Luz, but the main thrust would be made by Hill on the right bank of the Nivelle and Beresford on the left bank, towards St Pee and Amots. Hill's corps of 26,000, including the 2nd, 6th and Portuguese Divisions, would attack Urdax, drive d'Erlon from the defences around Ainhoa and advance on D'Erlon's main line of defence extending eastward from the bridge of Amots.

Beresford, on Hill's left, with 36,000 men, including the 3rd, 4th, 7th and Light Divisions and Giron's Spaniards, had as his first objective the strong defences around Sare, for which he had the support of eighteen guns, after which he was to drive Clausel's men from Amots and posts between that town and Ascain. West of the Great Rhune, Freyre's Spanish corps (9,000) was to advance north-east from the Mandela heights towards Ascain, to tie down Soult's small reserve at Serres.

On the Allied left Hope, with 19,000 men, including the Anglo-German 1st and the Anglo-Portuguese 5th Divisions, supported by more than half the ninety-four guns and by naval gunfire, were to drive the French from their positions in front of St Jean de Luz. They would advance to the Unxin stream and maintain their bombardment of St Jean with the intention of tying down Reille's corps of 23,000 and confirming Soult in his opinion that this was to be the decisive point of attack. For this purpose Hope was to attack first, opening fire at six o'clock, which was to be the signal for a general attack, to be relayed to the right flank by the firing of three guns from the Great Rhune. One other preliminary operation had to be carried out to protect the left flank of the attack on Sare and the defences covering it – was the taking of the Little Rhune by the Light Division.

The attack had been planned for the eighth but heavy rain postponed operations until the tenth. At 3 a.m. the 5th Division, advancing next to the sea with the 1st Division on their right, drove the enemy from the Sans Culotte redoubt, north of the Socorry hill, and Urrugne. The whole then advanced to the line of the Unxin from which position they kept up a smart bombardment of St Jean.

Under cover of darkness the Light Division got a line of riflemen and Cacadores close to the enemy defences on the Little Rhune, ready to assault at first light. This very strong position would be attacked from in front, and wound round the western flank of the French positions. In these operations the 43rd greatly distinguished themselves carrying one position after another. The French retreated precipitously when the 53rd turned their other flank.

On the right of the Light Division, the 4th Division successively made frontal attacks on the redoubts of St Barbe and Granada, covering Sare. While Giron's Spaniards and the 7th Division worked round the right and left flanks of that town, the 3rd Division advanced along the left bank of the Nivelle, took Amots, crossed the Amots bridge, and established themselves on the flank of D'Erlon's main position on the Harismindia ridge.

Hill's Portuguese Division cleared Urdax but was held up by strong opposition at Ainhoa until some of the 6th Division took the enemy skirmishing line in flank. Hill advanced up the right bank of the Nivelle, with the 6th Portuguese and 2nd Divisions echeloned back in line, against d'Erlon's position on the formidable Harismindia ridge, whose crest was crowned by three redoubts, one of which became the objective of each division. With the 3rd Division building up on their flank, the French did not fight for long after the attack went in shortly after one o'clock.

The Light Division, having cleared the Little Rhune, advanced rapidly towards the bridge at Harosteguia while Longa's and Freyre's Spaniards advanced towards that of Ascain. Colborne's brigade took the Signal Redoubt by assault, but at the cost to the 52nd of 250 casualties. Soon Clausel's forces risked being cut off south of the Nivelle, a danger which increased when the 7th and other divisions released from Sare came up. Receiving no assistance from Soult he had great difficulty in getting part of his force across the river and reformed.

Soult, as Wellington had intended, remained in St Jean until afternoon in anticipation of a major attack by Hope. By the time he joined his small reserve at Serres it was too late to change the course of the battle. Soult's concern that Wellington might cut off his right wing from Bayonne was growing but the cautious Wellington was also concerned that, if he let Beresford's corps and the Light Division advance beyond St Pee before Hill had come into line, they also would be vulnerable to attack from their left. He therefore held them back until Hill got up to St Pee about five o'clock, by which time only a limited exploitation was possible. D'Erlon had retreated through Espelettes to form a bridgehead on the left bank of the Nive covering Cambo, Ustaritz and the road to Bayonne. Here he was joined by Foy with his 10,000 men.

Foy had started the day by attacking Mina's Spaniards at Roncesvalles and nearly succeeded in capturing Hill's baggage train. However, when he heard the direction from which heavy firing was coming he realized that Wellington must have penetrated the French centre and he marched towards the sound of guns. While d'Erlon fell back towards the Nive, Clausel was trying to rally his men about Habacenborda. Wellington now ordered the 3rd and 4th Divisions forward to present Clausel rallying about Habacenborda. It was now too late to do more. Skirmishing went on into the night, while the Allies bivouacked on the battlefield.

Soult pulled back to the immediate defences of Bayonne. He evacuated St Jean under cover of darkness, having destroyed the bridge over the Nivelle. Wellington ordered an early advance for the following day. Hill was to advance on Cambo and Ustaritz but to halt at Souraide unless he saw an opportunity to cross the Nive without incurring more than light casualties. The centre under Beresford was to advance due north – Wellington still hoping for an opportunity to cut Reille's lines of communication – and Hope was to advance up the coast on to the high ground north of Bidart with Freyre on his right. It was soon realized that Reille had slipped away in the night but unfortunately it was after noon before the tide was low enough for Hope's men to ford the estuary.

On the twelfth Soult withdrew into the two fortified camps he had prepared, one each side of the Nive, south of Bayonne. D'Erlon withdrew under cover of fog and in the afternoon Hill started to bombard Cambo with the intention of fording the Nive between that town and Ustaritz. Then a torrential downpour which continued for eight days made the rivers unfordable and reduced the countryside to a sea of mud into which, on the by-roads, the infantry sank to mid-leg, the cavalry above the horses' knees and even to the saddle girths in some places. The artillery could not move at all.

The initial operations had gone entirely according to Wellington's plans. He had misled Soult and concentrated 50,000 men against 18,000 French around Amots and St Pee. The Allies had advanced over difficult, rugged clay terrain, tree-clad near the coast and moorland further inland, against defences which Soult considered must cost an attacker 25,000 casualties, and carried these works without check.

Although he had been cheated of decisive victory by the time it took Hill's corps to advance, Wellington believed that 'the Battle of the Nivelle was my best work'. Instead of 25,000 casualties the Allies had 2,700. Soult lost 4,000 in killed, wounded and taken prisoner, sixty-nine guns and all his field magazines. It was a remarkable achievement for which Wellington particularly praised the performance of the Allied gunners. From Bidart John Aitchison wrote:

Camp near the Bidout river
12th November 1813

My dear father,

    Providence evidently aids our cause and Bonaparte is being punished for his crimes; for while the powerful Army under himself, from defection of his Allies and the prowess of his enemies, is compelled to retreat to the frontier,[37] another Army in a different quarter is beaten within the territory of France proper.

    The weather continues fine and the whole army advanced and attacked the enemy in their position of the 10th – our column, which is the left, attacked only their outposts and having driven them into their entrenchments we halted: but the right and centre of the Army attacked the main position of the enemy and forced it with their usual gallantry, and the same day Ld Wellington crossed the Nivelle with 6 divisions. The heights above St Jean de Luz, which had been rendered almost impregnable by entrenchment, being thus turned the enemy abandoned them in the night, and yesterday we passed through that town to the heights which we now occupy.

    Today we have halted; and both armies are now on the opposite heights above the Rivulet (the Unzin), which at low water is nearly dry. The Cavalry is coming up from the rear, the heavy guns and Pontoons are already on this side of the Nivelle, and everything indicates our immediate advance. The enemy are at present on the only ground which favours them between this and Bayonne, from which place it is distant about 8 miles. But it would be too imprudent in them to wait a general attack, for their troops no longer fight with confidence and if they were beaten (as they certainly would be) with the Ardour in their rear the consequence would be ruinous to them. They will probably therefore retire on our advancing, which I suppose we shall do tomorrow if the weather keeps dry.

I cannot well describe to you the mingled feelings which I have experienced since yesterday. We have left the starving country of the Pyrenees behind us and we are passing into a country so beautiful and with a hardy and industrious population who require only a government like our own to make it as near a paradise as home.

I have just returned from St Jean de Luz which, and the road to it, presents spectacles which must excite the compassion of every feeling mind. The town has originally been large and rich but many houses have been suffered to decay, the harbour is blocking up with sand from want of commerce, warehouses have been turned into stables and everything indicates the tyranny of the Government. The people who remain suffer every misery – they have neither received us from hatred nor joy – they complain bitterly of their *governors* yet they retain a warm feeling for France, amiable in any people. They were advised to abandon their houses on our approach as we would *murder* them in revenge, but having been undeceived they are now returning with their effects.

13th November

We still remain where we were although the enemy have retired a league. It has rained all night very heavy and is still continuous without any appearance of stopping, but the cavalry which were up have crossed the rivulet, and we shall also we expect move forward either tomorrow or as soon as the cavalry, which is still a day's march in rear, shall have joined. We must soon be put into houses, for there are plenty all over this country and it is now too cold for tents. It is wonderful, however, how well the men keep their health, which I ascribe to being well fed – they have never been without meat and biscuit since July and seldom without rice, two ounces of which was last year added to the ration; being near the sea too they get plenty of potatoes to buy which have come in great quantities from Ireland and England and cost about 2 pence a pound – this you will consider dear though we think it cheap, but we hope to have a regular supply of everything in the winter from England which will lower the markets here. We are still very badly off for long forage; we have found a good deal in the houses but there is no quantity to last – there is plenty of Indian corn.

You will see by the Gazette that our part of the Army has had no fighting – the Coldstream Lt Company had one officer and a few men wounded in skirmishes, Marshal Soult expected that Ld Wellington would attack on this side and it is said was not so well prepared on his left. Our column I believe exceeds 20,000 men and is commanded by Sir J. Hope – we shall probably have the siege of Bayonne if it is undertaken – 180 pieces of ordnance are at Santander ready for it as soon as the weather will permit. My love to Mother etc.

ps *14th November* We are still awaiting the arrival of the Cavalry, the enemy are retired to within ten miles of Bayonne where they are in position – the weather is dreadful and we must drive off the enemy and get into quarters.

It was not only bad weather that had held up Wellington's operations until early December. There were serious political considerations as well. Following their victory at Leipzig, the Allied armies reached the Rhine as Wellington was preparing to cross the Nivelle. The war however was by no means over. Napoleon relied upon the divergent interests of the Allies and his own genius to afford an opportunity yet to snatch victory from defeat. When the Allies offered him peace on condition that France should be confined to her natural boundaries – the Rhine, Alps and Pyrenees – it was refused.

The Dutch rose, Blücher entered Holland and on 22 November the British government ordered an expeditionary force to Holland under Sir Thomas Graham, to uphold British interests. Three days earlier, at Frankfurt, the Allies agreed a plan for the invasion of France from two widely separated fronts, Holland and Switzerland. Designed to satisfy the multiplicity of national political objectives and ignoring all military principle, it seemed a perfect recipe for enabling Napoleon to defeat the Allies in detail, a strategy at which he was unsurpassed. Greatly alarmed, Wellington wrote, 'In regard to the operations on the Rhine, I confess I feel no confidence in what is doing. . . the Allies are not strong enough [to] do more than cross the Rhine in one great corps . . . the Allies don't appear to me to have reflected that everything was lost in Europe by the loss of one or two great battles, and that everything has been restored to its present state by their military success. . . .'[38]

Meanwhile Napoleon had started an intrigue to restore Ferdinand, still his prisoner, to the throne of Spain in return for the expulsion of the British. He was counting on the bad relations between Wellington and the Spanish government, which reached their lowest ebb on 27 November when Wellington wrote to Lord Bathurst:

> I recommend you to demand, as a security for the safety of the King's troops against the criminal disposition of the Government of Spain, that a British garrison be admitted to San Sebastian, with the intention that, unless the demand is complied with, the troops should be withdrawn; I recommend you to withdraw the troops, and if this demand be not complied with be the consequences what they may. The truth is that a crisis is approaching in connection with Spain and if you don't bring the Government and nation to their senses before they go too far, you will inevitably lose all the advantages which you might expect from the services rendered them.[39]

Wellington took the possibility of evacuation seriously, 'I think', he wrote, 'I should experience great difficulty, the Spanish people being hostile, in returning through Spain into Portugal . . . I might be able to embark the army at Passages in spite of the French and Spanish armies united; but I should be much more certain of getting clear off, as we ought, if we had possession of San Sebastian.'[40] Fortunately the Spanish government came to its senses, power shifted to men who saw through Napoleon's blandishments, and to improve relations Bathurst ordered the evacuation of British troops from Cadiz and Cartagena.

Besides these difficulties with the Spanish government, the conduct of the

Spanish troops towards French civilians continued to cause concern. After the battle of the Nivelle, murder, rape and pillage was the lot of towns in which Spanish forces were quartered, notably Sare and Ascain. The Spanish troops had been fighting well and Wellington understood both their desire for revenge and the compulsion to plunder put upon them by the failure of the Spanish government to pay or supply them, but he considered it essential to obviate the French organizing a resistance movement against the Allied occupation. This, he believed, depended upon the troops making it clear by their behaviour that the supporters of Napoleon and not the French people were the enemy. To Freyre he wrote, in French, after the battle of the Nivelle, 'I have not come to France to plunder; I have not lost thousands of officers and men killed and wounded in order that the surviving men may plunder. On the contrary, it is my duty, and the duty of us all to prevent plundering, particularly if we wish to subsist our armies at the cost of the country.'[41] To Bathurst, on 21 November, he wrote, 'If I could bring forward 20,000 good Spaniards, paid and fed, I should have Bayonne. If I could bring forward 40,000, I do not know where I should stop. Now I have both the 20,000 and the 40,000 . . . but I cannot bring any forward for want of means of paying and supporting them. Without pay or food they must plunder; and if they plunder they will ruin us all.'[42] Reluctantly Wellington sent the Spanish forces back to cantonments in Spain and surrendered his command of them, retaining only Morillo's well-disciplined division of 4,500. The Allied Army was thus reduced to 36,000 British, 23,000 Portuguese and 4,500 Spaniards, in all 63,500 men.

At the beginning of November, Soult had 72,000 men and in Catalonia Suchet had 46,000. Both were soon to be reduced by Napoleon's demands for experienced men to form the cadres on which to build new units from newly raised conscripts, mostly reluctant teenage boys, many of whom were having to be taken to the military depots in chains. Shortly also, as a result of his experience of having the Saxons change sides in the middle of the battle of Leipzig, all units of Spaniards, Poles, Portuguese and Germans in the French armies would be disbanded, though not until after the battles before Bayonne. In mid-November Soult was ordered to send two Italian brigades back to Italy. By December Soult's forces had been reduced to 54,500 men in the field army, organized into eight divisions and one independent brigade, and 8,000 garrison troops, and Suchet's to 23,000. About a third of these were inexperienced boys.

The territory gained by Wellington after the crossing of the Nivelle enabled him to put most of his men into cantonments between the river Nive and the sea, though this meant scattering them widely. Their better living conditions and good and ample rations resulted in a marked improvement in discipline, though the desertion rate continued to cause concern.[43] Wellington moved his headquarters to St Jean de Luz and the 1st Division were pulled back to Ciboure, a suburb of St Jean. Wellington kenneled his foxhounds in St Jean and whenever possible he and his officers hunted and on occasion killed a fox.

John Aitchison wrote home with a regimental officer's view of the situation:

St Jean de Luz
My dear father,   *28th November*

. . . There seems to be no general move of the Army in contemplation, as the Cavalry and most of the Artillery have been sent far to the rear and the greater part of the Spanish army to be better supplied, but we are in full expectation of taking the field again as soon as the weather shall have so dried the roads as to allow our right to advance. We shall then pass the Nive and once across that river and Ardour there will be nothing to stop us until we reach the Garonne. Soult's Army is very inferior to ours, both in numbers and composition, and they have become so dispirited by their frequent defeats as hardly to offer resistance even with advantage of ground, this was particularly shown in the last general attack, when the ground which they occupied at several points was so steep that men could hardly walk up it, yet it was carried with small loss.

We hear often from the interior of France and there are many reports of the difficulties of the government at present in managing the people, but they are so likely to be exaggeration that I shall not repeat them. There is, however, great reason to believe that much discontent does prevail amongst them, and in the army we know for certain that Marshal Soult has been obliged to take measures to prevent the return of the men to the country now occupied by us which they had abandoned on our approach.

The Mayors of two places have been ousted for not retiring on our advance as they were ordered but on the contrary for showing a disposition to assist us. This measure has made an impression on the people and they complain much of us in not proclaiming the policy which they mean to pursue. I am persuaded if we did so that we should ensure the neutrality of all the inhabitants of this part of the country who long for a change in their situation – they dread a change of *governors* yet they cannot live without trade – you would hardly believe this the same town it appeared a week ago – now every boat is in full employ and the Port of Sacoa, which is the chief harbour, is filled with vessels of private individuals of the Commissariat. All is bustle in the town – shops are open in every direction and they are well-filled with goods and customers. The markets begin to fall tho' they are yet high enough, whether the produce of this country or not, being at least twice as dear as in England. A good deal I think may be ascribed to avariciousness, or, for want of proper regulations, many things are allowed to be sold at 3 times as much as before we came and the Guinea is current for 2/6d less than what it always was in France, and at this moment is at Bayonne. We are however very comfortably off, the quarters in general being very good and having fireplaces in the sitting rooms as at home, and the French Army had the politeness to leave us in their entrenchments more dried wood than we shall burn in 5 years.

You will hear that Lord Wellington has been very angry with the Spanish Army for plundering and he has for that fault sent several corps of them away. Our own men I fear have not been so free from it as the general good decrees, and we hear that on the right several men have been hanged and shot for it. But there is another thing more to be regretted and very common, which is desertion, and I am very sorry to say it is true that a great proportion are from amongst our own countrymen. The French are said already to have formed a battalion of 800 men which have been marched to the north. We are all at a loss to ascertain to the real cause of this disaffection but it is mostly ascribed to the disinclination among the 7 year men to serve 3 years more – it is also true that every recruit is sworn to serve so much longer if desired but we know very well that few think of what they are about at the time of entering and few expect that they will be called upon. The proclamation too was so long delayed that nobody I believe expected it. One man of the Guards has deserted -- he was a Volunteer from the Irish Militia and belonged to the Coldstreams. Give my love to mother etc, etc.

THE NIVE

The English and Welshmen of Wellington's army were now on soil which for 300 years kings of England had ruled, and their own ancestors had garrisoned to which Bastide Clairence, eastward across the Nive, bore witness. On the main road from St Jean de Luz to Bayonne lay the village of Anglet, headquarters of the Black Prince after his victory at Poitiers. Northward of Bayonne, beyond a wide, inhospitable coastal strip of marsh and sand-dunes, lay the great city of Bordeaux where the Black Prince held court and Richard II was born. Later, in the reign of Henry VIII, an English expedition returned to the Bidassoa.

Wellington's army was now concentrated between the river Nive and the sea, along a front running from the ridge of Barrouillet, north of Bidart, eastward to that river and forming the base of an acute-angled triangle with the sea and the river as its sides. Near the apex, where the Nive ran into the Ardour, lay the fortified city of Bayonne, a minor arsenal which had given its name to the bayonet. The ancient fortifications of Bayonne, based on Vauban's plans, were not formidable in themselves but from the time Soult had taken command of the army of Spain, shortly after Vitoria, he had built about 600 yards beyond the city walls a modern line of defence. The Nive cut the city in two and within its walls was bridged in three places. The approach to the city, east of the Nive, was covered by the construction of the fortified camp called Mousserolles, which spanned the narrow neck of land in the angle between the Nive and Ardour; and from the south and west it was defended by an entrenched camp, including Marrac Castle, covered on the west by a marsh, called the camp d'Espana. Thus defended, Bayonne provided Soult with a base of great strength from which, using the bridges within the city, he could quickly concentrate his forces on either bank on the Nive.

Wellington's aim remained the destruction of Soult's army, for which the reduction of Bayonne was a necessary objective. The city was, however, far too strong to be taken by assault. It could only be reduced by a regular siege and this time he was prepared to wait until he could assemble all the necessary artillery and engineers' resources, which could not, however, be before the next campaigning season. In the meantime his forces were cramped for winter quarters and his cavalry short of forage; he needed to reconnoitre the city's defences and establish the possibility of crossing the Ardour below it. He also wanted to set up a battery on the banks of the Ardour, above the city, to restrict its supply by river.

Wellington felt a particular pleasure each time he outwitted Soult. Remembering how, in the battle for Oporto, he had led Soult to believe that he would cross the Douro at its mouth and had then surprised him by crossing above that city, he now planned to reverse the process. For this, a concealed reconnaissance of the lower Ardour was essential. To achieve his aims Wellington would have to cross the Nive and drive the French on both sides of the river back into their entrenched camps – an operation which Soult both expected and looked forward to, for, acting on interior lines, it would enable him to concentrate superior forces against the Allies on either side of the river, more quickly than Wellington could respond. On the day Wellington crossed the Nive, Soult wrote to General Paris, 'The enemy army is divided on the two banks of the Nive. Their general has lost his numerical advantage by extending himself in this way and I intend to attack him in the false position he has taken up.'[44]

By the end of November, Wellington was ready to cross the Nive as soon as the weather was favourable. He had about 63,000 infantry, while Soult had a field army of some 54,500, organized in eight divisions and Paris's independent brigade, and, in addition, 8,000 garrison troops in Bayonne. Reille, with two divisions and the Bayonne garrison, was responsible for the city's defences, the Camp d'Espagne and the lower Ardour; d'Erlon, on the east bank, had three divisions, two divisions being responsible for the Mousserolles camp and an outpost line between Villefranque and Vieux Mouguerre, Foy's division kept watch on the Nive from Ustarits to Cambo and Paris, away to the south, was stationed opposite Ilsatsou.

Wellington planned for Morillo's division to cross the Nive at Ilsatsou and drive Paris eastwards. Hill, with the 2nd and Portuguese Divisions, would ford the river about Cambo and drive d'Erlon within the Bayonne defences and establish a battery on the banks of the Ardour to prevent supplies reaching Bayonne. Beresford was to build a pontoon bridge just below Ustarits, under cover given by the 3rd and 6th Divisions who would then cross, the 3rd protecting the bridgehead and the 6th turning north and advancing on Hill's left flank against Villefranque. On the left Hope's corps, in conjunction with the Light Division, would drive Clausel's troops into the Camp d'Espagne, reconnoitre the defences of Bayonne, establish the possibility of crossing the lower Ardour, and return to their cantonments.

The ground over which these operations were to take place was deep, sticky clay, the country very close and broken, covered with small hills, copses, hedgerows, streams and lakes. The first week in December was fine and Wellington fixed the preliminary moves for the night of the eighth to ninth; the Nive was to be crossed on a signal about first light. Unfortunately it started raining on the eighth but Wellington stuck to his plans, though the roads were ankle-deep in mud. All went well and the Nive was crossed with very few casualties. The bridge at Ustarits was completed and Hill advanced to the line Villefranque–Vieux Mouguerre. Despite expecting such a move, Soult's men were surprised everywhere, except on the left where a deserter had alerted the enemy. As a result the advance of the 1st and 5th Divisions ran into considerable opposition; nevertheless, the French were driven within their permanent defences, the necessary reconnaissances carried out and, after dark, the troops returned to their cantonments, leaving forward posts on a line covering Barrouillet–Bassussany–Urdains.

On Hope's front Campbell's Portuguese Brigade held the outpost line, the 5th Division was at Bidart and the 1st Division, Aylmer's Brigade and his headquarters were back in St Jean. The troops reached St Jean exhausted after marching twenty miles in incessant rain and advanced for five across country in a sea of mud, in contact with the enemy. The Light Division, on Hope's right, had their picquet line north of Bassusary, its main body at Arcangues, with one brigade ordered to withdraw to Arbonne next day. Urdains was covered by a Brigade of the 7th Division. Wellington, Beresford and Hill were all east of the Nive. West of the river there was no overall commander, the forces were weak in front and scattered in great depth. Continued success had bred complacency and presented Soult with an unrivalled opportunity to inflict a serious defeat on the Allies. It would be true to say that, on returning to their cantonments, no one expected further action, as Johnny Kincaid put it, 'On our side were engaged in a continual skirmish until dark, when we retired to our quarters, under the supposition that we had got our usual week's allowance (of fighting) and that we should remain quiet again for a time.'[45]

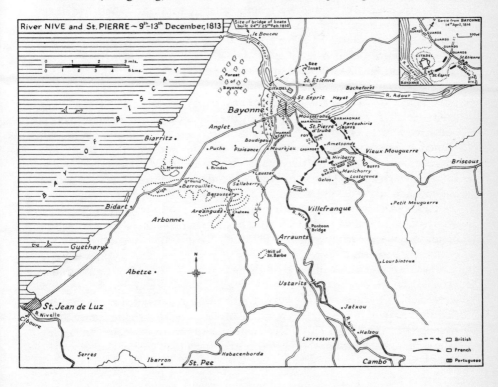

Soult acted with great speed and resolution. He decided to concentrate 50,000 men against the Allies west of the Nive with the intention of severing Wellington's communications with the sea and isolating his forces east of the river. D'Erlon, therefore, was ordered to leave his camp fires burning and bring his three divisions through Bayonne during the night to the west bank of the Nive; the eastern approach to the city would be covered by the garrison.

At dawn Soult marched south with Reille's corps of two, later increased to three, divisions along the axis of the main road to the St Jean. Clausel with three, later reduced to two, divisions marched on Arcangues; d'Erlon followed in reserve. Wellington planned to build a second pontoon bridge over the Nive, south-west of Villefranque; until then the only connection between the two halves of the army was by the Ustarits bridge four miles behind Hill's front line.

Dawn broke on the tenth with a thick drizzle making observation difficult. Nevertheless, the Light Division picquets, covering the Arcangues ridge, detected the French forming up for an attack. The French, however, came on in great numbers on both flanks, crying, 'En avant, en avant, Français! Vive l'Empéreur!' The picquet line was forced to retire on the main line of defence along the Arcangues ridge, which was accomplished without serious loss.

This ridge was topped by two strong points, the church and graveyard and, 200 yards further east, on the other side of the main road, the Château d'Arcangues. The 43rd held the church, the 1/95th and 3/95th the Château and the 3rd Cacadores the ground between. The defences had been strengthened with breastworks and by felling trees. Kempt and Alten had their headquarters in the Château. Echeloned back on the left was Colborne's brigade. Shortly afterwards Cole arrived at the Château and, on being given the situation, ordered a brigade of the 4th Division forward to support Kempt's right. In all 4,000 men supported by two Portuguese mountain guns were deployed on the ridge.

Though Clausel brought up twelve guns to play on the church and a heavy exchange of fire took place, surprisingly the French made no attempt to press home the attack. On the Allied left a far more serious situation developed. Hope's command was strung out thinly over a depth of seven miles. His outpost line was held by Archibald Campbell's independent Portuguese Brigade which covered the defile where the main road from Bayonne passed between the lakes of Mouriscot and Brindos. This brigade put up such stout resistance against greatly superior numbers that Robinson's Brigade from the 5th Division at Bidart had time to establish a very strong defensive position before the village of Barrouillet, in which the mayor's house became the centre of contention.

It was around this village that the outcome of the day's fighting was decided. To the front it was covered by a thick coppice and its approaches were such as to break up the assault into small groups of men so that the fighting became a mêlée. It was not until about noon that Reille launched his first attack on the village. This was carried out with two divisions, one advancing in a column of battalions from the north, the other converging from the north-east.

It was eleven o'clock before news of the attack on the outposts reached Hope in St Jean. Aylmer's brigade and the 1st Division were immediately put in motion and Hope set out at top speed for Barrouillet where he established his command post in the mayor's house. Soult now ordered a fresh attack by three brigades, one from each of Reille's divisions. In their advance the three columns became intermingled, but they pressed on despite heavy casualties and nearly surrounded the mayor's house, causing Hope to make a last-minute escape during which he was wounded. By this time Aylmer's brigade and Bradford's Portuguese had come up. Greville's brigade of the 5th Division was ordered into the battle. The 9th Foot wheeled inwards from the right towards the tail of the French attacking columns and the Portuguese from the left. The attackers broke and fled.

The afternoon was far spent but Soult was determined to make one more attempt on the village and called up the German Brigade, so soon to change sides, from the reserve, but at this moment the 1st Division was seen arriving and news came from Clausel that the 3rd and 6th Divisions had recrossed to the left bank of the river. Soult therefore ordered Reille to pull back. What now occurred on this part of the front is best told by John Aitchison, whose account differs in some interesting details from that of Fortescue.

Bidart
14th December 1813
6 o'clock

My dear father,

After five days of fatigue I sit down with much pleasure to tell you that I am quite well, though I had a *very* narrow escape, a musket shot having passed through the back part of my hat and grazed my head. I was a little stunned by it at the moment but I have suffered no other inconvenience from it, other than a headache which went off before the next morning. The result of our exertions has been glorious; Marshal Soult and all his army having been defeated with great loss and driven across the Ardour. Three German Battalions with their Officers, and in the most perfect state of equipment, deserted to us, and have been embarked for England.[46]

In my last letter I stated to you the advance of the Light Division and the intention of moving forward to the right of the Army as soon as the weather permits. Having been fine on the 5th, 6th and 7th, Lord Wellington determined to move on the 9th, and although it rained on the night of the 8th so as to make the roads almost as bad as ever he persevered in his intention. The whole army advanced at daybreak, each division attacking the enemy immediately in its front; the passage of Nive was effected almost without opposition and Sir Rowland Hill with his corps had soon established himself in the neighbourhood of Villefranque, where it was intended that he should halt.

The centre of the Army had difficulty in gaining their point; our corps (d'Armée) also had much to do, as the enemy were appraised of our intention to attack by a deserter who passed over to them about 2 in the morning, and instead of making a demonstration (as was intended) only, we had to carry every hedge and ditch till we reached the enemy's entrenched camps close to Bayonne. Here we halted, and as soon as dark we returned to our old quarter of St Jean de Luz and the whole army, but the right also returned to the quarters which they had previously occupied. There was no intention of advancing further and we would have allowed the French to remain quiet, but Soult advanced on the high road on the morning of the 10th and attacked the troops which covered it with an overwhelming force – after performing *prodigies* in the course of the day they regained part of the ground which they had lost and our division arrived in the evening to support – on the 11th Ld Wellington pushed forward and re-took, with the 5th Division and one Portuguese Brigade, the greater part of the ground which they had lost, and they kept it in spite of repeated efforts of the French with fresh troops to drive them from it – at 3 o'clock both armies were within *150 yards* of each other, and they remained so without firing a shot till dark when Ld Wellington ordered ours to retire by Brigades, meaning to leave only the picquets in advance, but the French seeing this advanced with all their force and drove our men back with loss to the ground which they had moved from in the morning.

Our guns had been ordered to the rear and it was a considerable time before they could be brought up again – the enemy were nearly gaining their point – but our two brigades being brought close up and all the other troops engaged – at dusk the armies occupied nearly the same ground as in the morning and we expected to be attacked at daybreak.

The 5th Division, which had been fatigued, was therefore relieved by the 1st and in the morning my regiment was put in advance. We had hardly been posted when the enemy opened a tremendous fire of musketry upon us and the rest of the Guards from the woods within 100 yards of our front, being better covered than ourselves by banks and ditches, they tried to drive us back for three hours and caused as much loss[47] *but they did not gain an inch* – Soult himself, we believe, was directing from hearing cheers at different times – he never repeated the attempt in this quarter and indeed was so well satisfied by what he'd got that he would not allow his men to cease firing for more than an hour after us, although we never showed an intention of attacking. Our object was to preserve the high road and the enemy to gain it, as had he succeeded our right and centre must of necessity have fallen back – Soult therefore never attacked either and Sir Rowland Hill extended his line to the Ardour and advanced a few miles.

Soult now determined to attack him, and having a very short line of communication he retired from before us in the night, and attacked with all his force yesterday morning before Sir Rowland could be supported – the Portuguese Brigade, which occupied an important hill, were obliged to give way but they rallied – attacked and carried it again in their usual fine style and they maintained it during two fresh attacks, when the enemy being driven down with immense loss, he began to retreat and was pursued till he passed the Ardour under the cover of Bayonne. In this battle the Portuguese took a proper revenge on the French, a number of whom being cut off treacherously fired before they offered to surrender and they were therefore *all bayoneted on the spot*. Everything is quiet today – Hd Qtrs have returned to St Jean de Luz and there is every chance of our being allowed to remain quiet till Ld Wellington chooses to advance.

I did not mean to say so much as I am writing in a miserable house with *borrowed* pen, ink and paper – but having had a warm by a good fire and some cups of that most refreshing beverage – *tea* – I found myself restored to my usual spirits. I will write to you the first moment after our return to our old quarters, which I hope will be soon – the 1st Brigade have already gone back and we hope to go tomorrow or next day, being only left as advanced here to support the troops at the outposts in case of attack – we are fortifying the heights in our front covering the road and we have sent up to arm the batteries with some of the guns which Marshal Soult was so good as to leave us in his entrenchments in front of the Nivelle. Good night, my dear Father, and give my love to my Mother etc and all my brothers and sisters.

ST PIERRE

Except for a continuous artillery duel, 11 December was a quiet day other than on the front of Hope's corps where at dawn a thick fog enveloped the village of Barrouillet. Arriving there from St Jean, Wellington ordered Hope to regain the ground lost the previous day. Since Soult had ordered Reille to withdraw, this was accomplished without dispute, though when the 9th Foot were later sent forward to reconnoitre the village of Pucho they fell into an ambush and suffered considerable casualties. Soon after noon, however, Soult ordered Reille to drive back the Allies again to Barrouillet. They advanced in force and, catching Hope's unprepared forces, were nearly successful. The tide of battle was, however, again turned and the day ended with the Allies back in their forward positions, the 1st Division relieving the 5th in the first line.

After visiting Hope, Wellington went to oversee the construction of the new pontoon bridge, of seventeen country boats, over the Nive south-west of Villefranque, which would enable him to move troops much more quickly from one front to the other. It was completed by the evening, apparently undetected by the French, and Beresford was warned to be prepared to prevent gunboats coming up the river and interfering with it.

Next day opened with a fierce and prolonged exchange of musketry between the French and the 1st Division. A considerable number of casualties were inflicted on both sides but the fighting abated at mid-day and, except for some skirmishing against Hill's flank and rear, there was little activity. Wellington suspected that Soult meant to switch the bulk of his army to the right bank of the Nive, a suspicion confirmed when Hill saw French forces across the Nive moving into the city. Wellington therefore ordered the 6th and 7th Divisions to be near the pontoon bridge, ready to move to Hill's support next day. Unfortunately heavy rain now swelled the Nive and during the night of the twelfth swept away the pontoon bridge; the older one near Ustarits was saved only by being dismantled.

During the twelfth Hill extended his flank to the Ardour, near Partouhiria, and established a battery to command the river. From Partouhiria his front formed a concave line covering Vieux Mouguerre and Gelos to the Nive. This was held by William Stewart's 2nd Division with Pringle's brigade on the left, Barnes's brigade and Ashworth's Portuguese Brigade in the centre, covering the main road to St Jean Pied de Port and supported by twelve of Hill's fourteen guns. On the right was Byng's brigade and in reserve, behind Barnes, was stationed Lecor's Portuguese Division supported by two guns.

During the night of the twelfth d'Erlon's corps was reinforced by six divisions. Next day the bridge having been swept away, Hill, found himself isolated with 14,000 men and fourteen guns facing d'Erlon's 35,000 men and twenty-two guns. Hill was deployed on a narrow front of three miles but d'Erlon, deploying from the Mousserolles camp, was on a still narrower one and could not make full use of his numerical superiority. There developed during the day some of the heaviest fighting of the Peninsular War, known as the battle of St Pierre.

At first light d'Erlon's columns advanced under cover of an early morning mist and by 8.30 had driven in Hill's outposts with great élan. The full weight of the attack now fell on Ashworth's Portuguese. Barnes sent the 50th to support them but, fighting valiantly, they were forced back, except for the 6th Cacadores who continued to cling to the Hiriberry copse. The 92nd now went to the support of the Portuguese Brigade and, charging uphill, threw back the enemy. The French soon recovered; and Barnes stepped in to steady his men and the centre held.

The flank brigades were now heavily engaged: on the left flank of Barnes's brigade, the 71st gave way; on the extreme right the Buffs, attacked by a brigade, abandoned the dominant but isolated Partouhira ridge. As a result Barnes's flanks were turned, Ashworth and Barnes were wounded and, but for the 6th Cacadores clinging to the Hiriberry copse, Hill's centre would have collapsed.

In this crisis Hill galloped to the 71st and rallied them, ordering them to counter-attack alongside Da Costa's brigade of the Portuguese Division. The 92nd charged, and regained the ground they had lost. Hill now rode to his right flank and ordered the Buffs, who like the 71st were keen to rally and retrieve their regiment's honour, to come under command of Buchan's Portuguese Brigade with the task of retaking the Vieux Mouguerre and Partouria ridges. By mid-day Hill had stabilized his front but had committed the whole of his reserve while only half of d'Erlon's forces had been engaged. But all was not well with the French. Their casualties had been heavy and, lacking space, they had fallen into disorder. The constant stream of fugitives and wounded spread panic among the rear and hindered the deployment of the reserve.

By one o'clock the bridge near Villefranque had been repaired and Wellington passed over with the 6th Division, followed by the 4th Division and a brigade each from the 3rd and 7th Divisions. The Vieux Mouguerre ridge regained, Hill ordered Byng to advance with his whole brigade and take the Ametsonde knoll which dominated the centre of his front. Arriving before it, Byng seized the colours of the 31st and led them to the top of the knoll. The French counter-attacked furiously but were beaten back by the brigade in fierce hand-to-hand fighting. Meanwhile Pringle had advanced the left flank to within half a mile of the Mousserolles camp.

By the time the reinforcing formations arrived the battle was already won. 'It was Lord Hill's own day of glory.' Galloping ahead of the column, the Duke rode up, shook our Chief by the hand and said, "Hill, the day's your own!"[48]

It had been a bloody day. In four days' fighting the French had suffered 6,000 casualties and lost 1,800 Germans – following the desertion of the other battalions, that of Baden had been disbanded. Allied casualties were about 5,000, Hill's on the thirteenth being 1,600. Both sides now went into winter quarters.

For the next two months there was little serious military activity. Soult's main concern was to keep open the Ardour for supplying Bayonne. Three of his divisions were on the north bank of that river, east of Bayonne, and two to the south of it with the task of threatening and harassing Hill's flank and rear from positions behind the Bidouse which flowed from Helette in a north-westerly direction into the Ardour. In the first week in January Soult created alarm by crossing the Bidouse and marching on the Nive with the intention of threatening Hill and chasing his forces away from the Ardour. Wellington broke away from a day's hunting to investigate and ordered the army from its cantonments; the 1st Division left St Jean. However, Soult's advance guard, which had crossed the Joyeuse, was soon driven back and Wellington, who had no intention of bringing on a general action, ordered the troops back to their billets.

It was a winter of quickly alternating spells of fine, crisp, sunny weather with cool, stimulating breezes off the snows of the Pyrenees and torrential rain which at times raised the rivers so far as to maroon the forces of both sides, accompanied by strong gales which hazarded the shipping off the coast. In the small towns and villages outside St Jean de Luz, there was little to entertain the officers or men and a considerable degree of fraternization grew up between the two sides, creating such a *modus vivendi* as sharing watering-places for their horses, bartering tea for brandy, and so on.

St Jean de Luz was a different matter. Sometimes referred to as 'The Paris of the Basques', it was a town of some elegance and had enjoyed great prosperity to which the large number of magnificent merchant houses, many now in decay, bore witness. The town had declined through a combination of natural events, the silting up of the harbour and the erosion of the sea front, against which Napoleon had built a substantial sea wall. The walls of its better houses were still covered with paper from China and Paris, the latter reproducing scenes from paintings by Vernet and Claude.

Under the French Army's occupation, as Larpent, who had been brought there as a prisoner, bore witness, the town had been gay and glittering. Now there were few social occasions, but to encourage friendly relations with the local civilians Wellington persuaded the mayor to issue invitations for a ball to celebrate the Queen's birthday, 18 January. Some forty women attended, of whom six were English and all but one of whom 'declined to dance French dances or the waltzes and there was nothing else but one country dance and that went off ill'. The star turn of the evening appears to have been a middle-aged French policeman who danced a hornpipe! To make up for the shortage of female company, there were present some two hundred officers, including all the field officers of the six battalions of the Guards and about fifty other Guards officers and all the generals and the headquarters staff, 'forming a very smart squeeze'.[49] There was a fashionable daily promenade along the sea wall, between four and six, which was

> ... quite gay, for all the great men of business, up to Lord Wellington himself, generally appear there at that time and the Guards also, though the exertion of walking, which we men of business are used to exercise at a true twopenny postman's long trot, is too great for them, yet they are formed about in knots and groups, sitting on the wall, or gently lounging on it, and though they stop the way very much they add to the gaiety of the scene.[50]

At this time Wellington was still seriously concerned about the affairs of the Coalition. Austria was getting increasingly alarmed by the growing influence of Russia and Prussia. With Austria's dynastic ties with Napoleon, Metternich was prepared to see a Bonapartist peace. The British government was adamant about the restoration of the Bourbons. Wellington would be prepared to accept a Bonapartist peace provided France could be confined within acceptable boundaries. He found among the French a great longing for peace but none for the restoration of the Bourbons. Larpent probably echoed Wellington's views as well as his own when, as a lawyer, he wrote, 'He [Napoleon] has done much for them on a great scale. The Code Napoleon has been a great work, and from what I hear is much liked; instead of being governed, in fact, and oppressed by the rich, as they were before, they are governed by the law, and that a good law.'[51]

Napoleon still hoped to profit through disagreement among the Allies. On 11 December he signed the Treaty of Valençay with Ferdinand VII who, in return for his restoration to the throne of Spain, would eject all British forces from his dominions; French forces would also withdraw. The Treaty was conveyed to the Council of Regency and as a gesture of goodwill Napoleon released Palafox, the national hero of the defence of Zaragoza. Wellington, appraised of this conspiracy, continued to feel concern until he heard that, on 8 January, the Council had refused to ratify the Treaty.

Because of Napoleon's need for troops elsewhere, his dismissal of all his Italian and German units and his belief that Spain was about to switch alliances, Suchet's army was reduced to 28,000, of whom only 15,000 were available to take the field. The efforts of Lieutenant-General Sir William Clinton, commanding the Catalan Allied forces to take advantage of this situation were, however, frustrated by the deliberate dilatoriness of Capon, who favoured the Treaty. On the other hand, when Soult's emissaries expressed surprise to Mina that he did not receive them as allies, Mina stoutly denied all knowledge of the matter, saying that he owed his allegiance to the Duke of Ciudad Rodrigo (Wellington).

Soult tried to get the Basques to organize a guerrilla war against the occupying forces, but with scant success. Wellington was winning the battle for the minds and hearts of the local peasantry who, much to Soult's concern, were voting with their feet to live under Allied occupation in preference to living in the territory occupied by their own army.

The winter had seemed a long one. As usual, Wellington was under pressure from home and from the Allies to do more. On 21 December he wrote to Bathurst, asking him to assure the Russian Ambassador that he would do all that could be done with the force under his command but 'in military operations there are some things that cannot be done, one of these is to move troops during or immediately after a violent fall of rain'.[52]

Wellington had already decided upon his strategy for the coming campaign, which it was hoped would be his last. In February he got down to detailed planning; he was helped by the arrival from the Horse Guards of Colonel Henry Bunbury, who had been sent out to study Wellington's requirements and make financial provision for the 1814 campaign.

CHAPTER SIX

1814
The Finale

ON New Year's Day Blücher crossed the Rhine at the head of a
Russo–Prussian army (75,000 Prussians, 35,000 Russians), while
Prince Schwarzenberg advanced on Paris from the south-east with an
Austrian army of comparable size. In four weeks the Allies penetrated 250
miles into French territory and occupied a third of the country. Ex-King
Joseph was in charge of Paris, with Marmont and Mortier under him.
Napoleon had some 83,000 troops, of whom about 40,000 were under his
direct control, most of them young and inexperienced conscripts.

Napoleon had rejected an Allied proposal for peace on condition that
France returned to her 'natural' frontiers – the Alps, the Pyrenees and the
Rhine – a proposal about which Castlereagh had strong reservations regarding the lower Rhine. On 29 January, before Blücher and Schwarzenberg
could join forces, Napoleon with 18,000 men attacked 30,000 of Blücher's
men, driving them from Brienne. Two days later the Allied armies were
virtually united and Blücher drove the French from La Rothière. Napoleon
was now outnumbered by four to one and was contemplating seeking the best
terms he could when the Allied armies again diverged. Blücher continued his
march on Paris along the Marne, while Schwarzenberg took his army up the
Seine toward Bar-sur-Seine and Sens, thus presenting Napoleon with an
opportunity he was not slow to take.

Turning first against Blücher's three widely separated corps, Napoleon
almost annihilated a Russian corps at Champaubert on 10 February, won a
further victory at Montmirail the next day, fought at Château-Thierry on the
twelfth, and defeated Blücher yet again on the fourteenth at Vauchamp. In all,
between 10 and 14 February Napoleon inflicted 17,000 casualties and captured a considerable quantity of artillery. Having halted Blücher's advance,
he now turned against the Austrians whom he defeated at Montereau on the
seventeenth, re-entering Troyes on the twenty-fourth. The Allies asked for an
armistice and again offered peace on the basis of France's 'natural' frontiers,
but the fighting continued.

On 21 February, Wellington renewed his advance into southern France,
and a week later Blücher continued his march towards Paris. Napoleon
harassed Blücher's left flank and with only half his strength attacked him at
Craonne on 7 March and at Laon on 9–10 March. Both battles being
indecisive. Time for Napoleon was running out and on 9 March, for the first

time in more than twenty years of war, his opponents signed an undertaking to continue the war until he capitulated. Castlereagh also obtained an agreement that the terms of peace should include the reduction of France to her 1792 boundaries, thus freeing the Netherlands.

On 12 March, Beresford, detached by Wellington, entered Bordeaux, the second city of France, accompanied by the Duc d'Angoulême, and the mayor of Bordeaux immediately declared for Louis Bourbon. On the twentieth Napoleon attacked the Austrians again – 23,000 men against 60,000 – at Arcis-sur-Aube, but failed to halt their advance towards Paris. On the thirtieth the Allies were before its gates with 110,000 men, while within Marmont and Mortier commanded 20,000, mostly National Guardmen. Next day the Russian and Prussian artillery was deployed on Montmartre, from where it dominated the city. The city capitulated and Joseph fled, though Marmont fought on skilfully until 4 April.

The Tsar and the Allied commanders entered in triumph on 1 April. Talleyrand called the Senate together and persuaded them to depose Napoleon and the Allies to accept the restoration of the Bourbons in the person of Louis XVIII. Meanwhile 'the great disturber' was at Fontainebleau. He still had some 60,000 men, and decided to march on Paris, but when he put his plan to his marshals they – led by Ney – refused to support him. On Marmont's surrender the Allies demanded Napoleon's unconditional surrender. This he agreed on 6 April. He signed his abdication on the twelfth and that night took a dose of poison so strong that he vomited it up. On the twentieth the Allied commissioners came to take him to Elba and he took a moving farewell of the Old Guard from the steps of the Palace of Fontainebleau. The long years of war were over and on 7 April messengers left Paris with the proclamation of peace, too late unfortunately to prevent bloodshed by Wellington's men in the battle of Toulouse and in repulsing a sortie from Bayonne.

Meanwhile it is appropriate to turn to a more detailed consideration of events in the south of France.

In the south Soult, as well as Suchet, had had to yield experienced men to Napoleon and to lose his foreign corps. This left him in February with 37,000 infantry, 3, 840 cavalry and forty-three guns besides the 11,000 garrison of Bayonne; Wellington credited him with having considerably more. Convinced that the passage of the Ardour below Bayonne was impracticable and that Wellington would attempt to cross the river above the city, Soult deployed his forces to take in flank any such attempt. Abbé with his division was made responsible for the immediate defence of the city for which, including the garrison, he had some 16,000 men. On the north side of the Ardour, as far east as Port de Lannes, Soult deployed three divisions . He deployed his remaining four divisions south of the Ardour behind its tributary, the Joyeuse, a line which his cavalry extended to St Jean Pied de Port, where the French were in contact with Mina's Spaniards, now constituted as a regular brigade.

Wellington, having resumed command of the Spanish forces, had ordered Freyre's corps of 9,000 forward to Ascains. In February the Anglo–Portuguese army numbered 70,000 supported by ninety-four guns and Wellington had a call on 30,000 Spanish troops. To take Bayonne by assault would be a bloody and hazardous business, requiring the whole resources of the army. Keeping to his aim of destroying Soult's army, Wellington had detached Hope's corps of 28,000 to invest Bayonne, for which he at last had enough artillery and engineer resources. This left him with a field army of 42,000 infantry and 3,000 cavalry organized into two corps under Beresford and Hill. This he would use to turn Soult's right on successive river lines, manoeuvring Soult away from Bayonne where Hope would bridge the Ardour below the city, and set siege to it.

Wellington had complained frequently to the Admiralty of the inadequate protection given to the shipping on which he relied for reinforcements and supplies, but he maintained good relations with the local squadron and during the winter Commodore Sir George Colville had taken every opportunity to see the army in action; unfortunately, as he complained, whenever he advanced the French retreated! At the beginning of February Colville was relieved by Rear-Admiral Charles Penrose, who was immediately invited by Wellington to a conference at St Jean, which would set in motion detailed planning for the intricate joint service operation to bridge the lower Ardour. Because little bloodshed was involved and because peace was declared before the battering guns had opened on the city, this extremely interesting and imaginative piece of planning and inter-service co-operation has received less attention than it deserves, but since John Aitchison was closely concerned in its execution it is worth mentioning.

Wellington now waited for favourable weather. The opening event of the 1814 campaign came on 14 February when Hope deployed his corps forward to a line from Biarritz, then a small village, to the Nive. Beresford's corps was in the centre. On the right Hill's corps moved east to drive Soult's right wing from the Joyeuse and Bidouse, tributaries of the Ardour.

On the sixteenth Beresford marched against Bidache and Hill took St Palais, further up that river. Soult now established a line behind the Gave d'Oloron and lower Saison, leaving the garrison of Bayonne shut up in isolation. The Allies advanced against the new French line on the eighteenth but the weather broke, suspending all operations. Wellington set out in a snowstorm for St Jean to review the progress of the plans for investing Bayonne.

The problems that had to be solved before the 1st Division could be established on the far bank of the Ardour and connected by a bridge that would later have to take the siege train and accompanying engineer stores were numerous, technical and daunting. There was also a military problem for, although Hope originally had 25,000 men, after 27 February he was reduced to 15,000; these were split in three ways by the Ardour and the Nive, enabling the 11,000 garrison, with their excellent internal communications to concentrate superior forces for a sortie against any one sector.

Bayonne on the south side of the Ardour was covered on the north bank of the river by the Citadel of St Esprit. A square fort with 120-yard sides occupying a height from which it commanded both the Ardour and the bridge which carried the main road to the north and requiring, according to Aitchison, a garrison of 4,000. Below this bridge were anchored the sloop of war *Sappho* and a few gunboats. Wellington planned to invest the city and pass the 1st Division and his siege train across the lower Ardour. They would then complete the investment of the city and set up battering guns on the right bank of the river.

It was not unreasonable for the French to believe it impossible to bridge the Ardour below the city. The river here was 300 yards wide, deep and with a swift current which, in times of heavy rains and when the snow melted in the spring, became a torrent. It was subject also to tidal changes, with a rise and fall at spring tides of fourteen feet. Below the city it ran between high retaining walls twelve feet thick whose top was fourteen feet above the river with a drop of ten feet on the land side. There was an entrance, whose buoys had been removed, through a shifting shingle bar at the entrance to the estuary, over which the sea broke in great confusion when the wind was onshore. The approaches to the left bank were sandy but beyond the wall on the far side was a marsh.

It was at once obvious to the planners that no ordinary pontoon bridge would solve their problem. They would have to improvise a special bridge from local material. As a general concept they selected a site two and a half miles below the city bridge round a bend in the river which would hide the new bridge from the defenders. This site would be a mile and a half from the sea leaving room to moor from 200–300 transports below it. The bridge would need to be protected by two lines of flexible booms laid in parallel above it to prevent fireships and other craft being used to destroy it. These booms would have to be protected in turn by a battery on each side of the river, and by having rowing boats with grappling irons permanently manned and ready to intercept any craft approaching the booms.

As for the bridge itself, it would be constructed of decked vessels of from thirty to fifty tons burden (chasse-marées), anchored head and stern at thirty-foot intervals, from centre to centre. Since there was insufficient timber to build a wooden bridge, it was decided to construct five lines of cable, out of sixteen thirteen-inch cables provided by the Navy, which would span the river from bank to bank and be secured to each of the boats. To anchor the cables at each end and to keep them taut under all tide conditions presented a special problem. On the near side of the river the cables would be anchored to a long wooden frame, buried in the sand and held in position by sixty tons of sandbags at the end furthest from the river. The far end would be anchored by attaching to each an eighteen-pounder gun, each weighing two tons. These would be hoisted over the wall and allowed to bury themselves in the marsh. To adjust the tension on the cables, to allow for stretching and the rise and fall of the tide, capstans would be set up on the near bank.

Twenty-five to thirty chasse-marées would be required, but to guard against accidents Admiral Penrose undertook to hire forty-eight; likewise, five eighteen-pounders would be required for the cables but ten would be available. So Coa became a hive of industry. Here the flotilla of chasse-marées and the engineer and special stores they were to carry were prepared and assembled. The frame for anchoring the bridge and the booms for hoisting out the eighteen-pounders over the sea wall were prepared and shipped. The Royal Sappers and Miners, artificers from the Guards and those of the Royal Staff Corps, together with large working parties, provided by the Royal Navy, worked under the direction of Elphinstone.

The laying of two flexible booms was the responsibility of the Royal Navy and these were carried on two transports and a sloop. Each chasse-marée was loaded with engineer stores. Ten of them each carried an eighteen-pounder gun and the means for hoisting them out over the sea wall. Six additional ships were loaded with the capstans and other stores for anchoring the bridge on the near side of the river. Each chasse-marée had on board two Royal Sappers and Miners. They were told off in five divisions, each under an Engineer officer. After the commanding Engineer had decided the exact site for the bridge, specific engineer officers were made responsible for the boats being anchored in the right place and for anchoring the cables at each end of the bridge. The flotilla of chasse-marées would put to sea under the command of Captain Dowell O'Reilly R.N. of the *Lyra,* who was reponsible for the navigation until they were within the Ardour. Admiral Penrose in the *Porcupine*, a twenty-four gun frigate, with the *Lyra* brig and five gunboats would give naval gunfire support.

Preparations were going ahead well when, on 13 February, a freak storm threw up such a bank of shingle at the mouth of the Nivelle that it was impossible for any vessels to enter or leave it. Fatigue parties of Guardsmen were employed for several days digging a channel to let the boats through. When Wellington returned to St Jean to review the plans he decided on 20 February as the day for crossing the Ardour, but another violent storm again prevented the boats getting out. Fearing that his prolonged absence from the front would be noticed by the French, and disclose his intentions, he returned to the field army, leaving the conduct of the investment to Hope.

The preliminary moves were to be made by the 5th Division, east of the Nive, and Campbell's Portuguese Brigade and Aylmer's brigade west of the Nive, driving the French within their fortified camps. The naval flotilla would take at least sixteen hours to arrive off the mouth of the Ardour and by that time it was necessary to have established a force on the far side of the river and to have sunk or driven the French sloop and gunboats up the river out of range.

The 1st Division turned left off the road before reaching Anglet, and under cover of night advanced across-country through the pine woods to arrive on the banks of the Ardour without being detected. Here, by daylight, the 1st Guards Brigade had established themselves with a battery of four eighteen-pounders. The 2nd Guards Brigade, including the 3rd Guards, remained in sand dunes under cover of the pine woods as did the King's German Legion who were to follow them across the river.

The eighteen-pounder battery was to cover the crossing but had, as its first task, in conjunction with the rocket troop, the destruction or driving up-river of the French naval flotilla. A portable furnace has been brought forward and attempts were made, without success, to set the *Sappho* on fire with red-hot shot, but the vessels were driven off as required, with the rockets, as one artilleryman described it, 'skipping about the water like mad things and dancing quadrilles in every direction but the right one'.[1]

The pontoons from Bidart failed to appear but five with the division were dragged forward by artillery horses. Since these and the four jolly-boats were the sole means of crossing there was a pause during which the French were driven from Anglet and the rest of the wood and confined to their fortified camp. Finding that the enemy had only a small picquet on the far bank, Hope decided at 11 a.m. to make the crossing with the slender means at his disposal. Fifty men of the Light Company were ferried across in the jolly-boats and a hawser was stretched across the river and secured. The pontoons were formed into rafts but were not used until 2 p.m. as it was still hoped that the remainder of the pontoons would come up (they arrived at midnight and were used as boats). It was now past slack water and the 3rd Guards started crossing in difficult circumstances because of the strong current. What occurred is best told in John Aitchison's diary.

Diary
23rd February 1814

The division having made a night march which began at 9 o'clock, arrived before daybreak on the banks of the Ardour near its mouth where we were detained three hours for the pontoons which, stuck in the sand, could not be drawn out by *20 horses.*

The 3 row boats attached to them were therefore taken off the carriages and carried by men forward to the river, where no enemy having seen this were launched about 7 o'clock and preparations made for crossing. The Brigade of Guards which headed the column moved by its left, and it thus fell to the 3rd Regt to cross after the Light Infantry. No opposition was made but at about 3 o'clock notice was brought to us that the enemy were marching troops out of the Citadel of Bayonne, apparently for the purpose of attacking us, and every exertion was therefore made to send over men to the assistance of the Lt Company. But the current of the river from the influx of the tide had become so strong that only 4 companies had been got across by $\frac{1}{2}$ past 5, at which hour the enemy began an attack with about 1,500 Infantry, in 3 columns – only the centre one came into action, which however obliged our Lt Company to retire which they effected in admirable order – closing to their flanks as they came near to the four companies which were drawn up in line. Supported by two small batteries of 10 Rockets each.[2]

The enemy advanced without skirmishers and their column were so annoyed by ours that their men became unsteady and fired even from the front of the column which had reached within a 100 yards of our line when the Pickets opened the bonnet, and our 8th company having at the same instant fired a volley, they halted where confounded and fled. The Light Infantry immediately advanced and the Rockets also and firing with elevation had a terrific appearance, it being by this time nearly dark.

The whole of the Guards were got over in the course of the night and part of the German Legion. Cold very severe – keen frost. Slept on the sand which we dug into 6 inches for warmth. Got a small fire from wood cut off some transport *that had been wrecked here.*

Light and contrary winds held back the naval flotilla until the twenty-fourth when it blew hard on shore, driving a heavy sea before it and raising a high and turbulent surf on the bar, which made it very difficult to locate the shifting and unbuoyed channel into the Ardour. John Aitchison's diary for that day records:

24th February 1814

The weather all yesterday having been windy and dead off shore, the fleet of boats which were to form a bridge could not come in, but this morning they were close to the shore at the mouth of the Ardour but they could not discover the entrance to it, owing to the high surf. Towards 8 o'clock Captain O'Reilly of the Royal Navy, in charge of the fleet, approached the shore with the pilot in a long boat to find out the place to enter, but failing he determined to land at all hazards, and accordingly hauled down sail and pulled straight for the shore. But unfortunately the sea struck the boat and upset her – driving her at the same time on the beach, from which accident one artillery man and three sailors were drowned. A smaller boat with a Midshipman and 4 hands was more lucky and ran through the surf in safety for the shore, from whence she was dragged across to the bank of the Ardour and launched in it. The entrance was soon found out and marks put up for the boats which began to enter, notwithstanding the tremendous surf. The whole got in within the course of the day. This arduous operation was not performed without loss and 3 boats floundered, all hands on them perishing and several men were killed in a gunboat and two others which were stranded.[3]

We lay upon our arms all day but were not molested by the enemy, and in the afternoon occupied Le Boucau, a small village half a mile from our ferry. Regular gangs of Rowers for the boats [were] turned out by the brigade, and were employed incessantly bringing out stores etc. A boom moored across the river to stop any fire vessels being sent down upon our boats. Weather fine and clear.

25th Feby. Moved forward to the high road leading to Bayonne and bivouacked in an open wood. The bridge begun, to be formed of boats, generally of 20 tons (declared) and ropes.

26th – remained in our camp, we got our baggage across the river by swimming the animals.

Bad weather held up the arrival of the Navy with the ships to form the bridge, so Hope started ferrying men across. By the evening of 24 February the whole of the 1st Division was across the river. The sappers worked throughout the night and by noon on the twenty-fifth the bridge was reported passable and many troops and some guns crossed over. At the same time the Navy had been constructing two flexible booms, which were completed shortly after the bridge. 'A battery of 18 pdrs was thrown up on each bank of the river to sweep the approach to the boom and four gunboats were stationed on its flanks; whilst row boats with fire grapplings were kept constantly manned in readiness to meet and anchor any fire or other vessel that might be drifted down the stream, and lighter boats plied in observation higher up the stream.'[4]

Throughout these proceedings the 5th Division east of the Nive and Aylmer's brigade and Campbell's Portuguese Brigade west of the Nive kept up a fire on the city's defences. Freyre's Spanish corps moved forward to Anglet and remained in reserve. A reconnaissance on the twenty-sixth disclosed that the French had been busy constructing outworks to the citadel. These consisted of four redoubts about 500 yards from and connected to the citadel by covered ways. They in turn were covered by strong points in the villages of Montegut, St Etienne and St Esprit, but were not completed. During the day Campbell's and Bradford's Portuguese Brigades were brought over the north bank and the following day, after noon, a converging attack on St Etienne was carried out by three columns. The 1st Brigade of Guards comprised the left, the 2nd Brigade of Guards and the King's German Legion the centre, and a Portuguese Brigade the right-hand column. The enemy were strongly posted but the village was cleared and two counter-attacks mounted to recover a gun taken by the King's German Legion were beaten off. Allied casualties were about 400, 300 of these being sustained by the five battalions of the German Legion.

John Aitchison recorded in his diary, 'After cooking, moved a little forward to the ground occupied by the Legion, which advanced and attacked the village of St Etienne, which was carried after a severe resistance and our posts established in it at 300 yards' distance from the enemy's fortified camp. Heard of Lord W. having gained a victory at Orthez.

North of the river the investing forces now held a line centred on St Etienne, with its right on the Ardour at the mill of St Bernard and its left on that river some 2,000 yards above the suburb of St Esprit. A sunken road parallel to their front was turned into an effective covered way for the picquet line, by means of traverses, etc, and was never forced. Leaving Sir John Hope to get on with the investment of Bayonne and the preparations of plans for its siege, we must return with Wellington to the main front.

The countryside between Bayonne and Bordeaux was largely barren and incapable of supporting an army, so Soult withdrew eastwards, taking up positions on successive river lines. Wellington followed up on 24 February with Beresford's corps on the left and Hill's on the right. That day Hill turned Soult's position on the Gave d'Oloron and the French withdrew across the Gave de Pau, blowing up the bridges except for those at Berenx and Orthez, which they mined.

Hill followed up on the road to Orthez and on the twenty-sixth, unknown to Soult, Beresford crossed the Gave de Pau by pontoon bridge near Peyrehorade and marched towards Orthez. As soon as Soult learnt of Beres-

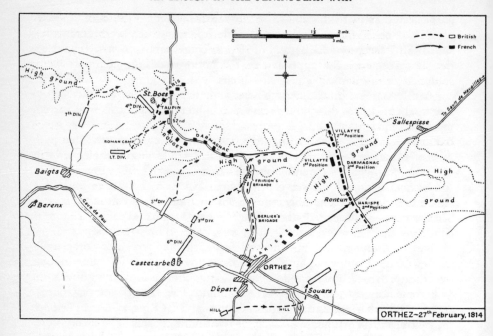

ORTHEZ~27th February, 1814

ford's move he concentrated his force of 36,000 men and forty-eight guns and deployed them in a naturally strong position on a ridge north-east of Orthez across which ran the Orthez–Dax road. A number of steep-sided spurs, with deep coombs between, provided excellent positions from which to enfilade any force moving along the ridge. The westerly spur ended in an eminence crowned by a Roman camp, from where Wellington directed the battle.

Wellington had about the same number of men and rather fewer guns. He ordered Hill to demonstrate from the south side of the river towards Orthez and to find a way over to turn Soult's right flank when the time was ripe. This he eventually did at Souars. Beresford was to attack the right of the French line (Reille) at St Boes with the 4th Division supported by the 7th Division. The 3rd Division, supported by the 6th Division, was to demonstrate against Soult's centre (d'Erlon) by way of the centre spur. The Light Division was in reserve with Wellington at the Roman camp.

About 9 a.m. Cole's 4th Division attacked St Boes and carried it against stiff resistance. They were then held by devastating artillery fire and, after three hours' fighting, were pushed out of St Boes. The 3rd and 6th Divisions fared little better against the centre. The battle seemed to be going in favour of the enemy. Wellington now saw that, in pushing back the 4th Division, Reille had opened a gap between his forces and d'Erlon's. Into this gap he sent the Cacadores of the Light Division and when they were held he sent in the 52nd.

Meanwhile Inglis's brigade of the 7th Division had advanced through the 4th Division, formed under very heavy fire, and charged. D'Erlon's centre gave way and by prodigious effort the British artillery was brought up the hill and for the first time the French fire could be kept in check. The 52nd now got across the Dax road and raked the right flank of Reille's left-hand division while the 3rd Division assaulted its left flank. The division broke and retired and the panic spread to Reille's centre. D'Erlon withdrew his corps eastwards, taking up a position across the Sault de Navailles road behind which Reille's corps could rally.

Here Clausel's corps came to extend the left of the position. Hill now crossed the river through Souars and came up on the left flank of the French position which was attacked by the whole of Wellington's force and by six o'clock the whole French line was in disorderly retreat towards the next river line, the Luy de Bearn. The country was unfavourable to cavalry, and in addition Wellington's sword was struck by a spent bullet, severely bruising his hip and striking him to the ground. He remounted but was in great pain and but for this accident the pursuit might have been more strongly pressed. Despite great confusion, Soult got his forces across the Luy de Bearn by nightfall with the loss of 4,000 men, more than 1,000 being prisoners.

Soult now moved north to St Sever on the Ardour. Here he was faced with the choice of retiring toward Bordeaux or Toulouse – he did not have sufficient troops to cover both. As Bordeaux was the second city of France its port would be of great value to the Allies. On the other hand it was known to be strongly anti-Bonapartist and the countryside was barren and incapable of supporting an army; such a move, too, would preclude the possibility of uniting his forces with Suchet's. Soult therefore decided to withdraw towards Toulouse.

Wellington, following up, was faced with a similar decision. Bordeaux would be a glittering political prize and he had received a communication from within the city that if he were to send 3,000 men the city would declare for the Bourbons. His aim remained that of destroying Soult's army but such an opportunity could not be ignored and he decided to send Beresford with the 4th and 7th Divisions, 12,000 men, accompanied by the Duc d'Angoulême. This left him with about 29,000 with which to pursue Soult, who he feared might already have received 10,000 reinforcements from Suchet. He therefore decided that he must bring up Freyre's Spanish corps; he also wanted to see how the operations against Bayonne were progressing so, halting the army, he went to St Jean with a letter to Freyre saying that his men would receive the same pay as the British forces and be rationed by them to whatever extent was necessary, after taking into consideration what was available in the Spanish depots.

At St Jean he held a conference to agree the steps necessary for forwarding the siege of Bayonne. Historians express surprise at the apparently languid pace of these operations but bringing forward the necessary artillery and engineer stores from Passages was a major administrative operation. In addition, Wellington had allowed all the gun platforms built for the siege during the winter to be used up in building the bridge over the Ardour. When asked how they were to be replaced he had replied, 'Make new ones out of the pine woods near Bayonne'[5] – a time-consuming task. On 7 March, Wellington approved and signed the detailed orders for the siege.

For the first time there were adequate artillery and engineer resources for conducting a siege. For the siege twenty-six 24-pdrs, twelve eight-inch howitzers and twenty coehorn (four and two-fifths inches) mortars were to be brought from Passages to St Jean, where they would be disembarked and dragged forward by 700 artillery horses.

Ammunition for eight days' firing would also be brought to St Jean. Half would be moved by road, while the other half together with half the engineer stores would be kept afloat in the Ardour. There were 39,000 rounds of artillery ammunition and 4,050 barrels each containing ninety pounds of powder. The ammunition and engineer store depots were established at Le Boucau on the north bank of the Ardour.

Soult was left in peace for ten days while Freyre's corps came up, accompanied it is supposed by the rocket troop. Beresford and the Duc d'Angoulême entered Bordeaux in triumph on 12 March, amidst an outbreak of white cockades. Wellington ordered the 4th Division to rejoin him and, following up Soult, he nearly trapped him on the 17th in a 'short but wonderfully fierce and violent' fight at Tarbes on the upper Ardour. No longer able to stand up to Wellington in the field and having received no co-operation from Suchet, Soult shut up his army in Toulouse.

TOULOUSE

On 19 February Wellington renewed his march. Beresford's corps was sent to Bordeaux, while Hill on the right wing advanced through Samadet and on 1 March encountered the French rearguard at Aire in an untidy affair in very wet weather. Soult now withdrew to a strong position at Tarbes where Wellington, having been reinforced by Freyre's Spanish corps and the return of the 4th Division, hoped to trap him. Soult escaped the trap but, despairing of getting the better of Wellington in the field, shut up his army in Toulouse.

Wellington's advance guard came in sight of Toulouse on 26 March. The city stood on the east bank of the Garonne, a wide and at times swift-flowing river, with only the fortified suburb of St Cyprien on the west bank. The Languedoc Canal, which entered the Garonne below the city, circled it to the north, then, bending south through the eastern suburbs, ran more or less parallel to the Garonne. The main road south from the city to Carcassonne via Villefranche ran between the two. Further east, running south to north and parallel with the canal, was the smaller but unfordable River Ers.

Toulouse was an important arsenal surrounded by ancient walls and battlements. The key to the city was a long ridge running down its eastern side and extending some 2,000 yards north and south of the city walls, called the Rave or heights of Calvinet. Towards its northern end was a sharp declivity, carrying a road, and beyond this the hill of Pujarde. Once an assailant had mounted artillery on the ridge, the city would be at his mercy. Soult had been employing forced labour to improve the defences and the main Calvinet ridge was crowned by four strong redoubts. Between the foot of the ridge and the Ers was a narrow strip of land, the northern half of which was marshy, and the southern part ploughed.

Soult, who had some 42,000 men and the National Guard, supported by about eighty cannon, of which half were of heavy calibre in permanent

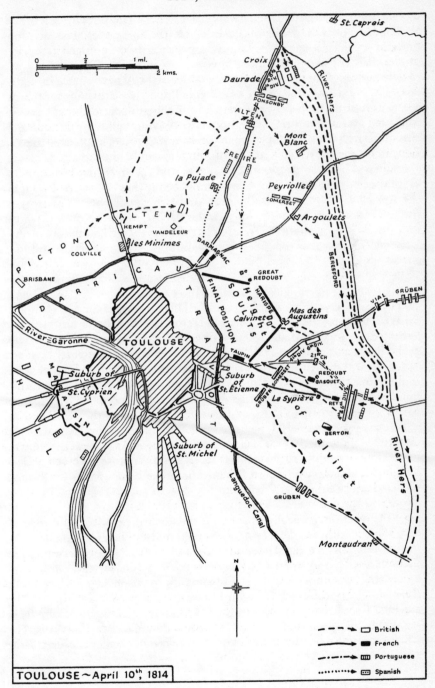

TOULOUSE ~ April 10th, 1814

emplacements, deployed four divisions, more than half his force, in defence of the Calvinet ridge and hill of Pujarde. Of the remainder, one division defended St Cyprien, one the canal covering the northern approach to the city and another, consisting largely of raw recruits, lined the city walls.

Soult enjoyed great tactical advantages. The city was unassailable from the west. To take it from the south would entail two river crossings for which there was insufficient bridging material, so Wellington decided that he must mount his assault from the north and east. Leaving Hill with the 2nd and Portuguese Divisions (12,000 men) to threaten St Cyprien, he planned to pass the remainder of the Allied Army across the Garonne below the city. This was no easy task, because the weather was foul and the river high. A pontoon bridge was, however, got across eleven miles below the city, and on the night of 4 April 18,000 men (three divisions and two cavalry brigades) crossed without opposition. Next day flood water carried away the bridge, which could not be restored until the eighth. For three days Soult had the opportunity to concentrate vastly superior forces against the Allies east of the Garonne, but did nothing.

The bridge restored, Wellington proceeded to deploy 32,000 men facing the city from the north. Picton's 3rd Division was on the right, and Alten's Light Division between the Garonne and the hill of Pujarde. Immediately north of that hill was Freyre's Spanish Corps and on his left towards the north, across the bridge of Croix Daurade over the River Ers, was Beresford's corps of two cavalry brigades, the 4th and 6th Divisions and a Portuguese infantry Brigade.

Wellington's plan, timed for first light on the tenth, was for Hill to make a holding attack on St Cyprien and Picton to threaten the line of the canal, while Freyre and Beresford would respectively take the hill of Pujarde and the Calvinet ridge. The Spaniards would attack the hill from the north-east as soon as Beresford was ready to attack the ridge from the south-east.

Beresford's task meant that he had to make a long march across the front of and in close proximity to the enemy. Its hazardous nature was well understood by Wellington who wrote, in a memorandum composed in 1838 when Gurwood was editing his dispatches:

'The position, naturally strong, was the strongest that could be formed by all the additional defence that art could devise. The canal could not be attacked by main force. The country beyond the Ers has been reconnoitred and it was found impossible to manoeuvre on it, for the purpose of repairing or forming new bridges with a view to the passage of the river. It was necessary to march between Mount Calvinet and the River Ers, the distance not being greater from the works on its summit, anywhere from 2,000 yards, diminishing to 1,000 yards and in places to 500 yards. The distance (to be traversed) was less than two miles under the fire of the enemy's position.'[6]

Beresford's march was greatly slowed by the boggy nature of the ground, across which it was impossible to take his field guns though the Rocket Troop carried their light equipment forward. The field batteries were therefore deployed to give distant covering fire, and it is thought that their opening fire, as well as the Spaniards' thirst for glory, may have led to Freyre launching his attack long before the 4th and 6th Divisions had reached their forming-up positions. Accounts of the Spaniards' action vary according to the prejudices of the authors, but all are agreed upon the gallantry with which the first attack was carried out.

Freyre's first attack was met with musket fire not only from the hill of Pujarde but from his right flank, under which the advance wavered and the French Voltigeurs advanced and poured fire into the Spaniards struggling up the slope of the hill so that they broke, leaving upwards of 1,000 casualties behind them. After this first attack the Light Division was moved to a position to support the Spaniards. While Beresford's men were laboriously marching for two miles across the front of the enemy in deep mud and under continuous artillery fire, Gruben's cavalry brigade of the King's German Legion was sent wide to the east to take the Pont de Balma and then move south to cover Beresford's left flank during the assault on the Calvinet ridge. Beresford's movement took several hours to complete and his troops became dangerously strung out. By the time Cole's 4th Division had reached their forming-up place near the Château d'Ers, Clinton's 6th Division was an hour's march behind. Soult had been able to watch this movement throughout and as soon as Beresford's intention became clear he sent Taupin's division to reinforce the right, ordering it to remain concealed behind the ridge. Soult's plan was to surprise and overwhelm the tired Allied force with fresh troops, numerically superior, striking from a commanding position with strong artillery support. While the French infantry would charge downhill at Cole's men struggling up the steep grassy slope of the ridge, slippery after rain, the French cavalry would attack both flanks.

Taupin led the French charge down the slope. Long subjected to an ordeal by fire, weary and momentarily surprised, the 4th Division nevertheless closed their ranks and stood firm as a rock. The front rank quietly loaded, took steady aim and poured a devastating volley into the French column. It was to be the last demonstration in the Peninsular War of the superiority of Wellington's line over Napoleon's columns. Taupin fell, pierced by three bullets. Meanwhile the two supporting lines had formed square on their flanks to repulse the cavalry whose attacks on the right, because of sunken road, never went home. The discomfiture of the French was completed by the Rocket Troop who put them to flight with their rockets, 'weapons', in Napier's words, 'whose noise and dreadful aspect were unknown before'.[7]

Repulsed, the French turned and we so hotly pursued up the steep, slippery slope that they were tumbled out of the southern redoubt, La Sypière, before they could rally. Soult now withdrew his right so that it rested on the central redoubts of the Calvinet ridge and short secondary ridge between it and the canal. Beresford's corps was now formed in line, the 6th Division having come up in line on the right of the 4th Division. About 2.30 p.m., around the time that Freyre's second attack went in, Beresford launched Pack's brigade of the 6th Division against the central Augustins and Colombette redoubts. These were carried by the 42nd and 79th Highlanders, but with heavy losses.

Fighting stubbornly, the French retook both, only to be thrown out again by the 91st, from Pack's brigade, and the 11th from Lambert's in the same division.

Beresford now controlled three-quarters of the ridge and though Freyre's attack again failed and his men rallied only with the personal intervention of Wellington, Soult withdrew to the secondary feature already mentioned, without awaiting an assault on the great redoubt at the northern end of the ridge. The battle of Toulouse had been won. The town would be at Wellington's mercy as soon as the artillery could be dragged to the crest of the ridge. The losses had been severe – Allied casualties are estimated at 4,500 and Soult admitted 3,236. Of Freyre's Spaniards, 2,000 were dead or wounded. Picton, going beyond his orders and attempting an assault across the canal – some say because he was Picton and some that he was relieving the pressure on the Spaniards – suffered 400 casualties. He was to repeat this action later in the day. The heaviest losses fell on the four British battalions of the 6th Division assaulting the redoubts, in which action the 42nd lost nearly three-quarters of their strength.

Next day, while Wellington was getting supplies and ammunition to invest the city, Soult, who had sent a message to Suchet suggesting that they join forces, was planning to slip out of the city and make for Villefranche. This he did during the night of the eleventh, leaving behind 1,600 wounded. Next afternoon, Wellington entered the city at the head of the Allied Army by a route unexpected by the civic dignitaries.

An hour later, while Wellington was changing for dinner, Colonel Frederick Ponsonby galloped in from Bordeaux with the news of Napoleon's abdication. Like Bordeaux, Toulouse had always been a centre of Royalist sentiment. That evening the mayor gave a great civic banquet.

At Orthez and at Toulouse Wellington had divided his forces and presented the enemy with opportunies to defeat him in detail. This, however, was a well-calculated risk based on the moral ascendancy which the Allied troops had established over the French and upon the proven indecisiveness of Soult as a commander in the field. Nevertheless, it is astonishing that Soult made no attempt to destroy Beresford's corps as it plodded its way through the deep mud marching across the French front, hemmed in between the Calvinet ridge and the Ers. Armchair critics point to the retribution that such tactics would have exacted from Napoleon. This is to miss the point; no-one had a greater respect for the Emperor's generalship than Wellington – witness his remarks after the close-run battle of Fuentes de Oñoro – and had Napoleon been in command the Duke's tactics would, undoubtedly, have varied accordingly.

The bloodshed was not yet over. Thouvenot, governor of Bayonne, who had remained passive throughout the city's long investment, heard on the thirteenth an unconfirmed report of Napoleon's abdication and for some inexplicable reason decided to launch a sortie from the citadel at 3 a.m. that very dark night. Three French columns left the citadel: the right-hand one rushed the village of St Etienne and carried all but one of the houses, which was stoutly defended by men of the 38th Foot of Hay's brigade of the 5th Division; the centre column overwhelmed the picquets of the 3rd Guards and drove back those of the Coldstream, exposing the flank of the 1st Guards Brigade, who were already being engaged by the enemy's left-hand column.

Taken by surprise, the British were in a serious situation for a time – Major-General Andrew Hay was killed, Lieutenant-General Sir John Hope was wounded and captured and Major-General Edward Stopford was also wounded. Major-General Kenneth Howard took over from Hope and Colonel Guise took command of the 2nd Guards Brigade from Stopford, which brigade counter-attacked almost simultaneously with attacks made by Hay's brigade and the King's German Legion on St Etienne. The darkness, which had at first favoured the French, hindered them in exploiting their success and, according to John Aitchison, 'The enemy were driven back and our picquets re-established by 8 a.m.'. This unnecessary adventure cost the Allies 838 and the French 905 casualties. The 3rd Guards had thirty-five rank and file killed and Captains White, Schiffner, Mahon and Holbourne mortally wounded.

On 25 March, Aitchison had estimated the effective strength of the Anglo-Portuguese forces blockading and besieging Bayonne as 10,600. There were in addition 3,400 Spaniards and, presumably, about 900 ordnance troops (Royal Artillery and Royal Engineers) of which he makes no mention – say 14,900 in all. His estimate of the French garrison was 16,000, of whom 3,000 or 4,000 were supposed sick.

Soult was reluctant to accept reports of Napoleon's abdication and it was not until the seventeenth that an armistice was arranged. News of this only reached the governor of Bayonne on the twenty-seventh, when he surrendered the garrison.

After twenty-one years of almost continuous war France had a great preponderance of young women in her population, a situation the Allied troops were only too willing to take advantage of as the whole country gave itself over to celebrating the peace. Wellington's army, so long drilled in being ever ready to turn out and march at a moment's notice, took a little time to adjust to the security of peace. Nearly all longed for home, while at the same time taking full advantage of the social opportunities offered by a population which had long yearned for peace. The day after the occupation of Toulouse, Larpent records, 'The whole conversation of officers turns upon half-pay and starvation.' The gaunt spectre of peace was beginning to emerge for the less well-off officers and for the rank and file, many of whom had come from the gutter and would find no alternative but to return there. Another part of the army which, as the day for the British troops' departure drew near, and unromantic bureaucracy would neither allow their embarkation nor acknowledge any obligation toward them, saw peace as unmitigated calamity, were the hundreds of camp followers, Spanish and Portuguese women, many with children, who had suffered and slaved, loved and plundered for their fighting men and were shortly to be abandoned in an alien land.

Not all who longed for home were to go there, for the American war continued. Still larger numbers were to be left in peace for less than a year before being reunited with their old commanders under the Duke for that epic finish to the great Napoleonic adventure, the battle of Waterloo.

John Aitchison was to take part in neither adventure. At the end of June the

3rd Guards moved from Bayonne to the beautiful city of Bordeaux, where for five weeks they enjoyed the social round before embarking for Spithead where they arrived in August. From Portsmouth they marched to London and were quartered in the Tower. Thus they missed the fatigues imposed on the Household troops by the feverish celebrations following the arrival in London at the beginning of June of the Tsar; the King of Prussia; Prince Metternich, Chancellor of the Austrian Empire; Prince Hardenburg, Chancellor of Prussia; Field-Marshal von Blücher; the picturesque Hetman Platoff of the Cossacks; and innumerable German princelings, all at the invitation of the Prince Regent. Instead Aitchison was able to return to East Lothian and his family. Posted to Edinburgh as regimental recruiting officer, he set about his task with his usual attention to duty, and soon the following poster was to be seen displayed in the cities of Edinburgh and Glasgow:

GR

Household Troops, Non-Commissioned Officers

Wanted for His Majesty's Third or Royal Scotch Regiment
of Body Guards
Commanding General HRH Prince William Frederick, Duke of
Gloucester and Edinburgh

16 Guineas Bounty for unlimited and 11 Guineas
for limited service

Owing to the great number of Non-Commissioned Officers of the Third or Royal Scotch Guards promoted into other Regiments, there are now a few vacancies, and HRH the Duke of Gloucester and Edinburgh, desirous of Scotchmen for Non-Commissioned Officers and Privates, in this Gallant National Corps, has just ordered out Parties to receive those Young Heroes who shall offer themselves.

Having at all times so Gloriously distinguished themselves the Guards Corps now possess peculiar advantages, and they have higher pay than any other Corps. A proportion is always stationed in London, to do duty at the Palace of St James' and the whole of the men there, both Non-Commissioned Officers and Privates, are allowed to appear at all times in uniform, any Dress they please, when not on Duty, and to follow their own Trades and occupations all over London, and in the country ten miles around it.

All young men enlisting in the Third Guards Corps have an increase of Pay after every Seven Years Service, and at the end of only 21 years service, they may return to their homes with an honourable pension for life, of £18/5s per annum for a Private, £24/6/8 for a Corporal and £33/9/2 for a Sergeant.

With such superior advantages in the Third Guards Corps, the applications in England are so numerous, that none are now admitted into this distinguished Corps, but Young Men of good Character, and not exceeding 25 Years of Age. They must be 5 feet 6 inches high, if under 20, and 5 feet 7 inches if above 20 years of age.

All Aspiring Young Men, answering the above description will meet with every encouragement, by applying to
CAPTAIN AITCHISON
Sergeant M'Donald, Edinburgh or Sergeant Miller, Glasgow

Bringers of Good Recruits will receive Three Guineas Reward

GOD SAVE THE KING

On the 27 January, Wellington was to take his seat as Duke of Wellington, Marquis of Douro, Earl of Wellington and Somerset, Viscount Wellington of Talavera and of Wellington and Baron Douro of Wellesely in Somerset. He was, besides, Duke of Ciudad Rodrigo in Spain and Duke of Vitoria in Portugal, though not yet Prince of Waterloo. He was only forty-five.

Appendix

Selected Abridged Biographies

Wellington had only two subordinate commanders he was prepared to trust with independent commands:

Thomas Graham (1st Lord Lyndoch)
Thomas Graham of Balgowan, a cultured Scottish Laird and an excellent linguist had, perhaps, the most remarkable career of any British general. In 1792 drunken National Guardsmen broke open the coffin of his young wife Mary, daughter of Lord Cathcart, whose beauty has been perpetuated by Gainsborough and who had recently died in the South of France, when he was taking her home to Scotland. Graham swore vengeance on the French. He received his baptism of fire as a civilian ADC to Lord Mulgrave at the siege of Toulon in 1794. He subsequently acquired the honorary rank of Colonel by raising the Perthshire Volunteers at his own expense. He served as liaison officer with the Austrian armies in Italy and became a friend of Sir John Moore, who first met him in Toulon. He accompanied Moore to Sweden and then to the Peninsula as his ADC, and was beside him when he fell mortally wounded. He at last obtained a regular commission at Moore's request in 1810, in the rank of major-general.

A fine horseman, with a natural eye for country and an iron constitution, his finest hour came in 1811 when in command of the British troops in Cadiz he turned an Allied defeat into victory at the battle of Barrosa. Transferred to Lisbon as Wellington's deputy and commander of the 1st Division, Graham is usually depicted as having all the military virtues and as held in high esteem by all ranks. It is particularly interesting, therefore, that John Aitchison should be highly critical of his administrative ability by making it clear in his letters how much the rank and file suffered from administrative shortcoming during their long flank march to Vitoria.

On 8 October 1813, Sir Thomas Graham was invalided and went home sick. He was replaced by John Hope.

Rowland Hill (1st Viscount Hill)
Every one loved 'Daddy' Hill, for no man could show more genuine concern for the misfortune of others no matter what their rank. Like Graham, Hill had served in the siege of Toulon and in the Peninsula under Moore. Hill was a

quietly intrepid and highly intelligent man. His benevolent exterior hid a steely will, and his excellent strategic and tactical judgement made him a man who could be relied upon to act in independent command with the utmost energy and effectiveness without running unacceptable hazards. He demonstrated his mastery of organization and rapid movement when in independent command during the manoeuvring leading up to the battle of Busaco; in the affair of Arroyo dos Molines; in the storming of the forts at Almarez; and last but not least in the battle of St Pierre, near Bayonne.

John Hope (1st Baron Niddry, 4th Earl of Hopetown)

Sir John Hope came out to relieve Thomas Graham. He had great experience in the West Indies and Holland, and as Adjutant General in Egypt to Sir Ralph Abercrombie was beside his chief when he fell. He had been second-in-command to Moore in Sweden, and commanded a division under him in the Peninsula and during the retreat to Corunna. He commanded the 1st Division and the Corps that laid siege to Bayonne. In the operations leading up to that event Wellington wrote of him in his despatches: 'I have long entertained the highest opinion of Sir John Hope like everybody else, I suppose, but every day more convinces me more of his worth. We shall lose him if he continues to expose himself as he did during the last three days. Indeed, his escape was wonderful. His coat and hat were shot through in many places, besides the wound in his leg. He places himself among the sharpshooters without shielding himself as they do. Sir John was another very large man.'

Beresford, William Carr (1st Viscount Beresford)

William Carr Beresford was the illegitimate son of the Marquis of Waterford and a friend of Wellington. The latter recommended Beresford to the Portuguese government as a suitable man to raise, train and command the Portuguese army. Beresford, having a working knowledge of Portuguese, was acceptable to the government, who made him a Marshal. An able trainer and strong disciplinarian, Beresford was a huge man with rugged features and one useless and discoloured eye, making him a terrifying spectacle when roused.

Absolutely loyal to Wellington, he was often used by him to command a Corps in the field, but after the first siege of Badajoz and the battle of Albuera, Wellington decided that he could not be trusted with an independent command. Nevertheless, he finally detached him to make his way to Bordeaux, where Louis XVIII was first proclaimed.

John Colborne.

Colborne, who was to become a field-marshal, was put in command of the 66th Foot in 1809. He took over command of the 52nd in 1811 (at Sir John Moore's dying wish) and retained it throughout the Peninsular War and during the Waterloo campaign, in which he greatly distinguished himself. In 1838 he became a Lieutenant-Governor of Upper Canada, where he suppressed a rebellion. Created Baron Seaton the following year, he was appointed field-marshal in 1860.

Lowry Cole
Cole, the second son of the 1st Earl of Eniskillen, commanded the 4th Division from 1810–14, except when recovering from wounds received at Albuera and Salamanca, and the 6th Division at Waterloo. Sir Lowry later became Governor of Mauritius and of the Cape of Good Hope.

Stapleton Cotton (1st Viscount Combermere)
John Cotton had seen considerable active service before reaching the Peninsula, where he was to command the cavalry almost continuously from 1810–14. That he was not given greater opportunity for independent command can probably be put down to Wellington's firmly held opinion that British cavalry were likely to get into trouble whenever they were out of his sight. (Comparing Napoleon's generalship with that of Wellington, it was in the conduct of a relentless pursuit that the latter was most clearly outclassed.) Of Cotton, Wellington wrote, 'I do not know where we should find an officer that would command our cavalry in this country [the Peninsula] half as well as he does – but he is not exactly the person I should select to command the army.' Nevertheless, Comberemere, as he became in 1814, became commander-in-chief in India and was advanced to a Viscounty after overcoming the great fortress of Bhurtpore in 1827. He remained a great dandy to his life's end, receiving a field-marshal's baton in 1855.

Robert Craufurd
'Black Bob' Craufurd came to the Peninsula with a chip on his shoulder. Although he had much distinguished service, he had fallen behind in promotion from being a fluent German speaker and, like Graham, having been attached as a liaison officer to the Austrian army. A Member of Parliament, he spoke frequently on military matters with much sagacity – generally contrary to the official view. He first served in the Peninsula under Moore and soon proved himself, as commander of the famous Light Brigade, to be an outstanding commander of outposts. When in 1810 the brigade became the Light Division, he continued in command for nearly two years of outstandingly successful service. This was due not only to his power of leadership but to his grasp of detail and methods of training. His 'Standing Orders for the Light Division' remained a model for the rest of the army for many years.

A strict disciplinarian with a caustic and eloquent tongue and a quick and ungovernable temper, Craufurd was respected but not loved. William Tomdinson (*'Diary of a Cavalry Officer'*, p. 30) tells us of the Commissary of the Light Division complaining to Wellington that Craufurd had told him he would be hanged if the supplies of the Division were not produced on time, to which Wellington replied, 'Then I advise you to produce them, for he is certain to do it!' Craufurd's temper, combined with a thirst for glory, led him at times into errors of judgement and to disobeying orders, and Wellington would not trust him with independent command. He was killed in action on 19 January 1812 while supervising the storming of the lesser breach at Ciudad Rodrigo. Rifleman Harris of the 95th wrote, 'I do not think I ever admired any man who wore the British uniform more than I did General Craufurd.' He left as a memorial the Light Division, which continued to add to its laurels under lesser commanders than 'Black Bob'.

Thomas Picton

Wellington's attitude to Picton was similar to his attitude to Craufurd – a splendid subordinate so long as he obeyed orders, but not a man to be entrusted with an independent mission. As choleric as Craufurd, Picton bludgeoned his opponents not with sarcasm but with expletives. Wellington called Picton 'as rough a foul-mouthed devil as ever lived, but he always behaved extremely well [in battle]; no man could do better in the various services I assigned to him'. Like Crauford, Picton had lost out in 'promotion stakes' owing to a political row that had risen over the use of torture, on a Mulatto girl by a local magistrate operating under Spanish law, when Picton was commanding in Trinidad.

Picton commanded the 3rd Division for three years in the Peninsula, during which time, along with the Light Division, it had the lion's share of the fighting. Picton was another strict disciplinarian, but despite his quick temper and rough speech he was liked and respected by all ranks, for he had a great sense of justice, was approachable and was also ready to listen to any genuine complaint. A despiser of pomp and ceremony he was eccentric in his dress, wearing a broad-brimmed hat to shield his eyes in the Peninsula, and a tall beaver hat during the Waterloo campaign, when he commanded the 5th Division. Wounded at Quatre Bras he hid his wounds, the severity of which was only discovered when he had been shot through the head at Waterloo. His hat, with the bullet hole through it, is now in the National Army Museum.

Bibliography
and Acknowledgements

The bibliography of the Peninsular War is very extensive. The source notes at the end of each section of the book give some indication of this. A select, but by no means exhaustive, list of those books which I have found most helpful in the task of editing John Aitchison's letters and diaries, or have thought most likely to be enjoyed by the reader who wishes to pursue a study of the campaigns, is set out below.

a) The most important sources for a history of the campaigns are:
Lt.-Col. Gurwood's *Dispatches of Field-Marshal the Duke of Wellington*. The source references are to the enlarged edition of 1852 published in eight volumes; *Supplementary Despatches, Correspondence and Memoranda of Field-Marshal Arthur Duke of Wellington*, edited by the 2nd Duke; and *Wellington's General Orders*.
b) The most important histories of the Peninsular War, for those who want to study the operations in detail, are:
Major A. H. Burne, *The Enigma of Toulouse* (*Army Quarterly*, Vol. 13, No. 2. Jan. 1927). Sir John Fortescue, *History of the British Army*, Vols. VI–X, Macmillan, 1910–1920. (Referred to in source notes as Fortescue.)
Sir William Napier's *History of the War on the Peninsula and South of France*, published in six volumes in 1852. Napier was a participant and the publication of his magnificent history raised a great degree of controversy.
Sir Charles Oman's *A History of the Peninsular War*, published in seven volumes (1902–1930), supplemented by the authors.
Wellington's Army (Edward Arnold 1912, reprinted Francis Edwards 1968).
c) For specialist interest in the Artillery and Engineers:
Major-General B. P. Hughes, *Fire Power* (Armour Press 1974).
Colonel J. Jones, *Journal of the Sieges in Spain, 1811–1814* (1821).
Major J. Leslie, *The Dickinson Papers* (RA Institution).
d) Excellent modern but less detailed military histories of the war are provided by:
Michael Glover, *The Peninsular War, 1807–1814* (David & Charles 1974).
Jack Weller, *Wellington in the Peninsula, 1808–1814* (Nicholas Vane 1962, reprinted Kaye & Ward 1969).

e) For the broad sweep of the campaigns with their social and political background:

Sir Arthur Bryant, *Years of Victory* (Collins 1944). *The Age of Elegance* (Collins 1950).

Elizabeth Longford, *Wellington – The Years of the Sword* (Weidenfeld and Nicolson 1969).

f) The following published memoirs are recommended from a very large selection:

Curling, *Rifleman Harris* (Peter Davies 1928).

Kincaid, *Adventures in the Rifle Brigade* (Clay and Sons 1919).

Larpent, *Private Journal of F. S. Larpent, Judge Advocate* (Richard Bentley 1853).

Liddell Hart, *Letters of Private Wheeler* (Michael Joseph 1951).

Smith, *Autobiography of Sir Harry Smith* (John Murray 1901).

Tomkinson, *The Diary of a Cavalry Officer* (Frederick Muller 1894, reprinted 1971).

g) Some material has been used for the first time, including:

Letters and Diaries of John Aitchison.

Initial Orders for Storming of Badajoz, 3rd Division's copy.*

Letters of Joe Palmer, 27th Inniskillings, seconded to Portuguese Army.*

Letters to Admiral Edward Foot.*

Finally, I wish particularly to acknowledge the great assistance I have derived from the previous researches of Elizabeth Longford for *Wellington – The Years of the Sword* and of Michael Glover for *The Peninsular War, 1807–1814*, and also the unfailing courtesy and help of Mr Potts and the staff of the library of the Ministry of Defence.

* Referred to in source notes as Thompson MSS.

Notes

Abbreviations for source references:
Fortescue – *History of the British Army*, Sir John Fortescue
Napier – *History of the War in the Peninsula and South of France*, Sir William
Napier
NC – Napoléon 1er – Correspondence
W.D. – Wellington's Despatches (John Murray, 1838)
W. Supp. D. – Wellington's Supplementary Despatches (John Murray, 1860)

Introduction

1. Smith, *Autobiography*, p. 185.
2. In the Artillery he would have had a higher rate of pay and less to spend on social appearances than in the Guards.
3. Lack of interest meaning lack of patronage.
4. Had he lived a little longer he would have died a field-marshal, to which Queen Victoria had already agreed.

Prologue

1. Navy Record Society, *The Private Correspondence of Admiral Lord Collingwood*, p. 216.
2. Bryant, *Years of Victory*, p. 212.
3. NC xvi, 13327.
4. Oman, Vol. i, p. 85: 'This is what is meant by the old epigram, "in Spain large armies starve, and small armies are beaten".'
5. This must refer to the scandal of the Duke of York and his former mistress, Mary Anne Clarke, who had been taking bribes in the belief that she could influence the Duke to obtain military appointments and promotions. A number of the Duke's enemies conspired to get him implicated. Mrs Clarke issued a blackmailing letter in June 1808 and the following February the House of Commons set up a committee of Enquiry. The Duke, though exonerated, resigned as commander-in-chief.
6. Moore, *Diary*, Vol. ii, p. 272.
7. NC xviii, 14731.

1809

1. This included forty-three officers and eighteen women – it was customary to allow six wives per company and their children to go on active service – and civilian servants.
2. The Duke of York did his best to cut this down in Flanders in 1793–5, but it continued to be a problem throughout the Peninsular War.
3. Major-General Mackenzie's force.
4. Commander-in-chief of the Mediterranean Fleet.
5. Sir Robert Wilson had formed, at British expense, from Portuguese officers detained in England on their way to Brazil, the Loyal Lusitanian Legion of three light infantry battalions armed with rifles.
6. General William Carr Beresford was commissioned by the Portuguese Regency to command, organize and train a Portuguese army.
7. A brigade of artillery at that time would today be called a battery, and consisted of four or six guns or howitzers.
8. Refers to the heroic defence of Zaragoza by the Spaniards.
9. On 4 May, at Coimbra, Wellesley reorganized his force by attaching a company of the 60th Rifles to five of his seven infantry brigades, bringing rifles into his skirmishing line, and including five of the best Portuguese battalions, one to each British brigade other than the Guards and the 1st Brigade.
10. Spherical case shot, invented by Lieutenant Henry Shrapnel. It was first used in Surinam in 1804 and in the Peninsular War at Rolica in 1808. It consisted of a hollow iron sphere with a bursting charge set off by a fuse timed to act at a chosen point along its trajectory. When the shell was blown open it discharged a large number of bullets – between twenty-seven and eighty-five in the case of a six-pound shell. The French had nothing comparable during the Napoleonic Wars.
11. The Archduke Charles crossed the Inn frontier with 140,000 men on 9 April and advanced on Regensburg, which fell on the twentieth.
12. Aitchison did not yet appreciate the potential of guerrilla warfare.
13. W.D., Vol. v, p. 335.
14. W. Supp. D., Vol. vi, p. 431.
15. On 11 June, Wellesley received permission from the government to take British troops into Spain, provided the defence of Portugal was not hazarded by it.
16. This had been forced on Victor by lack of supplies.
17. Cuesta was old, proud and obstinate, though courageous. At Medellin, where he had been badly defeated, he had been ridden down by his own cavalry and now travelled in an old family coach drawn by six mules. On the battlefield he was hoisted into the saddle. During the Talavera campaign the British were auxiliary to the Spanish forces, and Sir Arthur found Cuesta a most difficult man with whom to concert plans.
18. Joseph had received orders from Napoleon in Vienna to place the corps of Ney and Mortier under Soult's command. As soon as Soult's army had been re-equipped his whole force was to move south and cut

Wellesley's line of communication with Lisbon if the British had moved into Spain.

19. Beresford and the Portuguese Army were to be responsible for the local defence of Portugal.

20. Napoleon had entered Vienna on 13 May. Between the twentieth and the twenty-third the Archduke Charles defeated the French at Aspern. This was the first defeat of an army under Napoleon's personal command.

21. One of Wellesley's greatest difficulties in co-operation with the Spanish forces was his almost complete lack of transport and of money to hire it. The British already owed the Portuguese £200,000 for various services and the troops had not been paid for two months. Wellesley entered Spain on the understanding that they would be provisioned by the Spaniards, an undertaking which was only partly fulfilled.

22. Robert Craufurd's Light Brigade, nucleus of the famous Light Division, only joined Wellington the morning after the battle of Talavera. They had marched forty-two miles in twenty-six hours in great heat and dust, and virtually without food or water, yet arrived on the battlefield with their bugles blowing 'merrily'.

23. It is interesting that a front-line letter should attribute Cuesta's reluctance to attack to its being Sunday. This is given as a reason in nearly all histories of the campaign, but Elizabeth Longford (*Wellington: The Years of the Sword*) quotes Wellington as having remarked to Stanhope: 'He made many other foolish excuses, but that was not one of them . . .' The notion, however, was given credence in drawing-rooms back home.

24. The British troops had been on half rations for some days and Wellesley refused to advance unless proper provision was made for supplying his army.

25. Bessborough, *Lady Bessborough and her Family Circle,* p. 188.

26. Hopier, *Passages in the Early Life of Sir George Napier*, p. 110.

27. Cuesta had advanced twenty-five miles along the Toledo road when he found himself faced by a French army under Joseph, incorporating Victor's and Sabastiani's corps, in all some 45,000 men.

28. Victor tried to take the Medellin on the night of the twenty-seventh by a silent coup-de-main, and owing to a misunderstanding and lack of intelligence on the part of Hill's 2nd Division, nearly succeeded.

29. Time was becoming a crucial factor. Joseph had received information that Venegas was threatening the line of the Tagus, where only light detachments holding the crossing-places lay between him and Madrid. Time was becoming vital for Wellington, though as yet he did not know it, because Soult, with Ney and Mortier under his command, was advancing on Plasencia from the north to cut the British line of communication.

30. John Aitchison was carrying the King's Colour.

31. Robert Craufurd's Light Brigade and the Chestnut Troop, R.H.A.

32. As usual not everyone found Wellesley's dispatch to their liking. Sir

Arthur's brother William wrote to him: 'I never read so clear or so modest a statement. I have but one fault to find with it – you are not warm enough in praise of your officers . . . I think you are particularly cold in praising the artillery. I have heard that Howarth had two horses shot under him, this might have been thrown in and would have gratified his friend in the Corps.' (Raglan MSS, No. 101). The future Duke of Wellington was evidently not impressed, for, although he was to pass some handsome comments on the work of the British artillery he omitted to mention the crucial role played by the artillery in his Waterloo dispatch!

33. For the grand push Joseph, on Victor's advice, concentrated 34,000 men against Wellesley's 20,000 while holding in check Cuesta's 30,000 Spaniards with some 3,000 dragoons. The main weight of the French attack fell on the British 1st and 4th Divisions, where at times it looked like succeeding.

34. Langwerth's King's German Legion was taken in flank and severely raked by Victor's artillery massed on the Cerro de Cascajal.

35. The Guards came up against Sabastiani's uncommitted reserve and were at the same time taken in flank, since Langwerth's troops had failed to advance. This is the only source I know of where the retreat of the 3rd Guards is said to have been carried out in two phases. The first, to the line of the Portina, was made 'in better order than we arrived'. This withdrawal was followed by fresh French forces, so a further withdrawal was ordered, which threw the Guards into some confusion. Seeing that the British line was in danger of being broken, Wellesley ordered the 48th Foot to move to their right, from the Medellin, and cover the retirement of the Guards and for Mackenzie, who was subsequently killed, to bring forward the 24th, 45th and 31st in support. The 48th having formed line, they wheeled to let the Guards through, then reformed. The Guards quickly rallied and with a hurrah came, according to Aitchison, into 'a more advanced line than at the commencement' of the action.

36. Aitchison made no reference to the crucial part the 48th Regiment played in enabling the Guards to rally – probably because, having been wounded, he was sent to the rear at this stage.

37. General service medals with bars for various engagements in the Peninsular War were not issued until 1848! Colonel I.A. Wallace of the Connaught Rangers, the 88th Foot, got permission for the private issue of medals to his rank and file in 1818.

38. One of the many valuable reforms introduced by the Duke of York. Previously companies could be purchased without qualification.

39. On 28 July the 4th Guards, out of a strength of 1,019 all ranks, lost 54 killed and 267 wounded.

40. This was the ill-fated Walcheren Expedition, Britain's major military operation of the year. Some 40,000 soldiers and 600 ships were sent to Walcheren island as a first step to the capture of Antwerp. Its aims were to support Austria by drawing French forces away from the Danube,

and to destroy the French Fleet in the Scheldt and the dockyard at Antwerp. It failed to achieve either, and fever and dysentery decimated the troops.

41. Portugal had a small population and, being throughout history threatened with invasion by more populous Spain, had long maintained a system of conscription for manning her regular and militia forces.

42. Robinson, *Wellington's Campaigns, 1808–1815*, p. 116.

43. Canning had been intriguing to get rid of Castlereagh as Secretary of War and to have him replaced by Wellington's elder brother, the Marquis Wellesley, then British Ambassador in Seville. Aitchison confuses the two men. Castlereagh and Canning fought a duel on 21 September and both resigned. The Portland government fell and was replaced by the Tories under Percival. Wellesley replaced Canning as Foreign Secretary.

44. Light companies of the Guards and line regiments, which in the Grenadier companies were picked men, were employed in the skirmishing line. They wore short coats, without tails, and wings, a sort of crescent-shaped epaulette such as are still worn by drummers in the Foot Guards.

45. Wellington's reconnaissance for establishing the famous lines of Torres Vedras.

46. Napoleon defeated the Austrians at Wagram on 10 July.

47. Fortescue, Vol. VII, p. 279.

48. There is a very full account of the lives of soldiers' wives in Godfrey Davies: *Wellington and his Army* (Blackwell).

49. The armistice between France and Austria led to a peace treaty signed at Schönbrunn signed on 14 October 1809.

50. John Charles Villiers, afterwards 3rd Earl of Clarendon, replaced Marquis Wellesley as Ambassador in Seville.

51. Aitchison is mistaken about Marshal Oudinot, Duke of Reggio. See Dann-Patterson's *Napoleon's Marshals*, p. 340: 'The Duke was fortunate in not being selected for duty in Spain.'

52. Napoleon criticized Joseph's conduct at Talavera for breaking off the battle before using up his reserve: 'To be repulsed when one has 12,000 men in reserve who have not fired a shot, is to put up with an insult.' (Robinson, *Wellington's Campaigns, 1808–1815*, p. 113). To claim, as Aitchison does, that this was due to the intimidating effect of the Guards' charge, seems an exaggeration.

53. Sherbrooke was made a Knight of the Bath at Talavera.

1810

1. NC xx, 16192.

2. NC xx, 16031.

3. W.D., Vol. IV, p. 436.

4. There was a strong faction in favour of bringing the army home. Rejoicing over the victory at Talavera was soon followed by criticism of the casualties and the subsequent retreat into Portugal. Combined with

the Walcheren fiasco it led to the fall of Portland's government and Wellington's competence and motives were questioned. Britain was in serious financial difficulties and the cost of maintaining an army in Portugal was unpopular. Percival and Lord Liverpool, the new Prime Minister and War Secretary, were determined patriots, the former felt Spain to be the best place to reduce French land power, and the latter was convinced of the necessity of concentrating British forces in one place. Accordingly the budget for the war was increased from £1 million to £3 million a year.

5. It is true that Wellington claimed that, even though he had withdrawn to Portugal, he was still assisting Spain by posing a threat to any southward move by the French into Andalusia.

6. Napoleon married the Archduchess Marie-Louise, daughter of the Emperor Francis II, on 2 April. Their son, born in March 1811, was given the title 'King of Rome'.

7. It will have been seen that this does not reflect the actual moves of the Spanish armies.

8. The 79th and 94th Regiments and drafts from Portsmouth under Major-General Stewart, together with the 2nd/87th Regiment and a company of artillery. Captain Owen's company of artillery from Portsmouth were sent on to Cadiz where they were joined by Captain P. Campbell's company from Gibraltar.

9. This may have arisen from Massena having said to his corps commanders, on arrival from Salamanca, 'Gentlemen, I am here against my own wishes.' A rough diamond risen from the ranks of the Royal Army, Massena was the best general the French had after Napoleon. He had seen almost continuous active service and had recently been badly shaken by a fall from his horse at Wagram.

10. A series of mutinies by officers of the Madras Army, which led to a number of courts martial in September 1809. In February 1810, Sir R. Farquahar in Madras wrote to Wellington that only his coming as governor-general and commander-in-chief could restore discipline.

11. Stewart's force arrived in Cadiz on 17 February.

12. The Spaniards had only 25,000 troops to cover 160 miles of front, though the passes were few.

13. Alburquerque had 8–10,000 troops. Soult's decision to enter Seville in force delayed the advance sufficiently for Alburquerque to get his force into Cadiz, hitherto virtually undefended.

14. Charles Stuart, afterwards Lord Stuart de Rothsay, took over from John Villiers as British Minister in Lisbon.

15. To buy his next step.

16. This and the preceding two paragraphs refer to the Light Brigade under Craufurd, which was continuously harassing the French east of the Coa.

17. The affair of the bridge of Barba del Puerco, was said to have been undertaken because the French general had been assured by a Spaniard that the British officers were drunk every night. Taking advantage of the

noise of the river the French were able to bayonet the two riflemen on sentry at the bridge. The 95th, however, being imbued with the standing orders of the Light Division by which all had to be ready to march within seven minutes, day or night, were not to be surprised. (Craufurd's Light Brigade had become the Light Division on 1 March).

18. Napoleon overran Hanover in 1803 and the Hanoverian army was disbanded. Many officers and men subsequently escaped to England and were formed into the King's German Legion. In time the Legion became diluted with other elements, but when it first went to the Peninsula in 1808 it was still predominantly Hanoverian. By 1812 the K.G.L. had four cavalry regiments, four infantry battalions and two companies of artillery in Spain. By then it had become considerably diluted by men from other parts of Germany, mainly recruited from British prisoner-of-war camps. After the war the K.G.L. provided the nucleus for the Royal Army of Hanover.

The 5th Battalion of the 60th Rifles (Royal Americans) was a predominantly German corps whose national balance shifted gradually towards the British, who by 1814 provided rather more than half its strength. Though the exact meaning of 'Freemen' in this context is problematic, I take it that it refers to men released from prisoner-of-war camps. The role of the 5th/60th was to provide a rifle company for a number of British infantry brigades. Another German corps, initially Prussian, with the same role was the Brunswick Oels Jager (see Glossary).

19. This was nearly correct. The defensive position on which the battle of Busaco was fought was a little further north, with the Allied right on the Mondego and not at the Ponte de Murcella on the Alva. This was because Massena had been expected to advance on the relatively good road south of the Mondego, but chose instead, through ignorance, the northern and very bad route through Vizeu.

20. During their time in the malarial Guadiana valley, after Talavera, the army's number of sick rose and on 1 November 9,016 men (28 per cent) were in hospital. Sickness declined during winter but on 1 April, of a total strength of 31,548, 909 were still sick in regiments and 4,971 in general hospitals (18.7 per cent).

21. Army reorganization had produced a system whereby a large part of the Army's recruits came through the regular militia into the 2nd Battalion of regiments which received all recruits and acted as depots. Occasionally both battalions of a regiment were sent abroad, creating difficulties, but the 2nd Battalion were intended to stay at home and keep the 1st Battalion overseas up to strength. It was a rule at this time that officers on promotion in 1st Battalions should go home to the 2nd Battalion, being replaced from these. Wellington complained that the system deprived him of his experienced officers, and as will be seen in Aitchison's next letter, the necessary change was soon made. Many 2nd Battalions were sent to the Peninsula because their 1st Battalions had returned from Walcheren riddled with fever.

22. *The Courier* was a paper much read by officers in the Peninsula. Unlike

The Times, which was a story supporter of the Government, it supported many of the criticisms of ministerial policy voiced by officers.

23. Vizeu is on an elevated plateau.

24. Consisting of 2nd Battalion, 1st Regiment of Guards, two companies of 2nd Battalion Coldstream Guards, 1st Battalion of 3rd Regiment of Guards, and two companies of 3rd Battalion, 95th Rifles.

25. W.D., Vol. VI, p. 124.

26. The Duke of Gloucester had succeeded the Duke of Argyll as General and Colonel of the 3rd Regiment of Guards. He was the younger brother of George III.

27. On 24 April, Liverpool wrote to Wellington that he was sending 8,070 reinforcements to Lisbon and 8,000 (including a Portuguese regiment) to Cadiz.

28. Julian Sanchez commanded a body of irregular cavalry drawn from horsemen who herded bulls – *garrochistas*. When they slipped out of Ciudad Rodrigo they were taken into British pay.

29. The French opened their bombardment of Ciudad Rodrigo on 25 June with forty-eight pieces of artillery. The garrison fought back gallantly, but surrendered on the evening of 10 July.

30. Fort Concepcion was a small work which Wellington had had repaired.

31. The Marquis de Romana was one of the Spanish generals to have learnt the lessons of the war. He had reorganized his army of some 20,000 into small groups of 3–5,000 for the harassment and pinning down of the French, thus giving every encouragement to partisan warfare.

32. Robert Craufurd's Light Division (4,000 infantry, 1,000 cavalry and six guns) was operating east of the Coa in the face of Ney's corps of 24,000 men and thirty guns. His orders from Wellington were to harass the French, obtain information, but on no account to become involved in a serious fight beyond the river. After the fall of Ciudad Rodrigo, Craufurd did not retire across the Coa but when Ney advanced he kept in close touch with the French and took up a position along a ridge running south from Almeida. Between here and the river, a mile away, the ground dropped very steeply and was broken by ravines and walled vineyards. Moreover, the only means of crossing the Coa was by a single very narrow bridge. Attacked on 14 July by vastly superior numbers of French, the Light Brigade held on for two hours and then carried out a most difficult retreat which was only saved from disaster by the remarkable fighting qualities of the troops and the tradition of Moore's matchless discipline. Craufurd lost in killed, wounded and missing some 333 officers and men – the 43rd and 95th each losing 129 men.

33. The investment of Almeida by Ney started on 15 August. Prior to this, to pose a threat which would make Massena concentrate his troops and thus increase his considerable problems of victualling them, Wellington moved forward the Light, 3rd and 1st Divisions and again advanced his headquarters to Alverca.

34. The best of the Portuguese units were with Hill. Those with Wellington were inexperienced.

35. Ox carts.
36. Commander of the Portuguese Division.
37. This is incorrect. To distract Wellington, Napoleon ordered that Mortier should be sent into Estremadura to threaten his rear. Reynier would meantime return to north of the Tagus and operate on the frontier between the Tagus and Mondego. Accordingly Mortier ordered a division under Girard to manoeuvre along the Portuguese frontier between the Sierra Morena and the Guadiana. Ballesteros understood better than any other Spanish general how to harass the French without accepting unnecessary risks to his own army, and when Girard marched against him he led the French a pretty dance, but always eluding him. On reaching Olivenca he met Romana, who, despite Wellington's warnings, had insisted on setting out from Badajoz on an offensive sortie into Andalusia. Separating from Ballesteros, he marched on Bienvenida, where on 11 August Girard caught his advance guard unsupported and routed it with the loss of 600 men. This seems to have been the incident to which Aitchison refers.
38. It took the French a long time to get their siege train forward from Ciudad Rodrigo to Almeida but on 15 August Ney's corps were ready to invest the fortress and on the twenty-sixth opened fire from eleven batteries against it. Almeida was a small, nearly circular town with a diameter of about 700 yards. There was a curtain wall with six bastions, a covered way, a dry ditch cut out of solid rock and six lunettes. It was difficult to construct approaches to Almeida as the rock was on or very near the surface; for the same reason the glacis was low, exposing the walls. The fortifications mounted 100 guns, and it had a garrison of 5,000 Portuguese (half regulars and half militia) and ample supplies. Brigadier-General William Cox, a capable and resolute soldier, commanded the garrison, which was expected to hold out for a long time. He had communication with Wellington by telegraph. One of the difficulties in reducing the fortress was that the French guns could only be brought to bear on the upper parts of the walls, thus bringing down masonry to reinforce the lower parts. For twelve hours the French guns battered Almeida without making any noticeable impression. A lucky shell then set fire to a train of powder which had carelessly been laid from a leaky barrel on its way from the magazine to the batteries. The magazine blew up with a terrific explosion and 500 of the garrison, a large part being artillerymen, were killed. The town was wrecked and the whole of the powder less a small portion on the batteries was destroyed. Through his glass Wellington could see that the steeple of the church had been destroyed. Following the explosion Massena sent some Portuguese officers on his staff to demand the fortress's surrender. Cox's officers threatened that if he did not agree to capitulate they would open the gates. On the twenty-eighth Cox and the garrison marched out and laid down their arms on condition that the regulars would be sent as prisoners of war to France and the militia allowed to return home on parole. Massena disregarded this agreement and

through his Portuguese officers started recruiting the garrison into the French service. Large numbers of both officers and men agreed to join the French and this cast serious doubt on the reliability of the Portuguese forces. It was, however, for the most part, a ruse to prevent their being taken to France and in a very short time they deserted in hundreds and rejoined their colours. The rapid fall of Almeida was a serious setback for Wellington's calculations. One of the two main gateways to Portugal was now in the hands of the French.

39. From the numbering of the letters, two written between 28 August and 12 September are missing.

40. Napoleon's chief of staff in Paris.

41. The rearguard action between the Light Division and Reynier's corps.

42. W. Supp. D., Vol. vi, p. 607.

43. Gratton, *Adventures with the Connaught Rangers*, p. 33.

44. Napier, *Passages from the Early Life of General Sir George Napier*, p. 142.

45. The French cavalry first reconnoitred the lines of Torres Vedras on 11 October. On the twelfth Junot's VIII Corps pushed back the British outposts from the village of Sobral, after a skirmish. Skirmishing continued, and on 14 October Junot tried to dislodge a regiment of the 71st from its station behind Sobral and Monte de Agraca.

46. The Marquis Romana brought 8,000 Spanish troops into the lines of Torres Vedras. They were stationed about Mafra.

47. This interesting incident seems to have escaped the notice of the biographers of that colourful character Lord Cochrane – radical politician, inventor, future admiral and 10th Earl of Dundonald. The nature of his proposals is unknown but must have been similar to those he put forward for the destruction of the French Fleet by means of 'Explosion' and 'Stink' vessels. These, examined in 1812 by a committee of admirals, were kept secret until the end of the nineteenth century. 'Explosion' vessels were to contain 1,500 barrels of powder on which were to be laid 250 fused shells and thousands of hand grenades. 'Stink' vessels were to discharge a suffocating cloud produced by laying sulphur on burning charcoal.

48. Lieutenant in the Foot Guards held the rank of captain in the Army, and captains in the Guards, commanding companies, that of lieutenant-colonel in the Army.

INTERMISSION

1. News of Graham's victory at Barrosa was telegraphed from Plymouth to the Admiralty, who passed it on to the Lord Mayor on 23 March. Two days later, at 9 a.m., the guns in the Park and at the Tower of London were fired in celebration. In April the Prince Regent, to mark their outstanding services at Barrosa, conferred on the 87th Regiment the title of 'The Prince of Wales's Own Irish Regiment' and decreed that

their insignia should be an eagle crowned with laurel standing on a harp, in addition to his own arms.

2. In April the Prince Regent sent a message to both Houses of Parliament recommending a gift of £100,000 to relieve the sufferings of the Portuguese. The proposal was carried without a division, and private subscriptions for Portuguese relief were opened in London, Edinburgh and elsewhere.

3. W.D., Vol. VII, p. 445.

4. W.D., Vol. VII, p. 445.

5. The success of the Portuguese army after it had been reorganized by Beresford and trained by British officers was such that Lord Liverpool 'recommended to the Spanish government the same system of introducing British officers, but their prejudices were not to be overcome.'

   Wellington took a different view, for he believed that however inefficient Spanish officers might be, it was they who kept the spirit of resistance to the French army alive among the Spanish people, and he concludes: 'We must not disquiet the officers of the Spanish army and so deprive them of their profession as to give the British officers effective control over their Army.'

6. Kincaid, *Adventures in the Rifle Brigade*, p. 56.

7. The *picquets* of the 1st Division, under Lt-Col Hill of the 3rd Guards, were not withdrawn at daybreak owing to a mistake or oversight, and were only ordered to do so when large numbers of enemy cavalry appeared. On receiving the order the Guards formed, but had scarcely done so before they were charged by the French cavalry, which they repulsed. They were continuing their withdrawal 'when a Scotch major rode up to Colonel Hill of the 3rd Guards begging, nay, ordering him to open his files and oppose the enemy's light troops. The men, carried away by their great desire to do everything against the enemy, of themselves extended, and they had no sooner begun to fire when another body of cavalry charged their flank and took Colonel Hill and twelve men prisoner.'

8. W. Supp. D., Vol. VII, p. 177.

9. W.D., Vol. VII, p. 591n.

10. Maxwell, *'Peninsular Sketches'*, Vol. I, p. 331.

11. W.D., Vol. VIII, p. 82 and p. 79.

12. The prospects of Wellington taking, or even attempting to take, Ciudad Rodrigo were regarded by John Aitchison, who was always at pains to decry the excessive optimism that every success of Wellington engendered in the minds of the armchair critics at home, with deep pessimism. He wrote in his diary, 'Ciudad Rodrigo held out five weeks defended by the Spaniards – it will make at least the same defence by the French [to Wellington's credit it fell in twelve days] and ere that time could elapse, the enemy would again be in such force as to overwhelm any force Lord Wellington could collect. But they are already so superior in cavalry as to make the idea ridiculous that Lord Wellington will expose himself by descending into the plain on which Ciudad Rodrigo stands. It seems

more likely that he will press operations in the south and, first, the siege of Badajoz.'

13. Grattan, *Adventures in the Connaught Rangers*, pp. 134–5.
14. Napier, *Passages in the Early Life of Sir George Napier*, p. 181.
15. Maurice, *History of the Scots Guards*, p. 358.
16. NC XXIII, 18496, 11 February 1812.
17. Marmont, Vol. IV, pp. 341, 345.
18. A copy in my possession, which from internal evidence must have been that addressed to the 3rd Division, shows that Picton's assault on the castle was no last-minute enterprise, as is sometimes suggested.
19. Cooke, *Memoirs of the Late War*, Vol. I, p. 144.
20. Smith, *Autobiography of Sir Harry Smith*, p. 64.
21. Thompson mss. John Palmer's letter – Badajoz 11 April 1812. This is a particularly interesting account because there is considerable confusion about the details of the 3rd Division's attack. Palmer makes no mention of the first attempt to escalade, which was made at the wrong place, between San Pedro and San Antonio bastions, and failed, Picton being wounded and Kempt taking command.
22. In a letter to Canning written in 1820. Quoted by Oman, Vol. V, p. 260.

1812

1. The cause of malaria, from which the troops in the Guadiana valley suffered greatly, was not then understood.
2. Of the major historians of the Peninsular War, only Oman mentions this interesting incident, and he gives a very different account from that of Aitchison. During the siege of Badajoz, Graham advanced his covering force of three infantry divisions and two cavalry brigades in two columns towards Llerena. Hoping to surprise d'Erlon he made a forced night march on 18–19 March, but when cavalry patrols reached Llerena they found it empty, since the French had withdrawn to the east. A captured letter revealed that a force of 1,800 French had become isolated at Llerena and on the night of the twenty-fifth Graham set in motion converging columns to trap them. He and his staff, riding ahead of the 7th Division, ran into a French cavalry patrol which charged them and sent them helter-skelter down the road towards the head of the 7th Division, who opened fire, killing two staff officers and narrowly missing the general. Forewarned, the French were able to avoid the trap.
3. The Royal Staff Corps was raised in 1801 to be the Army's engineers, as distinct from the Royal Engineers, who were a corps of the Ordnance. The Bridge at Alcantara was a very fine Roman one, which was blown up in 1809 leaving a broken arch seventy-five feet wide. Fortescue claims that Sturgeon's bridge was the first suspension bridge to be built in Europe.
4. 2nd Guards Brigade, 1st Division, was commanded by Graham until his health broke down at the end of June, when Major-General Henry Campbell took over.

5. D'Urban, *Peninsular Journal*, p. 244.

6. The Light companies in the battalions of Guards wore the same jackets as the other companies but without tails. The habit of distinguishing between the different regiments of Guards by the grouping of their buttons was already established. The 'wings' to which Aitchison refers were a kind of epaulette (explained in an earlier note).

7. A great tribute to Wellington's ability to keep the enemy in the dark regarding his plans.

8. There were three forts erected on Napoleon's orders. The most important, San Vincente, stood on a perpendicular cliff above the Tormes, at the south-west angle of the town; 250 yards south-east of it, across a deep ravine, stood the smaller forts of San Gaetano and La Merced. They had been represented to Wellington as being of no account. As a result it was not until the twentieth that adequate siege artillery became available, six large howitzers having arrived from Elvas. However they soon ran out of ammunition and it was not until the twenty-sixth that the siege was properly opened.

9. On the heights of San Cristobal, north of the town.

10. Brealmont, M., *History of the Life of Arthur, Duke of Wellington*.

11. Stanhope, *Notes on Conversations with the Duke of Wellington;* Fortescue, Vol. VIII, p. 462.

12. W.D., Vol. IX, p. 284.

13. Croker, J. W., *Correspondence and Diaries*, Vol. II, p. 120.

14. Combermore, *Memoirs and Correspondence of F. M. Viscount Combermore*, Vol. I, p. 274.

15. Fortescue, Vol. VIII, p. 462.

16. Leaving the Light companies of the Guards at the Arapil.

17. The 61st Regiment, in Hulse's brigade of Henry Clinton's 6th Division, had the heaviest casualties of any unit, losing twenty-four officers and 342 rank and file killed, wounded and missing.

18. The number of Eagles captured was two and it is generally agreed that the French lost twenty cannon.

19. In the village of Los Arapiles.

20. Leslie, *Dixon Manuscripts*, Vol. IV, p. 679.

21. Captain Clithero was commanding the Light company, though Major-General Sir Frederick Maurice, in his *History of the Scots Guards*, mentions only Captain Walker as being wounded on this occasion.

22. Diaz Martin, one of the greatest guerrilla leaders, whose orders were to harass Joseph.

23. John Shiffner, captain in the 3rd Regiment of Guards, who was mortally wounded at Bayonne on 14 April 1814.

24. Ellesmere, *Personal Reminiscences of the Duke of Wellington*, p. 146.

25. Fortescue, Vol. VIII, p. 574.

26. W.D., Vol. IX, p. 442.

27. W.D., Vol. IX, p. 457.

28. W.D., Vol. IX, p. 574.

29. W.D., Vol. IX, p. 464.

30. W.D., Vol. IX, p. 512.
31. W.D., Vol. IX, p. 573.
32. This was the responsibility of the quartermaster-general's department.
33. Don Pedro Villacampa was a guerrilla leader.
34. Compare Fortescue's account (*History of the British Army*, Vol. VIII, p. 574.
35. This early use of 'Shrapnel' to describe what was officially known as 'spherical case shot' is interesting, as it was not until many years later that it became the official – now much abused – designation.
36. Souham took over from Clausel temporary command of the Army of Portugal until the return of Massena, which had not yet happened.
37. 'Stanhope's Journal' (MSS) – Fortesque, Vol. VIII, p. 586.
38. Fortescue, Vol. VIII, p. 595.
39. W.D., Vol. IX, p. 514.
40. W. Supp. D., Vol. VII, p. 478.
41. Almost all diarists mention the early fall of darkness on 15 November.
42. *Memoirs of Lejeune*, Vol. II, p. 108, quoted in Oman: *Wellington's Army*, p. 277.
43. Colonel Lejeune was a notable artist, and a picture by him of this scene, witnessed when he was a prisoner-of-war of the Allies in Elvas, hangs in Paris.
44. Ellesmere, *Personal Reminiscences*, p. 156, quoted in Davies, *Wellington and his Army*.
45. W.D., Vol. IX, p. 570.
46. Donaldson, *Recollections of the Eventful Life of a Soldier*, p. 25.
47. Girod, De L'Ains, *Vie Militaire du General Foy*, pp. 192–3.
48. This appears to contradict the usual story that the wheels of the artillery were muffled to pass through the town.
49. Captain Mylne, under whose command John's brother Robert was serving in the *Impétueux*.
50. W.D., Vol. IX, p. 582.

1813

1. W.D., Vol. X, p. 240.
2. Larpent, *The Private Journal of F. S. Larpent*, Vol. I, p. 150.
3. Larpent, (Ibid.), Vol. I, pp. 118, 123.
4. Napier, *History of the Peninsular War*, Vol. V, p. 542.
5. The 1st/1st and 3rd/1st Guards. The former landed at Corunna in September 1812, while the latter came up from Cadiz with Major-General Skerrett and joined Hill on the Tormes.
6. Each company had one mule to carry the heavy iron camp kettles. During the retreat from Burgos much hardship was caused when, for one reason or another, the camp kettle mule was not at hand when wanted. Craufurd had advocated the use of tin kettles in 1810 but had been turned down by Wellington who wrote: 'In a regiment well looked after, it is certain that tin kettles would answer best, as the officers

would oblige the soldiers to take care of them . . . but in two thirds of the Army such care would not be taken; and whether the regiments would have kettles or not would depend upon that most thoughtless of animals, the soldier himself, and I should very soon hear that there were none.'

7.   Hill's orders were to advance on Salamanca from the south. Graham's were to move on Zamora from the north, while Wellington met Hill at Salamanca and advanced with him on Toro.

8.   This did not 'turn out true'. On the contrary, Napoleon had defeated the Russians and Prussians at Lutzen on 2 May, and on 8 May entered Dresden.

9.   Burgos was blown up by the French on the day this letter was written. To prevent them falling into Allied hands, 6,000 shells were half loaded and arranged so as to be set off by the firing of a mine. The explosion occurred without warning, and 120 French dragoons and a great number of horses were killed or wounded as they were passing the castle.

10.   This is not the first nor the last time that Aitchison criticizes Graham. Graham was a remarkable man, having taken up soldiering as a volunteer in the defence of Toulon at the age of forty-three. Fearless, energetic and with a good eye for country, he was a natural soldier, and also a gentleman and scholar. Sir Charles Oman wrote of him: 'I have never found one unkindly word about General Graham, in the numerous diaries and autobiographies of the officers and men who served under him.' Aitchison's criticisms are therefore the more interesting and lead to the conclusion that, for all his other qualities, he was a poor administrator in the field, in which he probably lacked interest and may well have been let down by his staff. His alleged lack of decision is also something that future biographers will need to note.

11.   Liddell Hart, *Letters of Private Wheeler*, p. 119.

12.   Robinson, *Memoirs and Correspondence of Sir Thomas Picton*, Vol. ii, pp. 208–10.

13.   Napier, *History of the War in the Peninsular*, Vol. v, p. 542.

14.   Leslie, *Dickson Manuscripts*, ms 91, of 1813.

15.   The Portuguese created Wellington Duke of Vitoria.

16.   Clausel's Army of the North was not involved. Clausel with 15,000 men was marching to Vitoria on the road from Zaragoza and reached Trevino, twelve miles south of Vitoria, when he heard of Joseph's defeat and returned to Tudela where he turned north and crossed into France.

17.   Larpent, Vol. i, p. 249.

18.   Larpent, Vol. i, p. 258.

19.   W.D., Vol. x, pp. 473, 496.

20.   Fraser, *Letters of Col. Sir Augustus Fraser*, p. 176. 'Viva Wellington!' was a popular song commemorating the victory at Salamanca. It is on record that Wellington enjoyed hearing it, and would even ask to have it sung.

21. Pancorbo, a small but strong fortress guarding the important pass by which the Burgos-Vitoria road crossed the Monte Obarnes. It surrendered to Spanish forces.

22. Sir John Murray was the fourth general officer to succeed Maitland in command of the Anglo-Sicilian detachment sent to Alicante from Sicily by Lord William Bentinck. Murray abandoned all his guns and equipment landed for the siege of Tarragona and re-embarked at Balaguer without telling the Spaniards, with whom he was supposed to cooperate. He was court-martialled for this in 1815, but acquitted of most of the charges. His failure at Tarragona could have had dire consequences for Wellington, as it freed Suchet to act against him about the time he reached Pamplona.

23. W.D., Vol. x, pp. 587, 591.

24. Larpent, Vol. II, p. 65.

25. This refers to five under-strength battalions which were sent to Stralsund, at the request of Bernadotte, King of Sweden, freeing Swedish troops for service in Germany.

26. In eastern Spain Bentinck had started in July to advance by land from Valencia against Tarragona. On hearing that Suchet, who had some 40,000 in all, intended to blow up Tarragona, Bentinck embarked William Clinton, who was shortly to succeed him, with a division to lie offshore ready to occupy the city. Clinton, hearing that the French garrison of Tortosa, on the Ebro, were about to withdraw, landed at Balaguer to cut them off. By 29 July Bentinck's force was across the Ebro and two days later Tarragona was blockaded, but as Suchet's main force was near the siege train was not landed. On 15 August Suchet advanced in force, drove off the Allies, relieved the garrison and on the eighteenth, having blown up the defences at Tarragona, Suchet withdrew to the line of the Lobregat, covering Barcelona. Aitchison's report of the blowing up of Tarragona was, therefore, premature.

27. The Basques, whose independent spirit remains characteristic to this day.

28. Following the failure of the 5th Division's first attempt to storm San Sebastian, a great deal of bickering broke out which stopped as soon as the town was again besieged. Wellington, however, came to hear of it and wrote to Graham and Bathurst that he feared 'that I shall be obliged to disgrace the Fifth Division. I hear that the General and superior officers were so indiscreet as to talk before their men of the impossibility of success . . . I shall make him continue the operation of the siege and bring other troops to storm the place . . . who will not find success impossible.' (Oman, Vol. IX, p. 353.) Forty volunteers were called from each battalion of the 1st, 4th and Light Divisions 'to show the Fifth Division how to mount a breach'. Leith, who had just returned to the command of the 5th Division, was furious. He used the volunteers to provide covering fire for the assault and act as a reserve.

29. This may refer to Austria's decision to join the alliance.

30. Owing to the demands of the war with the United States and the

government's decision to send a British Fleet into the Baltic, American privateers were operating off Corunna and in the Bay of Biscay.

31. Stanhope, *Notes of Conversations with the Duke of Wellington*, p. 107.

32. Quoted in Fortescue, Vol. IX, p. 394.

33. W.D., Vol. XI, p. 168.

34. Major-General Kenneth Howard commanded the 1st Division, and Major-General the Hon. Edward Stopford commanded the 2nd Guards Brigade (Aitchison's old commanding officer). The battalion had just received a draft of 153, bringing its strength to 1,127.

35. On 12 November, Larpent recorded that: 'The Spanish oxen were so starved, and thin, and weak, that in a league I think I counted about eleven lying down to die. . . . Then there were ten or fifteen poor women belonging to the baggage of the division lamenting over their dying donkeys and mules, whilst others were being beaten to death because they would go no further.' (Larpent, Vol. II, p. 159.)

36. Smith, *Autobiography of Sir Harry Smith*, p. 142.

37. News of Napoleon's decisive defeat in the Battle of the Nations at Leipzig, 16–19 October, reached Wellington hard on the heels of his defeat of Soult on the Nivelle. The Bavarians had deserted Napoleon on the fourteenth and two days later 300,000 Russians, Prussians and Swedes, supported by more than 1,300 guns, closed in upon 190,000 French, Italians and Saxons near Leipzig. On the eighteenth the Saxons and a cavalry division from Württemburg deserted Napoleon and joined his enemies. Napoleon retreated towards the Rhine with his main body of some 40,000, leaving a strong rearguard to hold Leipzig and cover his retreat. However the bridges over the Elster were blown prematurely and the whole rearguard was cut off. By the time Napoleon reached Mainz, on 2 November, and crossed the Rhine, he still had about 40,000 men but had had to abandon 150,000 in isolated garrisons to the east. All Germany now rose against him. Jerome fled from Cassel and the Kingdom of Westphalia collapsed. Murat, who had fought valiantly in the battle, returned to Naples where, on having that Kingdom guaranteed to him by Britain and Austria, he declared himself neutral. Holland now rose, Blücher reached Arnhem, and Britain sent an expeditionary force under Graham to support the Dutch. Napoleon was an emperor without an empire.

38. W.D., Vol. XI, p. 365.

39. W.D., Vol. XI, p. 327.

40. W.D., Vol. XI, p. 326.

41. W.D., Vol. XI, p. 287.

42. W.D., Vol. XI, p. 306.

43. It may seem surprising that desertion among British troops should have been a problem at this time. Wellington had noted it in August, and it increased during periods of inactivity. An additional cause not mentioned by Aitchison was the desire to escape for a time from the rigidity of regimental discipline. This seems to have been felt particularly when the men were living in very hard conditions in the mountains.

44. Vidal de la Blanche, *L'Evacuation de L'Espagne et L'invasion dans le Midi*, Vol. II, p. 163.
45. Kincaid, *Adventures in the Rifle Brigade*, p. 187.
46. Soult's army included a German brigade of four battalions from the Confederation of the Rhine. Two battalions were from the Régiment de Nassau, one from the Régiment de Frankfurt and one from the Régiment de Baden. The brigade commander and the men of the regiments of Nassau and Frankfurt owed allegiance to the Grand Duke of Nassau, who, when the Confederation of the Rhine broke up, sent a major through France to order his subjects to forsake the French and go over to the Allies.
47. The 3rd Guards had their adjutant, Captain H.R. Watson, and seven rank and file killed, and about fifty other casualties. Larpent went to the sale of Watson's effects: 'I bought a very tolerable saddle, with holsters, about half worn, for eighteen dollars which is here considered cheap. I bid 15s for a curry comb and brush, bad, but of English make, and in England worth about 3s or 4s – it went for a guinea! I also bid for a Suffolk Punch horse up to two hundred dollars but Major Daring outbid me, though it was certainly very dear.' (Larpent, Vol. II, p. 210.) The local exchange rate of the dollar was seven shillings.
48. Bell, *Rough Notes of an Old Soldier*, Vol. I, p. 140.
49. Larpent, Vol. II, p. 261.
50. Larpent, Vol. II, p. 249.
51. Larpent, Vol. II, p. 255.
52. W.D., Vol. XI, p. 384.

1814

1. Maxwell, *Peninsular Sketches*, Vol. II, p. 151.
2. Rockets had been used for many years in wars between Indian states before being taken into British service. In the Indian armies these highly erratic weapons were carried by infantrymen and used against elephants in much the same way as the modern infantryman used guided missiles against tanks.

   Colonel William Congreve, was a protégé of the Prince Regent and among many inventions he developed the Congreve Rocket. He first tried to get his rockets adopted for naval purposes. The Duke of Wellington saw little use for these weapons while they remained so inaccurate, However, in 1813 two rocket troops were formed in the Royal Artillery. The 2nd Rocket Troop played a part in the battle of Leipzig. The 1st Rocket Troop was the one which supported the Guards. For the crossing of the Ardour it had the advantage that its equipment was man-portable, a characteristic which was again apparent at the battle of Toulouse. Before rockets were used operationally trials took place before Wellington and other spectators, including Larpent who reported, 'The ground rockets, intended against the cavalry, did not seem to answer very well; they certainly made a tremendous noise, and were formidable spitfires – no cavalry could stand if they came near them but there seemed the difficulty, none went within half a mile of the intended object, and the direction seemed excessively uncertain ... some instead of going one thousand four hundred yards as intended, were off in a hundred and some pieces of shell came back even amongst us spectators. . . .'

3.   According to Jones, thirty-four chasse-marées entered the river without accident. Of those that failed, one grounded on the bar, one was driven ashore and twelve returned to St Jean. The transports with the book got into the river successfully, but the sloop and gunboat were driven on shore and fell to pieces. It was largely due to the insistence of the engineers on board each chasse-marée that their civilian crews were made to persevere under very difficult conditions. In a dispatch on 25 February, Rear-Admiral Penrose paid this tribute: 'That so many chasse-marées ventured this experiment, I attribute to there having been one or more sappers placed in each of them, and a captain and eight lieutenants of engineers commanding them in divisions. The zeal and science of these officers triumphed over the difficulties of the navigation, and I trust that none of their valuable lives have fallen a sacrifice to their spirited exertions.' (Jones, *Journal of Sieges in Spain*, Vol. ii, p. 121.)

4.   Jones, *Journal of Sieges in Spain*, Vol. ii, p. 122.
5.   Larpent, Vol. ii, p. 306.
6.   W. Supp. D., Vol. viii, p. 756.
7.   Napier, *History of the War in the Peninsula*, Vol. vi, p. 644.

Glossary

Barbette   A three-foot-high parapet over which guns fire.

Bastion   Part of the inner enclosure of a fortification with an outward-pointing angle made by the conjunction of two walls. Its communication with the interior of the fortification was through a gorge.

Bat and forage   An allowance for the cost of moving an officer's or senior warrant officer's personal baggage. It was moved on a bat-horse attended by a bat-man.

Battering train   The men, guns, ammunition and specialist equipment to move and mount siege artillery for laying siege to and breaching a fortified place.

Brunswick Oels Jager   Formed from Prussian officers and men who had escaped to England after the collapse of the Duke of Brunswick's revolt in 1809. Know as the Black Brunswickers on account of their uniform. Like the King's German Legion they were later diluted with less desirable recruits, mostly from British prisoner-of-war camps. In the Peninsula they provided a rifle company for a number of infantry brigades.

Cacadores   Portuguese Light Infantry armed with rifles. They were mainly recruited from the north of Portugal.

Chevaux de frise   Large joists or beams stuck full of wooden pins armed with iron, or nails or sword blades, to stop up a breach or secure entrance to a camp against enemy cavalry.

Counterguard   A work placed in front of the bastions and sometimes in front of ravelins.

Covertway   A broad way around the works of a fortified place protected by a seven-and-a-half-foot parapet.

Curtain   Curtain walls join one bastion to the next.

Embrasures   Openings made in the flanks of a fortification or of a breast work for guns to fire through.

Escalade   To carry the walls of a fortress by means of ladders instead of by making a breach.

Fascines   Bundles of branches of about six or eight inches diameter, tied in two or more places, to retain the earthen walls of trenches or in batteries.

Fausse braye   A low rampart surrounding a fortified post not more than three feet hight.

'Forlorn Hope'   A small group that went ahead of the storming party into the breach to cover the emplacement of ladders etc.

Fraise   Stakes or a palisade placed horizontally on the outward slope of a turf rampart to prevent the work being taken by surprise.

Gabion   A cylindrical basket open at both ends, about three feet wide and of equal height, and filled with earth. Used to provide above-ground cover along the approaches to a fortification during a siege.

Gorge   The part of the work next to the body of the place where there is no rampart or parapet.

Glacis   The outward part of a fortification, beyond the covertway to which it acts as a parapet, outwardly terminating in an easy slope.

Hutting   Troops were either billeted, encamped or hutted. The building of huts from branches of trees was a well-practised drill in most units.

Hornwork   A fortification composed of a front and two branches or horns, two demi-bastions with a curtain in between.

Juramentados   King Joseph's Spanish guards. Sometimes used of any Spanish troops fighting for the French.

Lunette   A work made on both sides of a ravelin, and on occasion elsewhere.

Ordenanca   Portugal had had to be ready to defend herself against the far more populous Spain, and her government had for generations held power of conscription. Behind her regular forces stood the uniformed militia, and behind the militia was the Ordenanca, irregulars called out to help in local defence.

Palisades   Stakes made of strong split wood about nine feet long, fixed three feet deep in the ground, in rows about six inches apart. Normally placed in the covertway about a yard from the parapet of the glacis to prevent a surprise attack.

Parallel   Or place of arms. Deep trenches fifteen to eighteen feet wide from which troops working on the approaches to a fortified place can be supported. It was usual to dig three such parallels in the course of approaching a position to assault a fortified position.

Park of artillery   A place chosen by a commander for the assembly of his reserve artillery, ammunition and associated equipment, ready for use when required.

Pounder (pdr)   Cannon were classified according to the weight of their solid shot. Thus a 24 pdr threw a shot weighing approximately twenty-four pounds.

Piece of ordnance   A gun, howitzer or mortar.

Ravelin or demi-lune   A work placed in front of a curtain wall consisting of two faces meeting in an outward-pointing angle, enabling flanking fire to be brought against an enemy approaching the curtain wall.

Salient angle   The outward-pointing angle of a defensive work, a part either of a fortress or of a system of defence.

Sap   A trench dug to give cover to the besiegers approaching a fortified place.

Stand of arms   A complete set of arms for one infantryman.

Vedette   Mounted sentry placed in front of an outpost.

Index